H D Scott

LITH. OF SARONY & Cº NEW YORK.

LITH. OF SARONY & Cº NEW YORK.

O CATETTE

BRAZIL AND LA PLATA:

THE

PERSONAL RECORD OF A CRUISE.

BY

C. S. STEWART, A. M., U. S. N.,

AUTHOR OF

"A RESIDENCE AT THE SANDWICH ISLANDS," "VISIT TO THE SOUTH SEAS,"
"SKETCHES IN GREAT BRITAIN AND IRELAND," ETC., ETC.

"Sail forth into the sea, O ship!
Through wind and wave right onward steer!
The moistened eye, the trembling lip,
Are not the signs of doubt and fear.—
Sail forth, nor fear to breast the sea!
Our hearts, our hopes, are all with thee!"
LONGFELLOW.

NEW YORK:
G. P. PUTNAM & CO., 321 BROADWAY.
1856.

John F. Trow,
Printer and Stereotyper, 377 & 379 Broadway,
Corner of White street.

TO

MY DAUGHTERS,

THIS VOLUME

DRAWN FROM MANUSCRIPTS ADDRESSED TO THEM,

IS AFFECTIONATELY

Inscribed.

PREFACE.

Two inducements have led to the publication of the following volume: one, the favor with which similar works from my pen have been received; the other, the belief that a book of fact, for light reading, would be welcome to many, amid the floods of fiction of the present day.

It was with no purpose of making a book, that the record from which the volume is drawn was kept; on the contrary, the chief difficulty I have found, in fitting it for the press, has arisen, from its being so strictly personal and private. To remodel the manuscript so as to change its character in these respects, would have been a labor which I was unwilling to undertake; and to select from it such matter as might be at once suitable for publication, and acceptable to the general reader, without affecting the connection and unity of the whole, has proved a task not easily acomplished. In attempting it, I may have erred in judgment by putting into print, in some instances, what might better have been omitted ; and again perhaps, in others by omitting what would have been welcomed by the reader.

Besides such matter as was essential in giving an outline of the cruise of the Congress, and such observation of the places visited by her, as would be expected in a work of the kind, I have thought it proper to retain of that which related specifically to the ship, sufficient to convey a general idea of life on board a man-of-war ; and also, of that which referred to myself in my office, enough to throw light upon the position, duties, and influence of a chaplain in the naval service.

Should the volume meet with any degree of acceptance from the public in general, I shall be grateful ; and should its circulation be limited to the decks of a man-of-war, or to the forecastle of a merchant-ship, the object in its publication will not be entirely lost.

C. S. S.

Riverside, 1856.

CONTENTS.

CONTENTS.

CHAPTER VII.

CHAPTER VIII.

CHAPTER IX.

CHAPTER X.

CHAPTER XI.

CHAPTER XII.

CHAPTER XIII.

CHAPTER XIV.

CHAPTER XV.

CHAPTER XVI.

CHAPTER XVII.

CHAPTER XVIII.

CHAPTER XIX.

CHAPTER XX.

CHAPTER XXI.

CHAPTER XXII.

CHAPTER XXIII.

CHAPTER XXIV.

CHAPTER XXV.

CHAPTER XXVI.

CHAPTER XXVII.

BRAZIL AND LA PLATA.

CHAPTER I.

U. S. SHIP CONGRESS, CAPES OF VIRGINIA.

June 8th, 1850.—The time for my promised record has arrived: the Congress is at sea. This afternoon, with light and baffling winds, in a most lazy and listless manner she gained a distance of ten miles outside of Cape Henry, where, a breeze springing up sufficiently fresh to insure an offing before nightfall, the pilot took his leave for the land and we filled away upon the sea.

The 8th of June thus becomes for a second time an anniversary with me. Twenty years ago to-day, amid the bright beauty of a summer's afternoon, I entered the bay of New York from a voyage of the world. But, in what wide contrast were the feelings of that hour with those of this in which I now write! Then, the sunshine of the soul, beaming from face to face and reflected from eye to eye, outrivalled the brightness of the joyous scene around. We were safely at home, after a long and adventurous absence, and within reach of the salutations and embraces of those we most loved. Now, there is sunshine neither without nor within: without, a thick and gloomy haze obscures its smiles, and within, the sadness of separation for years from home and country, with all the uncertainty of its issues, entirely beclouds them. There is nothing joyous to us in the "glad sea:" it does not dance in our eyes as it was wont, or as we have, at times at least, imagined it to do.

Little do they who may envy the lot of an officer in the navy—in its opportunities of varied travel, the knowledge it affords of men and things, and observation of nature in her most impressive forms—know at what a sacrifice of the affections, in their choicest exercise, and by what a penalty of wearisome duty, in irksome routine, the privileges of the position are bought. A sacrifice and a penalty which, when the novelty of travel and

"The magic charm of foreign land"

are passed, and the enthusiasm of youth is chastened by the experiences of maturer years, are felt with a keenness which, to be justly appreciated, must be personally known. The long conviction of this has been impressed afresh upon my mind by an incident of the passing hour. Mr. B——, a gentleman of wealth and distinguished social position in one of our principal cities, has for some days past been a guest of the ward-room mess, as the close friend of a fellow officer. He chose to accompany us to the open sea, and risk the discomfort of a night on board the pilot boat in a return to the shore, rather than take leave at an earlier moment. While the little craft was still hovering around us, waiting the signal to approach and take off its master and his passenger, the officer referred to, in momentary expectation of this second leavetaking of home, as it were, in parting from one who was going directly to his family, approaching me, exclaimed, in a spirit of half desperation—"Oh! Mr. S——, if I were in circumstances to live on shore with my family independently of my profession, I would go straight over the sides of the ship into that boat, and throw my commission to the winds. When I think of my wife and children, I feel as if I would dig and grub—do any thing for an honest living—rather than thus for three years leave them for a drudgery so distasteful to me as life on board a man-of-war in time of peace, with scarce an object but to get through an irksome duty." Such must be the feelings, in a greater or less degree, of every sea-officer who has reached the meridian of life; and such would be my own, were there not connected with my office and its duties, issues, in hope at least, sufficient to outbalance all earthly considerations.

June 10th.—Little worthy of record, even in a journal for home, can be anticipated in a passage to Cuba; yet an incident has already occurred, which I would not pass over without notice. When Mr. B—— and the pilot left us on Saturday, the shades of a sombre evening were settling around us, and, as is customary on board a man-of-war in ordinary cruising, we reefed topsails for the night. This done, as the lighthouse fires began to gleam over the dark waters, from Cape Henry at one point and from Cape Charles at another, all hands were called to our first evening prayer on the quarter-deck. The deep twilight and the gloomy sky made the service the more impressive. Few on board, even among the officers, knew of the intention of Captain McIntosh with the sanction of Commodore McKeever, to have daily evening worship. One or two of those who did, had never witnessed such an observance on board ship, and doubted its expediency. But the impression made by it was at once effective and conclusive on the minds of those even who had most doubted. This they readily admitted to others as well as to myself: and while saying that it was the first time they had ever been present at such a service in the navy, added a hope that it would never be discontinued on board the Congress.

I was cheered by this frank avowal from those whose judgment I prized, and whose high-toned character carries with it predominating influence among their associates. Long experience warrants me in regarding this appointment as a most important auxiliary in the work of a chaplaincy, and an efficient promoter of discipline and good order on board a man-of-war. It is honorable to the principles and moral perceptions of those who framed the existing laws of the navy, that the second article in the code enjoins a daily service of worship on board every ship having a chaplain; and it is to be regretted that an injunction so salutary, in the moral economy of a crew, and in its general tendency, should in so few instances have been carried into effect.

The evening worship of the Cotter's fireside—where,

> "Kneeling down to Heaven's Eternal King,
> The saint, the father, and the husband prays,"

presents a picture which might well call forth the inspiration of the poet. In every grade of life, the social altar, encircled in the sincerity and simplicity of the Gospel, is in like manner an elevating and a touching sight. But if impressive in the comparative security of the shore, far from the fitful changes and dangers of the sea, how much more so when exhibited in the floating dwellings of those whose "home is on the deep." If He, who alone "commands the winds and the waves, and they obey"—He, who "rides upon the whirlwind and directs the storm," is the receiver of our thanksgiving and the only hearer of prayer, who sooner than the sailor should be found in supplication, or who be more frequent, or more fervent than he in praise?

Whatever may be the ultimate results in individual cases of such a service, few persons have for a first time witnessed it, without bearing testimony to its impressiveness on the eye, whatever may have been the influence felt upon the heart. But, it is not without cause, that I ever look for something more from it. The man-of-wars-man with all his recklessness, and, too often, degrading vices, has, in many cases, moral sensibilities and affections which bring him, where the means of grace are enjoyed, within the pale of hope; and I have never yet been long on board a ship where, to the preaching of the Gospel on the Sabbath, there has been added this daily evening prayer, without hearing from some troubled spirit the inquiry, "What shall I do to be saved?" followed, not unfrequently, by the resolution of the repenting prodigal, "I will arise and go to my Father, and will say to him, Father, I have sinned against Heaven and in thy sight, and am no more worthy to be called thy son."

The excitement incident to our departure and the tedium of a listless day, with little progress till we were at sea, disposed all on board not on watch, to retire early; and for the most part such were soundly asleep, myself among the number, when suddenly aroused at midnight by the cry, "A man overboard!" There was little wind and not much sea; but the darkness was Egyptian; the rain poured in torrents; and while the booming thunder of an approaching gust rolled heavily over the deep, occasional flashes of vivid lightning added double intensity, in the intervals, to the blackness around. The rescue of the perishing man seemed hopeless. Supposing him of course to be one of the crew—perhaps the most active and gallant of their number, who had lost his foothold in some effort of duty in preparation for the coming squall—I felt disheartened by so sad a casualty at the very outset of our cruise. I thought of our evening prayer, and of the deep feeling with which, in its brief worship, we had supplicated the defences of the Almighty, and in confiding trust committed ourselves to his protecting care. Had the Lord not had respect to our offering—had the Almighty not regarded our prayer?

In the midst of thoughts such as these, it was a relief, though a melancholy one indeed, to learn that the wretch overboard was not any of the fine fellows whose physical aspect and general bearing had already won from me, in my position, a deep interest, but a poor drunkard, who had been brought on board in a state of delirium tremens, from the receiving ship, the day we left Norfolk; and who had at once been consigned, in care of the surgeons, to the sick-bay. In a paroxysm of madness, he had now rushed from his keepers below to the gun-deck; and, knocking down with a billet of wood caught up at the galley, one in pursuit, had plunged headforemost through an open bridle-port, to be seen and heard of no more.

The life-buoys were cut away, the ship put about, boats lowered and sent off, at the risk of life both to officers and men, in the pitchy darkness and rapidly approaching squall: blue lights were burned, and repeated shouts through a trumpet made, in hope of some response, but all in vain, in rescuing him from his doom. After the first plunge, nothing was seen or heard from him. A miserable madman from strong drink, the accompaniments of his end on earth—the midnight gloom, the angry lightning, the muttering thunder, and the moaning wind, were befitting the fate of an immortal spirit "unanointed—unannealed," thus passing into the eternal world. He was an old man-of-wars-man, and, three years ago, in a similar condition and near the same place, jumped overboard from a frigate the first night from port, and was with great difficulty saved. How faithful the admonition, "He that being often reproved hardeneth his neck, shall suddenly be destroyed, and that without remedy."

Yesterday, the Sabbath, was a bright and beautiful day, with favoring winds and a smooth sea. The quarter-deck, screened from the sun by awnings, was our chapel; the capstan, spread with the stripes and stars of an ensign, our reading desk and pulpit; and the band, with sacred music, both our organ and choir. My sermon, suggested by the incident of the preceding night, was an exposition of the evils, physical, moral and spiritual, of intemperance, and the frightful condition of such as become its hopeless victims. The fatal proofs of the truths advanced, in the bodily and mental state of him who had just perished before our eyes as it were, caused the most fixed attention to be given to what was said, both by the officers and men.

I was happy to be told by the captain, immediately after the service, that it had been officially reported to him the day before, that more than three hundred of the crew, or two thirds of the whole number of foremast hands, did not draw the ration of rum furnished them by the government: this of their own voluntary choice, no persuasion having yet been used on board to influence any one on the subject. An encouraging fact certainly, at the offset, in this essential point in the morals of the sailor, and one that ought to be suggestive to our national legislators of the duty of striking at once from the list of naval allowances, a poison tending to the destruction of both body and soul. The day was a happy one to me, in the retirement of my own little room, as well as in the public discharge of my duties. A long and kind letter from an officer, in answer to a note with which I had returned one given to me to read, was so encouraging to me in my office, and so full of promise spiritually for himself, as deeply to affect me. I could but regard it as a token of grace from Him in whose hands are all hearts, and as an intimation of the good that may be accomplished on board, even in the most influential quarters.

Our worship, at sunset, was commenced, after an air of sacred music from the band, by the reading of Addison's beautiful hymn—

> "How are thy servants blest, O Lord!
> How sure is their defence!
> Eternal Wisdom is their guide,
> Their help, Omnipotence."

To-day we are crossing the gulf stream under a fresh breeze amounting almost to a gale: a "smoky southwester" with a short and high sea, into which the frigate plunges deeply, taking in large quantities of water forward. This rushing aft, as the ship rises, makes the gun as well as the spar-deck wet and uncomfortable. The wardroom, with all the stern and air-ports closed, is dark and stifling in its atmosphere, and every thing on board partakes largely of the disagreeable at sea. The motion is so great that nothing can be left by itself; and, at breakfast, each of us secured, as best he could, the very indifferent fare that came in his way: bread like so much lead; biscuits which, bagged and netted, might have passed inspection as grape-shot; rancid butter; addled eggs; and execrable stuff under the names of tea and coffee! As I cast my eyes over the mess-table and its surroundings, in the gloomy twilight falling from the hatchway above, and upon a disconsolate-looking and silent set of companions, I could not avoid contrasting the whole, involuntarily, with a breakfast room in my mind, on shore, in the fresh beauty of a morning in June—with a brightly gleaming lawn in front; the mingled bloom of the rose and the honeysuckle at the windows; the cheerful family group; and the varied fare fresh from the garden, the farm-house, and the dairy—and sigh at the difference in the pictures. Such a day as this, on shipboard in the gulf stream, with its discomfort in almost every form, would be enough to make a landsman content, for the rest of his life, with the blessings of the shore.

Apropos of our steward. We have been sadly imposed on by the professed qualifications of this important functionary. Claiming to be perfect in all, we find he knows nothing of any of his appropriate duties. The day we left Norfolk he gave a characteristic proof of his fitness for the office. It was at dinner, our guest Mr. B—— being of the number. Among the courses was a salad dressed by our *maitre d'hôte.* Mr. B—— was first served with it. I was the next to take from the dish, and in doing so, happening to look towards the visitor, was struck by a very peculiar expression of the eye and countenance as he tasted it—a blending of surprise, comical inquiry, and effort at self-command, while the fork was very quietly returned to his plate, as if he were done with it. Suspecting the salad to be the origin of all this, and hastily testing the point by a mouthful, I found to my utter disgust, that, in obedience to the direction of the caterer to use plenty of oil in the dressing, he had, in ignorance of any other, dashed the whole most copiously with the vilest lamp oil! The effect upon the palate can be more readily imagined than described.

June 12th.—A breeze from the north-east, which set in last night, promises to prove a regular trade-wind, and we are running rapidly before it on our course. You may easily follow our track, by marking, on a map, a pretty straight line from the mouth of the Chesapeake to the channel of the sea, between the Islands of St. Domingo and Porto Rico. It is our intention to pass between these, by what is named on the charts of the West Indies, the Mona Passage, and then lay a course by the south side of Cuba to Havana. Should it be asked why we go, seemingly, so much out of our way and so far round; I answer, that for a large ship, it is not only the safest, but, in point of time, the shortest route. The strong and adverse current of the gulf stream, and the intricate and hazardous navigation of the Florida channel, are the objections to the direct course along the coast. The weather is now fine—in strong contrast with that last described; and, at night, we have a splendid moon, enticing to constant visits in thought and affection to Riverside. Beautiful as moonlight is at sea, I must confess to a preference, in the enjoyment of it in the month of June, for the south-west corner of a verandah on the banks of the Hudson.

I have, thus far, been giving my time chiefly to visits through my floating parish—from the quarters of the Commodore to those of "Jemmy Ducks," and "Jack of the dust," as the feeder of the pigs and poultry, and the sweeper of the Purser's store-rooms, in shipboard nomenclature, are respectively styled. Almost every day, since coming on board, I have discovered here and there a shipmate of some former cruise; and perceive hourly evidence of having through these—in part at least—already gained the marked good will of the crew. I am quite at home in all my walks among them; and have every reason to be more than satisfied—to be truly thankful—in my official relation with them.

The Congress, a fifty-gun ship, is one of the finest vessels of her class. She is a model of strength and symmetry in hull and spars, and of imposing and effective equipment in her batteries and armament; never failing to attract the notice of all who have an eye to appreciate a chef d'œuvre in naval architecture. She is, too, a swift messenger over the waters, as well as a tower of strength and beauty on the sea.

The intellectual and moral tastes of many of my immediate associates and equals in naval rank, are such as not only to make them agreeable companions, but also to give to our mess in general, by their example and influence, a high-toned and elevated character; and I regard it a providence of special kindness that, in those chief in authority and executive power, I find cordial friends personally, and firm supporters in my duty officially. Their views, too, and their purposes, in regard to discipline and naval reform, harmonize with my own, in the persuasion that kindness is the surest key to the human heart; and that, in government, the law of love is more effectual than the rule of fear. I felt this particularly, in a long conversation with the commodore this morning, during a walk on the quarter-deck, and at breakfast with him afterwards. On this point I like his views much; and augur great good from them, in the support they will lead him to extend, officially, to the executive officer of the ship, in carrying out a system of internal rule based upon the principle of kindness and good will, of the practical well-working of which he is entirely persuaded.

The crew, physcically, are a fine set of men: healthful, athletic and young, the average age of the four hundred foremast hands scarcely exceeding twenty-five years. This general youthfulness of the ship's company encourages me to hope much from them as subjects of moral culture. They are more likely, than seamen of a more advanced age, to have had the benefit of a religious training in the Sabbath schools now so universally established in most sections of our country; and, thus, be more susceptible to moral impressions and persuasion, should they not have already felt the influence of the general improvement in the character of sailors which, confessedly, has taken place within the last ten or fifteen years. Still, at best, a man-of-war is a sterile and rocky field for spiritual labor. There is ever on board a large ship of the kind, a greater or less number of reckless and desperately wicked men: some who have been convicts and the inmates of state prisons and penitentiaries, and more who, long under the surveillance of the police, and pressed by close pursuit, have sought refuge at the rendezvous and receiving ship, from the merited penalties of the law. Of these last we are certain of having quite a company, composed pretty equally of 'Southwark killers,' 'Schuylkill rangers,' 'Baltimore rowdies,' 'Bowery boys,' and 'Five Pointers.' The whole number of both these classes, however, does not amount to more than fifty; the hundreds of others on board are either honest-hearted and true sailors, or inexperienced and raw landsmen: 'good men,' according to the ethics of the sea. The "baser sort," though comparatively so few in number, are ever first in gaining prominence and notoriety on board, by bringing themselves, through a manifestation of their evil propensities, in contact with the discipline of the ship, while the true sailor and old man-of-wars-man, in the quiet discharge of their duty remain for a time unappreciated, and perhaps personally unknown.

To an inexperienced eye, a man-of-war with her crew of five hundred, seems only like a bee-hive full of confusion and uproar, while, in truth, there is throughout in every department perfect organization and order. Every individual has his class, his number, and his station; the duty of each in his place is clearly defined; and whatever is to be done is accomplished with much of the regularity of a machine operating through the same number of wheels. To the same eye there would appear no signs of caste or grades of distinction, moral or social, in the general mass: there would be only so many hundred sailors, seemingly alike in all respects. Little would be dreamed of the extremes, not only of moral character, existing among them, but of social distinction also—from the exclusives of the "upper ten," priding themselves on moving only in the first circles, through three or four marked sets to the canaille, utterly below recognition or social intercourse. There is a marked difference, too, among many, in the outer man. Though the dress of all is uniform in color and general material, still there is often the widest difference in the quality, fitting, and make of the entire wardrobe; and, while one is so careless and slovenly in his attire, as to require the daily inspection of an officer, others are perfect sea-dandies, as fastidiously neat and clean in person, as the whole series of brushes known to the toilette-table can make them; and as fond of being assured of this, by repeated inspections and last glances in the miniature mirrors carried in their hats, or about their persons, as a beau of the first water on shore, before a Psyche in preparation for the ball or opera.

After the public worship of the last Sabbath, Mr. T——, the first lieutenant, who has had long experience in Sabbath schools, both as a teacher and superintendent, aided me in the formation of one among the twenty-four boys on board, from ten to fifteen years of age: each of us taking charge of a class of twelve. The value of a voluntary agency of this kind, from an officer of commanding influence, can scarcely be over-estimated. My next attempt, as a means of good, will be the establishment of Bible classes among the men. If successful in this, I am happy to know that others of the officers stand ready to assist me in the like manner.

It is an interesting fact, and one strikingly illustrative of the improved and elevated tone of morals in the navy, that of the fourteen gentlemen constituting the wardroom mess, five are professedly religious men of consistent and exemplary character.

CHAPTER II.

AT SEA.

June 19*th*.—Two days ago, at noon, land was descried from the mast-head. We were approaching the Bahama Islands, not in the direction of the Mona Passage, but in that of the Caycos, more to the west, the wind having headed us off from our first course. During the previous night, we had passed over a point on the ocean, memorable in its historic interest, where, on the very eve of joyful triumph, the illustrious discoverer of the western world suffered the severest trial of his daring voyage. It was here that the discouragement and fears of his followers in their frail barks, approached desperation and open mutiny; and confident hope had well nigh ended in disappointment, and triumphant success in failure. It was impossible to traverse the same waters, without recalling vividly to mind the scene of trial and conflict which they had witnessed more than three hundred and fifty years before, and sympathizing afresh with the great navigator in his distress; or to hear the cry, "land ho!" without recurring in thought to the devout exultations of his heart, when, in the watches of the night, the interrupted glimmerings of a distant light peered upon eyes eagerly searching its gloom, dispelling for ever the fears of his companions, and crowning his adventurous enterprise with imperishable honor.

The land descried aloft, soon became visible from the deck. It was the great Caycos, the most eastern of the Bahamas, a low, flat island of sand, surrounded by extensive shoals. There was little to interest in its appearance; a mere tufting of bushes on the water, along the line of the horizon, of which we soon lost sight. The next morning, and for the rest of the day, the west end of St. Domingo was in view, furnishing in its turn abundant subjects for musing in the tragic scenes of the revolt of 1791. Before nightfall the eastern extremity of Cuba was also in sight. Both are lofty and mountainous, but less picturesque in general outline than the islands of the South Seas. The sail of the afternoon and evening was delightful,—the perfection of its kind. The trade-wind was fresh and balmy, and so steady, that the lofty mass of canvas we spread to it was as motionless as if it were a fixture on the sea; while the ocean, of the most beautiful tint of marine blue, was every where gemmed with white-caps of the brilliancy of so much snow.

June 20th.—Hitherto the duty of the ship has been carried on admirably under a kind and humane discipline. The lash, formerly in such constant requisition on board a man-of-war, in bringing a new crew under ready control, has neither been heard nor seen. A fight, however, which came off a day or two since, between two of the marines, led to a kind of drumhead court-martial, yesterday, and to the punishment of the parties this morning, with the cat-o'-nine-tails. It is the first instance with us of such a revolting spectacle, and I most devoutly hope it may be the last. I am sure it will, unless there be those on board so incorrigible and so determined to subject themselves to it, that no other mode of discipline will meet their case. Before we left port, Captain McIntosh, in an excellent address, after the first reading in public of the "articles of war," assured the crew with deep feeling, that nothing could give him greater pleasure than to return to the United States and have it in his power to report to the Navy Department that a lash had never been given on board the Congress during the cruise. He reiterated the same sentiment this morning to the ship's company, mustered to witness the punishment, with the fresh avowal of his utter unwillingness to resort to so degrading a mode of chastisement: adding "that the existing law, however, made the duty imperative upon him as an ultimate means of enforcing his command, and protecting his ship from insubordination and misrule; and that it should be remembered by all, whenever the necessity was forced on him of administering this punishment, that it would only be through the deliberate purpose and choice of any one subjecting himself to it."

The cat-o'-nine-tails, as a mode of punishment, is a relic of barbarism disgraceful to the age in which we live, and antagonistic to its entire spirit. The wonder is, not that men-of-wars men are scarce, and recruits for the navy few, but that, with such a barbarous punishment legalized, an American sailor can be found willing to place himself in a position in which he can, by any contingency, be exposed to the disgrace of its infliction.

In place of attempting a description of the spectacle, as just witnessed by us, I will substitute one, which happens to be before me, of a similar scene, from the pen of an officer in the British Navy. It is more graphic than any I could furnish, and as truthful to the reality, in its leading features, as can well be pictured. It is drawn from his early experience as a midshipman. "I had not been many days on board," he says, "before I heard a hollow sound reverberating round the frigate's decks, and which seemed to bring a shade of gloom over the faces of all around me. Again the words were repeated, "All hands, Ahoy!" I eagerly inquired the meaning of this mystery, and was answered by a lad about sixteen years of age, 'It is all hands to punishment, my boy; you are going to see a man flogged.'

"The idea of a *man* being flogged at all, under any possible circumstances, had never before entered my brain. I had as yet no notions that such a degree of barbarity could exist; I had indeed known that boys were flogged, but how they could *horse* a man was to me a mystery. My reflections were broken in upon by observing all my messmates busily engaged in putting on their cocked-hats and side-arms. And as this was the first time I had sported my new dirk, I felt very strange and mingled sensations, as I stepped forth on the quarter-deck. The marines were drawn up on the larboard side of the deck, with their bayonets fixed, and their officers with their swords drawn, and resting against their shoulders. On the main deck the seamen had all assembled in a dense crowd around the hatchway, and the said hatchway was ornamented with several gratings fixed up on one end, evidently for some purpose which I had never yet seen accomplished. The officers in their full uniforms, with swords, and cocked hats, were pacing the decks: but all was still and solemn silence. At length the captain came forth from his cabin, the marines carrying arms at his first appearance on the quarter-deck. The first lieutenant, taking off his hat, approached him, and reported that 'all was ready.'

"As the captain came up to the gangway, he removed his hat; which was followed by all the men and officers becoming uncovered. Then, taking a printed copy of the articles of war, he read aloud a few lines, which denounced the judgment of a court-martial on any person who should be guilty of some particular offence, the nature of which I did not understand. This done, he ordered Edward Williams to strip; adding, 'You have been guilty of neglect of duty, sir, in not laying in off the foretopsail yard when the first lieutenant ordered you; and I will give you a d——d good flogging.' By this time the poor fellow had taken off his jacket and shirt, which was thrown over his shoulders by the master-at-arms, while two quartermasters lashed the poor fellow's elbows to the gratings, so that he could not stir beyond an inch or two either way. It was in vain that he begged and besought the captain and first lieutenant to forgive him; protesting that he did not hear himself called, in consequence of having a bad cold, which rendered him almost deaf. His entreaties were unheeded; and at the words, 'Boatswain's mate, give him a dozen,' a tall, strong fellow came forward with a cat-o'-nine-tails, and, having taken off his own jacket, and carefully measured his distance, so as to be able to strike with the full swing of his arm, he flung the tails of the cat around his head, and with all the energy of his body brought them down upon the fair, white, plump back of poor Williams. A sudden jerk of the poor fellow almost tore away the gratings from their position; he gave a scream of agony, and again begged the captain, for the sake of Jesus Christ, to let him off. I was horror-struck on seeing nine large welts, as big as my fingers, raised on his back, spreading from his shoulder-blades nearly to his loins; but my feelings were doomed to be still more harrowed. For as soon as the tall boatswain's mate had completed the task of running his fingers through the cords to clear them and prevent the chance of a single lash being spared the wretched sufferer, he again flung them around his head to repeat the blow. Another slashing sound upon the naked flesh, another shriek and struggle to get free succeeded,—and then another and another, till the complement of twelve agonizing lashes was completed. The back was, by this time, nearly covered with deep red gashes; the skin roughed up and curled in many parts, as it does when a violent blow causes an extensive abrasion. The poor man looked up with an imploring eye toward the first lieutenant, and groaned out, 'Indeed, sir, as I hope to be saved, I did not hear you call me.' The only reply was on the part of the captain, who gave the word, 'another boatswain's mate!' 'Oh, God, sir, have mercy on me!' was again the cry of the poor man: 'Boatswain's mate, go on; and mind that you do your duty!' the only answer.

"The effect of one hundred and eight cuts upon his bare back had rendered it a fearful sight, but when these had been repeated with all the vigor of a fresh and untired arm, the poor fellow exhibited a sad spectacle indeed. The dark red of the wounds had assumed a livid purple, the flesh stood up in mangled ridges, and the blood trickled here and there like the breaking out of an old wound. The pipes of the boatswain and his mates now sounded, and they called 'all hands up anchor!' The gratings were quickly removed, and of all the human beings who had witnessed the cruel torture on the body of poor Edward Williams, not one seemed in the slightest degree affected. All was bustle and activity and apparent merriment as they went to work in obedience to the call."

In this account there is no exaggeration: no exaggeration of the usual manner of inflicting such punishment; no exaggeration of the trivialty of the alleged offence; no exaggeration of the earnest asseveration of innocence; no exaggeration of the hardening effect of the scene upon the spectators. I have known men to be thus flogged for acts or omissions equally if not more trivial —not only singly, but, in one instance at least, a dozen at a time, and that, too, where it was known that one only of the number was really in fault. Because some one of a quarter watch in the top did a careless and lubberly thing, in the estimation of an officer, though doubtless, from the circumstances of the case, accidentally, and none of his topmates would give up his name, the whole watch were ordered on deck, and, in succession, received a dozen lashes each.

The entire experience of the writer of the above account, as to this punishment, corroborates fully the opinion I have formed from my own observation as to its effects—that in all its bearings it has a tendency to demoralize and harden rather than to reform. He proceeds to state that the captain under whose command the case of flogging described occurred, changed ships not long afterwards with one who abominated the system of corporal punishment; and adds, "For four years I served under his orders, and witnessed no more of the inhuman practice. The men were allowed to go on shore frequently sixty and seventy at a time, and in all respects were treated so kindly that but one case of desertion occurred during all that period. The captain made it a point to visit the whole crew when at dinner, to see, himself, that they had every thing they required to make them comfortable. This he did every day; and the sick were always fed from his own table. The result of this was that our ship was the smartest frigate on the station, and fought one of the most glorious actions which ever graced the annals of the British Navy."

His experience in the matter did not end here. He thus proceeds: "I joined another ship, the captain of which was wont to say, 'I never forgive a first offence—for if there was no first offence there could be no second.' Profane swearing and drunkenness, he never by any accident forgave. The result was a flogging match every Monday morning, and very frequently once or twice in the week besides. The crew grew worse and worse from this treatment, till, at length, there was scarcely a sober seaman or marine on board the ship, though her complement was about six hundred men and boys. The more drunken they became the more he flogged them; but the crime and punishment seemed to react on each other, and the ship became at last so very notorious for the cat that he was jested upon it by his fellow captains, and the men deserted at every opportunity."

I believe the experience, thus presented, of these two ships, to be a fair exposition of the general and direct tendency of the two systems. Revolting as punishment with the 'colt' and 'cat' ever has been to me, and often as my blood has been made to boil in witnessing it, a want of practical knowledge in the case led me, for a time, reluctantly to acquiesce in the opinion universally held, so far as I could discover, by those most experienced in naval rule, that it was indispensable as a means of discipline on board a man-of-war. But the teachings of my nature, that this is an error, have been corroborated by long observation; and had no previous conviction of this been fastened on my mind, the success of the executive officer of the Congress in devising and substituting more humanizing modes of punishment for transgressions of law and delinquencies in duty, would have gone far in persuading me to it. I doubt not that should the law of the lash be abrogated by our national legislature to-morrow,* and the change be met by the enactment of a wise and philanthropic code of naval rule, the discipline and efficiency of the service would be more perfect than ever before.

* Flogging was abolished, both in the navy and mercantile marine, a few months after the above was written.

June 24th.—

> "The twilight is sad and cloudy,
> The wind blows wild and free,
> And like the wings of sea-birds
> Flash the white caps of the sea."

So sings Longfellow, and such is the imagery around us from the passing of a heavy squall. The rushing wind and the dampness brought with it, from the approaching rain, are welcome and most refreshing, after two or three days and nights on the south side of Cuba, sultry almost to suffocation. Whether correct in our recollections or not, all hands agree that, in no part of the world in which we have been, either on land or at sea, have we before suffered so much from the intensity of the heat. Notwithstanding, I was never in the enjoyment of more vigorous health or in more elastic spirits.

In the afternoon of my last date, we had a distant view of a part of the island of Jamaica, as well as of San Domingo and Cuba: a sail, too, was in sight, and the smoke of a steamer marked on the horizon—all taking much from the solitariness of our position. The next morning we were slowly advancing westward, along the lofty, but mist covered and cloud obscured mountain range of the Sierra de Cobra, beneath a point in which lie the port and city of St. Jago de Cuba. At sunset the same evening we were directly abreast Cape de Cruz, in full view of the coast, but at too great a distance to make out the distinctive features of the landscape, even with the best glasses. We are now off the Isle of Pines, famed in the annals of the Buccaneers of the olden time, and a haunt of pirates in our own day.

Light and baffling winds, with alternate calms, have made our progress slow. The tedium of the time has been relieved in part by a first interchange of dinner parties between the wardroom mess and the commodore and captain. The kindest feeling exists among the officers of all grades on board, and these reunions, where the formality of official intercourse gives place for the time to the free interchange of thought and feeling, and of sympathy in intellect and taste, are salutary in their influences on both mind and heart. The Sabbath is the day usually chosen on board a man-of-war for these courtesies; but it has been unanimously decided, by our mess, that the entertainments given in the wardroom shall be on a week day.

During the continuance of moonlight in the evening and early part of the night, the enjoyment of it on deck in quiet musings, after the heat of the day, seemed the prevailing mood of the ship's company. The band in whole or in part, at times, added music to the sympathies which were sending our thoughts and affections homeward by the way of the moon. But now that she is on the wane, and reserves her beams for the later watches of the night, the sailors cheer themselves in the darkness, by singing on the spar-deck, grouped in their respective limits from the fife-rail to the forecastle. Last evening, even the quarter-deck was invaded, under the sanction of an officer, by a party of negro minstrels: not such mock performers as are heard on shore under the name, but of the genuine type, consisting of the servants of the wardroom. For half an hour or more they sang, in practised harmony and with effect, many of the more sentimental and popular of the negro melodies; while forward and in the gangways there was echoed forth, in varied song, the feats of warrior knights and the love of ladies fair. Others of the crew were, at the same time, listening in groups between the guns along the entire deck, to a rehearsal by their shipmates of tragic stories of shipwreck, piracy and murder; to recitations from tragedies and comedies; to close arguments on various topics—navigation and seamanship, politics, morals and religion—and, at one point, to a lecture on history, of which I overheard enough to learn the subject to be the life and achievements of the brave Wallace, dilated upon in the broad dialect of the "land o' cakes!"

Light-heartedness and contentment seem every where to prevail, and all manifest by their conduct, as well as by word, that they feel themselves to be on board a favored ship.

Had I time for the record, you would be amused by many things I hourly hear and see, in my walks of leisure. To-day, while on the quarter-deck after the men's dinner, I overheard one of the messenger boys, who had just come from this meal, say to a companion, "I tell you what, Jim, I couldn't eat much of that dinner: old mahogany and hard tack, is what I call pretty tough eating. To-morrow too is bean day, and I wouldn't give a penny for a bushel of them." A sprightly young sailor who completed an apprenticeship in the service, happening to pass at the time, stopped for a moment, and with an assumed air of indignant reproof, exclaimed, "Why, you ungrateful young cub!—you growling at Uncle Sam's grub? why you ought to be down upon your knees thanking God that you have so good an uncle to give you any thing!"

Just afterwards, I fell into conversation with an old salt who had been with me, in the Delaware line-of-battle ship, in 1833. After mutual inquiries of various officers and men who were shipmates with us then; what had become of this one and what of that—he said, in all honesty of heart, and with a most lugubrious expression of face, "And there was Lieut. M—— too: they tell me, sir, *he stepped out entirely*, the other day at the Hospital!"—meaning that he had died there. I never heard the expression in such a connection before, and could not avoid being struck, not only with its oddity, but also with its force.

June 29th.—Just at nightfall, on my last date, we doubled Cape Antonio, the extreme westerly point of Cuba, at a distance of ten or twelve miles. It is long and low, covered with dark woods, and, in general aspect, not unlike the coasts of Long Island and New Jersey, as seen from the sea. As soon as our course was turned northward for Havana, the regular wind became adverse to us, and the next morning we were in the Florida Channel, far from the land and a hundred miles and more from our port. The tediousness of a dead beat to windward was relieved, however, by the greater freshness and elasticity of the air, in comparison with that on the south side of Cuba. For two or three evenings, here, the sunsets were among the most gorgeous I recollect. The whole western hemisphere, filled with fantastic and richly colored clouds, glowed with a brilliancy and glare of crimson light, as if the entire sea beneath were one vast bed of volcanic fire.

After two days we again made the land, with fine views during the afternoon, of two lofty ranges of mountains in the interior of the island—the Sierra del Rosario and the Sierra de los Organos or Organ mountains; but it was not till last night that we reached the parallel of Havana. At 10 o'clock the Moro light, at the entrance of the port, was descried, some fifteen miles distant. Its brilliant flashings, through the darkness of an unsettled sky, came cheerily upon the sight over the troubled water, in the assurance they gave of our true position, amid the changing currents and hazardous navigation of these straits.

Before daybreak this morning we fell in with and spoke the sloop-of-war Germantown, Captain Lowndes, cruising off the harbor. I was early on deck. The morning was fresh and beautiful, but the shores less bold and striking than I had anticipated; and the mountains in view were more remote. Still the landscape was pleasing in its verdure, though neither varied nor picturesque in its outline. Having been lying to for the night, we were still eight or ten miles from the entrance of the harbor; but the Moro Castle and city were in distinct view—the former, surmounted by its pharos towering loftily on a precipitous cliff of rock on the left of the entrance, and the latter stretching beneath it to the right, in a long line of whiteness on a level with the sea.

The scene increased momentarily in interest. A fresh trade-wind, creating a sea which, in the brightness of the sun, tossed up jets of diamonds on every side, hurried us rapidly forward, under topsails and topgallant-sails only: the Germantown, a beautiful craft, followed closely in our wake, fluttering over the water with the lightness and buoyancy of a bird. There were besides some eight or ten square-rigged merchant vessels in sight, under various degrees of sail—some entering and others leaving port. While in the midst of these, the Germantown and Congress interchanged salutes, with pretty effect on the general picture.

The wind had now increased to a half gale; a pilot had boarded us, and we bore away with a rush for the Moro, which immediately overhangs the entrance to the port. This is narrow —very narrow; seemingly a mere creek, a few ships' length only in width. It runs at right angles with the line of coast along which we were flying. This made it necessary in entering, to haul suddenly, from a free course, closely on the wind. We did so, at the speed of a race-horse, almost grazing the surf-lashed rocks over which tower the frowning battlements of the Moro, and within biscuit throw, as it were, of the batteries of the Punta on the opposite side—the pilot, momentarily alternating the exclamation "Hard a port!" "Hard a starboard!" "Steady—steady!" kept the men at the helm on the full spring in shifting the wheel from side to side; while at the same time the yards were filled with the crew reducing sail to bare poles, as if by magic, under the trumpet orders of the first lieutenant. I thought it one of the most exciting moments, and one of the most beautiful sights, in the navigation of so large a ship, I had ever witnessed.

In less time than is required thus to state it, we were transferred from the tossings of a rough sea, to the glassy surface of an apparent river. The scene on either hand was picturesque and animated. On one side, were the terraced heights adjoining the Moro, grim with the defences of war, relieved here and there by sentries and groups of soldiers, lounging about the batteries; and, on the other, level with the water, a range of stone quays, lined with shipping and coasting craft, and covered with sailors, boatmen, negro porters, and stevedores. Beyond rose the buildings of the city, painted in every variety of light and gay colors, and overtopped by the time-stained domes and towers of the churches and other public structures. The aspect of the whole was so entirely transatlantic, that I could scarce resist the illusion that I was again in old Spain, and that it was "fair Cadiz" I saw stretched before me. The gallantry of our entrance had attracted the gaze of the thousands crowding the quay in its whole length, and murmurs of admiration were every where heard at the beauty of our frigate, and the dashing style in which she glided rapidly along under the headway brought in by her from the sea.

At the end of half a mile, the straight and narrow inlet expands into a round basin, five or six miles in circumference. Near the centre of this we dropped anchor: having the city and its defences towards the sea on one side of us, and green hills tufted with palm-trees and dotted with cottages and country seats on the other. The harbor is a gem of beauty, capable of containing the navies of half the world. Five Spanish men-of-war, including a ship-of-the-line, are moored within pistol shot of us, and the Germantown immediately at our stern. The dropping of the anchor was followed by salutes from our batteries of twenty-one guns to the flag of Spain, seventeen to that of the Spanish admiral, in command, and nine in honor of Mr. Campbell, the American consul, who soon boarded the Congress.

CHAPTER III.

HAVANA.

July 1st.—The object of a visit by the Congress to Cuba, before proceeding to her station on the coast of Brazil, is to bring to a close the negotiations which have been for some time pending with the authorities here, in reference to our filibustering compatriots, the prisoners of Contoy.

The report made by Captain Lowndes of the Germantown, on boarding us in the offing, and by Mr. Campbell afterwards, of the state of public feeling in reference to these, and to the citizens of the United States in general, led us to apprehend there would be great difficulty in securing an amicable arrangement of the point at issue—the disposition to be made of the prisoners. The excitement and indignation of the Spanish population of the city, on the subject of the attempted invasion, had been great; and manifested especially, within a few days, against Mr. Campbell, for sentiments on the subject, exposed in a correspondence between him and the Secretary of State, recently called for by Congress, printed in the newspapers in the United States, and republished here. At one time the consulate was believed to be in great danger of violence from the mob; and the excitement is still far from being allayed. In view of this representation we apprehended a long delay. The first interview, however, between Commodore McKeever and the captain-general, the Conde d'Alcoy, relieved us from all fear of this. Every disposition was manifested to receive favorably the mission of the

Congress; and the belief is that the special matter of negotiation will be speedily adjusted.

The commodore and suite were received, at the vice-regal palace, in the most frank and cordial manner, and the personal relations of the treating parties placed, at once, on a friendly footing. The governor-general treated lightly the fear that had been suggested, of violence to the consulate, avowing that all property and life in the city and island were in the keeping of the government; and that safety in both was more sure to none, than to the representatives and citizens of the United States. Summoning the chief of police at once to his presence, the following dialogue in substance took place between them. "Have you heard, sir, of an apprehended attack by the populace upon the American consulate?" "No, sir." "Do you believe, sir, that any such danger exists?" "No, sir." "Could a project of the kind be in agitation without your knowledge?" "No, sir." "See to it, sir," added the count, with an intonation of voice not to be mistaken, as he dismissed the functionary, "that nothing of the kind takes place!"

The truth is, the warmth of sympathy felt by some of our fellow-citizens for the would-be revolutionists within Cuba and the marauding filibusters without, backed by visions of national and it may be personal aggrandizement, through annexation, lead them to magnify every grievance imaginary or real, and to fan into a flame each spark of ill will elicited by the collisions that occur, in the hope of embroiling our government with the crown of Spain; and, through conflict and conquest, of making sure to us this choicest gem left in her colonial tiara.

That the Cubans are most fearfully oppressed by the vice-regal rulers here, and that the government under which they suffer is the most rigorous military despotism in the civilized world, no one with the slightest knowledge of the condition of the island can doubt. The simple fact that twenty-four millions of dollars are annually wrung, by various forms of taxation, from a white population of little more than six hundred thousand, proves it, without an enumeration of the different unjust monopolies, the prohibitory imposts upon the first necessaries of life, the depreciating levies on all the products of labor, and the vampire presence of a foreign soldiery, sufficient to furnish a constant sentinel, it is said, to every four white men in the country; or, a reference to the fact that there are no common schools—no liberty of the press, no liberty of speech, and scarce the liberty of thought. Still, sad as the truth of such a condition is, it does not justify piratical invasion from without, or agitating and revolutionizing influence on our part within.

The probability is that the stay of the Congress will be very brief; and that, consequently, my personal knowledge of Havana and the Habaneros will be limited to a hasty glance, through such loop-holes of observation as I may accidentally light upon.

The beauty of the panorama from the anchorage is so varied and so striking, that in the enjoyment of it, I have been satisfied thus far without a visit to the shore, though this is the third day, including the Sabbath, since our arrival. While examining closely with a glass again and again, every feature of the open country to the east and south, I could but indulge in many a reminiscence of tropical life at the Sandwich Islands and South Seas, awakened by the plumed palm and broad-leafed banana, the brightly gleaming hill sides and velvet-like slopes characteristic of the scenery. On the opposite sides of the harbor, the city and its fortresses,—its private dwellings and public buildings, its towers and domes and embattled walls,—are open to like inspection through the same medium, a sea-telescope of surpassing excellence.

While in the midst of these observations this morning, screened from the mid-day sun by the well-spread awnings of the poop-deck, my attention was drawn to a movement near at hand on board, occasioned by a succession of visits of ceremony from the "powers that be" in this viceroyal dependency, to our commander-in-chief and our captain. I am told, whether correctly or not, that the same policy which of yore prevented Ferdinand

and Isabella from keeping faith with Columbus, in his appointment as viceroy of the New World with undivided power, is still adhered to by the Spanish throne. The supreme authority, in place of being vested in one representative of the crown, is distributed among three—one at the head of the civil affairs, another chief in those that are military, and a third supreme in the control of the marine. Each is in his own department independent of the other, and keeps check on his compeers in any assumption of undue authority. The captain-general, however, has precedence in matters of ceremony, and is the nominal head of the government. He does not visit vessels of war, and the courtesy on his part is expressed through an aide-de-camp. The visitor in his stead on this occasion, was the Conde Villeneuva, a fine-looking young man, in a richly embroidered dress of blue and silver, but without military decorations. He had scarcely been ushered on the deck, with the usual ceremony, when a barge, still more stately in the number of its oarsmen and the dimensions of its banner of "blood and gold," than that by which he had arrived, was reported by the quarter-master. This bore the Intendante, or Military Chief, who crossed the gangway in full costume, with a magnificent star on the breast and three or four crosses and badges of knighthood at the button holes. Neither name nor title was announced with sufficient distinctness to be heard, and in view of the number and brilliancy of his decorations, I felt authorized in giving him precedence of the count, by at least one grade in the peerage, and set him down for a marquis: especially as the state in which the next dignitary approached would lead to the supposition that he could be nothing less than a duke—a grandee of the first rank. He came in a superb sixteen-oared barge of the purest white, picked out in gold. He was a most stately old gentleman, portly in person, fresh in complexion for a Spaniard, and of the most courtier-like and finished manners. Three magnificently jewelled stars decorated his left breast, with the crosses of twice as many orders pendant beneath, and over all the broad ribbon and insignia of the Golden Fleece. It was the Commandant-general of Marine, or Naval Chieftain. These visits of mere ceremony were brief, referring in conversation to the most common-place topics, followed by a departure in the order of arrival.

The weather since we have been here has been like that of the finest days in June on the Hudson: the sun very hot, the sky glowingly bright, the breeze fresh and seemingly pure, with heavy showers occasionally in the afternoons. In the evenings and at night the scene from shipboard is striking and impressive. Long lines of brilliant gas-lights, marking the walls of the city abreast of us, with the gleamings of others from fortress and tower reflected by the glassy waters of the bay in streams of gold, and a glorious canopy of sparkling stars above, compensate in a degree for the absence of the moon; while a fine military band stationed on the ramparts nearly opposite us discourses eloquently, till nine o'clock, the compositions of the masters in opera.

July 8th.—My first visit on shore was in company with my messmate F——, after the heat of the day had begun to pass. The low quays of a yellowish stone which face the water, are thickly lined with the smaller craft, engaged in the commerce of the port. We made our way along these for some distance, through an atmosphere redolent of tar and pitch and cordage—coffee and tobacco,—amid soldiers and sailors and throngs of brawny negroes, more than half naked and reeking with perspiration, in the labor of loading and unloading cargoes. On turning into a narrow street leading into the city, we soon discovered, that the buildings which from our moorings meet the eye so strikingly in their gay tintings of sky-blue, pea-green, peach-blossom, lemon and straw colors, with their mouldings, cornices and balustrades of the purest white, are thickly interspersed with others, dingy, shabby, decayed and dirty: barn-like, stable-like and prison-like. To an untravelled visitor from the Northern States, this last characteristic would be the first peculiarity in the aspect of the houses to attract his attention. Every man's dwelling here is literally his castle, the defences of which give to its exterior, on the ground floor especially, the appearance of a jail at home. The heavy doors opening on the street, are of the most massive make, and bossed and studded with iron so as to be bullet-proof, while the lower windows are universally guarded from top to bottom by strong bars and network of the same material. The general style of building is the Spanish-Morescan, many of the dwellings being only one story in height. The streets are straight and regular, but very narrow, scarcely admitting two vehicles to pass each other, while the sidewalks, as termed by us, are on a level with the way for carriages, and a foot or eighteen inches only in width.

A short walk from the point at which we left the quay, brought us upon a small but pretty and artistic square called the Plaza de Armas. It is enclosed with a handsome iron railing, is regularly laid out in walks, bordered with gay flowers and shrubbery overhung by the silvery trunks and long pendant branches of the palm-tree, and ornamented in the centre with a fountain and statue of Ferdinand VII. of Spain. Its southern side is faced in its whole length by the palace of the governor-general, a spacious and handsome quadrangular structure of stone, stuccoed and painted sky-blue, with pilasters, cornice and balustrade around its flat roof, of white.

Our chief object in going on shore was the enjoyment of a drive outside the walls. The vicinity of the Plaza furnished us with the opportunity of a choice of equipage for the purpose. Lines and groups of vehicles were standing along its sides and at the corners. An omnibus of American fashion and manufacture was seen on its route, and a carriage of modern style passing here and there, but those on the stand were exclusively the common vehicle of the city and country, the volante—a two-wheeled clumsy-looking machine of by-gone times drawn on ordinary occasions by one horse. The body is larger than that of an American gig or chaise, hung very low like an old-fashioned phaeton, and so delicately poised on springs of great elasticity as to sway about, under the slightest impulse, with a most buoyant and luxurious motion.

I find even a pen-and-ink sketch so much more satisfactory than verbal description, in conveying just ideas of novelties such as this, that I am more than half disposed to attempt one here, at the double hazard of defacing my paper and bringing in contempt my skill in the arts. I will try it. The experiment is not quite so successful and effective as I could wish it to be, but it will answer the purpose. Do not think it, however, defective in the proportions exhibited, either in regard to man and beast, or to the distance of both from the body of the carriage. The wheels in their size and height, in comparison with the top of the volante, the length of the shafts, and the bulk of the black calesero, or postillion, in contrast with that of the little pony he bestrides, are all true to the reality, rather underdrawn than exaggerated. You must not suppose either that the little horse is without a tail: for though not very distinctly visible in the sketch, the tail is there; neatly plaited and closely twisted round the hip, like the braid of a lady's hair around her ear, and made fast by a gay ribbon to the postillion's saddle.

The colors of these carriages, in body, shafts and wheels, are more varied than those of the rainbow: scarlet, yellow, blue, green—in endless tintings, contrasting showily with mountings of silver or silver-gilt, in greater or less profusion and massiveness, according to the rank or riches of the owner. The harness to our eyes appears complicated and heavy. It also is ornamented more or less elaborately with silver or gilt platings. As to the postillion, picture to yourself the most perfect personification of Congo blackness you ever saw, in the form of a stout muscular negro, with features and heels to match; put him in a very short-waisted jacket—scarlet, blue, yellow or parti-colored, and gay with worsted lace for livery, and into very high riding boots, large enough for Goliath, and with the sketch, you will have a tolerable idea of the equipage in which F—— and I set off from the Café

Dominica, not far from the Plaza de Armas, for a drive in the suburbs.

At the end of a half mile, it may be, through the narrow streets, with shops and counting-rooms and dwellings on either side, widely open and within reaching distance by the hand, we came to the principal gateway in the western walls, leading directly upon the Paseo de Isabella II., the fashionable promenade and drive without the walls: the Hyde Park and Champs Elysee of the Habaneros. This extends the whole length of the western side of the city, and is garden-like and beautiful in its trees, shrubbery and flowers. Two broad carriage ways run from end to end with four or more gravelled walks between them; a fountain ornaments either extremity, and in the centre is a statuette of Isabella II., erected shortly after her succession when a child: the more welcome from associations of purity and innocence, which an image of her majesty in later years would be little calculated to suggest.

A range of stately buildings on the west, faces and overlooks this point of aristocratic and fashionable reunion: an opera house and palatial café with other imposing structures, giving quite a metropolitan air to the scene. The first two mentioned bear the name of Tacon, in honor of the captain-general of that name, during whose rule they were built, and whose administration a few years ago, was distinguished by such signal reforms in the police of the city, and the entire suppression of the cut-throat outrages before so common. The enlarged views, public spirit, energy and determination which characterized his measures, stamped his name indelibly on the city; and to these is the population indebted, not only for the effectual suppression of crime, but for much also of the ornamental architecture which it boasts.

South of the Paseo is the Champ de Mars, an extensive parade ground, lined with spacious barracks and other governmental buildings. Passing these we drove three or four miles over a broad and well-kept macadamized avenue, filled with animated life in every form, and lined with suburban residences luxuriant in the richness and beauty of tropical growth in tree, shrub and flower: all in such wide contrast with scenes witnessed in a drive of like length in the suburbs of a city with us, as to excite the wonder, why more of our citizens of wealth and leisure do not take the short trip to Havana in the winter, to be amused and instructed by its novelties, and charmed by the blandness of its climate and the splendor of its vegetable life. Although the soil in this section of the island is of an inferior quality to that of most other regions, there are evidences on every hand of the richness and beauty which have secured to Cuba the proud and winning title of "Queen of the Antilles," and make her the choicest colonial possession left to Spain.

From the heat of the climate, the construction of the houses, in general, is such as to make them little more than so many open pavilions, from which as you drive by, you unavoidably catch not only the

> "Manners living as they rise,"

but many, if not all, the habits of life of the inmates. The eye penetrates at a glance, as it were, the entire domestic economy of the household. The dwellings are, for the most part, one story only in height, with a tower or mirador at one end or corner, for a "look-out." Externally they seem all door and window. These are very wide, and extend from the ceiling to the floor, on a level with the street. Thrown widely open in the cool of the day, the interior becomes fully exposed: furniture and inmates—the whole family group in full dress or dishabille as the case may be—a scene on the stage of life, as open to inspection as one from a drama on the boards of a theatre. This is as true of the dwellings of the rich as of the poor. In seeing the whole diagram of the interior thus exposed without any appearance of bed or bedroom, the wonder in my mind was where the people could sleep? On expressing some curiosity on this point, I was told that in many cases, the beds of the family consist of mats or mattresses, spread at night on the floor, or in cots in the reception-rooms, while in most houses an inner court is encircled by small sleeping and dressing-rooms.

Many of the residences of the gentry and moneyed aristocracy in the suburbs are luxurious and princely; exhibiting long suites of spacious and elegantly furnished apartments, with floors of polished marble and the oriental luxury of jetting fountains and clustering flowers, endless in the variety of their tint and perfume. The gardens attached to some of these are laid out with taste, and kept in the nicest order, filled with an exuberance of choice plants known to us at the North only in the dwarfish and stunted growth of the conservatory. Indeed, many which are cherished exotics with us, are here seen in rank profusion in the hedges and by the roadside, like the thorn and the thistle of our ruder climate.

By the time of our return, the hour for the drive and promenade of the citizens had arrived; and, as we approached the Paseo, we were met and passed by great numbers of equipages of varied style. Some were altogether American and European in their appointments; but most were the native volante in greater or less elegance and richness—some with one horse only, and others with two. When two are used, the second is placed abreast of the one in the shafts and ridden by the calesero. Each carriage contained from one to three females, in full dress as if at a party—low necks and very short sleeves: to which may be added, very fat figures and very dark skins. Bonnets are not worn of course with this costume, nor indeed with any other. The coiffure at this season is of ribbons, gauzes, laces and other zephyr-like materials, with flowers and jewelry; but, in the winter, I am told, these give place to head-dresses of velvet and satin, with ostrich plumes, pearls and diamonds. As the volantes pass and repass along the carriage drive, salutations are exchanged between the ladies in the vehicles with each other, and with acquaintances and friends among the gentlemen on foot or on horseback, by the eyes, the fan and hat, more than with the voice; but, so far as I observed, the ladies did not alight as is the custom in Europe in many places of the kind, to join in the promenade on foot, or form groups for conversation. At nightfall there is a return to the city, where, for an hour or two, the ladies amuse themselves in driving from shop to shop, to have such articles as they ask for brought to their carriages for inspection, or, proceeding to the Plaza de Armas, again join their associates of the beau monde in display and flirtation by lamplight or moonlight as the case may be, while a regimental band in front of the governmental palace gives a free concert of instrumental music till nine o'clock. The evening on this occasion was delightful, and we prolonged our stay and observations till that hour.

So well pleased was F—— as well as I with this first peep on shore, that we repeated the visit two days after, driving as far as the Bishop's garden, the principal attraction of the kind in the neighborhood of the city. Since then there has been much heavy rain. The trade wind at the same time ceased, causing a closeness of atmosphere that has been very oppressive, and made me more than content to remain for the most part quietly on board ship: I say for the most part, for I went once into the city, on a solitary pilgrimage to the tomb of the good and great, and ever to be honored, discoverer of the New World. As you know, his remains were removed at intervals of time of various length, from Valladolid where he died, to Seville, and from Seville to St. Domingo, the resting-place designated for them in his will. On the cession of that island to France in 1796, they were brought to Cuba, and deposited with great ceremony in the cathedral of Havana. A medallion likeness in marble, with a short inscription on a mural tablet, marks the spot in the chancel near the high altar where they have found, as it is to be hoped, a lasting sepulchre. No American can stand near them unmoved: or without a recurrence in thought to the sublime vision of an unknown world, which so long filled the mind, and amid endless discouragements and disappointments sustained the hopes and energies of the adventurous navigator, till it issued in a glorious reality; or without deep sympathy in the vicissitudes and trials of his after life, and the neglect and injustice which brought his gray hairs with sorrow to the tomb. Near by are exhibited—I was about to say the ignominious, but I recall the epithet—the ennobled fetters with which an ungrateful monarch permitted a jealous rival and enemy to manacle his limbs.

On another occasion I left the ship after night, for a row across the harbor with Lieut. T—— in his gig. It had been our intention to pass the evening in the city, in a visit to some families of his acquaintance to whom he wished to introduce me, but the heat and dampness of a debilitating and sickening atmosphere during the day, determined us to postpone this till the return of a more invigorating and elastic air. Our row was from the anchorage of the men-of-war through that of the merchant ships, at another point in the harbor, to a landing near the town of Regla opposite the city; a place of no enviable notoriety, in times past, as a kind of city of refuge through the indulgent winkings of government officials, first for the pirates who once infested these regions, and more recently for dealers in the slave trade. Here also is one of the principal amphitheatres for the exhibition of the favorite national amusement, the bull fight. The special object of the trip, on the part of my companion, had some reference to the disposition of the *slush* of the Congress, if you can comprehend the import of so elegant a term in a ship's economy: mine partly the pleasure of his company, and partly to inquire the state of the sick in a private hospital for cases of yellow fever, and to learn the practicability of visiting any American seamen, who might be suffering there from this pest of Havana, already beginning its annual ravages.

The night was very dark for a tropical region, and the most striking imagery discernible, as we threaded our way amidst the shipping, was the black masses of spars and rigging pencilled against the sky above us; the long line of brilliant lights marking the walls of the city reflected in streams of fire on the glassy water; and the alternate dim glimmerings and blinding flashes of the revolving pharos, surmounting the lofty tower of the Moro.

July 10th.—Bright weather has returned, and with it the regular trade wind from the sea. We rejoice in this, not only from the greater comfort it insures, but also from the promise it holds out of continued health in our ship's company. The change induced Lieut. T—— and myself to make our contemplated visit on shore last evening. For a couple of hours before nightfall, we drove in a volante a circuit of some miles through the environs, amid scenes and scenery of unceasing novelty and endless variety, embracing the attractive and beautiful; the grotesque and ludicrous; elegance and magnificence, filth, nakedness and degradation, strangely commingled. Here, a splendid equipage as perfect in its appointments as any to be met in New York or London; there, a vehicle as rude and clumsy as if belonging to the birthday of invention. Here a cabalero admirably mounted, riding a blooded horse with all the stately solemnity of a grandee of the first order; there, a negro or montero, in rags and half nakedness urging onward, at a most sorry pace, as broken down a skeleton of a pony or jackass as ever contrived to put one foot before another. Here a squad of well-equipped soldiers; there a gang of manacled and ruffian-looking galley-slaves—thus without end, exciting alternate admiration and disgust, smiles and pity. Before commencing the visits of the evening, we took a bird's-eye view of the fashionable movements in the Paseo, from the upper balconies of the Café Tacon which overlook it, and of the magnificent panorama of the city, the surrounding country, and the sea, commanded from the leads of its flat roof, and then proceeded to meet an engagement at the consulate for tea.

July 11th.—It has been known for two or three days past, that the object of our visit was well nigh accomplished, and that the prisoners of Contoy were to be delivered to the keeping of our flag, on the condition of their immediate transportation to the United States. The U. S. steamer Vixen came into port yesterday, bringing Commodore Morris as an additional agent of our government in the negotiation of this matter, but too late for the object of his mission, the work being already done.

At twelve o'clock this morning, the prisoners were brought on board the Congress in the boats of the Spanish ship-of-the-line near us. They are some forty-two or three in number, appearing a sorry-looking set of adventurers indeed, as they crossed the ship's sides to be mustered in the gangways, and turned over to our charge by the Spanish officer bringing them. Most of them are young—many mere boys—and a majority evidently scapegraces, including a few wild-looking, muscular and wiry Western men, tall Kentuckians and Mississippi black-legs. They have been well fed and well taken care of, it is said; but they all looked pale, and some seemed nervously agitated. This is to be attributed, it is probable, to the uncertainty till the very moment, of the result of the sudden summons they had received from their keepers to prepare for some event of which they were kept ignorant, and which they had more reason to fear might be death under the fire of a platoon of soldiers, than liberty beneath the flag of their country. During their captivity they had been denied all intercourse with others, and had no means of learning their probable fate. At times, the most intelligent among them had been subject to threats of immediate execution, seemingly in the hope of extorting some confession differing from the general attestation, that they had been entrapped into the expedition, under a contract of being conveyed to the isthmus, on their way to California, and on discovering the imposition had refused to take part in the attempted invasion. The most cheering hopes that had reached them were derived from the salutes, in honor of the 4th of July. They inferred from these the presence of American men-of-war of heavy metal, and that their case was neither forgotten nor neglected by the American government. I well recollect thinking and feeling, at the time, that the repeated thunder of the heavy batteries of the Congress, from sunrise to sunset on that day, re-echoed by all the men-of-war in port, must have brought them hope with no uncertain sound, whether it reached their ears in the hold of the guard-ship or the dungeons of the Moro castle: for even the place of their confinement was withheld from us. At three o'clock this afternoon, the whole number was transferred to the sloop-of-war Albany, for passage to Pensacola. She is to sail to-morrow morning at daybreak, and it is announced that the Congress will leave the harbor in company with her, and proceed to her destination on the coast of Brazil.

Great credit is due to Commodore McKeever for the speedy adjustment of this difficulty. His courteousness and amenity at once made smooth the way to negotiation. He is a man of peacefulness and good will, more disposed to pour the oil of kindness on troubled waters than to cast in any new element of agitation, and to his firmness and gentleness combined, are to be attributed the early and desirable result attained.

Thus terminates this filibustering invasion of Cuba. But is it the end? The enterprise, as projected and fitted out, was most ill-judged and piratical. But is it true that its origin and means of equipment were entirely from abroad? Is there no deep sympathy with such an adventure among the Creole inhabitants of the island themselves? Is the spirit of patriotism and of liberty here dead? Are there no groanings beneath the galling chains of a cruel and grinding despotism? No sense of degradation, no purpose to be free, among the intelligent and aspiring of the native population? It is impossible that there should not be. The prosperity and the glory of the unfettered nation immediately facing them are too near, and too brilliant, not to be reflected eventually in attractive splendor, through every valley, and over every mountain top of this gem of the seas. An atmosphere of freedom so near, must impart something of its elasticity and its power even to the depressing vapors of such a despotism. The Cuban in his summer visits of business or of pleasure to the United States, inhales and carries it back with him, and the American in his winter sojourn here, insensibly bears it wherever he goes. The breath of liberty has been, and will continue to be inspired by the natives of the island; and unless the mother country, with timely wisdom, changes her colonial policy and ameliorates her iron rule, restlessness, agitation and revolt, must be the issue, and Cuba become independent in self-rule, or free by voluntary annexation to the nation to which, geographically at least, she rightfully belongs.

CHAPTER IV.

GULF OF FLORIDA.

July 12th.—True to the announcement last night, all hands were called to weigh anchor at daybreak this morning; and, by sunrise, under the double impulse of a light land breeze, and the oars of a long line of man-of-war boats having the Congress in tow, we made our way, through the narrow entrance of the port, to the open sea.

Many merchant ships also were taking their departure. The shrill calls of the bugle from barrack and fortress; the unfurling of signal and banner from mast-head, battlement and tower; strains of military music from different points; the lively movement in all directions of boats and small craft on the water; and the rising hum of active life from the city, gave exciting animation to the picture, while the purple hues of the morning and its balmy breath, added a fresh charm to the whole.

After enjoying the scene till we were outside the harbor, I went below, intending to return to the deck in time for a farewell view, not only of the island, but of the Moro castle and city also. So rapid was our course, however, from a strong current, as well as a fresh breeze, that, on reaching the poop for this purpose, "the blue above and the blue below" were alone to be seen; and undisguised satisfaction was every where manifested that, not only the sickly, though beautiful port, but the entire island had been left out of sight behind us.

The first object that met my eyes this evening, at the close of our accustomed worship on deck, was the silver crescent of a new moon beautifully defined in the empurpled sky; and, I interpreted the mild and benignant beamings sent down upon us, from its young course, as an omen of good in our voyage across the wide sea.

July 22*d*, N. Lat. 37°, W. Long. 59°.—We made our way gently and pleasantly through the Straits of Florida: sighting, during successive nights, on either sides of the channel, while making long stretches against a head wind, the lights of Key West and Sand Key, Carysfort Reef, and Gun Key. These numerous beacons speak the perilous navigation of the region. It is peculiarly the empire of the wreckers, whose lives are spent in constant search along the reefs, which for two hundred miles here edge the coast, for the vessels which in great numbers are yearly cast upon them by storms, or the treacherous currents of a calm. The value of the commerce which annually passes through the Gulf of Florida is estimated at four hundred millions of dollars, of which not less than half a million, each year, is lost by shipwreck, notwithstanding the vigilance and prompt exertion of the amphibious and heroic race, whose business is the rescue of the lives and property here endangered.

For three days after regaining a latitude which admitted of plain sailing, we had boisterous weather and a wild sea, but an unclouded sky. The elastic and invigorating atmosphere attending it, was most welcome after the heats of Cuba. At such times the ocean, in its ever-varying forms of beauty and changing shades of prismatic light in the sunshine, often outrivals in attractiveness the still life of a wide-spread landscape on shore. There is, too, a voice of music breathing over it; for, not less truthfully than poetically, has it been said of the ocean, there is

"In its sleep a melody,
And in its march a psalm."

Now, however, in place of the

"Restless, seething, stormy sea,"

we have on every side an illimitable plain of the deepest blue, with scarce a perception of those giant heavings from beneath, which ever, in a greater or less degree, tell of an unfathomable abyss of waters. Over this we are hurried, without a consciousness of motion, at the rate of ten miles the hour, by a breeze as balmy, if not as fragrant, as the zephyrs of "Araby the blest." Add to these surroundings, the moon, at night, riding the heavens above in sublime tranquillity, and you will not be surprised, if, at times at least, I am ready with the poet to exclaim—

"Oh! what pleasant visions haunt me,
As I gaze upon the sea,
All the old romantic legends—
All my dreams come back to me!"

July 29th.—Happily I am not unfitted for mental occupation; by being on shipboard, as is the case with many, and, with the prospect of a voyage of fifty or sixty days, I have set myself closely to work. The early part of the day I give to the graver studies of my profession, and the later to lighter reading; visits to the sick, when there are such; exercise on deck with some fellow-officer; and such "walks of usefulness" as I can light upon among the crew, in different parts of the ship in the evening, fill up the intervals of leisure till bed-time.

One of our young officers, Midshipman L——, has the misfortune to be incapacitated for duty, by a nervous affection of the eyes and head, the consequence of three separate attacks of fever in the Gulf of Mexico. The surgeons interdict to him all use of the eyes; and, to relieve the ennui into which he is thus thrown, I have invited him to my room for an hour or two every day, that by my reading aloud he may have the benefit of such works as I am running over; travels and biography—Maxwell's Russia, Irving's Mahomet, and the excellent books of Miss McIntosh, the accomplished sister of the captain of the Congress, interspersed with those of a more serious character, such as Angell James' "Young Man from Home" and Pike's "Persuasives to Early Piety"—have thus far occupied these hours. The touches of deep feeling frequently met in the writings of Miss McIntosh, in her lifelike and instructive delineations of character, have been the means of bringing into exercise sympathies, the involuntary betrayal of which to each other, has led to quite an intimate friendship, considering the disparity of our years.

For a week after leaving port, we had every reason to hope that it had been with entire impunity, in regard to health, that we had been exposed to the burning sun, and, at this season of the year, pestilential air of Havana. But on the eighth day, just as we were congratulating ourselves on the certainty of our escape from all infection, a light fever made its appearance among both officers and men. Some dozen in number were brought down by it. It was the yellow fever, but of so modified a type, that, in a few days, all were convalescent and no new cases occurred.

Sickness, whether of a serious nature or not, presents an opportunity of approach, and often gives access to the confidence which I am careful to improve. I was much interested, a day or two ago, in an interview with a fine-looking young man of the crew, under the influence of the prevailing epidemic. He had evidently been familiar with better associations than those of a man-of-war; and, I soon learned from him that he was the prodigal son of a pious mother, by whom he had been carefully trained and cherished, and was a child of many prayers. The first glance of his eye, as I approached his cot, told me by the starting tears —not from alarm, for no danger was apprehended in his case, but from remembrances of the past—that he was in a state of mind to open his heart to me; and, in the admissions and confessions of a long conversation, I became deeply interested in the penitence and purposes of future well-doing which he avowed.

In a hammock near by I found a middle-aged Scotchman, of intelligent and respectable appearance, who was equally open to religious conversation. He told me he had been long deeply sensible of his guilt and misery as a sinner, and greatly troubled in mind and conscience; that a conflict had been going on in his soul, as if a good and an evil spirit were ever in contest there for the mastery over him: but that the good at last had gained the triumph, and he was "at peace with the Father, through the Son and Spirit, and feared no evil—not death itself."

August 7th, N. Lat. 12°, W. Long. 38°.—Delicious seems the only epithet descriptive of the atmosphere we are now breathing, and "delicious—delicious!" is the stereotyped exclamation of every one, as he mounts to the deck from below and drinks in the pure ether, as if it were the very elixir of life. The morning is in all respects lovely. The heavens have a look of infinity. A snow-white cloud alone floats here and there in them; and, as, rushing over the blue sea, before the fresh trade-wind, we dash the foam widely from our prow, unnumbered flying fish spring into the air, and skim the surface of the water before and around us, like so many birds of silver gleaming brightly in the sun.

August 28th, N. lat. 3° 30′, W. Long. 25°.—The region, through which we have been making our way, for the last ten days, is known among seamen by the very unsentimental name of the "doldrums." The origin of the epithet it might be difficult to trace. It is an equatorial belt, characterized by light weather and head-winds; by alternate calms and squalls, clouds and rain. Hence every thing on board and without, is, and has been, in as wide contrast as possible with that of my last date. The whole ship is saturated, both on deck and below, with rain, and the washings of the sea through the ports and hawser-holes. The air on deck is close and oppressive, and below stifling and musty, and the tossings and pitchings and rolling of the ship any thing but agreeable to the fastidious stomachs of many on board—especially to my friend T——, who, though familiar for more than twenty years with the caprices of the deep, is in a most annoying state of discomfort at every return of rough weather. The progress made on our course is small, averaging not more than twenty-five or thirty miles in the twenty-four hours, though we sail by tacks in that period, from a hundred to a hundred and fifty. We are navigating by Lieut.

Maury's wind and current charts, and notwithstanding the seeming tedium of our progress, in beating against what he denominates the south-west monsoons of these latitudes, are satisfactorily demonstrating the truth of his theory and the correctness of his sailing directions in conformity with it.

It is now some six or eight years since this distinguished young officer, whose attainments in abstruse and practical science have reflected such high honor not only on his profession but on his country, conceived the idea of collecting as many of the log-books of navigators as could be secured, with a view of collating them, and of projecting upon charts, to aid in the better navigation of the sea, the general experience in winds and currents, at all periods of the year, in the different regions of the ocean. He at the same time urged upon the masters of ships, the importance of adding to the usual subject-matter of their logs, the temperature of the water, the set of currents, and the depth of the bed of the ocean when it was practicable to obtain soundings. As an incentive to the trouble of thus keeping a log, and of furnishing an abstract of it to the National Observatory at Washington, the promise was given that each shipmaster complying with the suggestion, should receive gratuitously from the government, a copy of the charts and sailing directions which might be the result.

Not fully alive to the object or aware of its great importance, the response was slow and imperfect. In the course of a few years, however, sufficient data were secured; and the first practical result was the shortening by ten days of the voyage to the equator, and consequently to Rio de Janeiro. From the earliest times this passage, from North America, had been made by running obliquely across the Atlantic to the longitude of the Cape de Verde Islands, before venturing to strike the north-east trade-wind. A traditionary report and belief in the existence of strong adverse currents along the South American coast, and the fear of not being able to double Cape St. Roque, should the equator not be crossed far to the East, led to this. It required no little moral courage and determination in one of a class proverbially wedded to custom and subject to superstition, to venture the trial of the new route. Such an one was found, however, and the result was most satisfactory. The opinion is now firmly entertained by many of the most experienced navigators, that by following the direction of the wind and current charts, the length of the voyage is diminished one fifth. This is an immense saving of time in a commercial point of view. Doubtless the patient perseverance of the accomplished astronomer, in this new field of discovery, with the aids which are now rapidly placed in his possession, will lead to similar results on all the grand routes of navigation over every ocean, and place the commercial world in indebtedness to his genius for savings in time, and consequently in money, of incalculable amounts.

Last night, from nine till ten o'clock, we enjoyed a beautiful spectacle, in a halo around the moon of colors as vivid as those of an ordinary rainbow, and in concentric circles most clearly defined. The moon, near the full, retained her face of silver in the midst of a field of gold, shadowing towards the outer edge into a delicate amber and then into the deepest maroon. A belt of the purest blue intervened, when the encircling colors were repeated in fainter hues; apparently, though not philosophically, a reflection of the first. The phenomenon was so striking, and so singularly beautiful, that Lieut R——, the officer of the deck at the time—one ever alive to the poetic and impressive in nature, as well as to the scientific and practical in his profession—dispatched a messenger hurriedly for me. The commodore and captain were also summoned, and soon, with most of the other officers, joined us on the poop, while the whole crew, from different parts of the ship, shared in the admiration excited by the scene. It is the first exhibition of any thing unusual in sky or sea that has thus far marked our passage. A humid atmosphere and a thin fleecy scud were its accompaniments.

August 23d.—In the course of the night of the 22d inst. we took the south-east trade-wind, three degrees north of the equator, and at once bade adieu to the doldrums. We crossed the line at high noon, yesterday, on the parallel of 28° 30′ W. long. without any very perceptible 'jolt;' and are rushing on our course at the rate of ten miles the hour.

Just in the edge of the evening, after hammocks had been piped down, the ship was hailed loudly from the bows, and it was reported to the officer of the deck, that "Neptune was alongside and requested permission to come on board." This was granted, and very unexpectedly to me this monarch of the seas, his queen and suite made their appearance on deck. They were soon enthroned on the forecastle, with an immense bathing tub filled with salt water in front of them, in readiness for the presentation of those of the crew who had never before been in this section of their watery dominions. The sun being long set, and the moon, for the time, obscured, I could not make out very well the costume of their majesties further than to judge it to be of the latest marine fashion. The most conspicuous article in that of Neptune was a full bottomed wig of white manilla grass, closely curled, like that of a lord chancellor on the woolsack, but covering not only his head, face and shoulders, but his entire figure, giving him the aspect in general of a polar bear with the head and mane of a lion. He bore himself with imperial dignity, while Madame Amphitrite, of very sturdy and Dutch-like make, sat meekly by his side, in a fashionably made dress of coarse canvas, or sacking, with a shepherdess hat of the same material, hair in long ringlets 'à l'Anglaise,' cheeks highly rouged, low neck and short sleeves, with bare arms which bore a very suspicious resemblance, in muscle and color, to those of one of our most brawny forecastle men.

The commodore, with whom I was walking on the poop-deck, being informed of the presence of the distinguished company, made his way to the forecastle, claiming courteously from the monarch the privilege of the entrée, from having crossed the equator already some dozen of times. This Neptune most graciously conceded, with the flattering remark that he "recollected his countenance perfectly, and was very glad to see him." The

3

interview, like most others on state occasions, was brief, concluding on the commodore's part by his saying, "he presumed the presentations of the evening would be numerous," Neptune replying "yes," that he had "never seen so many green-horns on board one ship in his life!" A call of the names of candidates for the honor was now begun, and the gentlemen of the court, disguised in dress and with blackened faces, began to drag from every hiding place many an unwilling, but vainly resisting subject, who had never before entered the southern hemisphere. Forced into the presence with good-nature and laughter, by overpowering numbers, and blindfolded and seated on the edge of the tub, the victim was hailed by Neptune with stentorian voice through an immense paste-board trumpet, in the questions—"What is your name?" "Where are you from?" "Were you ever in these parts before?" While in the act of answering each of these respectively, a coarse brush dipped in a mixture of tar, slush, and lampblack was hastily passed over the mouth of the respondent. The court barber was then called to do his duty in shaving the gentleman with No. 5, No. 9, or No. 15, referring to the qualities of the razor; this being determined by the degree of submissiveness and good-nature, or the surliness and resistance of the subject in hand. The lathering brush was something of the form and softness of a broom of split hickory, the lather the composition before described, and the razors, two or three feet in length, of different degrees of edge, from the smoothness of straight wood to the roughness of a jagged piece of iron hoop. When an order for dressing the hair was added, in penalty of special refractoriness and ill-humor, the brush used was formed of long wooden pegs fixed in a board with a handle, like a hatchel for dressing flax; the pomatum, tar; to which, in extreme cases, was added a powdering of flour in the style of "'76," the whole winding up with a sudden souse, backwards, heels over head into the tub of salt water. The presentation thus completed, the new courtier, half drowned, and dripping like a water god, was left at liberty to free himself at leisure from the tar and lampblack, and dry himself as best he could.

The case of all others, in which the least sympathy was elicited, was that of a young landsman, who, after long impunity, had been detected some time before as a thief—supplying his own wardrobe very freely from the clothes-bags of his shipmates. The answer to the usual question, "who is this?" when he was brought forward, "Jackson the thief!" was received with a general shout of applause, and the following dialogue ensued. "What is your name?" "Jackson." "Yes, sir; and the sooner you slip yourself out of one so illustrious the better." "Where are you from?" "O——." "And a disgrace you are to so respectable a place. Were you ever in my dominions before?" "No." "I knew it: and take care you are never found in them again; or, if you are, look out how you fill your bag with other men's clothes for an outfit!" "Barber, do your duty: give him No. 15, and see that you dress his hair in the first style!"

The striking of eight bells and the calling of the first night watch brought the rough sport to an end. I have not time to-night to moralize on the subject or to speculate upon the propriety of the indulgence. By whose authority it was sanctioned I do not know. Many of the officers regarded it I believe with disapprobation, as a species of saturnalia unsuited to the rigid discipline of a man-of-war, and liable to be abused, while others defended it on the ground of old usage among sailors, and as an amusing relief to the tedium of a long voyage. By a little management I succeeded in screening from observation, till all hands were called to duty, two or three youngsters who were anxious to escape the annoying process.

August 25th.—Sailing in the latitudes of the south-east trade-winds is the very perfection of life at sea. The waters, as smooth and level as a prairie, are of the deepest tint of blue, with the addition in certain declinations of the sun, of a dash of rose color, imparting to the whole, for a time, the appearance of a plain of velvet of the true Tyrian purple. Though moving with great rapidity, through a wide and deep furrow of sparkling foam cast up by our bows, the sails of our frigate, fully set from the deck to the royal-mast-heads fore and aft, sleep by the hour, without the slightest apparent motion, as if, in place of canvas spread to the breeze, they were a like quantity of chiselled marble. Then, at night, such a moon! with the southern cross in marked beauty inviting to the sublimest meditations. The Magellan clouds, too, are in sight: small spots of fleecy whiteness in the sky, similar in general aspect to the nebulæ of the milky way. Indeed, with the mercury by Farenheit at 66° the whole Southern hemisphere is in brilliant exhibition, many of the most conspicuous stars flashing on the eye, not only with the brightness, but apparently with the varying tints of the diamond.

The smoothness of the sea and steadiness of the wind have afforded a good opportunity for exercise at the batteries, and in the various evolutions incident to an engagement in battle. The station of a chaplain, in action, is with the surgeons in the cockpit in attendance upon the wounded and dying; or, at his option perhaps, on the quarter-deck, in taking notes of the conflict. In these sham engagements, at least, I prefer the deck: and have stood with the commodore and captain, while broadside after broadside has been fired, till the whole ship has been enveloped in smoke, and I found myself at the end as well powdered as a miller, though not in such whiteness. An evening or two since trial was made in throwing shell with the Paixhan guns. The explosion took place eight seconds after the discharge, with beautiful effect. The tendency of all these exhibitions, though only as an exercise, is ever to make me regard with fresh horror and abhorrence the entire system of war—its principles, spirit, implements and cruel results.

August 30th.—The prevailing thoughts and feelings of my mind and heart this morning, traceable to visions of the night, may be best expressed, perhaps, by the familiar quotation—

"Who has not felt how sadly sweet
The dream of home—the dream of home
Steals o'er the heart too soon—too fleet,
When far o'er sea, or land we roam!
Sunlight more soft may o'er us fall,
To greener shores our bark may come,
But far more bright, more dear than all,
That dream of home—that dream of home!"

Little as I may have confessed it, "Riverside!"—"Riverside!" is the constant echoing of my heart, and my home is ever in bright vision before me. I breakfast with you every morning, sit by moonlight with you in the verandah every evening: walk with you every day to "Prospect Rock"—to "Gortlee"—to the upper fields beneath the mountain, and drive with you, if at no other time, at least every Sunday to your little church, along the magnificent terrace of the river-road.

I say, I breakfast with you every morning. Did you know exactly the state of the larder and store-room of our mess, you would wonder that I do not include all my meals in the avowal. For some time past, on each successive day, the giving out of article after article for our table, has been reported, till nothing now remains but salt beef, so hard as fully to justify the sailor's cognomen of "Uncle Sam's Mahogany," and salt pork as rusty as the beef is hard. No potatoes or other vegetables, no butter better than rancid lard, and no bread fit to be eaten except the ship's "hard tack," are left. Dried beans and peas we have, but both filled with weevil, which the cook has devised no means of separating, before being served, from the article itself. The consequence is, that when they come to us in the form of soup, the floating insects drowned and overdone, are the most conspicuous part of the mess, and when baked, give to the dish the appearance of being already well peppered. I can join very cheerfully in a jest over such untempting fare, and think of home; but cannot, like some of my messmates, persuade myself into the illusion that the little black insects speckling our board are only a rich condiment to give zest to the repast, and with them partake of it *con gusto*.

Yesterday our last turkey, after having given flavor to a tureen of watery soup, was served as a boiled dish. As we were about taking our seats at the table, a suggestion, made either seriously or in mischief, that the poor bird had not waited for the cook to bring its head to the block, but had died unexpectedly of its own accord, put a participation of either soup or meat, on my part, out of the question; and led, by the time the report had made the circuit of the table, to a kind of impromptu Court of Inquiry in the case. The steward was at once summoned by the head of the mess, who, fond of a joke, and knowing that the fat and shining negro, now honored with this office, like many of the more imitative and aspiring of his race, was somewhat grandiloquent in his language, put to him the question—"Steward, are you quite sure that the old fellow under this cover was entirely vigorous when he was taken from the coop?" "No! sir, he wasn't wigorous at all! he was perfectly good!" "Why, steward, what do you suppose I mean by vigorous?" "I don't know, sir, but I suppose from the way you ask me, something bad." "Well, steward, I do not wish to be too particular in this investigation, but just tell me this much, could the old fellow really stand on his legs when he was killed?" "Sartain, sir, he could." "Then, gentlemen," says Mr. ——, addressing himself to the mess, "I go for the turkey," and lifting the cover disclosed to view a mere skeleton in a shrivelled bag of skin, with scarce an ounce of flesh on the whole carcass.

You must not infer, either from the feelings expressed at the beginning of this date, or from the dietetic disclosure into which I have been incidentally betrayed, that I am otherwise than entirely content and happy: as much so as I well can be in this world of imperfection and sin. This is attributable, however, chiefly if not solely to the conviction in mind and heart, that I am at the post of duty—

"The shepherd of a wandering flock
That has the ocean for its wold—
That has the vessel for its fold;"

and am, as I trust, in a spirit cheerfully and faithfully to meet its responsibilities. Whether to any high result or visible effect, it is not in the power of man to say. The sufficiency for this is of God alone. I am thankful that I feel no discouragement in the use of the means for moral reformation and spiritual grace in those around me. Nothing but personal experience could persuade one of the almost insurmountable obstacles that exist, on board a man-of-war, to the conversion of any of the crew, and to a life of godliness in one of their number, or make him credit without close observation, the number and the power of

"The secret currents that here flow
With such resistless under-tow,
And lift and drift with terrible force
The will from its moorings and its course."

Nothing less than a miracle, humanly speaking, could achieve such a result; but, as the conversion of any soul, and a life of godliness in any heart, anywhere, are miracles of grace, I do not allow myself to despair of such results ultimately through the word and Spirit of God, whether I ever know them or not. So firmly is hand joined in hand among the crew, against every thing savoring of a profession of or pretension to personal religion, that it would require no ordinary degree of moral courage, in any one—whatever might be his secret convictions, feelings or purposes—to disclose or avow it. Many cheerfully give countenance, both by their words and conduct to good morals in others; but all seem tacitly at least to say "thus far only shalt thou go." Though it is by no means unusual to see one and another in different parts of the ship reading a Bible or a Testament either alone or aloud to others; though tracts, and religious papers, and books, are eagerly accepted and seriously read, still, to get the name of a 'Bible-man' by joining a class for reading under the chaplain, or of a psalm-singing and praying man, from being known to practise such devotion, is as much dreaded as would be a scurrilous reproach. From this feeling it is, that I have thus far attempted in vain to establish Bible-classes or secure a meeting for moral and religious instruction, beyond the public worship of the Sabbath and our daily evening prayer: and from the same fear of man it is that one or two spiritually-minded members of a church, whom I have discovered among the ship's company, are unwilling to have their true character and profession known.

The purpose of those chief in authority, to abandon as far as practicable, in the discipline of the ship, the iron rule, and in place of the "cats" and the "colt," the kick and the curse, to substitute a treatment less degrading to man and more befitting him as a moral agent and an intelligent being, has been carried out. Thus far the experiment has been successful; and we have a cheerful, obedient, active and efficient crew. We are also demonstrating the fact by experience, that a crew can be content and happy without having served to them the ration of grog furnished by government. Knowing that two thirds of all the evil and misery to which sailors, as a class, are subject both at sea and on shore, arises from the use of strong drink, I, early after the commencement of our cruise, made efforts by private argument as well as by public addresses, to demonstrate the magnitude of the evils arising from intemperance, and to persuade all to follow the example of those who had stopped drawing rum. In securing so desirable an object, I have had the warm support of those in authority, whose opinion and influence would be likely to have most effect. Commodore McKeever and Captain McIntosh have both given me their aid; and the former has twice publicly addressed the ship's company on the subject. The consequence is, we shall enter port without the name of an individual on the grog list; with the universal admission that the ship's company, to say the least, are as content and happy without the rum as they were with it, and certainly more quiet and orderly.

In the course of my canvass on the subject, I had, not only, many interesting, but many amusing conversations and arguments with various individuals. Before yielding, there was a great struggle in the minds of some half a dozen old topers—old men-of-wars-men, perfect sea-dogs, who, for half a century have drunk their grog as regularly as the roll of the drum announcing its readiness was heard, and felt that they could not live without it. I really pitied some of these old fellows, in the mental struggle they suffered, between conscience and a desire to follow the advice of those they honor, and the continued craving of an appetite strengthened by the habit of a whole life. I fell in with two of these one day immediately after one of the addresses of the Commodore. They were looking most doleful—as a true sailor seldom does look except in some great moral extremity. Suspecting the cause, I opened a conversation in which one of them met my persuasions by saying, with a most appealing look, "Why, Mr. S——, I haven't been without my grog every day for fifty years. Why, sir, I should die without it. I was brought up on it; my father kept a public house, and I sucked the tumblers, sir, from the time I was a baby!" But the old man soon joined the rest of his shipmates in the resolution to banish the grog tub. He has now gone a long time without his rum; and, in place of dying from the want of it, as he said he should, came up to me yesterday, looking hale and hearty, and with a bright smile and sparkling eye, said, "Mr. S——, I wouldn't have believed it—but, it's true. I don't miss my grog at all. You told me I would live through it, if I did knock it off. And so I have, and I feel ten times better without it than I ever did with it!"

CHAPTER V.

RIO DE JANEIRO.

Sept. 4th.—Land was descried at ten o'clock, on the morning of the 1st inst., and before noon we had Cape Frio in full view, twenty miles distant. Isolated from other highlands of the coast, it stands out boldly and loftily in the ocean; and, after being once seen, is not easily to be mistaken in its outline. We were rushing onward, before a fresh trade-wind beneath a brilliant sky, at the rate of eleven miles the hour; and at twelve o'clock, hauling closely round the Cape to the westward, opened a lofty and picturesque mountain coast on our right.

The speed at which we were sailing was in itself sufficient to produce great exhilaration. Add to this, the beauty of the sportive sea—leaping, foaming, and sparkling around us; the varied and noble outlines of the shore; the objects of increasing interest coming hourly in view, with the assurance of an early termination of our passage, and you can readily imagine that by nightfall, the continued excitement became almost painful. As darkness began to gather round us, the faint outlines of the famed Sugar Loaf marking the entrance to the harbor of Rio, were discernible; and the first gleamings of the light on Rasa Island, some seven miles seaward from it, came cheerily upon the eye. The wind still continued fresh, and we had the prospect of entering the port at night; but, just as we were attempting to do so by heading into the channel, the breeze died suddenly away, and we dropped anchor on what is called the "rolling ground." The appropriateness of this name was fully demonstrated to us before morning, by a depth of rolling on the part of our good ship in a dead calm, which we had not before experienced in the heaviest weather at sea.

As for myself, I was more than content to pass a restless night from this cause, rather than lose the opportunity of entering the harbor by daylight. I was anxious to test the fidelity of the impressions received twenty years ago from the same scenery; and to determine how far the magnificent picture, still lingering in my memory, was justified by the reality, or how far it was to be attributed to the enthusiasm of younger years and the freshness of less experienced travel. The early light of the morning quickly determined the point. I was hurried to the deck by a message from Lieut. R—— already there; and do not recollect ever to have been impressed with higher admiration by any picture in still life, than by the group of mountains and the coast scene, meeting my eyes on the left, as I ascended the poop. The wildness and sublimity of outline of the Pao d'Assucar, Duos Hermanos, Gavia and Corcovado, and their fantastic combinations, from the point at which we viewed them, can scarce be rivalled, while the richness and beauty of coloring thrown over and around the whole in purple and gold, rose color and ethereal blue, were all that the varied and glowing tints of the rising day ever impart. No fancy sketch of fairy land could surpass this scene, and we stood gazing upon it as if fascinated by the work of a master hand.

The pyramidal hills on the eastern side of the channel are less lofty and less wild than these, but impressive in their massiveness, and beautiful in the verdure of various growth clinging to their steep sides and mantling their summits. Together they form a portal to Rio worthy, not only the city, but the vast and magnificent empire of which it is the metropolis.

There was full leisure for the enjoyment of the scene, for the sea-breeze did not set in, with sufficient strength to enable us to get under way, till after mid-day. In the mean time I secured a drawing, while a thorough ship-cleaning was going on, both inside and out. This was so satisfactorily accomplished by four hundred busy hands, before the breeze would allow of taking our anchor, that, with the crew freshly dressed in a uniform of white and new summer hats, we looked, on taking our position among the men-of-war at anchor, more like a ship on a gala-day in port, than one just arrived from sea.

The width of the entrance is a mile, though the loftiness of the granite shafts by which it is formed, gives the impression of its being much narrower. The Sugar Loaf on the left—the naked peak of a mountain of rock whose broad base lies far below in the great deep—rises, with a slight leaning westward, to an elevation of twelve hundred and ninety-two feet according to the measurement of Captain Beechy. The corresponding mass on the eastern side, less isolated and more rounded, is six or seven hundred only. At the base of this, upon a tongue of rock projecting into the channel, is the strong and massively built fortress of Santa Cruz, against whose Cyclopean foundations the swell from the open sea beats heavily. Its white walls and embattled parapets, pharos lantern and telegraph fixtures, with the imperial flag of green and gold flaunting in the breeze, are the first features of civilization meeting the eye: all else along the coast looks as primitive and untamed as on the day it was first discovered.

From the point at which we were at anchor, little within the harbor could be seen: a small fortified islet or two, the tall masts of the shipping at the man-of-war anchorage, distant five miles, and the faint outlines of the Organ mountains in the far north. But on passing the Sugar Loaf and fort the bay opens, and the extent and magnificence of its leading features are rapidly disclosed. The mountain group, which so impressed us in the morning and seemed to belong exclusively to the outside, is found to constitute in new aspects and relative positions, the grand outline of the western side within.

To these aspects of nature there was soon added the charm of art. Long lines of imposing edifices edge the shores; white cottages and villas sprinkle the hill-sides and crest the mountain ridges; while church steeples and convent towers and the thickened masses of building in the city gradually rise to view.

As our ship moved gently onward the effect was like the unfolding of a panoramic picture. First came the land-locked bay of Botafogo, backed and overhung by the lofty peaks of the Hermanos and Gavia—its circular shores and sweeping sand-beach being embellished with a palace-like hospital and numerous suburban residences of the aristocratic and wealthy. Then the green and picturesque valley of the Larangeiras, with cottages hanging like birds' nests on its hill-sides, beneath the wooded cliffs and naked summit of the Corcovado; followed quickly by the bay of Flamengo, the Gloria hill, the hills of Santa Theresa and San Antonio crowned by their convents, Castle hill with its Capuchin monastery and old bastions, the hill of San Bento, and the entire city overtopped by the mountainous range and bell-shaped peak of Tejuca.

While these objects on the left successively absorb the attention, on the right a precipitous range of granite hills, extending two or three miles northward from the fortress of Santa Cruz, falls sheer into the water like the Highlands of the Hudson. It terminates in a bold promontory which divides a deep, circular inlet, called the bay of St. Francis Xavier, from the chief harbor, and which from some points of view is strikingly in the form of a colossal lion couchant, with the head settled backward in stateliness upon the shoulders. At the further distance of a mile a picturesque cliff-bound little islet—evidently once a part of the adjoining mainland—marks the northern entrance to this inner bay. Surmounted by a white chapel facing the sea, dedicated to "our Lady of good voyages," the special patroness of the sailor, it is a conspicuous and interesting feature in the topography, the first and the last upon which the ignorant and superstitious among voyagers and seafaring men, have long been accustomed to fix their eyes on entering and on leaving port. Beyond this, upon a widely sweeping beach, stretch the populous rural suburbs of Praya Domingo and Praya Grande, immediately facing the city. These terminate in a lofty rounded hill, partly under cultivation and partly in wood, which cuts off all further view northward, except clusters of islands on the distant waters, and the far-off mountains rising six thousand feet against the sky. The whole was seen by us under the strong lights and shades of the afternoon, as with a light sea-breeze we floated gently up and dropped anchor abreast the city, midway from either shore. A cluster of men-of-war were moored inside of us, from whose mast-heads floated the national flags of England, Portugal and Brazil, but none bearing the stripes and stars of the United States.

Towards night the coloring thrown over mountains and valleys, city and bay, was most gorgeous. A light haze, like that of Indian summer at home, characterized the atmosphere; through this the sun shone in fiery redness, empurpling the mountains, gilding dome and steeple and convent tower, and spreading a crimson glow over the entire bay. I have been thus minute in the description of the panorama surrounding us, because these winding shores and curving beaches, these verdant hills and towering mountains, are for many months in two or three successive years, to be the objects of hourly observation and the haunts of my daily rambles. The Sugar Loaf and the Corcovado, the Gavia and the Peak of Tejuca, Gloria hill, Botafogo, Praya Grande and the Organ mountains, will become in my communications to you, familiar as household words.

Admiration of the natural scenery was not the only feeling of which I was conscious, in advancing up the harbor. Remembrances of the past came unbidden to my mind and heart. With the first opening view of the Praya Flamengo, I was quick in my search with a glass among its mansions, for the dwelling which during my former visit had been to me a happy home. It was easily distinguished in its unchanged exterior. But where was the brilliant and accomplished diplomatist, whose genial spirit and polished mind gave such charm to its hospitalities? Long a tenant of the tomb! and I could not but recall the fact, that, with him, every one whose acquaintance I had here made—an acquaintanceship which, in some instances, from after intercourse, ripened into mature friendship—was also in the world of spirits: Tudor, Otway, Inglefield and Walsh, all gone. A generation had well-nigh passed away; and all was changed. A new Emperor was on the throne—a new Bishop over the see: there was no one to meet, and no one to look upon, whom I had ever seen before.

It was the predominance of feelings such as these that led, in my first visit on shore, to a solitary pilgrimage to the former Embassy, to look once more upon its familiar portal—now in possession of strangers,—and on my return at eventide through the embowered pathways of the Gloria hill, to think what a dream is life, and how vain as an abiding good, the highest attainments and most honored positions gained by man on earth.

September 6th.—Rio de Janeiro, if not built like Rome on seven hills, can boast an equal number around the bases of which her streets and dwellings closely cluster. The bright verdure of these—in tufted groves and shrubbery and in gleaming turf—as they rise abruptly here and there, from one to two hundred feet above the red-tiled penthouse roofs of the dwellings and the sombre turret and towers of church and convent, adds greatly to the beauty of the city, whether seen from shipboard, or in vistas at the end of the streets, on shore. One of the most conspicuous and lofty is Castle hill, so called from being surmounted at one of its angles, by the ramparts and dismantled batteries of a small fort, erected by the first colonists. It is also called by foreigners, Signal hill—from being the telegraphic station to which the movements of all shipping in the offing is made known, by signals from other stations at the entrance of the harbor and along the coast. Besides the ruin of the ancient fortress and the fixtures of the telegraph, it is conspicuously marked by the double-pinnacled church of a former Capuchin monastery, and by the old college of the Jesuits, both now converted to the use of the public—the one as a military hospital, and the other a medical school. The hill juts so closely on the bay as to interrupt, for a half a mile, the line of the city along the water, and to leave room only for a single street. This is not built upon, but being open to the sea-breeze and commanding a fine water view, is much frequented as a drive and promenade in the afternoon and evening. Inland from Castle hill, and separated from it by what was once a deep glen, but now a densely inhabited part of the city, rises the hill of San Antonio, so called from being the possession of a brotherhood of that name, whose convent stands in massive dimensions on its brow. These hills occupy the centre of the city, while that of San Bento, also crowned by a stately convent; that known as the Bishop's hill, from being surmounted by the Episcopal palace; and the hill of Lavradio, are on its northern side. The hills of Santa Theresa and Gloria, thus named—the one from a nunnery, and the other from a church dedicated to our Lady of Glory, are on the south. All originally rose from and encircled a marsh, the site of the present metropolis. Till within the last half century, the whole city then containing only some thirty thousand inhabitants, lay between Castle hill and the hill of San Bento, a distance of less than a half mile as a water front, in a parallelogram of rectangular streets extending about as far inland. This section is still regular; but in most others since built, the streets follow the curvature of the hills at their bases, and straggle from these, in every direction, up the ravines intervening between the spurs running from the mountains to the plain. The streets in general are narrow, and roughly paved with cobble-stones: the sidewalks being comfortable for two persons only abreast. The population is now about 200,000—including the suburbs which are very extensive, and reach south some five miles and nearly the same distance west; while Praya Domingo and Praya Grande, on the opposite side of the bay, form quite a town in themselves.

The general climate of Brazil from its great equality has been regarded as one of the most salubrious and healthful of the tropical regions of the world. Before the Congress left the United States, however, it was known that within the last year the yellow fever had made its appearance along the seaboard, and had raged with great mortality in the principal cities; especially in Pernambuco, Bahia, and Rio de Janeiro. We were uncertain what the state of health might be on our arrival; and were thankful to learn, by the first boat boarding us, that the epidemic had ceased, after frightful ravages among natives and foreigners, both afloat and on shore. The business of the port was almost suspended by its virulence for six or eight months; the citizens in great numbers having fled to the country, while the shipping put to sea. The general health is now good, public confidence is restored, and the inhabitants have returned to their shops and dwellings.

The origin of the pestilence is a mooted point here, among medical men of the most distinguished talent and experience. Some contend that it was imported from Africa by slave ships; others that it was introduced at Pernambuco in a ship from New Orleans; and others again believe it to be of domestic generation, connected with atmospherical phenomena thus far inscrutable to the observations of man. This last opinion is supported by changes of a meteorological character universally acknowledged: one the interruption, amounting almost to an entire cessation, of thunder-storms in the afternoons, formerly of such regular daily occurrence, that appointments for business or pleasure were made in reference to them, as to taking place "before" or "after the shower." It is a fact also attested by medical men, that of late years, marked modifications for the worse have been observed in the types of fever prevalent, till their malignancy reached the climax just experienced. There was, too, at the commencement and during the continuation of the pestilence, a stagnation and want of elasticity in the atmosphere, from the cessation to a great degree of the fresh and regular winds from the sea, very perceptible and very oppressive: all confirmatory of the belief that the sickness was atmospheric and indigenous. History and tradition are also brought to support this supposition; nearly a century ago, a similar pestilence is said to have prevailed in Rio, with the same devastating effect; and records of the years 1666, 1686, and 1694, bear testimony to visitations of a like kind. There is reason therefore to hope that the scourge will disappear as it has done before, and not become annual and endemic as in the West Indies.

The weather now is as delightful as can be imagined, with a clearness and brilliancy of atmosphere like that on the Hudson in the month of June, throwing an enchantment around the scenery of the bay perfectly irresistible.

September 10th. The first two or three days after our arrival were marked chiefly by an interchange of visits of ceremony, between the officers chief in command of the foreign squadrons near us and our ship; accompanied by a succession of salutes deafening to the ears, filling the pure atmosphere of the heavens with smoke and sulphur, and awakening in tones of thunder the ten thousand echoes of the adjoining mountains. In no harbor in the world, perhaps, is more powder wasted in the course of a year than in this. There seems ever to be among the Brazilians some new occasion for a salute. On the day of our arrival, in the course of a half hour the Congress alone fired eighty heavily charged thirty-four pounders: all of which were answered in the same space of time, gun for gun. Two of the intervening days since have been fête days on shore, calling for three separate salutes—morning, noon, and night—of twenty-one guns from all the forts and Brazilian men-of-war in the harbor, and at mid-day a general one of the same number, from all the flag-ships of the foreign squadrons. A commutation for the powder thus annually wasted, would be a princely income for any one securing it.

These observances of etiquette afloat well through with, Commodore McKeever invited me yesterday morning to join him, Captain McIntosh and Lieut T——, in visits on shore to the American Ambassador, and others of our countrymen in official positions, and to Mr. H——, a leading English merchant, who had called on board the Congress early after our arrival. In 1829, and till within a year or two past, the principal landing was in the centre of the city upon an inclined plane of solid masonry, descending into the water so as to be accessible by boats at any state of the tide; this conducted to a fine mole of granite, parapetted with stone, and forming one side of the palace square. Against the flush wall of this mole the water rose high, carrying off into the current, in its reflow, the offensive matter, which in want of sewers is cast along the shores of the city at night. An extension of the square on the bay is now in progress, however, by the driving of piles and filling in with earth and rubbish; and the landing is at a temporary stairs and platform of wood, at an adjoining point, in the midst of outpourings of filth disgusting to the senses, and making impressions on the stranger most unfavorable as to the purity and civilization of the imperial city. A carriage had been ordered for us here, and in its style and appointments we had evidence, at once, of the improvement in equipages which has been made since my last visit. Then, the old-fashioned Portugese Calesa, or chaise, and a clumsy close-carriage on leathern braces, of a similar style and date, were universally in use. I do not recollect to have seen vehicles of any other kind, except the imperial carriages and those of the British Ambassador. Now, although the Calesa is still frequently met, and occasionally its con-frere in antiquity, the low open four-wheeled carriage of the fashion and finish of those most modern in New York, London and Paris, and equal to them in all their appointments, is in general use. Besides many livery stables at which these may be found, stands of them occupy the Palace Square and other public points at all hours of the day. Twenty years ago, mules only were driven, except in the instances above mentioned; but, now, fine showy horses are as often seen in the turn-out. The carriage we entered was drawn by a pair of spirited, sleek, long-tailed blacks. The coachman in a livery of sky-blue and silver, made aware, by the broad pennant of the many-oared barge in which we came on shore, and by the lace and epaulettes of my companions, of the rank of some of the party, dashed off with a flourish of whip and a prancing of his beasts that won the admiration of the bystanders. He kept for the whole morning a Jehu speed characteristic of the manner of driving here; and significant, it would seem, by its accelerated rapidity, of the degree of rank of those it hurries along, from the Emperor down.

The route we took, is one of the finest the city and its environs afford, leading three or four miles southward, immediately along the bay, by a continuous street bearing different names in different sections, to Botafogo, the most beautiful of the suburbs. The green and palm-tufted hills overhanging the way inland; the luxuriant little valleys receding, here and there, from it, and terminating in wild and inaccessible ravines; the flower gardens and shrubberies, encircling the better residences, with beauty in endless forms, and the perfume of everlasting spring; the gay coloring, novel, and in some instances fantastic architecture of the houses; the vases and statuary and statuettes around and surmounting them; and the stately and ornamental gateways, opening into fine avenues of old trees terminating in embowered perspective at inviting residences remote from the road, with magnificent views at one point and another of the mountains on the one side and of the bay on the other, made the drive both in going and returning inspiriting and delightful.

Botafogo itself is a gem of beauty: a seeming lake, three or four miles in circumference. The one half is as untamed and wild as granite-bound shores bristling into mountains can make it; the other, a semicircular beach of white sand overhung with trees, and lined by a succession of fine residences. From the curving street on which these stand others run westward, forming a village-like settlement. On one of them we found the mansion of Mr. H——, a spacious establishment with an air of aristocratic elegance approaching magnificence. Besides the lofty entrance hall and stately drawing-room into which we were ushered, there were glimpses through different vistas of a fine library, a music room, dining hall and billiard room of proportionate dimensions and appropriate appointments. Situated immediately beneath the pyramidal shaft of the Corcovado, with a view of other mountain peaks, the waters of Botafogo at near access on one side, and those of the ocean not far distant on the other, and bloom and blossom on every hand—the rustling banana around and the plumed palm above—the whole presented a tempting picture of a home in the tropics.

It was late in the afternoon before we again reached the city. On inquiring the charge for the carriage for the four hours we had it in use, I was rather surprised, notwithstanding the large number "eight thousand," that met the ear in answer, that the whole was only four Spanish dollars, the thousand being *reis*, a nominal term in the currency of the country, one thousand of which constitute a mille-reis, a silver coin of the size and about the value of an American half dollar.

CHAPTER VI.

RIO DE JANEIRO.

September 12*th*.—On returning from the drive of Monday, I did not accompany the party to the ship, but gave the remainder of the afternoon to a stroll in the city. Its two principal and most attractive streets are the Rua Direita and Rua Ouvidor. The first runs north and south, parallel with the water, forming in its course the western side of the Palace Square; the other is at right angles with this, running east and west from a point near the square. A central section of the Direita is quite wide, and beside the palace contains the imperial chapel adjoining it, the Church of the Carmelites, used as a Cathedral, and that of the Holy Cross: in it also are the Custom House and Exchange, the Post Office and Commercial Reading-rooms, and the offices of the principal brokers and money-changers. It is in fact the Lombard-street and the Wall-street of Rio; while the Ouvidor, a mile in length, filled from end to end with shops of all kinds—fancy goods and millinery, prints and pictures, jewelry, articles of vertu and bijouterie—is its Bond-street and its Broadway.

The Rua Ouvidor terminates in a small open square, having on one side the fine façade of the church of St. Francisco de Paulo, and on another a more modern and well built structure, in Grecian architecture, used as a military school. A short street leads from this into a larger square diagonal to it, called the Roscio, in which is the Opera House; and a quarter of a mile further west lies the grand square of the Campo D'Acclamacao, so named from the proclamation in it of the independence of Brazil in 1822. My walk extended to this. It is a rectangular common of large extent, but partially built upon, and is distinguished by some fine public edifices. On the side next the city are the Treasury, the Museum and the Courts of Justice; on that opposite, the Senate Chamber of the Imperial Legislature; and on a third, a long line of Barracks. Roads and foot-paths cross it irregularly in various directions; but, ungraded and unplanted, it offers little attraction to the eye, being covered with coarse grass and weeds, mud-puddles and rubbish. Though thus neglected and shabby in itself, the views from it of the encircling hills and more distant mountains are full of freshness and beauty.

The Senate Chamber, a large square building of stone, is without architectural beauty or ornament. Originally the private residence of a governor of Bahia, when in the metropolis, it was sold by him to the government for its present uses. In it, in 1829, I witnessed the opening of the Imperial Legislature by Don Pedro I.; and learning incidentally this morning when on shore, that the same body was to be prorogued to-day by the present Emperor, I turned my steps again in that direction: partly for the accomplishment of my purpose of a walk, and partly for such observation as I might secure as an outside spectator. It was too late to seek a ticket of admission to the house, at the Embassy or elsewhere, and the Brazilian who gave me information of the ceremony, thought I could not without one gain admittance to the interior, in the ordinary morning dress I wore. There would, however, it was probable, be a gathering of the populace to the scene; and with an opportunity of the study this might afford, I was content. It is the remark of a biographer of the brothers Humboldt, I think, that "however fertile nature may be, man is always its most interesting and its most important feature;" and, after the almost exclusive observation of inanimate objects, from their surpassing magnificence for a week and more, I felt doubly inclined to avail myself of the chance of scrutinizing my fellows in new aspects of life.

The first impression made on an intelligent stranger on landing at Rio would, probably, arise from the numbers, evident difference in condition, the variety of employments, dress and undress, almost to nakedness, of the negro and slave population. Such figures, such groupings, such costumes, as are exhibited by these on every side, it would be difficult to picture or describe: the rapid lope and monotonous grunt of the coffee-bag carriers, their naked bodies reeking with oily sweat; the jingling and drumming of the tin rattles or gourds borne by the leaders of gangs, transporting on their heads all manner of articles—chairs, tables, sofas and bedsteads, the entire furniture of a household; the dull recitative, followed by the loud chorus, with which they move along; the laborious cry of others, tugging and hauling and pushing over the rough pavements heavily laden trucks and carts, an overload for an equal number of mules or horses, all crowd on the observation. Others, both male and female, more favored in their occupation, are seen as pedlers, carrying in the same manner, trunks and boxes of tin, containing various merchandise; glass cases filled with fancy articles and jewelry; trays with cakes and confectionery; and baskets with fruit, flowers and birds. And yet again others of the same color and race, more fortunate still, in being free—the street-vender, the mechanic, the tradesman, the soldier; the merchant with the dress and manner of a gentleman; the officer in uniform and the priest in his frock; all by their contrasts filling the mind with speculation and opening channels for thought.

An impression which would follow this first one, in quick succession, would be derived from the fearfully mongrel aspect of much of the population, claiming to be white. Mulattoes, quadroons, and demi-quadroons, and every other degree of tinted complexion and crisped hair, met, at every turn, indicate an almost unlimited extent of mixed blood. This cannot fail to be revolting, at least to a visitor from the Northern States of our country; especially as exhibited in the female portion of the lower orders of the community, as they hang over the under half of the doors of their houses, gazing up and down the street, or lean—black, white, and gray, three and four together, in the closest juxtaposition from their latticed windows.

A striking exhibition of this incongruous mingling of races and mixture of blood, was presented in the first object upon which my eye fell, on entering the Campo D'Acclamacao on my way to the Senate Chamber. A squadron of dragoons in a scarlet uniform, had just been placed in line on one side of the square. A mounted band in Hussar dress of the same color was in attendance. I took a station for a moment near this. It was composed of sixteen performers; and in the number included every shade of complexion, from the blackest ebony of Africa, through demi, quarter, and demi-quarter blood to the purely swarthy Portuguese and Brazilian, and the clear red and white of the Saxon, with blue eyes and flaxen hair. Such, in a greater or less degree, is the mixture seen in every sphere of common life—domestic, social, civil and military; and scarce less frequently than elsewhere, in the vestibule of the palace and at the altars of the church.

With the exception of this body of horse-guards and its band, there was but little indication in the square of the approaching spectacle. Two or three hundred idlers only, in addition to the ordinary movements on the common, were seen loitering about. Those who had begun to assemble, however, were in clean and holiday garb. The Senate Hall, which last evening looked deserted and shabby enough in its exterior, appeared now in gala dress. All the lofty windows above and below, were decorated on the outside with hangings of crimson silk; and the doors, thrown wide open, were screened by draperies of green cloth, embroidered in the centre with the imperial arms in colors. A body-guard of Halberdiers, in liveries of green and gold, stood in groups about the entrance—their lofty spears, surmounted with glittering battle-axes, being at rest near at hand.

Numbers of well-dressed citizens began to arrive and enter the building by a side door. Perceiving among them one and another in costumes not differing much from my own, I made bold to follow, leaving it for the door-keepers to question my right of admission. I knew not where I might be led, and after a long ascent by a dark, circular staircase, very unexpectedly found myself in an open gallery in the middle front of the hall, in a line with the diplomatic tribune on one side, and that appropriated to the Empress and her ladies on such occasions, on the other. All the best places in this gallery were already filled. As I was looking about for a choice in such as remained unoccupied, a Brazilian gentleman, recognizing me as a stranger, though there was nothing in my dress to indicate either my nation or profession, immediately approached and insisted on relinquishing to me his seat. It was in vain that I objected to dispossessing him, till, overcome by his courteous manners and unyielding purpose of civility, I bowed my way into it. The point of view was one of the best in the house, being immediately in front of the throne and the chairs at its foot, for the ministers and chief officers of the household. Besides the whole interior, it commanded also, through a large open window, the avenue, by which the imperial cortege would make its approach in state from San Christovao, the country palace, three or four miles west of the city.

The Chamber has been remodelled since 1829. Instead of being oblong as then, it is now semicircular, like the Senate Chamber at Washington. The canopy and hangings of the throne and the draperies of the windows, are of velvet and silk in green and gold, the national colors.

The members of both Houses began soon to enter; many in magnificent attire—naval and military uniforms stiff with embroideries of gold, various court-dresses and priestly robes—and many in a full dress of black alone, with an abundance of glittering stars and crosses, and the broad ribbons of different orders. In the number were many men of mark, not only in name and title, but in talent and popular influence. There was no friend

near me, however, as on the former occasion, to point them out individually; and I had only the unsatisfactory assurance, from the circumstances of the case, of seeing before me not only the ministers of state and other officers of the government, but the leading politicians and ecclesiastics of the empire. Among them were many heads and countenances indicative of talent and unmistakable intellect, with a refinement and dignity of bearing that gave a most favorable impression of the whole as a legislative body.

You are aware that the government of Brazil is a constitutional monarchy, similar in its limitations and general organization to that of Great Britain. A Council of State consisting of three members holding office for life, corresponds to the Privy Council of Her Majesty. The ministry, composed of the heads of six departments—those of the Empire, Justice, Foreign Affairs, Marine, War, and Finance—is appointed by the Emperor. The Legislature consists of two chambers, the Senate and the House of Deputies, and is elected by the different cities and provinces. The Senators, titled and untitled, the proportion of each being limited by law, are fifty-four in number, and like the Counsellors of State hold office for life. The deputies amount to more than one hundred and serve for a limited time. Titles, of which there are a considerable number, of the various grades of Marquis, Count, Viscount and Baron, besides those of different orders of knighthood, are not hereditary, and there is no right of primogeniture in the descent of property.

The Legislature in its two branches, like the Parliament of England and the Congress of the United States, has cognizance of the entire business of the empire. Its discussions and debates on every subject, are as free as those of the two bodies named, and, I am told, are often marked with distinguished ability, varied learning and accomplishment, and true parliamentary eloquence. The temperament of the Brazilians is impulsive, and often leads to displays of impassioned oratory, on points eliciting the sectional jealousies of the Senators and Deputies. With an empire as widely spread as our own, and the centralization of the entire revenue at Rio, occasions often occur in which this feeling in regard to appropriations and other legislative measures is manifested. In times past, the ground of the strongest and warmest partisanship, was found in the early rivalry between the old Portuguese population and the native Brazilians, from the absorption by the former of the chief offices and emoluments of the country when a colony, and the patronage and favoritism extended by the crown to those who accompanied and followed John VI., in the transfer of the court from Lisbon in 1808. This cause of party irritation is now, however, rapidly disappearing. The native party with its purely native policy and views is entirely predominant, and can never again lose its power and influence.

A flourish of trumpets and a general bustle outside soon intimated the approach of the Emperor; and, through the open window before mentioned, I had a view of the procession of state. A company of lancers in rapid movement cleared the way. These were followed by a detachment of horse guards, in a uniform of white and gold with scarlet plumes, accompanied by a mounted band playing the national air; then came six coaches-and-six—each flanked and followed by its guard of honor—containing the great officers of the household. The state carriage of the Empress and her ladies, drawn by eight iron grays, next made its appearance; after which came the imperial state coach with a like number of horses; a long cavalcade of troops completing the cortege. Each pair of horses had its postillion, and each carriage its coachman and three footmen. All were in state liveries of green, stiff with lace and embroideries in silver. The postillions wore jockey caps fitting closely to the head, with lace and embroideries to correspond with the livery, and the coachmen and footmen, old-fashioned cocked hats broadly laced and fringed with white ostrich feathers. The postillions, mostly handsome young lads, and the coachmen and footmen wore powder, and the head of each carriage-horse was surmounted by three ostrich feathers arranged like the Prince of Wales' plume. The panels and top of the Emperor's carriage were of crimson velvet; but all other parts, the wheels included, of the heaviest carving, richly gilt;—the pattern and style of the whole reminding me of the state coaches of his great ancestor, Emanuel of Portugal, in the palmiest days of his reign, which I recollect to have had pointed out to me, as matters of antiquity, in the Royal Mews at Lisbon.

A procession of courtiers now appeared, in an upper corridor, open to view from the gallery, and, by a double line, formed a passage way for the Empress and ladies in waiting, to the tribune appropriated to her. This was screened in front by curtains. As Her Majesty entered these were drawn, and all in the gallery rising and bowing, remained standing. In the mean time the hall below became deserted, the senators and deputies having left it to escort the Emperor from the robing room. They returned in procession in a few moments, with His Majesty at the head in full coronation attire, wearing the crown and bearing the sceptre or gilded staff of state. While he mounted the steps of the throne the members filed off on either side to their respective places. Bowing to them, as he turned to face the assembly, the Emperor bade them be seated, and rested himself on his chair of state. A secretary then presented him with a sheet of letter paper in a portfolio, from which he read an address some five minutes in length. At its close, rising and again bowing, he descended and passed through the centre of the hall as he had entered, followed in procession by the entire body.

Don Pedro II., whom I saw as a child of three years, beside his father at a presentation on my former visit in Rio, is now a tall and stalwart young man of twenty-five, standing among those around him, like Saul in Israel, "higher than any of the people from his shoulders and upward." He is finely and massively built, with great breadth of shoulders and fulness of chest. His German descent, through his mother, the Archduchess Leopoldina of Austria, is strikingly manifest in his light hair, blue eyes and fair complexion. There is nothing either in the features or expression of his face to remind one that, on his father's side, he is a direct representative of the united blood of Braganza and Castile. His countenance, in repose, is heavy and inexpressive, and in the reading of his speech exhibited little flexibility. A fixed and, seemingly, determined indifference was all that could be inferred from his enunciations and intonations. I could not detect the slightest emotion of any kind or perceive a ray of feeling in his eye, as he went mechanically through it. How far this might be attributed to the subject matter, I am unable to say; it was in Portuguese, which I do not understand, and I have not yet seen a report of it in French in the daily journals. Still he is known to be a man of mind and character; has been most carefully and thoroughly educated; is extensively read; scientific in his studies and pursuits; and of exemplary correctness in his moral principles and character.

The Empress Dona Theresa is a Bourbon of Naples, a younger sister of the present King of the two Sicilies, and, of course, of Christina, Queen Dowager of Spain. She is apparently some four or five years the senior of her lord. In person she is short and stout, full in face, with well-defined features, and great amiability and benevolence of expression. Her walk and general mien, however, are not particularly marked with the high bearing and finished air, which give such grace and such prestige of regal birth and training to some of her compeers in rank, whom I have seen in Europe. She was in court costume—an under dress of white satin heavily embroidered with gold, with a profusion of rich lace falling deeply over the corsage and forming its sleeves. These were looped with bands of diamonds magnificent in size and lustre. The train was of green velvet with embroideries in gold, corresponding with those of the skirt. Her head-dress, with the hair worn in long ringlets in front, was a wreath of diamonds and emeralds, in the shape of flowers, rising into the form of a coronet over the forehead, and from which a white ostrich feather fell on one side gracefully to the shoulder. A broad sash, the combined ribbons of different orders—scarlet, purple, and green—crossed the bust from the right shoulder to the waist, above which a mass of emeralds and diamonds of the first water sparkled on her bosom. The ladies in waiting were also in dresses of green and gold of corresponding character.

By the time the gallery was sufficiently cleared to allow of a comfortable descent, the procession was formed for a return, in the same order in which it had arrived. The Empress was entering her carriage at a canopied doorway, as I gained the open air. Some amusing incident had just occurred, and in taking her seat she indulged in quite a laugh with her companions. This entirely confirmed the impression of her good looks and amiability. Ten years of apparent age were at once thrown off, and both vivacity of mind and sweetness of manner indicated by it. A pleasant break upon the frigidity of imperial etiquette, having the effect of a burst of sunshine on a cloudy day, over a landscape whose chief beauty till then had been in shade.

A lowering morning by this time began to settle into a heavy rain; and a heavy rain here is a rain indeed. It soon poured in torrents; and it seemed a pity, in an economical point of view, at least, as the long display moved off for a ride of three miles to San Christovao, that so much gilding and embroidery, so much lace and velvet, and so many fine feathers should be exposed to the peltings of the storm.

CHAPTER VII.

RIO DE JANEIRO.

September 16th.—There is no seaman's chaplain or other American clergyman, at present at Rio; and the religious services of the Sabbath on board the Congress, since our arrival, have been attended by many of our compatriots, both ladies and gentlemen, residents here, including the Ambassador and Consul and their families. Occasions occur not unfrequently both in the shipping and on shore, calling for the special services of a Protestant minister of the Gospel. This has been the case within the passing week. The commander of an American schooner spoken by us the day we crossed the line, but which did not arrive till ten days after the Congress, died suddenly of apoplexy the morning he entered port. The schooner was put in quarantine, immediately, by the health officer; and it was with great difficulty permission was obtained from the authorities for the burial of the body on shore. Mr. Kent, the consul, formerly Governor of the State of Maine, solicited my attendance officially at the interment. This took place at the Protestant cemetery at Gamboa, a northern suburb of the city, situated on a broad indenture on the western side of the bay. Here the body had been carried by water. Gov. Kent took me in a calesa by land. The drive is through a mean and unattractive part of the city, by a winding course from street to street, between the hill of San Bento and that surmounted by the Bishop's Palace.

This burial-ground was purchased by the foreign residents of Rio twenty-five or thirty years ago. It was then, and still is, comparatively, a secluded and rural spot, upon a hill-side overhung and crowned with trees, and commanding a beautiful view northward of the upper bay and its many islands; of the rich valleys to the west; and of the Organ Mountains sweeping majestically round in the distance. It is enclosed with high and substantial walls of stone, and is entered by an ornamental gateway of iron. From this a winding avenue of trees marks the ascent to a neat little chapel on a terrace near the centre of the ground. Here such religious services as may be desired, or can be secured, before committing the dead to the grave, are usually observed.

The morning was wet and gloomy, according well with the object of our visit, and the peculiar circumstances in which the burial was to take place. A funeral more sad in its desolateness could scarcely be: that of a stranger, in a strange land, unwept and unattended by any one who had ever seen, or ever heard of him when living. The consul, the undertaker, the grave-digger and I, as chaplain, being the only persons brought to the spot either by duty or humanity. The officers and crew of the schooner were in quarantine, and, from some omission or mistake in the arrangements, no representative from other American vessels in port was present.

The kindness of Gov. Kent, in giving his personal attendance, was at a sacrifice of feeling which could not fail to elicit my sympathy, though a stranger to him till within a few days past. It is but a very brief period, scarcely a month, since he committed to the newly-made grave near which we were standing, an only son of great promise just verging into manhood: one of the last of the victims of the late epidemic. The associations of the passing scene could not but revive in painful freshness a sorrow that has not yet lost its keenness.

The rain, and the wetness in every pathway, prevented all observation, except a general glance around, or any lingering among the memorials of those who rest here, far from the sepulchres of their fathers. It had been my purpose, before being called thus by duty to the spot, early to visit in it the tomb of my friend Tudor. This was the only one I now sought, to stand a moment beside it in remembrance of the dead, and, in thoughts of the living, who most loved him, but who may never be permitted to look upon his grave. It is marked by a plain white obelisk of Italian marble, bearing the following simple inscription:

Ossa
Gulielmi Tudor
Rerump: Fœd: Americæ Sept:
Legati.
Natus Bostoniæ A. D. MDCCLXXIX.
Mortuus est
Rio Janiero A. D. MDCCCXXX.
Multis ille bonis
flebilis Occidit.

September 18th.—The objects, at Rio, of historic interest to the stranger, or suggestive to him of thoughts of the past, are few. There is, however, at least one entitled in these respects to a passing notice from a Protestant. It is a small island, situated a short distance seaward from our anchorage, beneath the green heights of Castle Hill, a half mile from the shore. Its entire area is occupied by a fortress, whose white ramparts, demi-turreted angles, and floating banner, form conspicuous objects in coming up the harbor. My eye never consciously rests upon it without recurrence to a fact in the early history of Rio, inseparably associated with the name which both island and fortress now bear—that of Villegagnon. However imposing and aristocratic in sound, it is synonymous in its application here, with treachery, and not less surreptitious—to compare small things with great—as regards the name of the noble old Huguenot Coligny, first given to them, than that of Americus, borne by half the globe, instead of one in honor of the true finder of the western world.

Brazil was first discovered by Vincente Pinzon, one of the companions of Columbus in his first voyage, on the 26th of January, 1499. The land descried by him was Cape St. Augustine in the vicinity of the present city of Pernambuco. He took possession of the country in the name of the crown of Castile, whose flag he bore, and, coasting northward to the mouth of the Amazon, returned to Spain without forming a settlement. About the same period Pedro Cabral was fitting out a large fleet in the Tagus, to be conducted to India by the newly known route of the Cape of Good Hope. Fearful of the calms in the Atlantic off the coast of Africa, in pursuing the voyage, he ran so far to the west as to make, on the 25th of April, 1506, the same shores Pinzon had, some degrees further to the south. Entering a fine bay, in imitation of Columbus, he erected a wooden cross on the shore, before which he and his followers prostrated themselves, and high mass being performed, possession of the country was taken in the name of his sovereign Emanuel of Portugal. He gave to the bay the name of Porto Seguro, since changed in honor of him to Cabralia, and to the country that of the Terra de Vera Cruz—the Land of the Holy Cross. This appellation, however, was soon lost in that of Brazil, from the abundance of the wood of that name found in it and the high value placed upon the article in Europe: a result pathetically deplored by a pious Jesuit, in the lamentation that "the cupidity of man by unworthy traffic, should change the wood of the cross, red with the real blood of Christ, for that of another wood which resembled it only in color."

The harbor of Rio de Janeiro was not discovered till 1516. De Solis, in search of a western passage to the Pacific, looked into it, in that year, as he coasted his way to the Rio de la Plata where he lost his life. He gave to it no name, however, and it remained unvisited again till De Sousa entered it in 1531. Under the impression that it was the outlet of a great river, this navigator called it Rio de Janeiro, the day on which he made the supposed discovery being the first of the new year. It did not, however, particularly attract the notice of the Portuguese, and still remained unoccupied by them.

In the mean time adventurers and traders from France made their way to this part of the New World, and secured the good will and friendship of the natives. Among them was Villegagnon, a knight of Malta, who had seen service in the east, was an officer of distinction in the French navy, and had commanded the vessel which carried Mary Queen of Scots and her retinue from France on her return to her kingdom. His visit to Brazil inspired him with the ambition of establishing a colony at Rio. Desirous of the favor and aid of the crown in this project, and believing the influence of Coligny with the king the surest means of accomplishing this end, to win his confidence and co-operation he professed a deep interest in the condition of the Protestants of France, and avowed the purpose of making the proposed colony a refuge to them, from the persecutions to which they were subject at home. The king was led by his friendship for Coligny, to regard the proposition with such favor as to grant to Vilegagnon two vessels for the expedition, while the admiral interested himself in securing a number of respectable Protestants to accompany it as colonists.

On arriving at Rio in 1555, Villegagnon first took possession of the small island Lage near the mouth of the harbor; but soon finding this too much exposed to the sea, removed to one larger near the site of the present city, to which, with the fort erected upon it, he gave the name of Coligny. The vessels were sent back to France for reinforcements. Great interest in the enterprise had in the mean time been excited among the Protestants there. Two clergymen and fourteen students of theology had been selected in Geneva to secure the spiritual good of the colony, and were received, preparatory to their embarkation, at the chateau of Coligny near Chatillon, with great attention. Large numbers of respectable emigrants joined them, and sanguine hopes were entertained that the principles of the reformation would be surely implanted in the New World.

Early after the arrival of this reinforcement, Villegagnon,

believing himself sure of the support of the crown in the further prosecution of his object, under the pretence of having returned to his old faith, commenced so bitter a persecution of the Protestants, that, in place of the peaceful enjoyment of freedom of conscience for which they had been led so far from their native land, they found themselves in a worse condition in this respect than they were at home. They were driven, at length, to the determination of returning to France. The only vessel, however, granted to them for the purpose was so old and so ill found for the voyage, that five of the number, after going on board, refused to venture their lives in her. Of these, three were afterwards put to death by Villegagnon, and the others, flying for refuge to the Portuguese settlements, were constrained to apostatize to save their lives. The company who embarked reached France only after having suffered all but death from starvation. At the time of their return, ten thousand of their brethren were in readiness, under the auspices of Coligny, to embark for the new colony. The report brought by them of the treachery of him who was to have been their leader at once changed their purpose; and the project of a Protestant colony in 'France Antarctique,' as the region had already been styled, was abandoned. Thus it was that the religious and civil destiny of one of the richest sections of the New World was changed for centuries now past, and, it may be, for centuries yet to come.

With the remembrance of this failure in establishing the Reformed religion here, and of the direct cause which led to it, I often find myself speculating, as to the possible and probable results which would have followed the successful establishment of Protestantism during the three hundred years which have intervened. With the wealth and power and increasing prosperity of the United States before us as the fruits, at the end of two hundred years, of the colonization of a few feeble bands of Protestants on the comparatively bleak and barren shore of the Northern Continent, there is no presumption in the belief that, had a people of similar faith, similar morals, similar habits of industry and enterprise, gained an abiding footing in so genial a climate and on so exuberant a soil, long ago, the still unexplored and impenetrable wildernesses of the interior would have bloomed and blossomed in civilization as the rose, and Brazil from the sea-coast to the Andes become one of the gardens of the world. But the germ which might have led to this was crushed by the bad faith and malice of Villegagnon; and, as I look on the spot which, by bearing his name, in the eyes of a Protestant at least perpetuates his reproach, the two or three solitary palms which lift their tufted heads above the embattled walls, and furnish the only evidence of vegetation on the island, seem, instead of plumed warriors in the midst of their defences, like sentinels of grief mourning the blighted hopes of the long past.

The conduct of Villegagnon soon met its just recompense. The course he pursued towards the Huguenots led to the early and utter failure of his enterprise. Had he been true to his followers of the Reformed faith, the colony, in place of being weakened by the return of any to France, would have been so strengthened and established by the ten thousand prepared to join them, that the Portuguese would never have been able to dislodge and supplant them. Needing reinforcements, Villegagnon proceeded himself to France to secure more settlers and the further aid of the government. Every thing there was adverse to his object. He had forfeited the favor of Coligny, and put an effectual end to the emigration of Protestants to Brazil. The king was too much occupied with the civil war existing to give heed to him. While thus delayed the Portuguese fitted out a strong expedition under Mem de Sa from Bahia. This was successful. The French were driven to their ships, and the Portuguese, possessing themselves of the island on which they had been established, gained such foothold as never afterwards to be displaced. This occurred on the 20th of Jan. 1560, St. Sebastian's day, under the patronage of which saint the expedition had been placed: and in whose honor the city afterwards built on the mainland, received the name of St. Sebastian. This is now, however, entirely supplanted by that of Rio de Janeiro.

In 1676 the city had become so populous as to be made the see of a Bishop, and the palace now crowning the brow of the Bishop's Hill was built. At that time, and for more than a hundred years afterwards, Bahia was the seat of chief authority in the captaincies of Brazil; but in 1763, so greatly had the wealth and influence of Rio increased, from the discovery of the gold and diamond mines, whose products were poured into her bosom as a market, that the residence of the Viceroy was transferred from Bahia and became permanently fixed here.

It was not, however, till the arrival of the royal family of Portugal, in their flight from Lisbon before the French army in 1808, that the prosperity and true progress of Rio, and Brazil in general, may be said to have commenced. Till then, the whole country had been subject to the restrictive and depressing influences of the policy adopted by the mother country, in the government of her colonies: all foreign trade interdicted, heavy import and export duties imposed on the commerce with Portugal herself, grasping monopolies claimed by the crown at home, and extortionate perquisites exacted by its representatives on the ground. There were no press, no newspapers, no books, no schools. The whole country was in a state of darkness and ignorance beyond that of the Middle Ages; and Rio an unenlightened, unrefined, and demoralized provincial town. But with the Prince Regent of Portugal, the Queen mother, the court, and more than twenty thousand followers, European manners and customs, and the habits and usages of modern civilized life were introduced. Commerce was opened to all nations; and the press, literature and the arts established. The changes effected in Rio were almost miraculous; and so constant and so rapid have been the improvements to the present time, that she now presents to the visitor, in many of her leading features, an aspect becoming the metropolis of a great Empire.

The progress of enlightened government, enlarged liberty and extended commerce, has been commensurate with the advances in civilization, intellectual culture and the refinements of life. The measure of throwing the ports open to all nations, so wise and so essential, at once adopted and proclaimed by the Prince Regent—afterwards John VI.—in 1808, was followed by him in 1815 by the no less important step of elevating the colony in its united provinces to a distinct kingdom, on an equality in its rights and privileges with those of Portugal and Algarves, under the one crown.

In 1822, Brazil became an independent empire under Don Pedro I. with a constitution which guaranteed to her a representative legislature, and the largest liberty compatible with the immunities of the limited monarchy by which she is still governed.

This political progress was not made without obstacles and threatened anarchy and disaster. The return to Portugal of John VI. in 1821, was followed in 1831, by the abdication of Don Pedro I. in favor of his son, a child four years of age; and partisan conflicts, during the regency which followed, made necessary the sudden termination, in 1840, of the minority of Don Pedro II., at the age of 14, in violation of an article of the constitution fixing the majority of an heir to the throne at eighteen. Since then, however, general tranquillity and progressive prosperity have prevailed. After years of deficiency in the revenue there is now a surplus; the receipts of the imperial treasury for the last year being seventeen millions and a half of dollars, and the expenditures little more than fifteen millions. The national debt is sixty millions, but with increasing exports and an enlarging commerce this may soon be liquidated; and the finances of the country be placed in unfettered condition. The revenue is derived from duties on exports as well as imports; those on exports being applicable alike to the internal commerce of the empire between province and province, and to that with foreign countries. The export duty on coffee, transferred from one province to another, is ten per cent. On shipments of the same article for foreign ports, there is an additional duty of two per cent. Every product—rice, sugar, cotton, farina—is thus taxed. The export duty on mandioca, the staff of life of the country, is regulated by the market value of the article, and not by fixed per centage.

There is no direct tax on landed property, but, in lieu of it, a levy of ten per cent. on every transfer of real estate. There is also an annual tax on slaves throughout the empire at the rate of two milreis a head.

The greatest danger to which the empire seems exposed, arises from the vastness of its extent, and the obstacles which have hitherto existed to a ready intercourse, between its different sections and the central power at Rio de Janeiro. But steam navigation already established along its coast, and soon to be introduced on its northern rivers, with projected railroads and telegraphic routes, promises to overcome this difficulty ; and, as in the United States, so to facilitate communication, and so closely and firmly to bind the different provinces in a whole, as to secure the perpetuity and integrity of the empire.

CHAPTER VIII.

At Sea.

September 23d.—

"The sea again! the swift, bright sea!"—

and, at the rate of twelve miles the hour,

"Away, away upon the rushing tide
We hurry faster than the foam we ride,
Dashing afar the waves, which round us cling,
With strength like that which lifts the eagle's wing,
Where the stars dazzle and the angels sing.
We scatter the spray,
And break through the billows,
As the wind makes way
Through the leaves of willows!"

We had expected to meet at Rio de Janeiro, the frigate Brandywine, the ship the Congress came to relieve; but instead, Commodore McKeever found orders awaiting him there to proceed to Montevideo. In obedience to these we got under way, early on the 17th inst.; but, after dropping down the bay a couple of miles, the land breeze failed us and we again came to anchor. For three successive days, we made a like attempt to get to sea, but to no purpose; and, on the morning of the 21st, employed a steam tug to tow us out. The British Admiral had previously proffered the use of a small steamer, in attendance upon his flag;

and now sent her, to aid the little tow-boat in stemming with her stately burden, the tide just beginning to set in. When well outside we took a smacking breeze; and, though scarce two days at sea, have run five hundred miles—nearly half the distance to Montevideo.

There was no special reason for regret at the delay in getting off. The position we occupied while detained was the finest possible for the study of the imagery amidst which we lay. But for some accidental cause of the kind, we should not have had an opportunity of enjoying it, and I availed myself of the chance to secure a panoramic drawing, embracing points of beauty not commanded from the customary anchorage of men-of-war. During the detention, Captain McIntosh took me with him in two or three excursions upon the water in his gig, followed by walks on shore of interest and novelty. One of these was to Praya Grande, opposite Rio; and another to the bay of St. Francis Xavier, called by the English Five-fathom Bay, on the same side of the water, but nearer the sea.

The formation of the land on the eastern side of the harbor is less bold and lofty than that on which the city lies. The mountains are more distant, and the spurs from them come down in rounded hills, interspersed with valleys and broad interval lands. Praya Grande and Praya San Domingo form one gently curving beach on this shore, some three miles in length, extending northward from the fragmentary islet—on the bluff crest of which is perched the little chapel of Boa Viagem—to a beautifully rounded promontory jutting far westward into the bay. They are contiguous parishes, seemingly but one settlement, and are rural and village like. The green banks along the water side are overhung with trees, and the houses every where interspersed with large gardens and ornamented enclosures. The population of the two places amounts to about three thousand. The residences, for the most part, are well built, and many of them tasteful in architecture, and fanciful in their embellishment. In comparison with the city opposite, the whole district is pure and cleanly; and, in place of the villanous smells too often met there, abounds with the mingled fragrance of the orange, cape jessamine, heliotrope, and unnumbered other blossoms—constituting a sweetness more fresh and grateful than the choicest 'mille fleurs' of the perfumist. Wild roses, multiflora, and clustering flowers of varied hues, mantle the tops and fringe the sides of the hedges of myrtle and mimosa, aloes and cacti which border the roads, while many of the pleasure gardens, of which we had glimpses through the iron railings and open gateways, are adorned with plants and shrubs of novel forms and gorgeous bloom, amidst fountains of greater or less beauty.

We made our way into the open country, meeting, at one or two points, features in the scenery quite homelike: one—a meadow of coarse grass edged by a copse and thickets interspersed with single trees; and another, a large field on a hill-side having the earth freshly turned up, like newly ploughed ground with us, over which noble mango trees, with their thickly set leaves, and rounded tops, were scattered like oaks in an English park. On every hand there was a great variety of growth in shrub and tree, and it was with no slight degree of pleasure that I recognized among others, as old friends at the Sandwich Islands, not only the cocoa-nut, palm and banana, but also the bread-fruit, the tamarind, and *aluerites triloba*—or candle tree.

Not knowing how far the road we were following might lead, before it would again conduct towards the water, we were about to retrace our steps the same way, when, a question accidentally put to a negro passing, led to a return under his guidance over a hill, by a wild and romantic bridle-path. This was so overhung by densely interwoven growth, that the glare of midday soon became twilight to us, and the heat of a burning sun tempered to the coolness of a grotto. At many points of the entire walk, the views of the bay and city in the distance, and of the mountains overhanging them were of unsurpassed beauty. Indeed, there was no end to the forms of loveliness by which we were surrounded, and to the associations in memory and affection brought to my mind by them. With the expectation of spending many a tedious month of our long exile on the adjoining waters, it was a delight to know that walks of such freshness and beauty are so near and so accessible.

The row to the bay of St. Francis Xavier was made the succeeding afternoon. A bold and strongly defined promontory of granite, separates this sheet from the waters of the general harbor, and makes it so land-locked as to give to it the aspect of a secluded lake. Till we had doubled this, I had no idea of the depth to which the bay sweeps seaward behind the promontory, or of the feeling of remoteness from civilized life which its general features at once impart. The wild mountains, with a rude hut clinging here and there to their uncultivated sides; the primitive look of the lowly cottages of fishermen stretched along a distant beach; and the canoes drawn up on the sands, or resting lightly upon the water, again transported me to the South Seas, and I felt as if at the Marquesan or Society Islands, rather than within a half a dozen miles of the metropolis of a magnificent empire. Just so untamed, just so Indian-like, I am told, were the entire surroundings of the bay of Rio, till within the last thirty or forty years.

The eastern side of this inlet is formed by a long curving beach of sand, called the Praya Carahy. It fronts an extensive plain of low alluvial ground through which, at either end, two streams from the mountains make their way. Landing at the mouth of the most southern of these, with orders for the boat to meet us at that to the north, we walked upon the sands the intervening distance, in alternate admiration of the scenery inland, on the one side, and the sportings of a heavy surf on the other. This illumined by the rays of the declining sun, rose high in emerald masses, till, cresting into ten thousand diamonds, it thundered on the beach and came rushing to our feet in sheets of foam.

September 27th.—The fresh wind mentioned in my last date brought us, the next evening, on soundings off the Rio de la Plata. A change then suddenly occurred with every indication of heavy weather. The mercury in the barometer fell low; and during the night there was heavy rain, with a good deal of thunder and lightning, while meteors, called by seamen, compesant—a corruption of corpo santo or holy body—flitted about the yard-arms and mast-heads of the ship. All these were forerunners of weather more like a gale than any thing experienced since leaving Norfolk: indeed, a regular pampero, a storm of wind so called from the pampas or boundless plains between the Rio la Plata and Patagonia, over which the cold south and south-west winds from the polar regions sweep, corresponding in force and temperature to our fiercest north-west winds at home. The storm was not of long continuance, and yesterday afternoon we made the land near Cape St. Mary, the northern entrance to the river. We lay off shore for the night, and sighting the land again this morning, soon after made the little islet of Lobos, a chief landmark in entering the Plata from the north, seventy miles from Montevideo. It derives its name from the multitude of seal frequenting it. Many of these were seen, as we approached, basking on the rocky shores and swimming about in the water. A strong and offensive odor was also very perceptible. The island is a governmental possession of the Republic of Uruguay, but leased for a long term of years to a gentleman of Montevideo, and yields a handsome income in skins and oil.

The river is here one hundred and twenty miles wide. Its northern shore only, of course, is visible. This is low and sandy, marked here and there by a green hillock. With a glass, great numbers of horses, in vast droves as if wild, could be seen grazing in the distance; also the church towers of Maldonado, the town next in size in the Republic to Montevideo. From all we can learn, it is in such decay and depopulation at present, that the euphony of its name is its chief attraction.

Midway between the island of Lobos and Montevideo are the highlands of Monte Negro. The next landmark is the isle of Flores, surmounted by a light-house, fifteen miles distant from the anchorage. This light we are in momentary expectation of making.

Montevideo, October 1st.—On the night of the 29th ult., after having run a sufficient distance beyond the light of Flores to bring us abreast of Montevideo, we dropped anchor without having caught sight of any shipping in the roadstead, or discovering any signs of the town. On the lifting of a dense fog the next morning, the first objects discernible were the men-of-war of a French squadron about five miles in shore of us. Shortly after, the Mount—a conical hill situated on the western side of a circular indenture in the river, constituting the harbor—which gives name to the place, was disclosed; and lastly, the town itself on a point opposite, distant from it a mile or more, in a direct line across the water. The whole landscape is as different as possible from that at Rio de Janeiro. It is low and level, without rock or tree: a soft verdure covered the shore and gleamed in the sun, like so much velvet, as it came peering on the eye through the fog bank.

The Mount is an isolated hill rising gradually and regularly on all sides, at an angle of 45°, to a height of 480 or 90 feet. It is crowned by a small rectangular fortress, above which the lantern of a pharos rises some twenty or thirty feet. Being in possession of a besieging force, no light is shown from it, that additional embarrassment may be placed on the commerce of the port. Midway between the Mount on the west and the town on the east, a smaller hill rises two or three miles inland, in like manner in regular lines from the plain. This too is crowned by a little fort, which, like the other, is in possession of the besieging party. It is called the "Cerrito," or little hill, in contradistinction to the other, known as the "Cerro," or hill par excellence. The town is situated on a peninsula of tufa rock, a half mile in length by a quarter in width, rising gently from the water on three sides to an elevation of eighty or a hundred feet, much in the shape of a tortoise's back. From a distance it presents a mass of compactly built, white, flat-topped houses, one and two stories high, of Spanish aspect, with multitudes of small, square turrets or miradors overtopping them, from the midst of which, on the central height, rise the lofty roofs, dome and double towers of a cathedral.

It was in vain we searched among the shipping of the outer roads, where alone there is sufficient depth of water for a frigate, for the broad pennant of Commodore Storer. The sloop-of-war St. Louis, however, was recognized in the inner harbor. On communicating with her, we learned that the Brandywine had sailed for Rio de Janeiro ten days ago, again leaving orders for the Congress to follow. Our trip has thus been for naught. We sail again for Brazil, with the first fair wind, and I shall defer all observation in the city to the more favorable opportunities of an after visit.

The general view around us is more homelike than any thing seen by us since leaving the United States. The growth is no longer tropical. The sky, the temperature of the air, the tinting of the clouds at sunrise and sunset are all those of the Northern States. Yesterday, the Sabbath, was altogether like a fine, bright, fresh and transparent day in October on the Hudson; though, while October there is the gradual freshening of autumn into winter, here it is the softening of spring into summer. The mercury in Fahrenheit has not yet fallen below 50°; still the change from the heat of Rio was felt so sensibly, on reaching the latitude of the river, that flannels, cloth clothes, and overcoats were found comfortable, if not absolutely necessary. The region of the La Plata is famed for the transparency of its atmosphere in fine weather. To this probably is to be attributed, in part at least, the great beauty of the sunsets at this place. We have been delighted by two already gazed on; the one remarkable for the exquisite delicacy of its tints in blue and gold, amber, pink and pearl, and the other, equally soft and beautiful at first, but afterwards gorgeous to sublimity, from the reflections in crimson and gold of a canopy of fleecy clouds spread widely over the heavens.

AT SEA.

October 12th.—We made an attempt to leave Montevideo on the 2d inst., but succeeded in making a small change only in our anchorage. At the end of three days, we had scarcely passed the island of Flores, fifteen miles from the city, though we had weighed anchor not less than three times each day in the hope of taking a final departure. The difficulty was caused by a succession of calms, thick fogs, head winds and adverse tides characteristic of the season here. It was not till the 6th that we again passed Lobos and were fairly outside.

Since clearing Cape St. Mary, we have been experiencing all the vicissitudes of the sea: first in a long stretch, off our course, far to the south-east, close hauled upon a head wind; and, since the 9th inst., when this changed in our favor, in a rapid but boisterous run of more than half the distance to Rio de Janeiro. While thus careering on our way, in addition to the ever-varying rush and roar—the cresting, breaking and foaming of the billows behind and around us, we have found an interesting relaxation on deck in watching the sportings and unwearied movements of unnumbered sea-birds, following closely in the broad and troubled wake of our ship, in pursuit of the fragments of food thrown overboard from the different messes at all hours of the day. It is not often that so rich a windfall as the waste of such a ship falls to their lot. To this fact they seem fully alive, and were indefatigable in making the best of their good fortune. Amidst flocks of beautiful Cape pigeons, outrivalling in numbers the crows of Crum Elbow * in an autumnal evening, were to be seen the gigantic albatross, sweeping round on wide-expanded and motionless wing; the sea-mew and man-of-war bird, black as ravens; the booby, and any quantity of the stormy petrel, treading the water more confidently and more securely than did the unbelieving Peter.

* A well known point on the Hudson River, overhung by precipitous cliffs, a favorite resort of crows.

The Cape pigeon—*Procellaria Capensis*—is beautiful on the wing or as seen tossing gracefully on the water. Its size is that of a large dove. Its breast is snow-white, with back, wings and tail of slate color, thickly set with oval spots of white, having much the effect on the eye of a tasteful dress in second mourning. Several were taken with hook and line, baited with pork, and one by the mere entanglement of its wings in a line. They are not so pretty or symmetrically formed, on close inspection as at a distance; and in place of the gentleness of the dove, which they at first so much resemble, are as snappish and resentful in spirit against their captors as the most carnivorous of their species.

The albatross—*Diomedia Exulans*—is white, with wings and back varying in different birds from black to a light brown. It is an ugly-looking bird, about the size of a domestic goose, with large head and great goggle eyes. The wings are very long—from eleven to fourteen feet from tip to tip. This interferes much with the facility of rising when seated on the water. It is only with evident effort and an awkward floundering that they mount again after having alighted; but then, it is a wonder to observe the ease and rapidity of their flight, and their ability, with seemingly motionless wing, to sweep in wide circuit round and round the ship, and still keep up with her in her swiftest career; and this day after day, without apparent exhaustion or fatigue, though sailing at the rate of two hundred miles and more in the twenty-four hours. The fiercer the winds and the more tumultuous the towering and thundering of the waves, the more joyous are their sportings, and the more triumphant their mastery of the elements.

The booby—*Sula Bassana*—is somewhat like the albatross in general appearance, but less clumsy, smaller, more angular in outline and pinion, and less majestic in flight. The man-of-war bird—*Fregata Pelicana*—is less adventurous in its wanderings over the sea. Its form is more that of the eagle—hence one of its names, *Tachypetes Aquilas*—with long feathers on the wings and tail, and its color a jetty black. It owes its English name to a supposition of the ignorant, that in returning to the land it heralds the approach of a ship; but, only from the fact that, like the ship it seeks the shelter of the port on the approach of a storm, and makes an earlier and surer arrival.

The most constant in its companionship with us, in every latitude and in all states of the weather, is the little petrel—*Thelassadroma Pelagica*—a small swallow-tailed bird, about the size, with much of the appearance, of the common house martin. Wilson in his ornithology gives a graphic description of these birds as seen in a gale, "coursing over the waves, down the declivities and up the ascents of the foaming surge, that threatens to bury them, as it bursts over their heads; sweeping again through the hollow trough of the sea, as in a sheltered valley, and again mounting with the rising billow, skimming just above its surface, occasionally dipping their feet in the water and throwing it up with additional force: sometimes leaping, with their legs parallel on the surface of the roughest wave, for yards in succession; meanwhile continually coursing from side to side of the ship's wake, making excursions far and wide to the right and to the left—now a great way ahead, now shooting far astern and returning again as if the vessel was stationary, though often running at the rate of ten knots the hour."

The most singular faculty of these birds, however, is that of standing, and of running on the face of the water, with the greatest apparent facility. When any greasy matter is thrown overboard they instantly collect around it with greedy and clamorous chatterings; and, facing to the windward, with their long wings expanded and their little webbed feet pattering the water, eagerly seize the booty. It is the lightness of their bodies and the force of the wind against their wings that enable them so readily to do this. In calm weather they perform the same manœuvre, by keeping their wings just so much in action as to prevent their feet from sinking below the surface. According to Buffon, it is this habit which has given to the whole genus the name they bear, from the walking on the water of the Apostle Peter. It is amusing, and partly vexatious, to see a clumsy albatross or great booby come swooping down among them, while they are thus collected around their food, and, flapping them away with its monstrous wings, at one mouthful rob them of a whole meal. Greasy substances are their choicest food, and their little bodies become a mass of oil: so much so, that dried and strung on a skewer, they are burned on some of the islands of the Atlantic as a substitute for candles.

The boisterousness of the weather has made the frequent reduction of sail necessary—at times, almost to bare poles. This has afforded a more than ordinary opportunity of witnessing the exposure and daring intrepidity required from the sailor in the discharge of his duty. The taking in of sail and the reefing of topsails in so large a ship, by a crew of four hundred men, emulous of excelling in skill and expertness, is an exciting scene even in a moderate breeze. When this occurs amidst the rushing winds and howling storm, with such masses of heavy canvas as compose our sails, flapping seemingly in unmanageable force, and snapping like thunder in the gale, it is frightful to look aloft. While the masts are bending to the wind and the ship careening in the water, you see the yards covered with hundreds of the crew with no guard from destruction in the giddy height, but the habit of keeping their feet firmly on the foot-ropes, while their hands and arms are occupied in overcoming the fearful thrashings of the sails, and in gathering in the canvas and binding it down with the reef-points. Some of them on the upper spars, like birds in the topmost branches of a tree, sweep to and fro over the roaring gulf below; and, occasionally a man or boy is beheld clinging to a slender spar or single sheet at the very mast-head, two hundred feet from the deck, disentangling a halliard or conductor—causing one's nerves to shake under the apprehension of seeing him hurled, in some pitch or roll of the frigate, far overboard into the raging sea, or dashed to death at your feet on deck.

October 16*th.*—The mountains and islets around the harbor of Rio are in full view, and I will close this section of my record. In doing this, I must follow the subject matter of my last date—the birds of the sea—by a word on some of its fishes. In a calm yesterday we were surrounded by a great number of dolphin—*Cyrophæna hippuris*—certainly, as seen moving in its blue waters, the most beautiful of the inhabitants of the deep. When full grown, it is from two to three feet in length, elegant and symmetrical in shape, and brilliant in colors: the prevailing hue being mazarine blue, or Pompadour, shading from the back to the under parts into emerald and gold, with fins and tail of green running rapidly into a bright yellow. Its motions are easy and graceful, and were watched, in great numbers, under the advantages of a smooth sea and brilliant sun. Dolphin are so common in all tropical latitudes, and so frequently seen, that I might not have thought of taking note of them in this instance, but for an assertion respecting them recently met in a book on natural history, which, emanating from a fellow of Oxford, ought to be of good authority. After stating the fact that the shape of this fish, as given in heraldic and classic representations, is entirely poetical and untrue, the author—Wood—adds: "indeed almost the whole history of the dolphin is imaginary—very poetical, but very untrue. The red and blue of the heraldic lion are not less fabulous than the changing colors of the dying dolphin, so dear to poetry. Alas! our unpoetical dolphin, when we have harpooned him and brought him to the deck is only black and white, and all the change that he makes is that the black becomes brown in time, and the white gray." This assertion I know, from personal observation in company with many witnesses, to be an error. In the first voyage I ever made, I had an opportunity of observing and admiring the varying and beautiful colors of the dolphin while dying; and now, fully proved to myself the truthfulness of the record of it then made. Mr. G——, secretary to our commander-in-chief, caught one with a hook and line, and quickly drew him over the stern on deck. I happened to be present, and, though the dying throes even of a soulless fish can scarcely be looked on without sympathy, the effect on its coloring could not be watched without admiration. The first change which took place, after the fish reached the deck, was of the whole surface into a bright yellow or gold, spotted, like the speckled trout, with deep blue; then the whole became blue again, the spots of a deeper hue still remaining distinctly marked; a third change was into a pure and spotless silver, over which prismatic colors, like those in an opal under a shifting light, passed rapidly and tremulously for a few moments, when the beautiful dolphin became brown and gray like any other dead fish.

It is possible that, when struck with a harpoon, the violence of the shock may be such as to produce death so suddenly that these changes have passed away, before the fish can be drawn on board, as their duration is but momentary. Either this is the truth, or Mr. Wood is not authority in the case. You may still believe therefore that

> "The dolphin, 'mid expiring throes,
> More exquisite in beauty grows,
> As fades the strength of life:
> And tintings bright of sapphire blue,
> And rainbow lights of every hue
> More exquisite each moment shew,
> As fainter grows the strife."

Portuguese men-of-war—*Physalia physalis*—have also been floating past us. These are moluscæ with long feelers, and furnished with an air-bag which they have the power of inflating at pleasure when moving on the surface. This is provided with apertures at either end, by which they can expel the air, or take in sail, as a seaman would say, when they wish to sink. This air bag, when inflated, is of an oval shape, and of the tenuity almost of a soap-bubble, and exhibits like it, though in stronger shades, many of the hues of the prism. The beauty discoverable in many of these animals is said by naturalists to equal any thing in organic nature.

A passage in Montgomery's Pelican Island applied to the convoluted nautilus, which rises and floats on the surface of the water, but spreads no sail, is perhaps more truthfully descriptive of this man-of-war :

> "Light as a flake of foam upon the wind,
> Keel upwards, from the deep emerged a shell,
> Shaped like the moon ere half her horn is filled ;
> Fraught with young life, it righted as it rose,
> And moved at will along the yielding water.
> The native pilot of this little bark,
> Put out a tier of oars on either side ;
> Spread to the wafting breeze a two-fold sail,
> And mounted up, and glided down the billow
> In happy freedom, pleased to feel the air,
> And wander in the luxury of light."

Should you be disposed to think that such commonplace observations indicate the tedium and monotony of sea life—the paucity of its resources for occupation and amusement—and are not worth the time required for the record, I must take shelter from the reproach in the example of a voyager no less illustrious than Humboldt, who, at the end of forty years, confesses to the delight still afforded by reminiscences of such pastime on the sea. True, we may not, like him, mingle our admiration with thoughts of deep philosophy, or make our observations subservient to generalizations in science ; still, we can take equal delight in the varied phenomena of the sea, and, in humble adoration, thus "look through nature up to nature's God," and rejoice in the infinitude and perfection of his manifold works.

CHAPTER IX.

RIO DE JANEIRO.

October 20th.—On entering the harbor on the 16th inst. the lofty masts of the Brandywine were soon descried through a mist and vapor which, to a great degree, enshrouded the general scenery. Hauling down our broad pennant of blue, while yet three or four miles distant, that of Commodore Storer was saluted by us, and one of red was run up to the masthead of the Congress. To this only Commodore McKeever is entitled in the presence of a superior in command. The Brandywine at once returned the salute, and, soon afterward, greeted our arrival with "Hail Columbia" from a band, as, passing alongside of her, we dropt anchor under her stern.

The early return of the Congress was quite a surprise, the Brandywine herself having but just arrived. We had made the trip down and back again in the same number of days—eighteen—which had been occupied by her in the one passage. Though a surprise, it was, however, a greater joy to her officers and crew. They are more than three years from home, and have long been waiting a relief. Moreover, Commodore Storer had given the assurance, before we were sighted, that they should be under way, homeward-bound, the next day but one after the Congress should arrive. True to his word, his anchors were up with the early dawn of the 18th inst. The departure, with its associations, was quite an exciting scene. The mist and fog of the two preceding days had disappeared, and the whole panorama of city and bay was in the perfection of its beauty in light, shades, and coloring. As with the first rays of the sun the frigate swung from her moorings, the Congress gave a salute. With the first echoings of this, her rigging was filled by the crew, clustered together like bees in a swarm, sending forth three cheers for the homeward-bound, with a feeling and will that swept every chord of the heart. Then came "Hail Columbia" from our band: the whole quickly followed by the salute, the cheers, and the music of "Home, sweet home," from the Brandywine. By this time she was completely enveloped in a broad and lofty pyramid of convoluting and pearly smoke, beautifully illumined by the sun. I thought it a good time to bid her adieu, while thus lost to sight in a glory of her own creation, and descending to my state-room, left her to make her way out of the harbor as she best could.

The 19th inst. was a court-day at the palace. Commodore McKeever availed himself of it for a presentation to the Emperor and Empress, as the new commander-in-chief of the United States Naval Force on this station. I made one of his suite; and left the ship at noon for the ceremony, with a party of ten, including Lieutenant McKeever of the U. S. army, a son of the commodore, who, on furlough for six months after service in Florida, came to Brazil in the Congress on a visit to a brother connected with a principal mercantile house in Rio.

The palace fronts immediately upon the chief landing-place, a few hundred yards only from the water. It is an old building, originally the viceregal residence, appropriated to the court of Portugal on its immigration in 1808. It is of stone, stuccoed and painted yellow, in part two and in part three stories in height, and without architectural pretension. The front, occupied on the ground floor by a vestibule leading to the grand staircase, is scarce a hundred feet in width; but the building, enclosing a small quadrangle in the centre, runs back along the public square,

5*

about five or six hundred feet to the Rue Direita. Over this a gallery—thrown from the second story—communicates with a still older range of structures on that street, at right angles with the other, extending also some five or six hundred feet to the royal library and imperial chapel, both appendages of the palace. The rooms of state and the throne-room occupy the whole length of the second floor, on the side overlooking the square; and the imperial apartments and private rooms the whole of that on the other side of the quadrangle. The only use made of the palace is for receptions, at levees and drawing-rooms, and the giving occasionally of a state-ball: the family seldom if ever lodge in town. Having, in September, twice witnessed the arrival of the Emperor and Empress in state, from their residence at Boa Vista, I lost nothing of the usual spectacle on court-days, by not being on shore in time for this, on the present occasion. In both instances I happened to be crossing the square, when the approach of the cortege was signalled by a call, from bugle and drum, for the guard and bands in attendance to turn out for the reception. The degree of state and the splendor of equipage vary on different occasions. Sometimes mules only are driven; sometimes horses only—sometimes both attached to different carriages. The general display, at all times of ceremony, is much the same as that described at the prorogation of the legislature, a month ago. As the cavalcade approaches, the halberdiers with their battle-axes at rest, form, in single lines, on either side of the principal entrance, through the vestibule to the foot of the grand staircase. No objection was made to my taking a position, almost in a line with these, and within touching distance of their majesties as they passed. On the drawing up of the carriages at the entrance, the great officers of the household and ministers of the empire descending from the waiting-rooms, form a line on either side, within those of the guard, from the carriage door to the staircase. Immediately on the alighting, a kissing of hands by these is commenced. The Emperor, a step or two in advance of the Empress, presents his right hand for this purpose, first on one side and then on the other, the Empress following in the same manner with a constant short and quick bow of the head, and an expression of great kindness and benignancy. Both occasionally extend a hand beyond the courtiers to individuals among the halberdiers on the *qui vive* for the honor. As they thus pass, the grandees of the court close in after them, and the ladies and gentlemen in attendance, and in procession, mount the broad staircase.

This guard of halberdiers is not of hireling soldiery, but of volunteers of respectability from the middle ranks of life in the city; and the indulgence accorded by them of so near an approach of spectators as was allowed me, affords an opportunity for many a poor subject to place a petition in the hands of the Emperor or Empress, without the intervention of an official or courtier. I was pleased with the readiness and condescension with which two or three were received by the Emperor, from women of the humblest class in evident distress, and were placed in the crown of his chapeau, while kisses, tears, and thanks were showered on his hand.

On entering the palace we were received by Mr. Tod, the American ambassador, in the diplomatic saloon—the richest of the apartments excepting the throne-room. The imperial party were in the chapel at mass. Mr. Tod proposed to conduct us there, by the corridor over the Rua Direita, and we followed him in that direction, through a long succession of rooms, till met by several of the foreign ministers returning with the report, that the diplomatic tribune in the chapel was undergoing some repairs, and was closed. We therefore retraced our steps to await the close of the religious service. This was not long; and Don Pedro and Donna Theresa, followed by some twenty or thirty attendants, soon made their appearance on their way through the long suite of rooms to the audience chamber. The court dress of the ladies here, as in Russia, is a uniform: a white brocade embroidered in gold, train of green velvet with corresponding embroideries, and head-dress of ostrich plumes and diamonds. This is a sensible regulation promotive of economy, by an avoidance of the rivalry in expense and display, among the ladies, though at a sacrifice of the picturesque, from variety in taste and elegance in such a spectacle. Among the ladies in attendance was one more than eighty years of age, a venerable condessa, who accompanied the royal family from Portugal in 1808, and has been a leader of the fashion in the court circles, through the change of four dynasties, to the present time.

The Emperor led the suite a little in advance of the Empress. He is in stature truly a splendid specimen of humanity. The maturity of his countenance, as well as figure, leads to a supposition of his being full ten years older than he really is. An imperturbable gravity and unbending dignity contribute to this impression.

The diplomatic corps and our party fell into line on one side of the room, and saluted the Emperor and Empress as they passed by a bow, receiving a stately return from each, accompanied by a very decided look of scrutiny at such as were perceived to be strangers. A long range of apartments was to be passed through, before reaching the throne-room, and it was some minutes before a chamberlain announced to Mr. Tod—the senior ambassador in residence, and thus entitled to lead the diplomatic procession—that their majesties were on the throne.

The intervening rooms were thronged with Brazilians, representing in strong force the church, the army, the navy and judiciary, with many in civil life, in distinctive uniforms and varied court dress; but I missed in the throng much of the picturesque variety noticed in 1829. There were now no barefooted friars nor mendicant monks—no Augustines in white, nor Franciscans in gray, with corded belts and dangling cross and rosary. It was manifest that, at court at least, the monkish days are past: the high dignitaries of the church in purple and scarlet, in satins and lace, were the only representatives of the religious orders.

The state apartments in general appeared naked and unattractive compared with the recollections of 1829. The best paintings have been removed; one or two only worthy of attention remain. One, the martyrdom of St. Sebastian, is impressive, and the work of a master in the art. There are also some good battle-pieces illustrative of Portuguese history, in the olden times. The two largest pictures represent respectively the coronation of Don Pedro I., and the marriage of the present Emperor and Empress. They are coarse and inartistic in execution, but valuable from the number of portraits they contain, the principal figures introduced being from sittings to the painter of the personages delineated.

The throne-room is a large and magnificent apartment, the predominating colors in the finish and furniture being green and gold. The lofty, vaulted ceiling, among other embellishments in fresco, presents medallion portraits, real or fictitious, of all the sovereigns of the House of Braganza, from the establishment of the kingdom of Portugal to the present time.

The occasion of the court was the anniversary of the marriage of their majesties, and the address of congratulation, from the diplomatic corps, devolved on Mr. Tod. Entering the room with a bow,—followed by those to be presented by him—he advanced midway from the door to the throne, where making another bow, he took his station, with our party grouped around. He concluded his speech of felicitation by adding, that "Commodore McKeever, on assuming the command in chief of the U. S. Naval Force on this station, availed himself—with the officers of his ship—of the opportunity for a presentation to their majesties. The Emperor's reply in Portuguese was brief, and of course courteous. Immediately on its close, a band in the vestibule struck up the national air: and filing off before the throne, we each in succession bowed respectively to the Emperor and Empress, and moving backward in a semicircular sweep from the door by which we had entered, bowed ourselves, through another corresponding to it, from the presence to an ante-room. Being in clerical robes, I might perhaps have claimed the privilege of a straightforward exit. It is said that, owing to the fall backwards, in the royal presence, of a bishop-legate from Rome—a hundred and more years ago—

from treading on the tail of his gown, in retreating from the throne at a levee in Lisbon, a permit was issued excusing, thereafter, all clergy in robes from the established etiquette. Not having ascertained however whether the privilege had been transmitted to the court of Brazil, I thought it most safe to conform to the general usage, though at the risk, in accomplishing a distance of forty or more feet in the manner of a crab, of suffering a disaster similar to that of the bishop.

The rest of the foreign ministers and their suite followed us rapidly. After these came the hundreds of Brazilians, according to their rank and precedence, each kneeling on a step of the throne and kissing the extended hand of their sovereigns: a ceremony which, between wedding-days and birth-days, saints' days and days of independence occurs, on an average, at least once a month during the whole year.

This bow before the throne will doubtless be the nearest approach to personal intercourse with their majesties that I shall enjoy; and I may, at once, in connection with it, give such intelligence, in regard to them, as I have derived from those having the best opportunities for correct information on the subject. Their personal appearance I have before described. The power vested in the Emperor by the constitution is very limited: almost nominal indeed, with less influence through the right of appointments and political patronage in general, than is possessed by the President of the United States. So carefully restricted and so jealously guarded are the prerogatives of the throne, that the abuse of them, by despotic rule or usurpation, would be impracticable. The hereditary descent of the crown is the strongest monarchical feature in the government: and it is to this alone, doubtless, that Brazil is indebted for an exemption from the anarchy and bloodshed which have proved so destructive to the advance of liberty and civilization, in all sections of South America. While it places an effectual check upon the reckless ambition of selfish politicians and patriots, falsely so called, it forms a point of permanency around which the wise and good may rally, in the support and in the defence of true liberty. It is not impossible that the constitutional restrictions resting on the Emperor, and an accompanying feeling of irresponsibility, may cause, in some degree, the seeming nonchalance which marks his air and deportment in public, and also induce to some extent, at least, to the quietude and seclusion of his ordinary life. From all I learn, nothing can be more simple and domestic than the habits of himself and family. The library, and its cabinets, the pleasure-grounds and gardens of San Christovao, chiefly occupy their leisure-time, and are principal sources of their happiness.

Prudent and high-minded as a ruler, cultivated and accomplished as a scholar, benevolent as a man, and pure and irreproachable as a husband and father, the Emperor is justly regarded with honor and affection by his people; while the Empress, no less exemplary in all the relations of life, through her amiability and kindness of heart shares largely with him in general popularity and good will.

The annual stipend of the Emperor is four hundred thousand dollars, and the allowance to the Empress fifty thousand. The civil list is small, the ladies and gentlemen of the household being few in number. They live with prudence and economy; seldom entertain except by an occasional ball at the palace in town. With the lessons on the vicissitudes of empire and the instability of thrones, so frequently given in these modern times, it is wise in them thus to husband their resources, and to familiarize themselves of choice with habits of life which, by possibility, may yet become those of necessity. They have already been afflicted by the loss of two or three children; one, the Prince Imperial and heir to the crown. Though two young princesses are left to them, this may have had a chastening effect on their hopes in life, by placing the succession in a female, and thus rendering the perpetuity of their dynasty less certain, than if there were a male heir to the empire.

It must not be inferred from what I have stated of the outward bearing of the Emperor, or of his habits in private life, that he takes no interest in the policy of the government or active part in its executive administration. While content under the constitutional restrictions of his power, and with the prerogatives accorded to the throne, he holds his position and exercises his influence firmly and with a noble regard to what he believes to be the highest interest of the nation; and gives the strength of a mind, endowed with more than ordinary natural gifts, to the promotion of measures calculated to advance the honor, dignity and prosperity of the empire. This has been strikingly manifested recently, in successful efforts to persuade those around him of paramount influence in the various provinces, of the evil and reproach of a continued connivance—in disregard of national faith given by treaty—at the slave trade, and of the ultimate inevitable disadvantage and disaster to the country of a more extended slave population. So zealously and so wisely has he urged his views of public policy on this point—though in the face of long-established national prejudice as to the necessity of slave labor—that the legislature, sustained in the measure by their constituents, have pronounced the slave trade piracy, and enacted rigorous penal laws against it. This has been accomplished by demonstrating to the agriculturists of the empire, the economy and advantages of free labor, through colonization from Europe, over that of slaves, and by enactments for the encouragement of immigration from abroad. This is a most important and most desirable step forward in national good, and is sufficient alone to mark the reign of the young monarch with true and enduring honor.

October 22d.—Night before last, while walking the poop-deck, just before our usual evening worship, I met, engaged in some momentary duty there, a young man named Ramsey, whose frank and open-hearted face, bright smile, and confiding look and manner towards me had long ago attracted my notice, and led to more familiar intercourse with him than with most others of the crew. Stout in figure, and strong and muscular 'n limb, he might have been selected as a personification of health and buoyant youth. In various conversations I had learned something of his history: the place of residence, circumstances, and position in life of his parents and family. He had been religiously trained, was a teetotaler in principle and practice from the example of his father, and, so far as I could learn, free from the open vices which too often degrade the sailor.

In addition to the prepossession in his favor, from an attractive exterior, and from the promptness and activity with which he was observed to discharge his duty, he had early won the praise and good will of all on board, both officers and men, by saving, at the risk of his own life, that of a small boy, who fell overboard from the Congress when at anchor in the stream at Norfolk. The boy could not swim, and a strong tide was carrying him rapidly away when Ramsey jumped after him and succeeded in sustaining him half-drowned, till both were rescued by a boat.

A few evenings ago I had observed that one of his eyes was inflamed and swollen from a cold, and, now, in reference to this, asked him if he were well again. "Oh, yes, sir—all right—never better in my life," was his reply, as with his accustomed bright smile he passed down to the quarter-deck, where his shipmates were assembling for prayers.

My usual time for exercise on shore is in the afternoon, but yesterday, being engaged to the Commodore at a dinner given by him to the British admiral and family, I took the morning for a walk. On coming on board ship at three o'clock, Dr. Williamson, the fleet surgeon, mentioned to me that one of the crew had been taken ill with symptoms of the cholera. It was but a moment after hearing the name—Ramsey—in answer to the question who it was? before I was beside his cot on the berthdeck. He had been relieved from cramp and pain, by the treatment adopted; the pulse which had intermitted was restored, and he supposed to be altogether better. It was not yet twenty hours since I had met him seemingly in the fullest health; but how altered now, and how utterly prostrate! He looked rather than spoke his gladness at seeing me, and listened to my conversation with interest and satisfaction. It was evident that he was still under great physical oppression, and though endeavoring, occasionally, to rally his spirits, was dejected and sad—his eyes filling with tears as he pressed again and again the hand I had given to him at first, and which he continued to retain in his own as I remained by his side for a couple of hours, attempting to soothe him by words of consolation and by whispered prayer.

The sympathies which had been awakened by this unexpected scene forbade any enjoyment of the party in the cabin, and at the earliest moment practicable I excused myself from the table and returned to the poor fellow, not to leave him again till he should be out of danger. He was much in the state in which I had left him: had, if any thing, a stronger pulse and more natural state of the general surface. I again conversed tenderly with him and encouraged him to look in penitence and faith to Him from whom alone help cometh in time of trouble. I never witnessed greater submission and patience, and the tones of his voice and whole manner were as gentle as a lamb. In seeming apology for the irresistible depression he felt, though he considered himself to be relieved and better, he said to me with a look and accent I cannot soon forget—"Oh! Mr. S——, I was never sick before, and it makes me too down-hearted—too down-hearted!" Poor fellow! who under the same circumstances would not have been down-hearted—stricken down, in an hour as it were, from the very fulness of health and strength, and in the bloom and buoyancy of early manhood, to the feebleness of the merest infant, and to the very borders of the grave!

The surgeons had told me that every thing in his case depended upon the fidelity of those in attendance upon him to the directions given; and that there should be no failure here, I at once took the place of nurse in administering the prescriptions, and gave myself entirely to him. As the night wore away I could not discover the change for the better I wished, though I was not conscious of any for the worse. Dr. Howell, the assistant surgeon, who visited him every two hours, encouraged me to continued vigilance and hope. One, among other injunctions from the surgeons, was on no account to give any water to the patient, and only occasionally a mouthful of a tea prepared for the purpose. But he longed for water, and at one time well-nigh overcame my purpose of rigid obedience to the orders given. He had been almost covered with cataplasms, and had on him besides two or three large blisters; and the tenderness of his entreaty in gentle Scotch dialect, after having been once refused—as he looked up with pleading eyes and said, "Oh! Mr. S——, one wee drop, for I am all on fire!" touched my very heart. Poor fellow! from the best of motives and in the hope of soon seeing him better I reasoned with him and persuaded him to submission: but now lament it. The indulgence would have given him temporary comfort and could have done him no harm: for in a short time afterwards a return of cramps threw him into convulsions, and I saw that the stroke of death had been given. Unwilling unavailingly to watch the rapid changes which betokened too surely the flight of the soul, with the hand which so often during the day and the night by its warm pressure had given assurance of the comfort imparted by my presence still clasping mine, I kneeled by his cot, now surrounded by the surgeons and many of his messmates, and in tears and in strong though silent supplication plead with Him who alone is mighty to save, to spare the immortal spirit of the dying man from the sorrows of the second death. I do not recollect ever to have been sensible of a nearer access by faith to the only Hearer of prayer, and never saw more clearly how it is possible for Him, in the sovereignty and boundless riches of his grace, in the eleventh hour even to have "mercy on whom he will have mercy." At four o'clock this morning, he gently breathed his last without a struggle or a groan.

Such is the first of death's doings among us, and such was the last on earth of this poor sailor boy. I am devoutly thankful that though he died in a foreign land far from his home, I have it in my power to assure those who most loved him, that while all was done that the highest professional skill could devise to save him, but in vain, he did not die uncomforted, unprayed for or unwept.

His funeral took place this afternoon. Captain McIntosh, with the Christian kindness of heart characteristic of him, led the procession in his gig—the flag of the Congress, as well as those of the boats leaving the ship, being at half mast. The body was buried in the beautiful cemetery of Gamboa,

> "where palm and cypress wave
> On high, o'er many a stranger's grave,
> To canopy the dead; nor wanting there
> Flowers to the turf, nor fragrance to the air."

CHAPTER X.

RIO DE JANEIRO.

November 2d.—This is "All Souls day," an anniversary of the church of Rome in commemoration of the dead, when masses are specially said for the repose of their souls; or, as an Irish servant, in explaining its character to me, says, "the day when all the dead stand round waiting for our prayers." It is one on which here, as in other Catholic countries, the living also visit the tombs of their departed friends. As the observance is universal, and all the churches are open, we thought it a good opportunity, not only for viewing the interior of the principal edifices themselves, but also for observations of the people; and a party left tho ship for this purpose early after breakfast.

The number of churches in the city amounts to forty-five or fifty. Scarce a half dozen of them, however, are worthy of notice either for their external architecture or internal decorations in sculpture and paintings, especially to those familiar with the treasures, in these respects, of the churches of Italy, Spain, and other European countries. The imperial chapel and a church adjoining it, formerly belonging to the barefooted Carmelites, and now a cathedral; the church of the Candelaria, so named from its being the chief place for the consecration of candles on Candlemas Day; and that of San Francisco de Paulo at the head of the Rua de Ouvidor, are the principal.

Having been told that the Emperor and Empress would attend mass at the church of San Antonio, where the remains of their infant children are deposited, we made our way first there. This church is attached to the convent of that name, and forms one end of the extensive and imposing establishment which so conspicuously crowns, with its lofty and massive walls, and terraced gardens and shrubberies, the hill to which it gives name in the centre of the city. The broad platform in front of the church and convent, paved and parapetted with stone, commands magnificent views of the city and bay; as does the entire front of the convent. This is three stories in height, with a tier of balconied windows running the whole length of each. Within, each story opens upon a cloistered quadrangle; while the church with two or three smaller chapels, various vesting rooms, sacristies and corridors form another end of the pile. Every part of the building on this occasion was open to inspection. The floors of the corridors surrounding the quadrangle, and those of the churches and chapels are formed of loose planks, six feet in length and of the width of a grave; each being fitted with a mortised hole at one end, that it may be the more readily lifted for the deposit beneath of body after body of the dead: so that none walk here without literally

"Marking with each step a tomb."

That which first arrested the eye on entering was the range, on either side through the church, chapels and corridors, of miniature cabinets, urns and sarcophagi of ebony and other valuable wood, containing the bones of the dead thus preserved, after having been freed from the flesh by the action of quicklime. These receptacles are of various sizes, forms and degrees of elaborate workmanship. Each bears a plate of silver or gold with an inscription, and is furnished with a door which gives access to the ghastly memorials. They were arranged—some on rich tables and platforms and others on the pavement and floor—with more or less display of ornament: lighted wax candles in massive candlesticks of silver, interspersed in some instances with other pieces of silver plate, were clustered around them, and the whole garlanded and festooned with wreaths of the purple globe amaranthus and other flowers of the tribe "immortelle." Each cabinet, or urn, was in charge of a well-dressed negro servant or other humble domestic of the family to whom the relics appertained. I was forcibly reminded by the scene of the custom of the Sandwich Islanders, in their heathen state, of preserving the bones of the dead in a similar manner. It was this usage, and the care and veneration with which the relics of their monarchs and chiefs were guarded, that enabled Rihoriho—Kamehameha II—to restore to England, on his visit to that country in 1825, the skeleton of Captain Cook. After his assassination the principal bones of his body were prepared according to their custom, and placed with those of their race of kings.

The principal church and the adjoining chapels were decorated profusely with artificial flowers, and with hangings of silk and velvet, and of gold and silver tissue; the high altars, shrines, tribunes, and organ-lofts of all were one blaze of wax lights. One of the chapels is covered throughout with elaborate carvings in wood trebly gilt. In the centre of this a lofty catafalque was erected, surmounted by a colossal sarcophagus covered with a superb pall. A mass was in progress as we entered; after which a procession of monks headed by a party of ecclesiastics—each bearing a wax candle of the size and length of a stout walking stick, and all vociferating a chant—marched slowly from chapel to chapel, and from shrine to shrine, through the corridors lined with the memorials of the departed, stopping at various points to scatter incense and utter prayers for the dead. Every spot was thronged with spectators; but I could detect no feeling of devotion, no sensibility in the affections, no solemnity in any one. The only object of the assemblage seemed to be to witness a show, and to examine with the curiosity observable at a fair, or the exhibition of an institute, the varied ornamental display. Three fourths of the crowd were negroes, male and female. Here and there, in two or three instances, I recognized a party of ladies in full dress in black with mantillas of lace, but a majority of the Brazilians and Portuguese present was evidently of the lower orders. We afterwards entered the churches of San Francisco de Paulo, the Candelaria and the Carmelites, where the bishop of Rio was officiating, but without witnessing any thing essentially different from what we had already seen.

All observation of the day confirms me in the impression before received, that a great change has taken place, since 1829, in the respect paid by the people to the superstitious ceremonies of the religion of the country. There is now little in the general aspect of things in the streets, even on days of religious festivals, to remind one of being in a Romish city. A monk or even ecclesiastic is scarce ever met, and whenever I have entered a church during service, a few poor negroes, sick persons, and beggars have constituted the principal part of the assemblage.

November 4th.—I have just accomplished quite a pedestrian feat, in the ascent of the Corcovado. After two days of such rain as the tropics only often witness, the weather this morning was as fine as possible, the atmosphere clear and transparent, very like the most brilliant days of June in the Northern States, when the wind is from the north-west. Lieutenant R——, Mr. G—— (secretary of Commodore McKeever), Prof. Le Froy of the British flag ship, and I, were induced by it to attempt the excursion, though it was not in our power to set off before two o'clock in the afternoon —a late hour for the accomplishment of a walk of nine miles, to the top of a mountain, two thousand three hundred and six feet high, according to the measurement of Beechy, and two thousand three hundred and thirty-nine, by that of Captains King and Fitzroy.

The Corcovado is one of the lofty shafts of granite which, in a greater or less degree of isolation, are characteristic of the geological formation in this region. Its relative position to the range of mountains of which it forms so conspicuous a part, and the height to which it towers above it, can best be compared, perhaps, to a colossal buttress standing against a massive building, with a pinnacled top rising high above the adjoining roof. As looked up to, from its eastern base in a green valley by the sea-side, it appears, as it there really is, an utterly inaccessible mass of perpendicular rock. On the west, however, it is so joined to an angle of the general range for two thirds of its height, as to be comparatively easy of ascent. The first half of the distance from the city may be made by either of two ways: the one, through the valley of the Larangeiras, and the other, by the spur of mountain along which the aqueduct descends into the heart of the town, near the nunnery of Santa Theresa. We chose this last. At the outset, the ascent is a sharp pitch, but after gaining a height of one or two hundred feet, is so gradual for four miles as scarcely to be perceptible. The way leads along the flattened ridge of the hill by a bridle path immediately beside the aqueduct, the refreshing sound of whose waters, as they murmur and rumble in their covered channel, is a pleasant accompaniment to the sea-breeze sweeping by. It is overhung by embowering trees which, while they form a screen against the sun overhead, are too lofty to interfere by their branches with a full view of the prospects on either hand. These, for the whole distance, surpass in beauty and variety any of a similar nature I recollect ever to have met. As we gradually gained terrace after terrace of the spur, the pictures opening immediately beneath us in the ravines on the right —up which the suburbs straggle in tasteful dwellings and blooming gardens; in the broad and bright valley of Engenho Velho beyond, thickly sprinkled with the country residences of the wealthy, and adorned by the imperial palace; in the city itself—the upper bay and its islands; the Organ Mountains and whole panorama, are beyond the powers of description. At the end of two and a half or three miles, the aqueduct, sinking to a level with the surface of the ground, crosses the ridge which it has thus far been following, and leaving the course of this, runs along the face of the mountain at an elevation of a thousand feet. The pathway follows it, and I can compare the suddenness in the change of the prospect to nothing that will give a better idea of it, than a new combination in a kaleidoscope, by a turn of the instrument. It is entire. By a single step, as it were, in place of the above pictures, which are at once lost sight of, you have the southern sections of the city—Gloria Hill, Flamengo, Catètè, Larangieras and Botafogo, the lower bay with its moving imagery, the Sugar Loaf and its companion at the entrance of the harbor, the islets in the offing and along the coast, and the boundless sea. The walk for a mile here, with this picture beneath you on one side, and the beautifully wooded mountain cliffs above, on the other, is a terraced avenue worthy of fairy land itself. Of it Dr. Walsh justly remarks—"Without exaggeration, it may be said, that there is not in the world so noble and beautiful a combination of nature and art, as the prospect it presents."

Five miles from the city, near a natural reservoir in a ledge of granite where the aqueduct originally commenced, the direct pathway to the summit leaves the water-course and strikes steeply up the mountain. Here it is stony and rough, and was now wet from the recent rain. The angle of elevation, equal to that of an ordinary staircase, made the ascent fatiguing: but it is adorned at points by noble specimens of the primeval growth of the forest, reminding me of the finest of the old elms occasionally left standing by the pioneer settlers in Western New York, as I recollect to have been impressed by them thirty years ago. A mile and a half through this wood brought us to a clearing of some extent, with a rancho or cottage, formerly a place of refreshment for those making the ascent. It has been purchased recently by the Emperor, and the land is designed by him for a plantation of foreign pines and other evergreens, which he is introducing. It lies in a dip or notch between the general chain of mountains and the peak of the Corcovado; and the cottage, in full view from the city and harbor, forms a picturesque object from the anchorage of the Congress, though seemingly, in its airy height, but a bird's nest clinging to the wooded cliffs.

Here the ascent of the Corcovado proper commences—the distance to the summit about two miles. The way is steep and wearisome, especially after so forced a march over the preceding part, as we had made; but we pressed on, notwithstanding the heat and fatigue, cheered by the exhortation and promise of the poet—

"Let thy foot
Fail not from weariness, for on the top
The beauty and the majesty of earth
Spread wide beneath, shall make thee to forget
The steep and toilsome way. There thy expanding heart
Shall feel a kindred with that loftier world,
To which thou art translated, and partake
The enlargement of thy vision."

In less than three hours from the city, the bare peak rose directly before us—a pinnacled platform of rock scarcely twenty feet square, separated from the general mass by a broad and deep fissure, over which a rude wooden bridge is thrown. As the peak has been known to be frequently struck by lightning, it is supposed that this chasm was originally caused by a thunderbolt. A rail, supported by iron posts soldered into the solid granite, furnishes a guard on three sides to the precipices descending perpendicularly from them.

The panorama commanded by it, embracing as it does all the imagery that combines in securing to Rio de Janeiro its world-wide celebrity for wonderful beauty, could not fail—under the advantages of the brilliant atmosphere, bright sunshine and lengthened shadows in which we gazed on it—to meet our expectations. The entire city and its suburbs lay at our feet; and, like a map, the bay—near a hundred miles in circuit—its many picturesque headlands and islands and the Organ Mountains and chain along the coast, the peak of Tejuca, the Sugar Loaf reduced to insignificant dimensions, the Gavia, the outer islets and the illimitable sea! The silence one is disposed to keep, in view of such a scene from such a point, best expresses perhaps the kind of admiration felt. Had Bryant in an inspiration of his genius stood with us, he might possibly have given utterance to a description more sublime but to none more graphic or minutely true to the scene, than one already recorded by his pen—

> " Steep is the western side, shaggy and wild,
> With mossy trees, and pinnacles of flint,
> And many a hanging crag. But to the East,
> Sheer to the vale, go down the bare old cliffs—
> Huge pillars, that in middle heaven up bear
> Their weather-beaten capitals, here dark
> With moss, the growth of centuries, and there
> Of chalky whiteness, where the thunder bolt
> Has splintered them. It is a fearful thing
> To stand upon the beetling verge, and see
> Where storm and lightning, from that huge gray wall,
> Have tumbled down vast blocks, and at the base
> Dashed them in fragments, and to lay thine ear
> O'er the dizzy depth, and hear the sound
> Of winds that struggle with the woods below,
> Come up with ocean murmurs."

There is danger, in the impressiveness of a scene of such mingled beauty and sublimity, of forgetting the risk of taking cold, even in the finest weather—after the unavoidable heat and temporary exhaustion of the ascent—from the reduced temperature of the elevation, and the freshness of the sea-breeze sweeping over and around the rock in strong eddies. But reminded of this by a sense of chilliness, and aware of the lateness of the day, at the end of a half hour—grateful for the favorable auspices under which we had enjoyed the view—we gave a farewell gaze and turned our faces for the descent.

I omitted to state that, before reaching the plantation of the Emperor in the dip of the mountains, we had again fallen upon the line of the aqueduct. At this point it passes to the southern side of the range, which here makes an angle in that direction; and Mr. Lefroy, familiar in his walks with all the region, proposed that before descending we should follow it at least a short distance: with the assurance that we would find it equal, in picturesque wildness and beauty, to any thing we had yet seen. Though already pretty well fagged, and a walk of seven miles yet to be made in reaching the city, we readily assented; and most amply indeed were we rewarded. The scenery on every hand—above, beneath and around us, in the strong contrasts of bright sunshine and deep shade, was like pictures of fancy, with a variety and richness of foliage to be found only in the tropics. The aqueduct and path beside it, scarped on the very face of the precipitous mountain, wind round the head of a deep glen, at an elevation of two thousand feet above the valleys beneath and the surf of the ocean; and command uninterrupted views, far and wide, over land and sea, of indescribable beauty and grandeur. Parasitical plants and running vines add to the rich drapery of the woods overhead and beneath the feet, and hang in long pendants from the rocks and in festoons from tree to tree, while, here and there, the tree fern—a novelty to me till now—rises rankly to a height of twenty and thirty feet: throwing out its closely feathered leaves in an umbrella-shaped top, proportionate in size to the height of the stem.

Tempted from point to point, by one new object of admiration or another, we were led two miles amid this luxury of beauty before aware of it, almost to the very sources of the work. At one point, from the impossibility of securing space in the face of the precipice for stone work, the water is led along in small wooden troughs, and the footpath, constructed of planks supported by strong bolts of iron fastened into the rock, is suspended in the air, with a frightful depth beneath. There is no particular spring or fountain head, from which there is a supply of water, but from the beginning of the aqueduct, the smallest streamlet that trickles down the mountain summit is carefully collected by side troughs, and the drippings of every crevice, as well as the gushings of more abundant springs, fully secured.

This aqueduct is a magnificent work for the period at which it was constructed—a hundred and thirty years ago. It is of solid granite with a semicircular bottom for the water-course, and is four feet in width and the same in height; at places entirely above, and at others partially beneath the ground. It is capped with granite in the form of a roof, is furnished with ventilators protected by iron gratings at regular intervals, and is accessible for the use of the water at different points, by doors under lock and key. The honor of having projected and accomplished so important a work is due to Albuquerque, captain-general of the province at the period—1719–23. A record of this is made on a tablet on the front of the fountain of the Carioca, near the convent of San Antonio, above which is the reservoir in which the work terminates. The inscription is of a rudeness of outline and execution characteristic of the art of writing in Brazil a century ago; and undecipherable, except by an antiquarian like Dr. Walsh, familiar, from his favorite studies, with the abbreviations and readings without a division into syllables and words, of olden times.

The following is the translation of this inscription as given by Dr. Walsh. "In the reign of the high and powerful king Don John the Fifth, Ayrès de Saldanha and Albuquerque, being governor and captain-general of this place, by his directions this work was made, which was begun in the year 1719 and completed in the year 1723."

The most magnificent and costly section of the aqueduct—and one which the now well-known principle in hydraulics, that water will rise to the level of its head, shows to have been useless both in labor and expense—is a lofty arcade, a conspicuous ornament of the city, by which the aqueduct is carried across a deep valley from the hill of Santa Theresa to that of San Antonio opposite. It consists of two ranges of arches one above the other, the lower six hundred and the upper eight hundred and forty feet in length, and forty feet in height. Next to the Roman remains of the Pont du Garde in Languedoc, the aqueduct across the Alcantara at Lisbon, and the High Bridge at Harlem, it is the finest structure of the kind I have seen.

It was near sundown before we reluctantly turned our backs upon the surprising beauty which still enticed us forward. By a forced march we accomplished the stony and staircase descent through the woods, while there was yet sufficient daylight to make good our footsteps over the rough and slippery way. Safely at this point, though the night soon gathered around us, we had no difficulty in keeping the path under the brilliant starlight of the evening, and reached the city at eight o'clock, having accomplished the trip of twenty-two miles in six hours.

CHAPTER XI.

RIO DE JANEIRO.

November 9th.—Saturday more than any other is a day trying to my spirits. It is that which I appropriate to special preparation for my professional duties on the Sabbath; and with it, the hardness and seeming barrenness of my field of labor is, unavoidably, brought painfully to view. The moral condition of our ship is equal, probably, if not in advance of that of men-of-war in general, in our own or any other service; and the discipline and general order on board good. Indeed, we regard ourselves, and are regarded by others around us, in these respects as a peculiarly favored and a happy ship. But mere external propriety of conduct does not satisfy my expectation, or meet my hopes. I look for evidences of higher results, from the preaching of the Gospel and other means of religious influence established among us, but look in vain; and instead, especially when in port, find daily discouragements which would lead a spirit, less elastic than my own, utterly to despair of being instrumental in any spiritual good.

During the last fortnight, the crew in successive detachments have been on shore, on a general liberty of forty-eight hours. The drunkenness and debauchery of many, incident to this, unavoidably obtruded on my notice in a greater or less degree, have filled my heart with sadness, and my lips—at the end of a ministry of six months—with the desponding language of the prophet, "Who hath believed our report? and to whom hath the arm of the Lord been revealed?" This has not escaped the observation of the men themselves, and yesterday, one of them as spokesman of a group with whom I fell into conversation, said to me—"We are afraid, Mr. S———, that you will become so disgusted with our wickedness that you will leave the ship, and give us up to the devil altogether: but we hope not." To do this would be to act the part of a coward and a traitor; and knowing in whom alone is the sufficiency for these things, I must still labor—bear and forbear—preach with fidelity and love, pray without fainting, and hope against hope.

The privileges of the shore over, all were settling down into customary contentment and quietude when, by some means last evening, a large quantity of strong drink was successfully smuggled into the ship. There is ever in a man-of-war a greater or less degree of unmitigated rascality which, on such occasions, does not fail to manifest itself, giving the executive of the ship an abundance of trouble, and bringing reproach upon the better portions of the crew. The consequence of the successful strategy was a good deal of disorder last night among "the baser sort" of the ship's company, and a nervous headache and a heartache this morning to me.

One result of the liberty on shore, was the incarceration for drunkenness and riotous conduct, of a half dozen or more of our men, in the calabouça or common jail of the city. An early intimation of the dilemma in which these were placed reached me, with an appeal for aid in procuring their release. A visit to them for this purpose, gave me the opportunity of a personal inspection of the prison. While confessing and lamenting the folly which had brought them there, they complained most grievously, as well they might, of the horrible place. It is time indeed for some Howard to arise in Brazil; and I rejoice to learn that the state of her prisons and the subject of prison discipline, or rather the fact of an utter want of all discipline, is attracting

6*

the attention of some of her philanthropists and statesmen. Our fellows, at the end of two or three days, were almost starved. No food is served to the prisoners by authority. They are entirely dependent on their own resources, the kindness of any friends they may happen to have, or the supplies furnished gratuitously by some of the brotherhoods of benevolence in the city. I found those from the Congress—chargeable only with having broken the peace in a drunken brawl—in a filthy room of horrible smells, crowded with eighty or a hundred felons, black, white and colored of every hue. Among these were robbers, and murderers, and criminals of the most desperate character: without classification in age or crime—beardless boys, arrested for the most trifling and venial offences, being placed side by side with gray-headed veterans in vice. Our men had stripped themselves more than half naked, that their clothes might furnish no ambush for the vermin with which the place was filled; and gave pitiful accounts of the nights they had spent, in stifling heat, amid clouds of mosquitoes and other insects, with no beds but the rough plank of the floors, open in large crevices to the effluvia from the common cesspool of the whole prison immediately beneath. A civil and intelligent young man of their number told me that, till "this spree," he had not tasted strong drink for two years past; and had been well punished, for the indulgence, by a week in this frightful and disgusting hole. Giving them the means of relief from immediate hunger, I promised to do what I could for their liberation; and the youngster referred to, the last—from some mistake in his name—to gain a release, has just come thankfully on board.

November 12th.—A ball on board the Congress and a soiree at the American Embassy have afforded, within the week past, our first opportunities of mingling in the society of Rio. It required but a short time to transform the quarter-deck of the frigate from a grim battery into a brilliant ball-room. The guns having been run out of sight on the forecastle, the awnings screened by the flags of all nations, in flutings overhead and in festoons at the sides, and the decks artistically chalked in colors, the interior soon presented the aspect of a spacious and gay saloon. In this, at different points, muskets arranged in thick clusters with a candle in each muzzle, formed glittering and becoming candelabra; and pistols and bayonets similarly arrayed and mounted, made brackets for lights along the sides and chandeliers above, while a graceful amenity was thrown over these implements of death, by wreaths of evergreen intermingled with bouquets of flowers rich in color and perfume. The poop-deck overlooking this dancing room, was transformed by similar decorations into a lofty, tented pavilion, from which those not disposed to join in the amusement below, might view the spectacle and enjoy each other's society in conversation.

The ship was illuminated outside, by lines of lights running up each mast and by lanterns suspended from the yard-arms. While the company were assembling, rockets were sent up, to add to the brilliancy, and blue lights burned on the arrival of the most distinguished of the guests. Thus the effect without, in approaching in the dark, was scarce less striking and beautiful than the coup d'œil within, on crossing the gangway. The only interest I took in the preparations was in having the draperies, which separated these brilliant apartments from the forward deck, so arranged as to allow the crew—who would be kept from their hammocks till a late hour by the entertainment—to be spectators of the scene. This indulgence was readily accorded; and, during the whole evening, our hardy tars in a uniform dress of white and blue, clustered in thick rows from the mainmast forward, formed by no means the least striking feature in the spectacle. Indeed, their fine physical aspect and becoming deportment attracted much observation; and elicited the most complimentary remarks upon them, as a body of men, from the most distinguished strangers on board.

The company on this occasion consisted principally of resident foreigners, diplomatists, and their families, and the officers of the national ships in port. There were few native Brazilians among them. Under the impression that the entertainment given by Mr. and Mrs. Tod would embrace the higher circles of the native society, I joined the party from the ship attending it. The mansion occupied by the Legation is at Praya Flamengo, where I was so much at home in 1829. It is spacious and lofty, with a stately suite of reception-rooms on the second floor, which command fine views of the bay and its chief features near the sea. It was illuminated in front, and brilliantly lighted and tastefully decorated with flowers within. According to Brazilian custom on occasions of fête, the tesselated pavement of the vestibule and hall, and the marble staircase leading to the reception-rooms, were strewn with the fresh leaves of the mango tree and various aromatic plants which, under the pressure of the feet, send forth a grateful perfume. A garden in the rear, filled with myrtle and orange trees, and gay with the blossoms of the pomegranate and oleander, was also illuminated, and seen opening in perspective from the hall, with pretty effect. The company was large; exhibiting a good deal of dress among the ladies, in the latest modes of Paris, and some fine diamonds. There was, too, a sprinkling of title and nobility, and a little beauty, but nothing more distinctively Brazilian, or characteristic of nationality, than in the party on board the Congress.

At an early hour after the civilities of the reception, and a general interchange of salutations, dancing was commenced and continued to be the chief amusement of the evening. There was nothing in the scene with which I could sympathize, and I withdrew from the crowded and heated rooms to the terraced-walk fronting the beach. Here, a land breeze, deliciously fresh and fragrant, came fanning down the mountain's side; and I passed two hours and more in the enjoyment of it, in a promenade back and forth of a quarter of a mile, beneath a gloriously lighted sky, while every thing was hushed to a midnight repose, except the sounds of the distant music of the dance, and the rush, and roar, and the thunder at my feet of the foaming surf.

On returning to the house I met Mr. Tod in the lower rooms,

the supper-room being about to be thrown open. The banquet was profuse and luxurious. A chief novelty among its delicacies, at either end of the principal table, was the choicest fish of the adjoining seas—the garoupa. It is very large, and, on the present occasion, was baked whole and served cold. From the general demand for it, especially among the ladies, I should have judged the dish to be in high estimation, without the assurance of the fact. It is a rarity, and its market price very high. Sums, I am told, are sometimes given for it which I dare not venture to state, without further inquiry, lest either my veracity or credulity, or both, might be put in question.

November 15th.—Yesterday afternoon I accompanied Captain McIntosh, Lieut. P—— of the British flag ship, and Lieut. T—— of the Congress, in a drive of five miles to the country residence of Mr. R——, an English gentleman, a partner in one of the wealthiest mercantile houses in Rio. An invitation to an evening party had been received from Mrs. R——, a few days before, and the call we now made was in acknowledgment of the civility. The direction of the drive was westward, through the rich and broad valley which extends seven or eight miles from the city, to the foot of the mountains of Tejuca. High walls of brick and stone, or lofty hedges equally impenetrable to the eye, cut off the view of the pleasure gardens and grounds surrounding the residences in the suburbs, from those seated in the low carriages at present in fashion, and I chose a more elevated seat beside the coachman—though at the risk, in a black dress and white cravat, of being taken for a servant out of livery—rather than forego the advantage of this better point for observation; especially as there was no inconvenience from the sun, the afternoon being overcast and gray, such as do not often occur here without rain. But for this position I should have lost much of the enjoyment of the drive.

Half the distance is a continued suburb of the city; and the remainder a succession of cottages, villas, and mansions in a greater or less degree of proximity—the residences of the aristocratic and wealthy, both natives and foreigners. A predominating fancy with these seems to be the exhibition of showy entrances and gateways, little in keeping in their stateliness, in many instances, with the inferior style and dimensions of the dwellings themselves. Some of these last, however, are quite palatial. One of this kind was pointed out, as an evidence of the talent for business, and the prosperous fortunes of a colored man. The gardens and grounds on every side are luxuriant in the display of flowers, shrubbery and trees, and often tastefully embellished with vases, casts, statuary and fountains of graceful and classic model. The rapidity of vegetation in weeds and grass, as well as in more valuable growth is such, however, as to make perfect neatness and good keeping in the grounds difficult. One great defect in them, which cannot fail to arrest the eye unaccustomed to it, is the entire absence of the close sod and velvet turf, which give such smoothness and softness to lawns and pleasure grounds in the United States and in England. The burning sun of this latitude kills the roots of such growth, and there is no close set grass here. All that is native is coarse, tufted, and straggling. The site of the city was originally a marsh, and this interval land, between the bay and the mountains, is low and wet. The soil, a stiff clay, causes the roads in rainy weather soon to be so cut up as to become almost impassable, and in dry, to be both rough and dusty.

The residence of Mr. R——, crowning a gently swelling hill in the midst of a lovely valley, rises conspicuously to the view while yet a mile from it. It is an old Brazilian house of unpretending and cottage-like aspect, soon to give place to a new building: but looked rural and attractive, and commands a splendid panorama. Here the gateway is of a simplicity corresponding with that of the house. It opens, at the distance of a quarter of a mile from this, into an avenue of young mango trees, winding gradually up the ascent and bordered on either side by a hedge of the double scarlet hibiscus, whose polished leaves of green were studded with bright flowers.

A long and lofty saloon, so well furnished with windows as to be readily converted almost into an open pavilion, occupies the whole front of the house. A flight of stone steps at either end ascends from the carriage drive to this. A similar apartment in the rear forms the dining-room; while between these, and lighted only through them, is the drawing-room. In a colder climate an apartment thus situated would, in the day time, be dark and gloomy; but here, where for a great part of the year a glaring and glowing sun pours down upon every thing, it forms a welcome retreat into which the light comes only in subdued and grateful shade.

We had made the acquaintance of Mrs. and Miss R—— at the entertainments mentioned under my last date; and, on being ushered into the saloon were received by them in a most frank and courteous manner. Mrs. R——, though a native Brazilian, has been much in England, and Miss R—— has but lately completed her education there. Both are of pleasing address and most gentle and amiable. After a half hour in conversation a walk in the grounds was proposed, the freshness of the evening with a land breeze from the mountains having set in. We had already discovered the views in every direction to be lovely: embracing the rich valley through which we had driven, the mountains bordering it on one side and the fantastic peaks in which they terminate at its head behind; with cottages and country houses scattered thickly around, and the imperial palace of San Christovao encircled with plantations in full view. Glimpses of the city were caught in the far distance in front; and, with a glass, the tapering masts of the Congress, surmounted by her broad pennant, rising high above the tallest of its towers and steeples.

From the end of the saloon opposite to that at which we had entered, an embowered grapery leads to a stream at the foot of the hill, overhung with trees and beautifully fringed with the lofty and graceful bamboo. Along the green banks of this, the gardens, filled with the greatest variety of shrub and flower, spread widely among fruit-bearing and ornamental trees, including a succession of orange groves. Through these we sauntered with great delight, tasting of the various fruits; examining, in the fine display of the botanical kingdom around, things old and new; resting upon a rustic seat here and there; and finally becoming grouped in a picturesque bower of living bamboo, whose thickly clustered stems at the sides and feathery tops interlaced overhead effectually exclude the sun, and secure, even at midday, a retreat of refreshing coolness. Among entire novelties to us were the Jaca or jack fruit—*artocarpus Indicus*—or East India bread fruit, and the Brazilian plum.

We were here joined by Mr. R—— and his sons, by Lieut. F—— of our ship, and Mr. Lawrence McKeever, a son of the commodore, an attaché of an American partner of the house in which Mr. R—— is the English principal. Mr. R—— to the reputation of an able and successful merchant adds that of a well-read man, thoroughly furnished with intelligence in regard to all subjects of local and general interest in Brazil. His conversation is thus both interesting and instructive.

As twilight began to gather round us, we returned to the house, and were summoned to a tea-table in the dining-hall well spread as in the olden times at home, not only with every delicacy appropriate to the repast, but with such substantial dishes, also, as those who had been riding and driving and walking, since an early dinner, might be disposed to welcome. There was an air of genuine hospitality in the well-covered length of the board, which carried me back to the tables of our friends of Massena and of the Lakelands in former days, telling that like theirs it was no unaccustomed thing thus to be drawn out to its full length by the presence of some eight or ten unexpected guests, in addition to a large family circle. With a number of well-trained and neatly-dressed negro servants in attendance, the whole scene was more like that of an ordinary exhibition of American hospitality, as I recollect it in boyhood, even in the Northern States, than any thing I have for a long time witnessed. It was half past nine o'clock before we took leave; yet, such is the Jehu style of driving that we were not only at the landing in the city, where the captain's gig was in waiting for us, but safely on board ship by ten.

The rainy season is not so strongly marked at Rio as in many tropical regions, though at this period of the year more rain falls than at any other. To-day it poured in torrents from the early morning, while an impenetrable fog has been rushing from the sea, before a driving wind. The worst of this state of things, to some of us on board the Congress, was an engagement of several days' standing to a dinner with Admiral Reynolds, the English commander-in-chief on this station. We looked in vain as the appointed hour approached, for any abatement in the wind and rain, or the arrival of a messenger to say we would not be expected; and, at a quarter to six, the barge was called away and Commodore McKeever, Captain McIntosh and I, with such protection as our boat cloaks could give, were in the midst of the storm pulling for the flag ship. Fortunately the distance was scarcely more than a quarter of a mile. We escaped getting wet, and in the shelter and elegant appointments of the admiral's cabins soon forgot the discomfort of the pull on board.

The want of a higher grade of rank in the navy of the United States than that of post captain, while in the British service and that of other nations there is not only that of admiral, but six degrees of advancement in that rank, often leads to embarrassment and an unpleasant state of feeling between those bearing other flags and our commanders-in-chief. The preposterous expectation and, in many instances, pertinacious claim of equality in rank and reciprocity in official honors, where there is confessedly an inferiority of commission, and in contravention of the established rules of military etiquette, not unfrequently limit the intercourse between American commodores and European admirals to the cold formalities of an official visit. Where this is the case, the association of the officers of the respective squadrons is, in a greater or less degree, of the same character. Happily for myself

I have never been placed in this position. On the contrary, in all the ships to which I have been attached, the most friendly relations have been established with English ships of war, on the same station. Such is the case with the Congress and the Southampton. By mutual courtesy and good will, the official and social intercourse of the two commanders-in-chief was on our arrival at once placed on a desirable footing. The consequence is, that the officers of the respective ships are left to an unembarrassed association. This has proved cordial, and many in both ships visit each other with the intimacy and informality of congenial neighbors on shore.

Mrs. Reynolds accompanied the admiral from England and lives on board ship. She is a person of intelligent and cultivated mind and of frank and pleasing address; and the birds and flowers, the drawings and cabinets in natural history which, in addition to a choice library, adorn the apartments of the Southampton, at once bespeak the presence and taste of an accomplished woman. In addition to the military family of the admiral, which consists of the captain of the ship, the flag-lieutenant and the secretary who are regularly at his table, we had the company of two or three other officers, including the Rev. Mr. P——, the chaplain. Besides this gentleman, I was happy to meet in the party others whom I found to be enlightened and spiritual Christians, as well as agreeable and well-bred men. It is unnecessary to say that the entertainment was sumptuous: served in plate, with all the appointments of the table in the elegant keeping of English aristocratic life. The summons to the dining cabin was by music from a fine band; and with the removal of the cloth and her majesty's health, we had "God save the Queen," followed by "Hail Columbia" and a succession of passages from the choicest operas. Our reception was the more cordial, perhaps, from the badness of the weather; and the whole evening marked with such free interchange of thought and feeling that it seemed a family party at home. The effect to me of such an impression in this far off land, has been an irresistible fit of the "*mal du pays.*"

November 20th.—The Praya San Domingo and Praya Grande on the eastern side of the bay, continue to be favorite resorts with us, especially when Captain McIntosh is leader of the party. He holds in abhorrence the filth of the city side. The interest of our visits has been much increased by the acquaintance accidentally formed with a Portuguese family, shortly after the return of the Congress from the Plata. In a stroll we were taking there, we passed a plantation, the extent and thriftiness of which had before attracted our notice. The principal gateway now stood open, exhibiting, in long vista, an avenue of young palms, whose interlacing branches completely over-arched the walk beneath. A group of slaves were at work just within; and coupling our admiration with a question as to the privilege of entering, we had scarcely received an affirmative reply, before the proprietor, Don Juan M——, made his appearance from a wilderness of luxuriant growth on one side, courteously bidding us welcome, and becoming himself our guide. There is nothing artistic or particularly tasteful in the manner in which the grounds are laid out; but they are in high cultivation, and the variety and exuberance of the growth, and the novelty to us of many of its forms, made them very attractive. Fruits, flowers, and vegetables—shrubs, plants, and trees are so closely intermingled, as to shut out all view, except in each immediate path, or at the intersecting angles of the larger alleys. In other places endless beds, so arranged as to be easily irrigated, are filled with every kind of vegetable in the greatest profusion; while above wave the broad leaves of the banana and plantain, the feathery palm, and the closely set, and pinnated foliage of the mango. Many of the paths are bordered with coffee trees, now in full bloom. These are allowed to grow to a height of ten or fifteen feet, and are in the form of a bush. The blossoms, of the purest white, appear in general effect like those of the double jessamine. They cluster thickly over the branches, and contrast beautifully with the dark green of the polished leaves. Among the exotics are the cinnamon, clove, and nutmeg, and the climbing vine of the black pepper.

In the course of our ramble we came upon the wash-house of the establishment—an open, tile-covered lodge or verandah, supported by pillars of brick, and furnished with a wide and deep tank or reservoir of water, troughs, tubs and slabs of stone for the various operations of the laundry. Three or four negresses were engaged in the appropriate work of the place, with their children at play around. Near one of the mothers, in a flat basket on the ground, lay, kicking and crowing as if ready to spring out of its skin, an entirely naked and shining little negro, six or eight months of age—one of the brightest and cleanest looking little rogues I ever saw. It was black as the purest ebony, and in a perfection of form fitting it for the model of a cupid, or infant Apollo, or Adonis. It looked so healthy, and so wholesome, and so perfectly pure, as to be provocative almost of a kiss; and one of our party—who, in strong remembrance of his own little ones at home, has a perfect passion for every child he meets, whether black or white—was so delighted that I thought he would scarcely rest satisfied in his caressing, short of such an evidence of admiration.

At the end of a half hour we came again into the principal avenue, leading from the gate to the base of a steep hill, or rather cliff, overhanging the gardens, from the brow of which the dwelling of Don Juan looks down as upon a map. Detained already, it appeared, from an appointment of business by his attentions to us, he here apologized for the necessity of taking leave, but begged us to continue our walk up the hill, from which we would have a magnificent view; and called a negro lad to guide us. We willingly complied, and advanced by a winding path up the steep. Among the growth not before noticed, we here observed the peach, apple, and pomegranate, interspersed with grove after grove of orange trees, heavily laden with golden fruit. The house is a long, tile-roofed cottage of one story, surrounded by broad piazzas, opening upon flagged terraces. The pointed top of the hill has been cut down to a platform, sufficient only in extent for the area of the dwelling, with a shrubbery and flower garden on one side, and a dovecote and quarters for the house-negroes on the other. The whole is perched upon the angular point of a precipitous promontory overlooking the bay of St. Francis Xavier, from which a heavy surf rolls beneath, breaking, in part, amid a cluster of fantastic and columnar rocks, and in part upon a white sand beach. To reach the best point for a panoramic view at the end of the flower garden, we were conducted through the reception rooms, in the centre of the cottage, furnished with some showy articles of French manufacture—a piano, sofa, vases of painted china. The landscape and water view at every point are superb—especially on the garden front, with the wild surf beneath, and the islet of Boa Viagem for a foreground—its fantastic cliffs of strongly colored earths draped with bright verdure, and crowned by its picturesque little chapel. The varied movements of sail in the lower harbor; the bright gleamings of the city along the shores of Flamengo and Botafogo; with the Sugar-loaf and adjoining hills, and the Gavia and Corcovado in sublime groupings in the distance, formed together a picture of unrivalled beauty. The coloring, and effective shades of a sunset of crimson and gold, exhibited the whole with gorgeous effect; and we stood fascinated by it, till the gathering twilight hastened us to our boat.

Commodore McKeever and Mr. G—— accompanied us in a second visit which we were invited by Don Juan to make, a few evenings afterwards. We were welcomed with the cordiality of old friends, and after a walk through the grounds, were conducted to the house, introduced to Madame M——, and served with coffee, sweetmeats and liqueurs. We soon discovered the mistress of the establishment to be of the order of women, so graphically described by the wise man—"she seeketh wool and flax, and worketh willingly with her hands. She looketh well to the ways of her household, and eateth not the bread of idleness. Her children arise and call her blessed, her husband also, and he praiseth her." Through the open windows of the verandah, as we entered, we saw her busily engaged, amid a group of female slaves, old and young, in the cutting and fitting of garments which they were sewing; and learned from her husband that her agency, as well as supervision, was thus exercised in the whole economy of the establishment. In dress, she was in the dishabille common among the females, and males too, in this climate, at least till a late hour of the day; a loose wrapper with a colored silk pocket-handkerchief over the head. On the summons of Don Juan, she joined us without apology in regard to her toilette; and after the refreshments were served, while we were enjoying the view at the point of the promontory, gathered and arranged for each of us a choice and beautiful bouquet.

In acknowledgment of the kindness of thus throwing open their grounds and house to us, an invitation was given for a visit to the Congress. This was readily accepted, and they have since passed a morning on board. It was their first visit to a man-of-war, and they professed to take more interest in it, and to feel themselves more highly honored from its bearing the stripes and stars of the United States, than they could under any other flag. We scarcely recognized the Dona at first, under the aspect of a visitor. In place of the Portuguese negligè, in which we were received by her at home, she now appeared in the latest style of Parisian promenade costume: with silks and laces and expensive embroideries, in a correctness of taste and good-keeping, that proved her by no means unaccustomed to the elegancies of the toilette. Don Juan is a man of intelligence and of much practical good sense and observation. Among many things on board, which attracted his attention, aside from the equipment and peculiar character of our ship in military appointment, was a small homœopathic medicine chest in the captain's cabin. He is a warm advocate of this system, and a practitioner of it in his own family; and he informed us that in forty cases of fever, among his slaves, during the late epidemic, he allowed of no other treatment, and did not lose a single patient, though many negroes around him died of the pestilence under allopathic practice.

CHAPTER XII.

RIO DE JANEIRO.

November 26th.—The heat of the mornings on shore is becoming so intense as to make walking oppressive. Till the setting in of the sea-breeze about mid-day, the ship is altogether more desirable than any other place accessible to us. Moored in the direct line of the winds from the sea, her decks with awnings spread fore and aft, form a delightful lounging-place; one never without attractions, in the constant movements on the bay, and the varying and beautiful effects produced upon its imagery, by hourly atmospheric changes. This you can readily understand from daily experience at Riverside. Like the verandah there, the poop of the Congress here commands a wide-spread panorama of water, mountain, and valley, ever varying in its aspects of lights and shade, sunshine and clouds, tints and coloring, and tempting one to give too much time to mere admiration of the changing picture.

When the atmosphere is peculiarly brilliant, the mountains stand out with a nearness and strength of light that exposes to clear view the chisellings of their minutest features. With a good glass, every rock and tree, and almost every shrub, of the nearer ranges is then brought, seemingly, within touch; while the sublime chain, forty and fifty miles distant in the north, exhibits, through the same medium, not only the fantastic spikes and fingers from which it derives its name, but the minuter formations of the wooded sides also, furrowed by water-courses, and streaked here and there with the silver line of a cataract in a deep glen. Then again, the whole stand, with undistinguishable features, like massive walls of purple and blue, the upper profile only of their jagged outlines being marked boldly against the sky.

In the morning, the whole bay is smooth and glassy as a lake. one vast mirror, along whose edges are repictured in strong and unbroken reflection, mountain and city, church-tower, fortress, and convent, in minute fidelity, while all the men-of-war, and the little craft floating by with useless sails, lie in duplicate around. The sun glares hotly—not a breath of air is stirring, and every one is oppressed. But watching seaward, the topsails of the inward-bound in the far offing are seen, by and by, to be gently filling with a breeze; presently, 'cats-paw' after 'cats-paw' comes creeping through the channel and up the bay; till soon, in place of a glaring and oppressive calm, its surface is dancing with 'white-caps;' the lateen sail boats, careening to the wind and dashing the spray from their bows, rush past and around us like "playful things of life;" the inward-bound with wide-spread wings come hastening to the anchorage; every one drinks in with delight the welcome draught; and for the rest of the day, new aspects and new life are imparted to every thing and every body. At times, this sea-breeze is supplanted by a half gale from the same direction, causing so much of a swell as to raise breakers between us and the landing, and partially to interrupt communication with the shore. This was the case a day or two since, when the surf rolled along nearly the whole length of the city. The change in the temperature too, is frequently so great as to lead to the substitution of cloth clothing for that of light summer wear, and to the buttoning closely of the coat to avoid a sense of chilliness.

Towards evening the sea-breeze ordinarily dies away; and, by sunset, a glassy surface again reflects the gorgeous coloring which now mantles the mountains, and gilds with brightness the prominent architecture of the city. As the short twilight settles into darkness, regular lines of brilliant lamps gleam for miles along the shores on either side of the bay, and up the ridges and over the tops of the hills in the city; the bright radiance of unnumbered stars falls from above; and the land-breeze, gently fanning down the mountain sides, brings with it the freshness and fragrance of their woods and flowers.

Often a thunder-storm of thick blackness, with forked lightning, is seen raging among the mountain peaks without approaching nearer; and oftener still, magnificently culminating summer clouds, heaped pile upon pile above them, exhibit a play of electric light, of a beauty and splendor sufficient for the pastime of the evening. We had a remarkable display of this kind a night or two ago; the flashes were more vivid and more incessant than I recollect ever before to have witnessed. Masses of black clouds, towering to the zenith on every side, made the night exceedingly dark. In the momentary intervals between the flashes there was a darkness that might almost be felt—utterly impenetrable even at the shortest distance—and making inexpressibly grand and beautiful the more than mid-day brightness which instantly followed, disclosing to microscopic view every object far and near.

From the cause named at the beginning of this date—the heat of the mornings—my visits on shore, for the long walk which you know to be an essential daily enjoyment to me, are chiefly in the later hours of the afternoon and evening. As the last regular boat of the ship leaves the shore punctually at sunset, this necessity of choosing so late a period of the day would subject me to the inconvenience of coming off in a shore boat, and the disgust of breathing the atmosphere by which the vicinity of the common landing is nightly polluted, were it not for the social arrangements of the Commodore. Intimacy with the Ambassador and his family, and other American friends in the same neighborhood, leads him with Mr. G—— to pass most of his evenings at the Praya Flamengo. His barge awaits him regularly, at nine o'clock, at a sheltered and pleasant landing near the Gloria Hill. A seat

in this is always in reserve for me; and, whether visiting with him or not, I am sure of a passage in good season to the ship. I am thus left at liberty to range the hills and valleys at my pleasure towards the close of day, and to take my fill of such delights as nature, in her exuberance and ever-varying beauty in ten thousand forms, here affords. A chief drawback to the pleasure is the want of a companion in my rambles. Such of my messmates as have a round of ship's duty in their order, find sufficient exercise in pacing the decks in its discharge, and are often too much fatigued to start in search of the picturesque; others, though at leisure, less inured to fatigue than I am, think the beauty of the upland haunts I most frequent, scarcely worth the effort required at all points, in the first sharp ascent of a half mile, by which only they are attained. Hence my evening strolls of this kind are solitary: still—

> "My steps are not alone
> In these bright walks; the sweet southwest, at play,
> Flies, rustling, where the tropic leaves are strown
> Along the winding way.
> And far in heaven the while,
> The sun that sends the gale to wander here,
> Pours out on the fair earth the quiet smile—
> That sweetens all the year."

The row, at night, of two miles and more to the ship is of itself a pleasure: sometimes beneath a bright moon, with the palm-topped trees and convent towers of Santa Theresa on our left, marked in silver against the sky; sometimes amid a darkness which leaves nothing for our guide but the signal lanterns for the Commodore, at the peak of the far-off Congress; and sometimes again, amid a display of phosphorescence in the water, sufficient to excite both admiration and surprise. The regular dip of the oars, then, creates splendid coruscations: streams of apparent fire run from the uplifted blades, while the barge, under the impulse of fourteen stalwart oarsmen, rushes on through a wide trough seemingly of molten silver.

But I am forgetting the object for which I opened my journal —to say, that in despite of the heat, I have spent two mornings, within the past week, in a stroll along the shaded side of the Rua Ouvidor, in company with the Commodore, Captain and Mr. G——, on a visit of curiosity to the various shops with which it is lined. The show windows of these rival those of Broadway, in the display of rich fancy goods of English, French, and German manufacture, and of jewelry, articles of vertu, drawings, engravings, and bijouterie. Among the jewellers' shops which we entered was one, having for its sign the imperial arms and crown in rich gilding—thus indicating the special patronage of their majesties and the court. The person in attendance received us most politely, and, though we at once apprised him that our object was not to purchase, exhibited his choicest caskets, from those valued at a few hundred dollars to those at as many tens of thousands. Most of the contents were native diamonds and other precious stones tastefully arranged and artistically set. The workmen here are celebrated for skill in this respect, and for the delicacy and finish of their filagree in silver, and chasings in gold. Rio is also celebrated for the manufacture of artificial flowers from feathers. Those most valued are of the choicest and rarest humming birds. The changing tints of some of these are more rich and varied than those of the opal. Such are much prized and are expensive. The counterpart of a set recently ordered by the Princess de Joinville was as costly as so much jewelry. The manufactories are in large shops open entirely in front to the street, and, the artisans being chiefly young girls, are favorite resorts and lounging places of shoppers and idlers.

It must not be inferred that in thus spending a morning in shopping, we were encroaching on the prerogatives of the ladies of Brazil. The usage of the country denies them this pastime. Portuguese and Spanish views of the liberty of outdoor locomotion to be allowed to females—traceable to the Moorish estimate of their trust worthiness and virtue—prohibit to them here in a great degree the privileges of the street. In the early morning they may be seen, dressed in black, and attended by a servant or child, walking to and from church; and on the Sabbath, likewise, in long family procession, in performance of a like duty; but, to take a promenade as such, for pleasure or display, or to pass from shop to shop looking at fine goods by the hour, without finding the article sought, or any thing to suit the fancy, would be regarded as an indecorum, and an unmistakable mark of vulgar boldness. Native prejudice on this point, has doubtless been modified by the example of numerous foreign residents and visitors; still, when a lady is met in the streets in promenade, it may be safely inferred that she is not a Brazilian: if wearing a bonnet, it may be deemed certain.

Aside from the light thrown upon the general estimate of female virtue, by this prohibition, from usage, there are habits of indecency among the people, witnessed even in the most public thoroughfares, sufficient to justify it, so long as the nuisance is permitted; moreover, a lady in walking is subjected to an impudent stare and look of libertinism from shopkeepers, and clerks, and passers-by, which is in itself an insult, without the addition of the remarks of levity which at times may be heard. There has been an advance in civilization of late in this respect; still, effrontery enough is left in connection with it to offend the delicacy of a woman in walking, and to excite the indignation of any male friend accompanying her.

The native female of the better classes is, therefore, still to be regarded as a kind of house prisoner; she may stand against or lean over the railing of an upper balcony by the hour—as is much the custom—gazing in listless silence upon whatever is taking place in the street; but a promenade below, with the chance of a flirtation, is denied her.

How then, you will ask, is the shopping of the ladies for fine dresses and fine feathers accomplished? I answer, either by husbands and fathers, who I am told are well versed by experience in the business, or by a running to and from shop to drawing-room of boys and porters with pattern-books and pieces. A lady from the country will drive to the house of some friend, or secure a hired room, and, sending forth a servant, will put the errand-boys of half the shops in the city, in motion for the day.

On one of these mornings, we entered a common auction-room for a moment, and accidentally stumbled on the humiliating and reproachful sight of a sale of men and women by a fellow man. Not the sale, as till within a few years past might here have been the case, of newly imported captives from Africa, but of natives of Rio, thus passing under the hammer from owner to owner like any article of merchandise. They were eight or ten in number of both sexes, varying in age from boyhood and girlhood to years of maturity and middle life. They stood meekly and submissively, though evidently anxious and sad, under the interrogations and examinations of the bidders, and a rehearsal and laudation by the auctioneer of their different available working qualities and dispositions: their health, strength and power of endurance. All, in their turn were made to mount an elevated platform, to display their limbs almost to nakedness, and exhibit their muscular powers by various gymnastics, like a horse his movements and action, before the bidders at Tattersall's.

They were rapidly knocked down at prices varying from two hundred to a thousand and more milreis: that is, from one to five hundred and more dollars. As we turned away, the indignation of one of our party found vent in the exclamation: "Such a spectacle is a disgrace to human nature. It makes one sick at heart, and ready to fear that in the retributive justice of the Almighty the time may come, when the blacks here will put up the whites for sale in the same manner!" And why not? Why should the blood boil at the mere suggestion of the thought in the one case, and yet flow coolly and tranquilly on, in view of the other?

Happily Brazil has been aroused, through the influence of her Emperor and the wisest of her statesmen and legislators, to earnestness in that suppression of the traffic in slaves to which she has so long stood pledged by treaty. It is no longer in name only that the trade is a piracy. The landing of a cargo any where in the Empire subjects it to forfeiture. A high premium is given to an informer in a case of smuggling of the kind, and the law cuts off all recovery of payment for the proceeds of a sale that may have been effected. The consequence is, that the millionnaires of Rio, whose coffers have been filled to repletion with the price of blood, finding the government in earnest in the execution of the laws, are forsaking their gilded palaces here—some of them among the most luxurious and ornate residences of the city—for homes where they may pursue their nefarious business with less reproach to reputation, and less liability to the penalty of the laws. It is said that there are residents here, entitled by birth and citizenship to stand beneath the protecting folds of the stripes and stars of our country, who till now have been active agents in, and have shared largely in the emoluments of this wicked outrage on the rights of man.

December 10th.—The 2d inst. was the Emperor's birth-day, a chief gala among the anniversaries of Rio. His Majesty then completed his twenty-fifth year. The day was fine, and the celebration consisted of a grand military procession of regular troops and national guards through the palace square; a Te Deum in the imperial chapel, at which the Emperor and Empress assisted, as the phraseology is; a review of the troops by their Majesties from a balcony of the palace; a levee for hand-kissing afterwards, for such as are entitled to the entree; and at night a visit of the Court in state, to the opera. The whole accompanied by the firing, morning, noon and night, afloat and on shore, of unnumbered cannon.

I was in Captain McIntosh's party in going on shore. He has a horror of crowds, which to me afford some of the best opportunities of judging of the character of a people, and after seeing him comfortably seated in a balcony commanding the square, Lieut. T—— and I sallied forth "among the horses," as he expressed it, to be in closer proximity to the populace.

The Brazilians are manifestly an orderly, civil, good-natured, timid, and temperate people; contrasting favorably in their manners, language, indulgences and general deportment, on similar occasions, with the masses in large cities, in the United States. I saw nothing rude or coarse in any one, nothing offensive or insulting: no profanity, no intoxication, no quarelling, no call for the interference of the police.

In the course of the morning, among various other experiences, we elbowed his Majesty and the ministers of the household, the metropolitan and his chapter of the priesthood, and the great officers of state in the Imperial chapel; scrutinized the Empress and her ladies in their tribune; listened to the effective music of the Te Deum, performed by the chief singers of the opera company; witnessed the return of the court in procession from the chapel to the throne room; and gained a point of observation for the review, so near Don Pedro and Dona Theresa as to have been able readily to have carried on a conversation with them, had it been according to rule.

The regular army of Brazil consists of some twenty thousand troops. Very few of these are at present here. The great mass of those under arms on the present occasion, amounting to some five thousand, was of municipal guards, corresponding to the volunteer companies of New York. They were in neat and handsome uniforms, are well appointed, and well drilled; but are small and light in figure, without an appearance of much physical force, and most motley in complexion and the mixture of blood. An abundant supply of fine bands was in attendance. Negroes and mulattoes predominated in these, testifying to the gift of musical taste in the race here, as with us in the United States.

There was a partial illumination in the evening, but to no striking effect, except in the streets leading from the palace to the opera-house. The progress of the court in state through these was a showy spectacle. The glaring flambeaux of liveried outriders, preceding and flanking the open carriages, themselves brilliantly lighted, and the illuminated houses, exhibited the diamonds of the Empress and her attendants to great advantage.

The left breast of the Emperor's coat, too, flashed with the brilliants of the many orders with which it was decorated. The vivas of the multitudes were tolerably loyal, and the spirited strains of the national air, caught, as the cortege approached, from band to band, stationed at various points on the route, quite spirit-stirring. The music of this air is a composition of Don Pedro I., who was a master in the science. It is one of the most animated, spirit-moving national airs I know—equal almost in this respect to the Marseillaise. The words of the anthem to which it is set are said to be also from the pen of his late Majesty; and, in the native language, are scarce less incitive than the tune, to emotions of patriotism and valor—

> Iá podeis, filhos da patria,
> Ver contente a mai gentil,
> Iá raiou a liberdade,
> No horizonte do Brazil.
>
> Brava gente Braziliera
> Longe vai temor servil!
> Ou ficar a patria livre,
> Ou mourer pelo Brazil.

I could not be otherwise than amused by an incident, characteristic of the too widely spread spirit of my countrymen, which came under my observation just after reaching the shore. The court were alighting at the palace, on their arrival in state from San Christovao: the turn-out, in equipages and their appointments, the same as described at the prorogation of the legislature in September. The hurried rush across the square of the mounted guard in advance; the flourish of trumpets and striking up of the bands; the glitter of postillions and coachmen in livery, stiff with lacings of silver; the tossings of the plumed heads of the long lines of richly caparisoned horses; and the ceremonies of the vestibule, in the salutations and kissing of hands at alighting, were just occurring, as a rough specimen of our compatriots, in the character of a Yankee sea-captain happened by. He stood near me for a moment gazing at the pageant, evidently with less of admiration than of contempt, and, as he passed on with a significant " Humph ! " I heard him add in half soliloquy—" I tell you what, there is a little too much nonsense here; it is time this people were annexed ! "

To-day the weather has been wet and stormy. Notwithstanding, a Brazilian naval officer came on board the Congress before breakfast, to say that the Emperor would be afloat in an excursion on the bay. It is customary on such occasions for the national vessels in the harbor to fire a royal salute. That they may be in readiness for this, on the appearance of the imperial standard, the official notice mentioned is given. The Brazilian men-of-war man their yards also, and nine cheers are given for their sovereign as he passes. At 11 o'clock the firing was commenced by the Brazilian flag-ship; and, on going on deck I found myself surrounded by a blaze from guns on every quarter. At the same time, a procession of state barges was seen moving from the naval arsenal near the convent of San Bento, to a steamer not far from us. The barge of his Majesty, of white and green, was magnificently gilded, and furnished with a standing canopy of green and gold over the stern sheets, surmounted by the imperial crown. A naval officer in epaulets and chapeau acted as coxswain, the boat being handsomely pulled by twenty-four fine-looking oarsmen in a uniform of white. The object of the excursion was a visit in the steamer to a foundry and steam-engine manufactory at Praya Grande, on the opposite side of the bay; where, in proof of the rapid advancement of the empire in scientific works and national power, native talent and enterprise is successfully competing with foreign skill, in the construction and equipment of men-of-war and other steamers.

CHAPTER XIII.

RIO DE JANEIRO.

December 18th.—On the morning of the 17th inst. I was called to officiate at a marriage on shore. The ceremony took place at the American Consulate, where a *déjeuner a la fourchette* was given to the party by Gov. and Mrs. Kent. The groom, a native Brazilian, a young physician, had attended a course of medical and surgical lectures in New York. He became there a member of the Protestant Episcopal church; and was altogether so much interested in our institutions, as to file, in the proper office, an intention of becoming a naturalized citizen of the United States. These circumstances led him to desire a marriage ceremony in the Protestant form, under the American flag, though, the bride being a Romanist, they had already been united by the rites of her church.

While on shore on this occasion, I came near being a spectator, accidentally, of a more interesting scene of the kind. In passing the foundling hospital, which fronts an open, irregular space not far from the ordinary landing, beneath Castle Hill, I perceived the grated windows of the second and third stories to be filled with females of different ages, from childhood to maturity, in holiday dress, evidently awaiting the occupancy and departure of a couple of private carriages, drawn up before the principal entrance. Stepping into the open vestibule of the building—in one corner of which is the roda, or turning-box, for the deposit of the infants clandestinely left—I rightly conjectured from the white gloves, waistcoats, and breast-knots of two or three young men present, that the occasion was one of marriage, and learned that the ceremony had just taken place in the chapel of the hospital. This, which opened from the vestibule, was, however, now empty. An aged female of dignified appearance, in a monastic dress of white, was walking back and forth in a small corridor behind a grated door. She appeared to be waiting to unlock this. Almost immediately the bride and groom, in the significant garb of the newly wedded, were seen to approach from the interior. They were both quite young. An elderly lady, evidently of distinction, attired in purple velvet with a display of rich laces, jewelry and ostrich plumes, accompanied them, and was herself followed by a dignified and well-dressed gentleman, who appeared to be her husband. A crowd of the inmates of the institution quickly filled the entire corridor behind. The bride was in tears, as she hurriedly gave a farewell embrace to one and another of the youthful companions crowding around her, and, on coming to the aged female at the door, dropped on her knees, and covered her hands with kisses and tears. The groom hurried her from this scene to the first carriage, and drove off rapidly, followed by the second containing the fine folks, probably the god-mother and god-father, or the patron and patroness of the bride. The whole explained to me a usage, in connection with this establishment, of which I had heard. A recolhiemento, or female orphan asylum is an appendage of the foundling hospital, many of its *élèves* being selected from the inmates of the latter. In addition to the nurture and education of the orphans, care is taken to provide for their settlement in life, with the bestowment of a marriage portion, varying from one to two hundred dollars. That an opportunity may be afforded for young men of respectable character to make choice of a wife from the inmates, the establishment is open to visitors one day in every year—that of the anniversary of St. Elizabeth, the patroness of the asylum. Before a union is sanctioned, however, satisfactory testimonials of good character in the applicant for marriage must be furnished, and guaranties of ability to support a wife be given. Such was the origin of the marriage which had just taken place. The dress and lady-like bearing of the bride, the respectable appearance and manners of the groom, the rich attire, equipages, and evident position in life of those under whose patronage they appeared, all indicated, in this case, something in her lot above the destiny of common orphanage.

While the establishment of a home for the friendless young is one of the most self-commending of charities, the philanthropy which provides an asylum for the secret reception of foundlings is no longer questionable, in the judgment of the wisely benevolent and truly good. It is but to foster vice, and to encourage the unnatural and depraved in the abandonment of their offspring. This is well known here, and readily admitted to be the effect. The number yearly left in the roda, or turning-box, of this hospital, amounts, I am told, by those best informed, to five and six hundred—white, black and mongrel of every degree. More than half of these soon perish from diseases seated upon them before being abandoned; from the impossibility of securing natural nourishment for the feeble; and from the various ills to which early infancy under the most favored auspices is subject.

December 20th.—One source of agreeable excitement with us, is the daily anticipation and frequent arrival of sailing vessels and steamers, governmental and mercantile, from the United States and various parts of the world. The number of vessels entering the port of Rio annually, besides those engaged in the coasting trade, which are very numerous, averages about eight hundred: importing cargoes to the amount of some two hundred thousand tons. Of course, scarcely a day passes without the entry of two or three foreign vessels in the regular trade, besides such as merely touch for repairs or refreshment.

It is a remarkable fact—especially in view of the achievements in navigation, of the Portuguese of old, and the boldness and enterprise with which for centuries they sustained their part in the commerce of the world—that their descendants here should have yielded that of the empire, which is foreign, entirely to the vessels of other nations. It is extremely rare for a Brazilian ship to cross the Atlantic, or double Cape Horn, or the Cape of Good Hope; and I learn, from Gov. Kent, that not a single vessel of the country has cleared for the United States, since he has been consul here. Their trading vessels, though small, are generally well built, strong, and well modelled; and are navigated with care and safety along the extended coasts of the continent, from the Plata to the Amazon. But, as the consul remarks, "the native navigators seem afraid to compete on the high seas, with the vessels of this age of hurry and locomotion—with the reckless driving of the 'Flying Clouds' and 'White Squalls,' the 'Sea Witches,' and other wild birds of the ocean, and yield, without a struggle, the enterprises in foreign commerce to the hardy northmen—the unwearied and ever-present Yankee, and the pushing and exacting Englishman." The truth is, as he adds, the Brazilian is not by nature a trader or experimenter. He thinks it sufficient for him to raise coffee and get it to a market: he lacks the energy, the industry—the earnest, long-continued, unwearied effort which leads one willingly to sacrifice present ease, comfort, and quiet, to the prospect of future gain, and which makes the successful merchant. "Go ahead," "strive," "struggle," "compete"—are words not belonging to his vocabulary. He shrugs his shoulders at the very mention of them—not in contempt, but in despair; and prefers sitting in his easy chair, or lolling out of the window, to the tussle of life common with us, of which the very thought would throw him into a perspiration. "Let the negroes work," is his motto; "and let what they cannot do remain undone." The Yankee character, as exhibited here within the year or two past, in the rush by of the thousands of emigrants on their way to California, struck the people with astonishment. They were looked upon as most reckless and daring adventurers, who, born in snow-drifts and cradled in ice, had a hardihood and enterprise it was in vain to attempt to rival. But I am forgetting the subject with which I commenced.

The telegraphic station on Castle Hill, to and from which the appearance of all sail in the offing is reported, is in full view from our moorings. The quarter-masters of the Congress are furnished with explanations of the various flags used, and the combinations by which the nation, character, and position of the sail in sight are made known. Few moments of the day pass without a turn of the glass in that direction. The distinguishing flag for an American vessel is a long, pointed pennant of white and deep blue in closely-arranged perpendicular stripes, giving to it the appearance, as it flutters in the wind, of being ring-streaked. With a Yankee fondness for sobriquets having a political or national import, Jack has dubbed this pennant "the coon's tail," from a fancied resemblance to the well-known emblem of the party of which the great statesman of Kentucky was so long an illustrious leader; and, "the coon's tail is up!" or "there goes the coon's tail!" is the regular announcement of an American ship in the offing.

Among uncounted merchant vessels which have thus been reported since our return from the Plata, there have also been the frigate Raritan, storeship Relief, and sloops-of-war Saratoga and St. Mary of the navy. The St. Mary was especially welcome from the number of officers attached to her, closely associated in friendship with several on board the Congress. Captain Magruder, her commander, is of this number; and is justly held in high estimation. The intercourse on his part with our ship has been most intimate. After an interchange of civilities by various parties on board both vessels, Captain McIntosh and I took dinner informally with him to-day, with the purpose of a drive afterwards to the Botanic Gardens. These lie six or eight miles south-west from the city, on the sea-shore, beneath the range of mountains, of which the Corcovado and the Gavia are such conspicuous points. For three miles the way is the same described in a visit to Botafogo. The remainder does not differ materially from it, except that the suburbs of the place change gradually, by the greater distances intervening between the villas and country houses which adorn the sides of the road, into a thinly-occupied and open country. At the distance of five miles, the interval between the mountains and the sea is taken up chiefly by a lake or lagoon called Rodrigo de Freitas. A short drive hence over a sandy plain brought us to the gates of the garden. This was originally a pleasure-ground of the royal family in the time of John VI., and was appropriated by him to its present use, on the accidental arrival in 1809 of various cases of exotics from the Isle of France, in a vessel which brought to Rio a company of Portuguese prisoners. The collection was afterwards augmented, at the order of the king, by additions from Cayenne, then under his rule; and eventually by the importation of the tea-plant from China, with a company of Chinese laborers skilled in its cultivation and in the preparation of the leaf for use. The attempt proved a failure; not so much from a want of adaptation in the soil and climate, or from the quality of the tea produced, as from the expense above the cost of the imported article. Both here, and at Santa Cruz—an imperial estate fifty miles west of Rio, where also a plantation was formed—the culture has been abandoned; a few plats of stunted, mildewed, and neglected bushes only are left as a botanical curiosity.

The gardens cover some fifty acres of ground—an alluvial flat of rich soil, and constitute a nursery from which plants of the cinnamon, nutmeg, clove, camphor, allspice, and tea, originally introduced here, have been widely dispersed through the empire. Specimens of all these were examined by us.

The cinnamon and camphor trees are of the laurel family—the *laurus cinnamonum* and *laurus camphora*;—the nutmeg, clove, and allspice, of the myrtle. The cinnamon grows to a height of fifteen or twenty feet. The stem and branches are of a light green; the leaves, of the shape of the laurel, are also light green, and are pliant and tender. When they first bud forth they are of a light red, and gradually become green as they advance in growth. The blossoms are white. There is no perceptible fragrance, either in the stem or leaf, till bruised or broken, but both when bitten have the cinnamon flavor. The clove is the flower-bud of the *caryophyllus aromaticus.* The tree was in blossom and the bud very strong in its peculiar taste. Specimens of all these in branch, blossom, and fruit, were readily furnished by a negro in attendance, who expected a trifling gratuity in return.

Long avenues of the Sumatra nut—*vernicia montana*—furnish abundant shade, and yield great quantities of nuts. The mulberry tree is also introduced for the purpose of shade. The bread-fruit—*artocarpus incisa*—so familiar to me in the South Seas, was also conspicuous in the beauty of its strongly-marked, shining, and digitated foliage, and its ponderous fruit of light green.

The whole garden, though a national property, for the good keeping of which an annual appropriation is made by the imperial legislature, appeared in a neglected state. There is nothing strikingly tasteful or artistic in the arrangement or embellishment of the ground. At the western end, a mountain stream comes brawling down a rocky channel, and on reaching the level, meanders lazily eastward, between banks beautifully fringed with bamboo, and overhung by the dense foliage of loftier growth. Where this mountain stream enters, there is an attempt, on a small scale, at landscape gardening. A little basin of water with projecting points, and an islet or two, overhung by willows, represents a miniature lake; and near by, on an artificial and terraced mound, is a chapel-like summer house, formed of the flat cedar or arbor vitæ, so planted and so trained as to be perfectly architectural in its outline, and to appear to be an old ruin overrun with living green. That, however, which more than any other ornamental feature of the place attracted our notice, was an avenue of royal palms, a quarter of a mile and more in length, leading in a straight line from the principal gate, and crossed at right angles, midway of the distance, by another corresponding with it. The trees are at perfectly regular distances from each other; are all of one size, and, either by nature or by artificial training, rise from uniformly shaped swelling bases, into perpendicular shafts, forty or fifty feet in height. The silver-gray trunks, marked in their whole length by rings, showing the growth of each year, terminate in plumed capitals of true Corinthian magnificence. The effect of the perspective is very beautiful: strikingly like that which we would imagine a colonnade of equal length in Egyptian or Asiatic architecture to be.

As a botanical garden, the place is unworthy the name, and useless as such to the cause of science. The realization of one here, such as John VI. projected, would be exceedingly interesting and important. There is no empire in the world in which a botanical garden on a magnificent scale could be more readily established, or whose native vegetable kingdom is so rich, and so full of novelties to the scientific world.

When we left the city the weather was magnificent; the atmosphere clear and pure, elastic and bracing, and the lights and shades on the scenery in perfection. But ere we were aware of it, an entire change occurred. The Corcovado towers in gigantic altitude over the garden, and, almost without warning, a violent storm came rushing down its precipices, bearing with it masses of cloud of impenetrable blackness, surcharged with torrents of rain, which were poured upon us with unabating fury during the entire drive back to the city. Notwithstanding the individual discomfort incident to such showers, they are welcomed with joy by the people in general, as indications of continued health. Previous to the epidemic of the last year, they were almost as regular in their return as the afternoon itself. But during the pestilence they intermitted almost entirely. The regularity of the sea breeze also was greatly interrupted; and lightning and thunder for the most part ceased. Believing that these meteorological changes were connected in some way with the infection existing in the atmosphere, a return of the showers of old is regarded as an indication of the accustomed salubrity of the air.

December 27th.—The little chapel of Santa Lucia fronts the bay at the southern end of the promenade beneath Castle Hill. This saint is a kind of deputy-patroness of seafaring men, under Our Lady of Good Voyages, whose shrine crowns so conspicuously the little islet of Bonviagem. In my usual walk two or three evenings ago, I accidentally fell upon an anniversary fête here; the birthday of her saintship. The chapel is the parish church of the neighborhood, and I could scarcely have believed, without the ocular proof, that within hearing of the hum of the busy metropolis a gathering of people so entirely rustic and village-like, could have been brought together. Great preparation for the celebration had been made. Long avenues of young palm-trees, twenty or thirty feet in height, and from which brilliant lamps were suspended, were planted beside the road along the water; alternating with these, were lofty flag-staffs, from which varied colored banners and streamers floated in the breeze. Frameworks with complicated pyrotechnic preparations were placed thickly around, as in the parks and squares of New York on the Fourth of July. Indeed, the whole aspect of things—the crowds of people in holiday dress, the many venders of refreshments in fruit and confectionery, cakes, orangeade and orgeat, the talk and the laugh, and the general hilarity—was that of a general muster, or other similar holiday, in the United States. The little chapel was in a flutter of flags and gay hangings without, and within, gaudy in the profusion of gilt paper and tinsel, and coarse artificial flowers. It was, too, one blaze of light from a pyramid of wax candles on the high altar.

An animated sale of engravings of Santa Lucia was going on. These were in different degrees of artistic execution, and on various qualities of paper to suit the taste and finances of the purchasers. Men, women, and children, black and white, master and mistress, freeman and slave, crowded with equal earnestness around the priest, seated behind a counter for the sale, all seeming alike delighted to secure the consecrated likeness, as, depositing their money, one after another were served with it, and then struggled back through the throng.

A service of music took place at eight o'clock; and as this hour approached, the little church became crowded to suffocation. The females were admitted to a portion of the nave, nearest the chancel, separated from the rest of the area by a rail. They sat in full dress on the carpeted pavement, as closely crowded as possible, while the men outside of this separating line stood as thickly packed. The music, both instrumental and vocal, was that of a regular opera, and delightfully performed. The festivities continued till midnight: and, as we returned by boat to the ship at a later hour than usual, rockets in constant succession were seen rushing to the sky, and bursting in glittering coruscations of colored lights; balls of fire were flying through the air; Chinese crackers every where exploding; and fiery serpents hissing along the ground. But there was no intoxication, no quarrelling, no rudeness; in their stead, general civility, decorum, and light-heartedness.

On Christmas eve, I visited the cathedral on the Palace Square, and the church of San Francisco de Paulo in the square of the Roscio. The former was first open. It was of course richly ornamented with tapestries of brocade and velvet, and hangings of cloth of silver and gold, and was brilliantly illuminated with wax lights, amid a profusion of artificial flowers. The chancel was filled with the dignitaries of the church, in striking costumes of scarlet and purple silk, with any quantity of the richest lace in the form of capes and togas. The Bishop, wearing a mitre studded with jewels of immense size, and holding a massive gilded crosier, was seated on his throne on one side of the high altar: presenting, with the encircling groups of Dean and Chapter and officiating priests, a scene of hierarchical stateliness and splendor, befitting the palmiest days of papal supremacy. The music here is always of the first order: it was on this occasion, as usual, altogether operatic in style and execution.

The church of St. Francis is much more spacious than this

of the Carmelites. The interior is unbroken by galleries or colonnades, and the coup-d'œil, on entering, was now brilliant and effective. A ball-room for a civic fête could not have been decorated with more taste and richness, or with greater regard to effect on the eye. Lines of closely-arranged lights marked the general architecture of the whole interior; while, midway between the pavement and loftily-arched ceilings, beautiful clusters in brackets, gave a dazzling brilliancy to the walls. The display upon and above the high altar was magnificent. The music was fine; and the throng greater than at the cathedral, more mixed in its character, and full of levity. A third of the nave was appropriated exclusively to females. The various personal attractions and deportment of these, seated closely together in full evening dress, seemed chiefly to occupy the attention of the men; while innuendo, badinage, and loose remarks upon them were freely passed in whispers by one and another. The place seemed little like one of devotion, and any other than a house of God.

January 8th.—We are once more at sea. The weather for the last few days, though magnificent in clearness and brilliancy, has been too excessively hot for us to remain longer with comfort at Rio. A rumor, too, of the reappearance of the epidemic of the last year, was becoming prevalent, and the region of the Plata was deemed in every respect most desirable for the ship. At this season of the year, light winds and calms are characteristic of the weather at sea, in the latitudes between Rio de Janeiro and the Rio La Plata: it is probable, therefore, that our passage of ten days or a fortnight thither, will be destitute of any thing worthy of record.

The cordiality which I mentioned as existing between the officers of the Congress and those of the British flag-ship, Southampton, continued to the last. A banquet, surpassing in its appointments any thing upon so large a scale that I recollect to have witnessed on board ship, was given some time since by the officers of her gun-room to those of the Congress—embracing as guests, the commanders-in-chief and captains of both vessels; and night before last, Admiral and Mrs. Reynolds gave a farewell dinner to Commodore McKeever, Captain McIntosh, and one or two others from our ship. It was Twelfth-night, the last of the Christmas holidays; but it was in vain that I attempted to bring into exercise any associations of the season, in connection with my thoughts of home. While suffering here more than midsummer heat, it is difficult to reconcile even the imagination to a picture of festivities on the same occasion, with the accompaniments of howling winds and drifting snows—a frozen river in front of you, and a leafless grove behind.

This farewell entertainment was even more genial in its sympathies than any of those previously enjoyed. The company embraced a number of intelligent and spiritually-minded Christians. A seat between two of these fell to me, and I was most agreeably and profitably entertained. It is ever a delight to me to find intelligent piety openly professed and consistently maintained by a young officer, especially where an elevated position in social life, as well as the military profession, exposes the individual to peculiar temptations from the world. Such is the case with young W——, and such that of his chosen companions. He lent me, a few days since, a memoir of a young friend, an officer in the army, printed like that of your early companion, M—C——, for private circulation only. Like hers, it is a portraiture from life of gifted and devoted youthful piety. Lieut. St. J——, the subject of it, went to India on duty, in the war of Afghanistan. The cholera broke out in his regiment when on march there. Fearless of consequences, and trustful in faith and Christian hope, he gave himself up at once to unremitted, personal attendance upon the sick and dying soldiers. Though but a youth of twenty-two, the parting breath of many of these was spent in blessings upon him, as a minister of consolation and spiritual grace to them, till seized at last himself, he was carried off at the end of six hours, with the triumphant exclamation on his lips, "All's well!"

CHAPTER XIV.

MONTEVIDEO.

January 30th, 1851.—Our passage "down," as the phrase is, was devoid of incident. We arrived on the night of the 20th inst., and are at anchor in the outer roadstead. In October, I described the general aspect of the mount, the city, and the surrounding country from this; and reminded you of the existence of a civil war, and the close siege of the city, for eight years past, by Oribe, a citizen of Montevideo, and formerly President of the Republic of which it is the capital. The right to this office, though once resigned and abandoned by him, he still claims; and to enforce it, invaded the State with an army of Argentines, furnished by Rosas, Governor of Buenos Ayres, and minister of foreign affairs for the Argentine States. With this he would have gained possession of the town long ago, had it not been for the armed intervention, in 1845, of England and France; and the continued guardianship of the place by the latter, with a squadron, in the roadstead, and a body of fifteen hundred or two thousand troops on shore.

The principal European powers, rejecting the pretensions of Oribe, acknowledge the constituted authorities of the inside, or city party only, as the government of the Republic. The policy of the United States being a strict neutrality, Commodore McKeever pays a like respect to both; and, under an escort furnished by Oribe, has paid an official visit to him at his camp outside of the lines, as well as one to the President within, at the government house in the city.

When here in October, an armistice had existed for some time, in connection with the negotiations then pending between the belligerent parties and Admiral Le Predour, commander-in-chief of the French force. We had not heard of its termination: but a movement of the troops on shore at daylight, the morning after our arrival, attracted the notice of those on board on watch, and led to the supposition that an engagement was about to take place. A messenger from my ever mindful friend R——, the officer of the deck at the time, summoned me to witness it; and for an hour, with other officers of the ship, I gazed through a glass upon what seemed a spirited conflict, between the outside and inside forces. We learned afterwards, however, that it was only a sham battle between different parties of the French troops, and the Montevidean soldiery, composed of a foreign legion of Basques and Italians, and a native regiment of negroes. So far as the effect upon the eye, and, under our misapprehension, upon the heart was concerned, there was, in the manœuvres of the battle field—the rapid charge, the roar of cannon, the sharp rattle of musketry, and the flying through the air and the bursting of shells—much of the reality of an actual engagement.

Poor Montevideo, for nearly a half century past, has been singularly ill-fated, even for a South American city. The greater part of that period, it has been the victim of calamitous wars, either foreign or civil. In 1807, while yet a colonial dependency of Spain, it was besieged, bombarded, and carried by storm by the English, under Sir Samuel Achmuty. After the inglorious defeat of Gen. Whithead at Buenos Ayres in 1808, and the consequent expulsion of the British from the Plata, as a colonial city faithful to the crown of Spain it was besieged from 1810 to 1814, and eventually made to capitulate to the troops of the then revolted and republican province of Buenos Ayres. Shortly afterwards, the republican forces being withdrawn, it fell into the hands of the bandit Artigas, a native chieftain, so lawless and marauding in his rule at home, and in his depredations on the adjoining frontiers of Brazil, as to give just cause for invasion by the Portuguese of that kingdom, who gained possession of the city in 1817.

This occupation of the place led to a warfare of more than ten years, between the royalists of Brazil, and the republicans of Buenos Ayres, the chief disasters of which centred in Montevideo; till, in 1829, through the intervention of England, a peace was effected, by the withdrawal, by both parties, of all claim to the territory in dispute—known then by the name of the Banda Oriental—on condition that it should constitute an independent Republic, to be called Uruguay, after the great river which forms the western boundary between it and the Argentine States.

From that period till the year 1842, the territory enjoyed peace. Under a constitutional government, with a president, ministry, judiciary, and legislature of two houses, both city and country had great prosperity. The population of the city increased rapidly from fifteen to fifty thousand, and that of the state to two hundred and fifty thousand. The exports in a few years amounted to six millions of dollars, and the imports to five millions. Fortunes were readily accumulated; fine buildings in great numbers were erected within the city; and beautiful country houses, with tasteful and luxurious surroundings, spread over the environs without. Poverty and want were unknown, and the evil days seemed entirely past. But the civil war, into which the republic was plunged by Oribe, soon produced a sad change. The invading Argentines speedily devastated the entire country, and by the wanton destruction of vast herds of horses and cattle—the chief sources of its wealth and commerce in hides, jerked beef, and tallow—and the plunder of their estancias or farms, paralyzed the enterprise of the inhabitants, and forced them to emigrate; while the close siege of the town, intercepting all supplies for support and all means of commerce, at once sapped the sources of its prosperity, and drove the citizens by tens of thousands elsewhere for maintenance and life. The result upon the wealth and population of the port may be readily imagined. I do not recollect ever before to have been so deeply impressed with the desolateness of any place as on first landing here, and on taking a stroll through its streets, and the limited suburbs within the lines of defence. The mole, once alive with busy commerce, was as deserted and silent as a churchyard; and excepting at Pompeii, I never wandered through streets which seemed to be more truly those of a city of the dead.

This impression, however, I afterwards discovered to be in some degree deceptive, owing, partly, to the hour of the day; that for the universal siesta. Scarcely an individual was to be seen anywhere. With screened windows and closed doors, the inhabitants, young and old, rich and poor, were yielding themselves to the insinuating influences of the dolce far niente, or to the more oblivious indulgences of sound sleep. It is now midsummer here; the day was hot, for this latitude, and every thing in a state of Spanish repose customary in such weather, after an early dinner. The dilapidation and decay on every side, the manifest poverty, and the seemingly utter desertion of dwelling after dwelling, through whole streets, were so saddening and oppressive, that, for the time, I felt that I would never wish to visit the shore again. As to the suburbs without the walls, excavated Pompeii itself is scarcely more a region of ruin and desolation.

An hour at the American consulate afterwards—where our party received the most frank and hospitable welcome from Mr. and Mrs. Hamilton and family; an application there within fifteen minutes, for my official services from a stranger in the marriage ceremony—showing that bad as the state of things in Montevideo is, the voice of the bride and of the bridegroom is still to be heard in her streets—with other assurances of a better state in general than I had been led to infer, changed in some degree the current of my sympathies. Still, however deceptive the first impressions on landing may have been, there is too much

8

reality in the wretchedness to which hundreds and thousands of the inhabitants are reduced, to allow them to be at once dispelled.

The city is finely situated upon a peninsula of granite, which, in its form, has been compared, not inaptly, to the shape of a tortoise's back: an area a half mile square descending gradually on three sides, from a central height of a hundred feet or more, to the level of the surrounding water. This, though only a river, is seemingly a sea; for, a hundred miles in width, it presents a horizon on the south as boundless as the ocean. Like most towns of Spanish origin, the streets are rectangular, with an open square or plaza in the centre, on which stand the principal church and the cabilda, or town hall and prison. It is well built. Many of the private residences are spacious, and the principal public buildings, the cathedral, and an unfinished hospital, are rather imposing in their architecture. From long disuse the streets are in many places tufted with grass, and in others, the pavements are so torn up and broken as to be impassable with wheels.

One redeeming fact, in regard to the general want of interest in the place, has very unexpectedly presented itself to me personally, in an invitation from the standing committee of the British Episcopal Church, to officiate for them in public worship on the Sabbath. This I have already done, and shall continue to do whenever the Congress shall be in the Plata. The English government, with commendable interest for the spiritual good of its subjects abroad, makes a liberal provision, under certain conditions, for the maintenance of the ministry and its ordinances where they may be. Its chief embassies in foreign lands are furnished with regular chaplains; and, wherever British subjects abroad contribute to a fund for the ministrations of the Gospel among them, the same amount, to a specified limit—four hundred pounds is the maximum, I believe—is allowed by act of parliament for the same object.

Eight or ten years ago, Samuel Lafone, Esq., a principal English merchant here, and a chief capitalist and landed proprietor in the Uruguay, secured from the authorities the privilege of erecting a chapel for Protestant worship. The site of an elevated circular bastion, overlooking the rocky shores of the river, on the south side of the town, was chosen for the purpose, and purchased by him. Upon this, at a cost of forty-five or fifty thousand dollars, he erected a fine edifice in Grecian architecture. It is of brick, stuccoed, and painted in imitation of Portland stone, and is ornamented in the front by a well proportioned pediment, supported by four lofty Doric columns, and altogether is one of the most conspicuous architectural ornaments of the city. The interior is spacious and lofty, the wood-work—the pews, chancel-railing, the reading desk, pulpit, and organ-loft—being of solid mahogany, and is capable of accommodating an audience of several hundreds. When completed, Mr. Lafone made an unconditional gift of it to the British community resident here. These joined by the few Americans engaged in commerce, raised a fund sufficient, with the governmental gratuity, for the comfortable support of a rector. The Rev. Mr. Armstrong officiated for several years in that capacity, and till ill health obliged him and his family, not long since, to seek a different climate. The Rev. Mr. Lenhart of the Methodist Church, my predecessor as chaplain of the American squadron on this station, was invited by the standing committee to occupy the pulpit thus left vacant: and now, with equal ecclesiastic liberality, on the part of the committee and church, I am invested with a like temporary rectorship.

It is customary to have but one service on the Sabbath. This takes place at one o'clock, the earliest hour practicable for me to be on shore, after the discharge of my official duties on board the Congress.

The interruptions to commerce, and the disasters attending the long siege, have reduced the Protestant residents of Montevideo comparatively to a mere handful, and the usual audience composed of English, Scotch and American worshippers, male and female, numbers only from sixty to eighty persons. Still it is a privilege to minister in holy things, even to so small an assemblage, with 'none to hurt or make afraid' amidst a people once wholly given to superstition and bigotry, and to witness a depth of interest and solemnity of devotion characteristic of spiritual Christianity. I have already been called to officiate at two marriages, and have twice administered the ordinance of baptism. Thus, though a Presbyterian of the 'straightest sect,' I feel it not only a privilege and happiness, but a duty, under the circumstances, to follow the prescribed ritual of the English prayer-book in worship, and—in surplice and bands—to pray statedly, not only "for all in authority," but specifically, for "the most gracious Lady the Queen Victoria, His Royal Highness Prince Albert, Albert, Prince of Wales, and all the royal family."

CHAPTER XV.

BUENOS AYRES.

February 21st.—I am unexpectedly in Buenos Ayres, having accompanied Commodore McKeever in an official visit to General Rosas, the sagacious but unscrupulous despot of the Argentine Confederation.

The distance from Montevideo is about a hundred miles due west. The intervening navigation is rendered intricate by sand banks and shoals, and the general shallowness of the river; and, for the last forty miles, is impracticable for a frigate. In making the trip, therefore, the broad pennant of the Congress was transferred to the sloop-of-war St. Louis, on board which the commodore and his party became, for the passage, the guests of her commander, Captain Cock. The U. S. Brig Bainbridge, Lieut. Manning, accompanied the flag.

We left Montevideo on the evening of the 18th inst. The run is usually made in a night, but the wind being light, the current strong, and the St. Louis not in sailing trim, we did not reach the outer roadstead here till the morning of the 20th. The passage was pleasant. Though it is midsummer, the temperature is cool and bracing, with clear skies and a brilliant atmosphere, remarkable for the magnificence of its coloring along the horizon, at sunrise and sunset. There is, too, a full moon at present; and though the river from mid-channel is often seemingly shoreless, and its waters of the veritable mud-puddle hue, the scene from the deck of the St. Louis, both by night and by day, was not without attractions: especially in the companionship of the Bainbridge. This is a beautiful little craft; and was as buoyant and graceful on the waters as a bird in the air, as with greatly reduced sail, to avoid passing us by her superior speed, she at times fell far behind, and then again, with newly spread wings, rushed forward closely in our wake. Various other sail were in sight, at greater or less distances, some ascending and some descending the river, with no little display of nautical evolution, in making the best of their way.

Early yesterday morning, Buenos Ayres was in sight, at a distance of ten or twelve miles; gleaming showily in the sun, from the whiteness of the general architecture, and the number of its lofty and finely proportioned domes and church towers. It is situated on a bluff, which extends along the river a couple of miles, and rises at the highest point eighty or a hundred feet above its level. At the distance, however, from which we first saw the city, this formation of the shore was scarcely perceptible: it seemed to be resting, like Venice, upon the water, while a tufting of tree-tops, in long stretches on either side, showed the general flatness of the surrounding country. The river is here twenty-five miles wide, and its northern shores, equally low as the southern, are not ordinarily visible. But for the smoothness of the water, and its muddy hue, we might have thought ourselves still upon the open sea.

A first surprise is the very great distance from the city—five, six, and nine miles—at which vessels of moderate tonnage even, are obliged, in the midst of such an expanse of waters, to come to anchor. A long shoal stretches out thus far in front of the city, preventing nearer approach, except by vessels of light draught. When the water is high, such can cross the shoal, and, at other times, find a channel by a circuitous route to an inner roadstead, where there is anchorage for vessels of different draught, respectively, one, two, and three miles from the landing. In the outer roadstead, for a distance of miles, tall masts rose above the waters like steeples on a populous plain, while quite a fleet of small vessels was lying three miles within. The St. Louis came to, six miles or more from the city; and, after an exchange of salutes with the flag of Buenos Ayres, and those of France and Sardinia, borne by ships-of-war of these respective nations near us, we left her in a procession of small boats.

The formation of the shore in front of the city, and for a considerable distance above and below it, is a flat tufa rock which extends irregularly, far out upon the sands. Its surface is fretted and broken, and, when the water is low, boats cannot approach the landing nearer than from a quarter to a half mile. At such times the intermediate distance is made in strongly-constructed, high-wheeled carts, drawn by two horses, one of which is mounted by a wild-looking postilion. These carts, like hacks at home, are in attendance in great numbers, for the transportation of passengers and freight from the boats to the shore; and often present a scene of strife and rivalry in the water, between the drivers, similar to those witnessed in the rush of carriages, the brandishing of whips, and the exercise of lungs at a pier in New York, on the arrival of a steamer. It seemed now to be high water, and we were apprehensive that we should miss this novel mode of debarkation, and thus lose, for the time, a spectacle characteristic of the place. Our fears were unfounded, however; for soon, a cocked hat of portentous dimensions, with other insignia of official and military dignity in the wearer—himself of no ordinary dimensions in height or rotundity—was seen rising above the water. It was that of Don Pedro Ximenes, the captain of the port, who had been deputized by his imperious master to receive the commodore; and was patiently waiting in a cart, far out in the stream, the approach of the barge. Mr. Graham of Ohio, the American Consul, was also in attendance. The floor of the clumsy, high-sided vehicle, was scarcely above the surface of the water, as we rowed 'handsomely' alongside its open back, and stepping aboard, were transferred from the protecting shadow of the broad pennant, to that of Don Pedro's cocked hat. In this novel reception-room, the ceremonies of an official introduction took place; and we were soon plunging and tumbling through the splashing waters—a wheel on either side rolling, first up and then down, over the rough tufa bottom—with an artistic lashing of whip and vociferation by the postilion, till, backed up, according to custom, in coal-cart style, we were dumped on an inclined plane descending ten or twelve feet from the Alemeda, or public walk in front of the city, to the water.

A large crowd had gathered to witness the arrival—foreign merchants and native citizens, soldiers, sailors, porters, peons and boatmen. In the number, were many in the demi-savage dress of gauchos—the peasants of the country. This is picturesque and showy; and, with many other things which met the sight, gave promise of a more novel field for observation than we had yet lighted on. A glaring red coach, something of the dimension and style of those employed by hotels in New York, in conveying guests to and from the steamboats and railroad stations, was in waiting, by order of the government, and quickly conveyed the commodore to the Hotel de Provence, in an adjoining street. Rooms had been secured for us there, and a hospitable welcome was extended to the party, including Captain Cock, to the mess-table of a private club, consisting of Mr. Harris of Virginia, American chargé d'affaires to the Argentine Confederation; Mr. Graham, American Consul, Count Frolich, Swedish Consul-general; and two or three American gentlemen, connected here with the principal mercantile houses engaged in the South American trade.

Every thing in the general aspect of the city is Spanish: with the addition to the universal whitewash on all that is stone of an equally universal display of red on all that is wood or iron. This color of blood has been for twenty years the prescribed signs of adhesion to the remarkable man who maintains here an undisputed reign of terror: hence the red waistcoats, red hat-bands, red breast-knots, universally seen—the red doors, red window-frames, red bases to the houses, red lamp-posts, red carts, red railings, and red fixtures on every thing.

The place is subject, at all seasons of the year, to occasional high winds of two or three days' continuance. Then the tumultuous seas which roll over the shallow bed of the river cut off all communication between the shipping and the shore; and the city and its suburbs are filled with driving dust. Weather of this character set in yesterday, shortly after we landed, and has kept us housed much of the time since, principally at the reading rooms of a club, where we were introduced, and where we found files of the American and European papers, and the latest magazines.

This evening, notwithstanding the wind, Mr. D—— of New York, one of the mess at the Provence, took me a drive in his tilbury. Our route was westward, along the course of the river, in the direction of Palermo de San Benito, the quinta, or country seat of Rosas. Policy—by such demonstration of courtly attention to the supreme chief—as well as pleasure, leads all who drive or ride, to take that direction; and as we descended from the heights of the town, through the Alemeda fronting the river, to the road along its banks, the whirl of carriages and gigs, and the prancing and galloping of gay riders on horseback, was quite metropolitan. The speed of all was very much that of Gilpin—the females being mounted in the in-door costume of short dresses, bare arms, bare necks and bare heads: with the exception, in some cases, of the partial covering of a silk handkerchief on the head, tied under the chin. I saw none in the hat and habit worn in England and America, though doubtless in a city where foreign fashions are so extensively introduced, these have been adopted, to some extent at least, by the higher classes.

On gaining the level of the beach, the road passes over a flat and marshy common, without any enclosure of fence or hedge on either side. Here, by the river's side on the right, was presented, for a mile and more, a striking spectacle, in hundreds after hundreds—I had almost said thousands of negro washerwomen, indescribable in their costumes—scrubbing, beating, slapping, rinsing, and bleaching ten thousand articles of clothing. It is a natural laundry, to which the soiled linen of the whole city is brought for cleansing. The soft rock of the shores is filled with holes, some natural and others artificial, which, on every flow of the tide, are filled with fresh water. These are converted into wash-tubs, and, after being used, are left to be emptied of the suds by the next flood, and to be refilled with clean water by its ebb. Each washerwoman has her own little reservoir of this kind, to which she gains the exclusive right, by the payment of a small fee to the government. The wind was blowing a half gale, lashing the river into foam, and dashing the spray far on the shore; while clouds of dust on the land were driven before it, like drifting snow in a winter's storm at home. When on our way back the whole company, spread along the banks for a mile or more, were preparing to return to the city; and such a Babel, in the varied intonations and chatter, the laugh and the wrangle, the shout and the jeer, I scarcely recollect to have heard; while the oddity of the packages and bundles, the trays and baskets, borne on their heads, the endless form and color of the rags and tatters they wore—their old hats and old shoes, presented a scene grotesque beyond description.

Another novel scene was vast numbers of the lofty, cumbrous, reed-sided and hide-roofed carts of the pampas, arranged in a kind of camp on either side of the road. They are "the ships of the desert" here, by which the whole produce of the interior, for hundreds of miles, is brought to the market, and by which the returns of foreign import are carried to the remotest districts of the Confederation. They constitute the only habitations and homes of their owners and their families: bear with them all the household furniture and worldly goods of these; and, in addition, often have lashed to their tops or under their axles the trunk and branches of a tree, for wood with which to prepare, whenever a halt is made, the indispensable maté, or native tea. Their wheels are from six to eight feet in diameter, and their covered tops rise fifteen feet from the ground. They are long and narrow, of most heavy and clumsy construction, with tongues of rough-hewn timber, each in itself a load for a beast. They are drawn by oxen, attached by ropes of hide, in any number of pairs requisite for the draught. As means of transportation, they correspond well in their massive clumsiness and ponderous weight with the elephant of India, or the burden-bearing camel of Egypt and Turkey: and as they move in long lines over pampas of almost unlimited extent, form a feature not less striking, and not less in harmony with the surrounding scene, than the caravan in the deserts of Arabia, or the elephant on the plains of Bengal.

February 24th.—On Washington's birthday, the 22d inst., Mr. Harris, the American chargé d'affaires, gave a banquet to Commodore McKeever, and others of his fellow countrymen, visitors and residents in the city. The evening of the same day had been appointed for the reception of the commodore by "the governor," as Rosas is here styled. A government-house, covering the area of half a square, in the centre of the city, has recently been completed by the chieftain. It encloses quadrangle after quadrangle of spacious and elegantly furnished apartments, but is visited only occasionally by him for a few brief hours, at uncertain times. His chosen, and, indeed, only residence, properly so called, is the palatial quinta, or country-house of Palermo de San Benito, situated in the midst of an extensive domain, on the banks of the Plata, three or four miles west of the city. I most readily accepted an invitation to be of the party, glad to avail myself of the opportunity for a sight of the tiger in his den. Pardon the figure, but I have heard so much of his bloody ferocity in subduing the people to his abject rule, that no other will so well express my sense of his nature, and of the mysterious and guarded retirement of his present life: an unchained monster, in the security of a well-protected lair. The prospect of the interview revived in fresh force all I had ever heard and read of his atrocious deeds; and the anticipation of being in his presence, was not without the superstitious feeling of being exposed by it to the hazard of the "evil eye." There was no certainty, however, notwithstanding the appointment, that an interview with him would take place. He is so arbitrary and so capricious in his imperious rule, as to pay little regard to the ordinary civilities of life; and makes not only his own ministers and people abide his whims and pleasure, but diplomatic agents and foreign ambassadors also, are often obliged to dance attendance by the hour in his ante-rooms, without an audience, if such be his will. In the exercise of this despotic habit, however, one redeeming, and—socially, if not diplomatically—compensating indulgence is ever granted to such persons: the presence and smiles, the spirited conversation and the winning grace and manner of his accomplished daughter, the Doña Manuelita de Rosas. Of a reception by her we were sure.

We set off at a sufficiently early hour to allow time for a view of the grounds of Palermo before nightfall; and followed the same route I had taken with Mr. D——. At the distance of a mile from the city, after having crossed the common along the beach, we entered a broad and straight macadamized avenue, scientifically constructed, and in fine order. It is enclosed on either side by a neat iron railing, and is bordered with plantations of willow, and furnished with handsome lamp-posts and lamps for the night. It is a public road, constructed by Rosas: commencing at Palermo and to be extended to the city, and is still in progress. At the end of a mile and a half, a similar, but more beautiful avenue branches from this, and forms the private entrance to the domain, leading directly in front of the palace-like domicil of the Dictator. It is a half mile in length, is lined with orange trees in addition to the willows; and, besides these, is separated from the public road which runs parallel with it, by a broad and deep canal of brick-work. This private road is formed of sea-shell, and is as white and hard as so much marble. All dust is kept down by the sprinkling of water; while the sward on either side, clipt with the care of an English lawn, through the same means is ever in living freshness. The orange trees are nurtured with great care, and are frequently washed with brush and soap-suds, leaf by leaf, by persons in charge of them. As we passed, numerous peons, in the gay and picturesque dress of the country, were seen engaged in this process on a kind of step ladder, by which access was had to every part of each tree. Equal care is taken of them in the winter season, by enclosing each in a temporary house, to guard against the effect of frost. A nearer approach brought us to a cantonment of soldiers, consisting of a village of regularly disposed brick huts, of uniform construction. A park of artillery was near by, and clusters of soldiers in scarlet *ponchos* and petticoat-like *chirepas* were grouped on every side. These multiplied in number to the very doors of the villa.

The first impression, as we drove rapidly through this imagery, was striking and peculiar : the picture, in its still life, was one of high civilization and princely expenditure not anticipated ; but one, strongly marked in all that gave animation to it, with evidences of a demi-savage state. But for these—the Indian-like costume, the dark and wild countenances, and the savage knives seen sticking in the belts of the soldiers and peons—one might almost have believed himself on the shores of the Zuyder Zee : so dead is the level of the ground ; while the broad and deep canals of finished workmanship, the artificial lakelets, aquatic plants and water-fowl, the gay parterres and embanked terraces, presented imagery answering well to a scene in Holland. Every thing, too, was in straight lines ; roads, canals, plantations, and the villa itself. This is a parallelogram, having a rectangular pavilion projecting from each angle. It stands on one corner of two intersecting avenues, presenting a façade of two hundred and sixty feet front and rear, by one of two hundred and fifty on either side. It is one story in height, and the architecture throughout uniform. A wide corridor, supported by heavy arches, runs around the whole. All the apartments open by doors and French windows upon this, as well as upon a quadrangular court within.

The roof is flat, and is surrounded by an iron balustrade, ornamented at regular and short intervals by a kind of demi-turret, having the effect of a like number of chimneys, a purpose to which many of them are, in fact, appropriated. The preparations for the reception, in a guard of honor, to present arms as the commodore should alight, were not at the principal front, but at the farthest angle of the most western pavilion, on the garden front. We thus passed two sides of the structure before being set down. We were then conducted through a spacious saloon of state, to the corridor or arcade on the east end of the building, again through the length of this to the extreme eastern pavilion on the front, past which we had first driven—thus making the circuit of the entire establishment, before being ushered into the private drawing-room of Doña Manuelita. We found her standing here with two female companions in waiting, and were received with the cordiality and affability of long acquaintance.

This daughter of " the governor " is probably the most remarkable woman in South America : certainly so, as the impersonation of a government, which she confessedly is, and the only visible agent of its influence and power. Rosas himself, in his official position, is a kind of invisible personage—never, on any occasion, or under any circumstances, making his appearance publicly. It is said there are thousands of people in Buenos Ayres who have never seen him. A sight of him may often be caught in his grounds, superintending a gang of workmen, or perhaps witnessing the punishment, even to death, of a soldier, or some victim who is suffering, justly or unjustly, the penalty of the law or of his displeasure. He may be seen, too, at times, talking and jesting with the fishermen along the shore of the river on his domain, or driving Jehu-like, in the dead of the night, from Palermo to the city, or from the city to Palermo: it being his habit, from motives of policy, to make his appearance suddenly, at an hour, and under circumstances least to be expected; but never in public, in his appropriate place as chief magistrate and head of the people. On all public occasions, and in all public places, Manuelita alone appears as his representative; and as the embodiment of his will and the channel of his favor, receives the homage of sovereignty. While she acts no unimportant part in the negotiations of diplomacy and in foreign affairs, she is, virtually, the minister both of the "Interior" and of "Justice" in the government, tempering with mercy, as far as in her power, every act of oppression, and diffusing, in name at least, a semblance of benevolence wherever her influence reaches. Four hours of each morning are appropriated by her, to the receipt of petitions, the hearing of individual grievances and applications for redress. For this object, a bureau with a regular set of secretaries is established, where records are made of all cases brought before her, for her own decision, or for the intervention of her influence with her father. As may be rightly inferred from these facts, she is a woman of talent and judgment, and of infinite tact. Her age is thirty-five. She is of good height and fine figure, has regular and good features, black hair and eyes, with a beaming and benignant expression, and in complexion is a Spanish brunette. Her manners are graceful and winning, her conversation animated and playful, with a word of complaisance and a smile of kindness to all who approach, and are around her. Though a polished and elegant woman, she affects nothing of the stately dignity and lofty bearing of some of the aristocratic and high-bred whom I have seen—but has the easy, self-possessed, frank and cordial air, often met in every-day society. She is said to be exceedingly popular, and to be sincerely beloved by the people: as well she may be, if she does, indeed, exert the immense influence for good, which is reported of, and claimed by her friends for her, in softening, by acts of clemency and womanly mercy, the iron rule of her father.

Scarlet, or the veritable blood-tint, is the prescribed color of the government, and the silent, though exacted pledge of allegiance to the chief in power. Every man and boy under his rule, must don at all times the scarlet waistcoat, scarlet hatband, and the scarlet breast-ribbon, stamped with the motto of death to his political opponents. Women and girls, also, of every rank and all ages, must exhibit the scarlet ribbon in their hair or head-dress. It was no surprise, therefore, to see the Doña and her ladies, on a hot evening in midsummer, arrayed in scarlet silk bareges of large plaid, over under-dresses of white, with the scarlet ribbon and its savage motto, streaming among the tresses of their black hair. The predominating hue of the reception room—in the hangings of the walls, the draperies of the windows, and the carpet, was of the same color. This apartment is lofty and spacious. A grand piano and harp were conspicuous among its furniture.

The usual apology was made,—the pressure of important business—for the delay in the appearance of the governor, with the gracious assurance, however, that he would give audience to the commodore; and it was proposed, in the mean time, to take a view of the grounds, before nightfall. This we did, under the guidance of the sprightly and accomplished mistress of ceremonies and her ladies. They are very extensive, in a perfection of order, and in many respects novel and striking; but are too full of straight lines for beauty and artistic effect. The whole domain is a dead level—a swamp redeemed by draining and embankments from the overflowings of the river, and the quagmires of a marsh. The sums expended in transforming it into a paradise, compared with every thing around, are beyond all estimate; and make the place, at least in the outlay of money and labor, the most princely estate in either North or South America. The predominating growth in trees is the willow, imparting to the whole a sombre aspect; but the flower-gardens and shrubberies are brilliant in the display of colors, and sweet in the variety and richness of their perfume. A paved court extends along the arcades around the whole building. On the two sides communicating with the lawns, this court is enclosed by parterres of choice flowers, elevated three or four feet upon walls, and ornamented at regular distances by classically modelled urns and vases, also crowned and festooned with floral beauty. The effect of both is ornamental and pretty.

A rustic arbor with a dome-shaped top, overrun with clustering roses, woodbine, and sweetbrier, and encircled with busts in marble on pedestals, and one or two full-length figures in plaster, was specially commended to our notice, as the favorite retreat of Doña Manuelita. Not far from it, on the lawn, is a humble whitewashed cottage—the first domicil of Rosas on taking possession of the estate. It is scarcely superior, in its aspect and accommodations, to the rancho of a common peon : but is retained in its original state as a memento of the past, or possibly for contrast with the courtly splendor of the present establishment.

Some years ago, an American brigantine, at anchor in the river, was driven by a violent storm and flood, high and dry into the woods of Palermo. Its restoration to the water was impracticable. She was still stanch and uninjured, both in hull and spars, and Rosas, in place of permitting her to be broken up for the sale of the material, purchased the craft with the purpose of converting her, as she stood, into a pavilion of pleasure. Brought to an even keel, she was substantially underpinned; and thus firmly moored, and, remodelled between decks into a dancing saloon and refreshment rooms, is a favorite place for the entertainment of select parties in summer. It is situated a half mile from the house, and our walk extended to it.

As we returned to the quinta, the shades of the evening were beginning to fall. Two of the pavilions mentioned as being attached to the angles of the main building—those on the garden front—are unenclosed by walls, each forming an open saloon, furnished with ranges of crimson sofas, on which beneath the protecting roof, the cool of the evening may be enjoyed with uninterrupted views on every side. Into the most retired of these we were now conducted; and, while standing in a group in the centre, with our faces directed to the lawn and shrubbery, I perceived a figure stealthily approaching from behind, without the warning even of a footfall, till a little pliant riding-whip of polished whalebone, mounted with red coral, was playfully tapped on the bare shoulder of the Doña. Turning suddenly, as if in surprise, she exclaimed in a tone of pleasure and affection—"Tatita!" a diminutive of fondness by which she addresses and speaks of her father; and following her example in a change of position, we found ourselves in the presence of the far-famed Ruler. Though the place and circumstances of our presentation were seemingly thus accidental, both doubtless were of previous arrangement, to give greater informality to the audience. Rosas is now a thick-set, portly man of sixty, of medium height, with finely marked and well chiselled features, and of florid complexion. In youth and middle age he is said to have been remarkably handsome. The feature which first and most deeply arrested my attention was a piercing, restless, fiery eye of grayish blue. Whether from previous prejudice or not, to me its expression seemed singularly devoid of ingenuousness and benignity—indeed, to be positively sinister and tiger-like. His dress was a round-jacket of dark blue, with small military buttons; the inevitable scarlet waistcoat, ribbon, and motto; and an undress military cap, with the visor drawn low over his eyebrows. His manner and address were common-place and familiar, without any mingling of the dignity of the Spanish Hidalgo in high position.

After an interchange of salutations, and some brief conversation on indifferent topics, he led the way, with Commodore McKeever by his side, through the long, intervening arcade to the drawing room in the front pavilion, in which we had first been received. Here, seated in an angle of the lofty apartment, with the leading gentlemen of our party on his right, and his daughter and her ladies on the left, he at once took the lead in conversation, running loquaciously from subject to subject of trifling importance, and often interlarding his statements and opinions with low anecdote and vulgar details, unfit "for ears polite," much less for the hearing of women of delicacy and refinement.

So full of conversation was he, and seemingly so anxious to please, that our stay was prolonged beyond all expectation; and we were disappointed in the pleasure of an evening with Mr. and Mrs. C——, whose country-seat lies between Palermo and the city.

CHAPTER XVI.

BUENOS AYRES.

February 25th.—The Argentine confederation, composed originally of thirteen states, joined together in compact, but not by constitution, under the style of the United Provinces of La Plata, has become practically consolidated and merged in the State of Buenos Ayres. Being the only province possessed of a sea-port, and enjoying an extended commerce, she was encharged by the others with the management of the foreign relations of the confederacy. This naturally made her the controlling power; she increased while the rest decreased. The result was a division of the people of the provinces into two parties, and speedy conflict and anarchy. At this juncture Rosas raised his standard, and subdued the whole to his sway; and though nominally only governor of the city and province of Buenos Ayres, encharged with the sole ministration of the foreign affairs of the confederacy, he is, in fact, the despotic ruler of the whole.

He is the most remarkable chieftain in South America; possessing all the elements of character essential to the successful despot: firmness, energy, shrewdness, subtlety, unscrupulous purpose, and unfaltering cruelty. Sprung from a Spanish family of respectability in Buenos Ayres, the recklessness of his early youth led to his removal by them to what is here termed the "Camp"—the open country of the pampas, over which are scattered the estancias, or estates of landed proprietors, for the raising of cattle, sheep, and horses. Here, among the gauchos, or demi-savage peasants of the interior, he was made an overseer by a wealthy relative in Buenos Ayres. Adopting the usages and habits of savage life of the people, he became, in the course of years, thoroughly a gaucho; and distinguished himself by the control he acquired over his associates, and over the scarcely more untamed Indians of the southern territory. He excelled in all the personal qualities and feats of skill most prized by them, and gained their unlimited favor. The reputation thus established, first called the attention of partisan leaders in the confederacy to him; and secured for him, as early as 1820, from the party in power the appointment of colonel of the militia of the southern frontier. In this position he gained additional reputation and new popularity; till, fired with ambition, he began in 1829 to lay the foundations for the despotism which he has since exercised. Having secured the favor of the good among the people, by the evidences he had given of a power to win the confidence and to control the will of the wild men around him, he is charged with the determination of gaining that of the evil, by making his camp the sanctuary of every class of criminals; and thus surrounding himself—with the deliberate purpose of making the use of them he afterwards did—by an organized band of assassins. Whether this be true or not, it is an undoubted fact that, after being placed at the head of the government, he soon put an end to all hazard of rivalry in power, by processes of bloodshed and assassination through such minions of his favor, almost beyond belief. Volumes might be written, as volumes already have been, upon the tragedies with which, from time to time in his early rule, he startled and terrified the community, till every one was brought to the subjection of abject fear: all this, too, under the pretence and plausible plea of sustaining the law and securing public quietude and order.

The justification which he himself pleads, for acts of cruelty which are admitted, is that "the Argentines can only be governed with the knife at their throats;" and the highest vindication of his character which I have heard from some foreigners, who do not believe in the extent of the atrocities with which he is charged, and are disposed even to admire him as a man and a ruler, is that his faults are to be attributed to the defects of his education and his habits as a gaucho—that he is but a type of the people. This may be true; but what is the state and character of the people—the gauchos of whom he is the type? The best description I have seen of them, is in a pamphlet by the Chevalier de St. Robert, a French gentleman, who visited the Plata officially. This you may not be able to refer to, and I furnish the extract in point.

He says: "There is nothing to be found in the Pampas—those immense plains which extend over a space of more than seven hundred leagues, from the extreme north to the extreme south of the Argentine Confederation—but *estancias*, or farms, scattered here and there, which form so many petty republics, isolated from the rest of the world, living by themselves, and separated from each other by the desert. Alone in the midst of those over whom he is a complete master, the *estanciero* is out of every kind of society whatsoever, with no other law than that of force, with no other rules to guide him but those that are self-imposed, and with no other motive to influence than his own caprice. There is nothing to disturb his repose, nothing to dispute his power, or interfere with his tranquillity, except the tiger that may lurk about his grounds, or the wild Indian that may occasionally make a hostile incursion on his domains. His children and his domestics, *gauchos* like himself, pass the same sort of life; that is to say, without ambition, without desires, and without any species of agricultural labor. All they have to do is to mark and to kill, at certain periods, the herds of oxen and flocks of sheep which constitute the fortune of the estanciero, and that satisfy the wants of all. Purely carnivorous, the gaucho's only food consists of flesh and water—bread and spirituous liquors are as much unknown to him as the simplest elements of social life.

"In a country in which the only wealth of the inhabitants arises from the incessant destruction of innumerable herds and flocks, it can easily be understood how their sanguinary occupation must tend to obliterate every sentiment of pity, and induce an indifference to the perpetration of acts of cruelty. The readiness to shed blood—a ferocity which is at the same time obdurate and brutal—constitutes the prominent feature in the character of the pure gaucho. The first instrument his infantile hand grasps is the knife—the first things that attract his attention as a child, are the pouring out of blood and the palpitating flesh of animals. From his earliest years, as soon as he is able to walk, he is taught how he may with the greatest skill approach the living beast, hough it, and, if he has strength, kill it. Such are the sports of his childhood: he pursues them ardently, and amid the approving smiles of his family. As soon as he acquires sufficient strength, he takes part in the labors of the estancia; they are the sole arts he has to study, and he concentrates all his intellectual powers in mastering them. From that time forth he arms himself with a large knife, and for a single moment of his life he never parts with it. It is to his hand an additional limb—he makes use of it always, in all cases, in every circumstance, and constantly with wonderful skill and address. The same knife that in the morning has been used to slaughter a bullock, or to kill a tiger, aids him in the daytime to cut his dinner, and at night to carve out a skin tent, or else to repair his saddle, or to mend his mandoline.

"With the gaucho the knife is often used as an argument in support of his opinions. In the midst of a conversation, apparently carried on in amity, the formidable knife glitters on a sudden in the hands of one of the speakers, the *ponchos* are rolled around the left arm, and a conflict commences. Soon deep gashes are seen on the face, the blood gushes forth, and, not unfrequently, one of the combatants falls lifeless to the earth; but no one thinks of interfering with the combat, and when it is over, the conversation is resumed as if nothing extraordinary had occurred.

No person is disturbed by it—not even the women, who remain as cold, unmoved spectators of the affray! It may easily be surmised what sort of persons they must be, of which such a scene is but a specimen of their domestic manners.

"Thus the savage education of the estancia produces in the gaucho a complete indifference as to human life, by familiarizing him from his most tender years to the contemplation of a violent death, whether it is that he inflicts it on another, or receives it himself. He lifts his knife against a man with the same indifference that he strikes down a bullock. The idea which everywhere else attaches to the crime of homicide does not exist in his mind; for in slaying another, he yields not less to habit than to the impulse of his wild and barbarous nature. If perchance a murder of this kind is committed so close to a town that there is reason to apprehend the pursuit of justice, every one is eager to favor the flight of the guilty person. The fleetest horse is at his service, and he departs, certain to find, wherever he goes, the favor and sympathy of all. Then, with that marvellous instinct which is common to all the savage races, he feels no hesitation in venturing into the numerous plains of the pampas. Alone, in the midst of a boundless desert, and in which the eye strains itself in vain to discover a boundary, he advances without the slightest feeling of uneasiness: he does so watching the course of the stars, listening to the winds, discovering the cause of the slightest noise that reaches his ears, and at length arrives at the place he sought, without even straying from it, for a moment. The *lasso* which is rolled around his horse's neck; the *bolas* suspended from his saddle, and the inseparable knife, suffice to insure him food, and to secure him against every danger, even against the tiger. When he is hungry, he selects one out of the herds of beeves that cover the plain, pursues it, lassos it, kills it, cuts out of it a piece of flesh, which he eats raw, or possibly cooks, and thus refreshes himself for the journey of the following day.

"If murder be a common incident in the life of a gaucho, it often also becomes the means to him of emerging from obscurity, and of obtaining renown among his associates. When he has rendered himself remarkable by his audacity and address in single combats, companions gather round him, and he soon finds himself at the head of a considerable party. He 'commences a campaign,' sets himself in open defiance of the laws, and in a short time acquires a celebrity which rallies a crowd about him, and makes him a chieftain." Such are the people of whom Rosas is the type, and such the processes, in a qualified degree at least, by which he attained, and still holds his supremacy.

Are you not afraid of your life even in Buenos Ayres? you will be ready to ask, after reading such a description of the people who surround, and have the military guardianship of the city. I reply, that there probably is not a city in the civilized world, in which all, not suspected of political or partisan offense, are more perfectly secure in life, limb, and property. The police is perfect. The stranger and foreigner especially, may move about the streets at any hour of the night, with perfect impunity. Theft, robbery, and burglary are unheard of; and a pocket-handkerchief or purse dropped in the street, if bearing any mark which indicates its owner, will be sure to be returned to him, or quickly be found in the keeping of the police.

February 26th.—The impressions made by Buenos Ayres in its external aspect, are increasingly favorable. The plan of the town is rectangular, like that of Philadelphia. Every street is of the same width, and every square of the same dimensions. The streets are narrow, just wide enough for two vehicles to pass each other, and the sidewalks comfortable only for those moving in Indian file. In walking two abreast, or arm in arm, there is a constant jostling against passers-by. In some parts of the town the sidewalks are elevated two or three feet above the level of the carriage-way. The city being a dead level, and the streets straight, long vistas in them are every where commanded. Some of these are striking, and where the domes and fine towers of the old Spanish churches come in as leading features, are quite European. These stately old structures are scattered about in various localities, and, with the citadel on the highest rise of ground overlooking the river, are the chief, if not the only sombre objects in the architecture of the place: still retaining the natural color of the brick of which they are built, or exhibiting time-stained surfaces of stone or stucco, and roofs covered with moss, lichens, and grass. Till within a few years, the houses were uniformly one story only in height. This is still the case in many quarters, but in others, successive blocks and almost entire streets are now composed of those of two stories. The general plan of all is the same: the Spanish, or rather Moorish quadrangle, upon which all the apartments open, with a cistern, and sometimes a fountain in the centre. In many of the establishments of the wealthy, there are a succession of these quadrangles. Filled with shrubbery and flowers, and often ornamented by a fountain, the view from the street through them, terminating not unfrequently in an assimilating scene in fresco against a wall in the far perspective, is quite impressive in stage effect. The custom of constantly applying fresh whitewash to buildings new and old, gives to the whole city a clean and bright look. Here and there, however, in almost every street, a quaint and antiquated building is seen, contrasting with later structures, in the manner of the old Dutch houses still remaining, a few years ago, in New York and Albany, with those of modern date. These are a single story in height, with slanting, instead of flat roofs, covered with tile. Over the central door, however, there is a kind of demi-tower, furnished with a window and projecting balcony, as a look-out and place of parley with an outsider whose motive for demanding admittance might be questioned. In many cases these look-outs are quite tasteful in their architecture, and pleasing to the eye from the air they bear of the "olden time." Lichens, air-plants, and tufting grass clinging to the cornices and mouldings and ornamented pinnacles, give to them a venerable, moustached, and bearded aspect, that cannot fail to arrest the eye of the lover of the antique.

Great improvements have been made of late years, both in the external architecture and internal arrangements of private dwellings. Many of the mansions recently erected would scarcely suffer, in point of richness and elegance, by comparison with some of the most luxurious of the Fifth Avenue in New York. This is especially true of one just being completed by Gen. P——, the minister of war: though the lofty and massive entrance-gates, in complicated and artistic patterns of cast-iron bronzed, and the colonnades of Moorish arches surrounding its quadrangular courts within, would not entirely harmonize with the prevailing architecture of that street of palaces.

Every house here is necessarily a castle, having its windows on the street barred and grated, with portals not easily to be forced, and parapets, upon the flat roof, capable of effective defence against assailants below. Being without cellars or basement-rooms, the level of the floors is elevated but little above that of the street, and as no railing or area intervenes between the side-walks and the large windows, which descend to the floors, the interior of the room is as open to the inspection of the passers by, as to the inmates themselves. In some residences of wealth and taste, a vista of room after room in long suites, richly furnished, is thus exposed to view. The apartments on the street, with scarcely an exception, are reception and drawing-rooms; and, in the afternoons and evenings, the promenaders in the street are thus furnished with a succession of tableaux vivans of females—not occupied as with us in conversation, or reading, or fancy work, or other employments of leisure and taste, and grouped with husbands, and fathers, and brothers, and sons, and other male friends—but seated in formal rows, or in a semicircle around the windows, in a greater or less degree of 'full dress,' with little interchange of conversation among themselves, and evidently for the mere purpose of seeing and being seen. Every thing in their dress and manner shows the studied purpose of exciting admiration. These exhibitions, however, are only in hours of costume. Till late in the day the ladies of the country in general are invisible; very much in undress, lounging, and idling, and sipping Paraguay tea through the silver tube of the maté cup.

An American or Englishman cannot fail to be struck with the seemingly slight intercourse of the male and female members of a family. The latter are to all external appearance without husbands, fathers, brothers, or sons. You meet them in numbers in the morning, going to and returning from mass, followed by a servant or servants, but seldom, if ever, attended by a male relative. The evening is a favorite time for shopping, and the streets are often crowded in some sections, with ladies thus engaged, but unattended by a gentleman in escort. And in the hundreds of parlors and drawing-rooms into which I have looked in passing, I do not recollect ever to have seen a gentleman, old or young, in the groupings of a family circle.

A week being the extent of the leave of absence which I feel willing to take from my charge on board ship, and from the voluntary duty I have assumed at the chapel in Montevideo; with the purpose of returning to the Congress to-morrow, I gave therefore the mornings of yesterday and to-day to calls in acknowledgment of the civilities from our fellow-countrymen, and various foreign residents, in which, as one of Commodore McKeever's party, I have shared. In the course of these, I accompanied the Commodore and Mr. G—— in a visit to the Conde de Bessi, bishop of a diocese of unpronounceable name and unknown region, and nuncio from the Pope to Rosas. The disregard which Rosas has shown in ecclesiastical matters for the supremacy of the Pope, and the sacrilege, in the view of the Romish Church, of some of his acts, led long ago to his excommunication, and the withdrawal by the Papal States from all diplomatic intercourse with him. The Conde de Bessi has recently arrived, with overtures of reconciliation. Though every civility has been paid to him in his official character, by the government, and a house elegantly fitted and furnished been appropriated to his use, with other marks of courtesy—carriages and horses at his service—he has not yet been admitted to an audience, and, it is believed, will not be. The preliminary to negotiation which the nuncio demands—the release of the clergy from the obligation of wearing the red ribbon, stamped with the motto of death to the political opponents of the dictator, which they are forced to do, even while officiating at the altar—is one that will not be accorded; and unless the legate yields on this point, he will fail in his mission.

Our visit being announced, we were ushered into the cabinet of his excellency—first through a large and elegantly furnished saloon, and then through a smaller apartment, fitted as a chapel with all the appliances of Romish worship. The reception of our party by the count was most courteous, and the conversation in French which ensued, animated, and on his part, most complimentary to the United States, as to her prosperity and her power. He appears to be about forty years of age; is very plump and healthful, with little that is ascetic in look or manner. He is very handsome, with a face as fresh and smooth and round as that of a female, and an expression beaming with benignity and high breeding. His voice and intonation are of the most silvery softness, and his whole manner as feminine and polished as that of a duchess. Indeed, so remarkably was this the case, that as I looked at him in his silken robe of purple reaching to the heels, and with a cap of velvet on his head, of corresponding color, I found it difficult to disabuse myself of the impression that the interview was with one of the fair sex.

CHAPTER XVII.

MONTEVIDEO.

May 30th.—Scarcely any duty in naval service can be more destitute of interest, than such as the Congress is performing off Montevideo at the present time. To the close investment of the city by land, a practical blockade is added, from a decree of Rosas, by which every vessel touching here on her way up the Plata is denied entry at Buenos Ayres. The consequence is—there being little demand for imports and nothing to export at Montevideo—that no vessel in the trade of the Plata comes into the port except from necessity, and the arrivals are limited, for the most part, to a man-of-war, occasionally, and the regular mail-steamer from England, by the way of Rio de Janeiro, once each month. My chaplaincy on board, and the additional service of worship each Sabbath on shore, furnish the only variation in my duty; and an occasional row or sail to the city for a walk or the visit of an hour, in a limited circle of acquaintance, my only recreation. For opportunities of visiting the shore I am indebted chiefly to the kindness of Commodore McKeever: Captain McIntosh, so frequently the companion of my walks at Rio, here scarcely ever leaves the ship.

The recent arrival in which we were most interested was that of the U. S. storeship Southampton. It brought Dr. C—— to the Congress as fleet surgeon, in place of Dr. W——, who returned home invalided, shortly after our arrival on the station. This loss to the medical corps of the ship and to our mess was regretted. In the substitute furnished, we are greatly favored. As a physician and surgeon Dr. C—— is worthy of all confidence; and as a gentleman and Christian, carries with him predominating influence. The value of such an accession to a naval mess-table and to the associations of the gun-room of a man-of-war, can scarcely be over-estimated.

Another circumstance connected with the Southampton, in which we felt great interest, proved less happy in the issue. The Congress, through a mistake not discovered till she was at sea, left the United States without a suitable library for the use of the crew. As soon as this was known, I took measures to have one sent after us. This was shipped by the Southampton and arrived safely here; but from an oversight of the officer in charge, was carried again to sea by her, on proceeding to her destination in the Pacific. The disappointment to the crew is great, and only to be remedied by patiently waiting for the return of a fresh order to the United States.

My visits on shore are most unvarying in their character. Sometimes I take a solitary stroll through the less public streets of the city; but never without feelings of commiseration for the depressed and suffering condition of the poorer classes. The pale and haggard faces of the females, seen at the doors and windows, tell one story of privation and want—of listless despondency and gloom. The extent and degree of destitution, from the long suspension of all business, is fearful, among those even who have been accustomed to independence, if not to affluence and luxury. Among such, the poorest scraps that fall from the tables of the more fortunate are most thankfully received; and any kind of employment is eagerly sought. Females of the first respectability are glad to be employed in making up linen in a most finished style, at a half dollar a shirt, and at six and eight cents a collar. The demoralization among all classes, in consequence of the pressure of want, is very great, I am told, and of a character fatal to the purity and self-respect of individuals and whole families.

The only semblance of general cheerfulness observable, is in the daily evening promenade to witness the relief of guard. This takes place at the inner lines without the walls, every evening at sunset. During the previous hour, in fine weather, hundreds of the better classes of the citizens both foreigners and natives, in a greater or less display of dress, may be seen issuing through the ancient gateway of the northern wall, for the walk of a mile through the broad and straight street, leading from it to a battery where the relief of guard takes place, and to listen to the music of the bands with which this is accompanied.

I have mentioned the presence here of fifteen hundred or two thousand French troops with their officers. They are quartered in barracks, a part within and a part without the walls of the old city; and may be seen in groups and small parties in the streets at almost all times of the day and evening. Well dressed and well fed, young and athletic, fresh and healthful in look, and cheerful and animated in movement and manner, they constitute quite a redeeming feature in the aspect of the city. They have a parade-ground just without the walls, and are regularly and severely drilled, but take no part in the military duty of the place, and perform no patrol. This devolves exclusively upon the Montevidean soldiery. These, amounting to three thousand, consist chiefly of a foreign legion, composed of emigrants—Italians from the vicinity of Genoa, and from Piedmont, and Basques from the frontiers of Spain and France; and of a negro regiment under the command of native officers. The negroes, till the commencement of the war were slaves; but were then liberated by a decree of the government, without compensation to their masters, on condition of entering the army for the continuance of the war, with a right to a bounty of land on the restoration of peace.

The foreign legion form the municipal or national guard. They consist of artisans, porters, laborers and boatmen, who, in successive companies are on duty as a patrol one day in three, and engaged in their various callings the rest of the time. The negroes are regular soldiers. They are said to be brave and faithful, and have proved themselves most reliable on post and in battle. The dress of the foreigners is that of their every-day labor—the jacket and trowsers and Pelasgic cap of the Basques; but the negro regiment are in uniform—the dress of the gauchos, or Indio-Spaniards, of the country. This is striking and picturesque, though Indian-like and savage in its general effect: at best barbarism, 'picked out,'—as carriage painters say—with civilization. It is composed of a red flannel shirt, beneath a poncho of red of the same material, lined with green; a green cheripa, or swaddling blanket for the loins and lower limbs; drawers of white cotton terminating in wide pantalets ornamented with insertings of lace work, and a deep fringe falling over the ankles and bare feet: the covering of the head being a conical cap of green cloth, without visor, laced with yellow cord. It is seen to the best effect at Buenos Ayres, where there is in the soldiers more of the Indian and less of African blood; and where, exhibited on horseback, the long black hair and streaming ponchos of the riders are in keeping with the flowing manes and tails of the horses, as they scamper with the fleetness of the wind along the beach and over the plain.

The free hospitality of two or three houses, both English and American, in addition to the Consulate, is extended to us; and usually, after the relief of guard, we join the family of one or another of these for tea. It is pleasant in a strange land thus to be received informally in a home circle, and to be made welcome, in this, the winter of the year, to the elegant comforts of carpeted floors and curtained windows—of the glowing grate of the fireside, and the hissing urn of the tea-table, and for the hour to share in the social enjoyments of conversation and music. The chief drawback to the pleasure, is the remembrance forced upon us by such scenes, of our distant homes, and the vision in fancy of what we there lose. This was particularly the case in the visits of the last evening. I made an early call at Mr. L——'s, and, on entering the drawing-room, found Madame L——at the piano. After giving the accustomed kind welcome, she was prevailed upon to continue at the instrument. Though the mother of a fine family of carefully educated and intelligent children—gathered at the time in various amusements round a centre-table of the saloon—she has not thrown aside her music, but is still in good practice. Her touch and execution are very much in the style of Mademoiselle R——, and in some fine passages from Verdi and other masters, brilliantly given, carried me at once to Riverside.

I do not recollect to have mentioned the romance of the honey-moon of Mr. and Madame L—— at Buenos Ayres, in the early days of the despotism of Rosas. Madame L——, previously the Signorita ——, a native of the city, and member of the Romish church, ventured to be married to Mr. L—— by an American missionary, without the consent of the Dictator. This was contrary to an existing law; and the consequence was that the bride was very unceremoniously immured for three months in a nunnery, while the groom and clergyman were as summarily arrested, and thrown into prison. Mr. L—— was then established in mercantile business at Buenos Ayres. But indignant at such an interference with the rights of conscience and personal freedom, on regaining his liberty, he withdrew with his wife to Montevideo, and is now a chief capitalist in this section of South America.

On joining the Commodore at Mrs. Z——'s, I found quite a party of the H——'s and other friends. The ladies were in more dress than usual; the rooms were well lighted; and the tea-table richly and elegantly appointed; and in the enjoyments of an evening of music, both vocal and instrumental, including some fine chants and psalmody, we were tempted for the time to forget our exile.

The private dwellings in Montevideo, whether only one, or two stories high, are all built in the Spanish-Morescan style, having a quadrangle within, enclosing a pateo, or open square in the centre. Upon this, where there is but one story, and upon an encircling verandah or corridor, above where there are two, all the apartments open, through doors and French windows. The pateos in the one case, and the verandahs in the other, are usually filled with running vines, and flowering plants and shrubs, in boxes of earth, or in urns and vases. The parapeted walls of the flat roofs are also often ornamented by vases, containing aloes and various cacti; and I have often been struck, on passing to the staircase in leaving, with the ornamental and picturesque effect of these—especially in bright moonlight—as they stand out in strong relief against the sky.

However good the promise of fair weather may have been in going on shore, we never take leave for a return to the ship at night, without a greater or less degree of uncertainty, as to the manner and circumstances in which we may get on board. The shallowness of the roadstead obliges vessels of the draught of the Congress to lie two or three miles from the shore; and even then, such are often cradled at low water in a bed of mud three or four feet deep; but the distance is a trifle, compared with the obstacle to a visit to the shore, either for exercise or pleasure, arising from the frequency and suddenness of the south and south-west winds, called pamperos. These often burst over the water with little or no warning, and by their fierceness and the sea they raise, cut off, for twenty-four hours or more, all communication between the ship and the shore. Twice within the first week of our arrival, a party in the Commodore's barge was detained a night and a day on shore under such circumstances; and other boats sent on shore on various objects of duty, at least as many times. Fortunately for some of us, Mr. Frazier, of the American house of Frazier, Zimmerman & Co., being without other family than the employées of the counting-room, had it in his power to offer some of us, on those occasions, an asylum in the well-appointed residence in which he dispenses a liberal and generous hospitality. The few hotels in the place, kept principally by Frenchmen and Italians, are comfortless, especially in their accommodations for sleeping.

A few nights ago, on reaching the mole, a high and piercing wind was blowing, very much from the point we wished to steer, tumbling a rough and wild sea before it. We could not lay our course for the ship within several points: leaving a long and heavy pull for the oarsmen, after we should take in sail. Close hauled upon the wind, and plunging into the head sea, all hands were well showered, even as far aft as the stern-sheets, by the spray dashed from the bows. In disgust at this winding up of the pleasures of the evening, the Commodore exclaimed that it would be "the last of his night expeditions from the shore;" that hereafter he would limit his visits to the daytime, and then to fine weather. However, the barge is a beautiful sea-boat, riding the swelling waves—whether propelled by oars or canvas—like a duck, and under sail, skimming the crested waters like a sea-bird. When obliged at last to take to the oars, the pull to the ship was not so long, or the trouble in getting on board on the lee-side so great, as we had apprehended. The next morning the weather was tranquil as a summer's day; and the Commodore, beckoning me to join him on the poop as he was taking a turn before breakfast, said, "Why, Mr. S——, the getting off last night was not so bad after all. I must take back my hard speeches about the place and weather, and recall my rash vows. I think we may still venture an evening's visit." This we soon did, and our return on board, for that and two or three successive nights, was the very perfection of every thing lovely in moonlight upon the water. The air was mild and balmy; the river, smooth and glassy as a lake, seemed beneath the moonbeams, a very sea of silver; a fair and gentle land-breeze kept the sails of the boat just steadily full—wafting us imperceptibly along, while every thing above, beneath, and around us, was so tranquil, so bright, and so pure, that we were charmed by it into a musing mood of the profoundest silence.

The prevailing weather, at present, is like that of the finest October at home, with which season—that of autumn—it corresponds. The mornings are cool, bracing, and brilliant; at noon, the temperature is almost hot, and the nights are humid and cold. The sunsets are equal, in the beauty and softness of the tintings and colors, to any I recollect to have observed in any part of the world. To judge from the apparent purity and elasticity of the atmosphere, it would seem that the climate could not be otherwise than healthful; yet the sick list on board the Congress, from catarrhs, inflammation of the lungs, and rheumatism, is greater than at any time since the beginning of our cruise. Some of the cases of pneumonia are very severe, and threaten to prove fatal. This increase of sickness and its character, are attributable, probably, to the frequent recurrence, amidst all this brightness, of wintry storms of two or three days' continuance: like a cold and boisterous equinoctial gale in the United States, with pouring rain and piping winds. Indeed, the anchorage here is a terrible place for winds at all seasons of the year: terrible, not from danger to the ships—for the whole bottom is a soft and tenacious mud, into which large vessels safely cradle—but in the discomfort on board in a storm, and the inconvenience of communicating with the shore.

The special interruptions to the monotony of a daily routine on my own part, have been a series of infant baptisms, in the families of various foreign residents, English, Scotch, and German; three marriages in which the grooms were foreigners also—American and English; and the funeral of an American lady, long a resident of Montevideo. The groom at one of the weddings was Dr. K—— of the navy, surgeon of the St. Louis; his bride, the Signorita L——, daughter of Don Juan L——, Secretary to the Senate of the Republic of Uruguay. The ceremony was private, Commodore McKeever, the captain of the St. Louis, one or two other naval officers, Madame L——, the godmother of the bride, and the immediate members of the family constituting the party. Another of the marriages was in the presence of a large company, and was followed by a general reception of the society of Montevideo, and a ball. The parties being

English, the presence of the representative of the British government was necessary, to give validity to the rite, according to act of parliament; and the ceremony was followed by the making out of a certificate, at a centre-table of the drawing-room, on a folio sheet of paper, to which, as first witness, the Hon. Mr. Gore, H. M. Chargé d' Affaires, attached his name officially. Nearly the whole company, both ladies and gentlemen, gave witness to the event in a similar manner, so that, in the end, the document, in its length of signatures, rivalled a Magna Charta or Declaration of Independence. It was the first occasion, except at the chapel, in which I had met so large a company of Montevideans, or in which there was a mingling of the native Americo-Spanish society. The ladies of this blood have been celebrated by travellers for their beauty, and for sprightliness and grace of manner; and justly, I would say, were I to judge in the matter, from one at least, of those present on this occasion: Mrs. R——, the wife of a young, but retired captain in the British navy, a son of Admiral Sir J—— R——. She is beautiful, and apparently truly lovely, with more of the bearing and manners of polished life than most other ladies I have met since I left the United States. Others equally favored may have joined the party afterwards, but of this I cannot speak. The general company were only beginning to arrive, as, under the guidance of Mr. Gore, I left for the British Consulate, to officiate in the baptism of a child, which had been appointed for the same evening.

The first funeral I have been called to attend, was at the house in which I performed the first marriage ceremony after our arrival. The mother of the young and lovely bride, an American lady, was, at the time, in so feeble a state from consumption, as scarce to be able to be present. She has failed rapidly since, and was buried on the 16th.

During the years of prosperity in Montevideo, a Protestant burial-ground was laid out, a half mile beyond the outer gate, along the edge of a narrow ravine and watercourse. It was enclosed by a handsome wall of brick, planted with trees and shrubbery, contained many tombstones and monuments of marble, and was one of the most attractive spots in the suburbs. It was found, however, on the commencement of hostilities, that the walls and trees gave shelter to the assailants, in their approaches to the city, and interfered with the effect of the batteries of the besieged. The walls consequently were razed, and the trees cut down by the inside party. The result is an entire ruin. The tombs and monuments are mostly overturned and destroyed, and the place, though still appropriated to its original use, is utterly desecrated. Scarce a stone is standing, and not a vestige of ornament or beauty remains. I could not avoid being struck, amid other objects in the scene—at the funeral, with the appearance of the hearse—the best the city now affords, and emblematic of all its attempts at display. Its curtains of velvet, once doubtless black, are now faded to a muddy orange, and are all tattered and torn; and what were, originally, plumes of ostrich feathers, nodding gracefully at each corner, are now only bristling quills, from which every feather has fallen in decay. It was drawn by two miserable, starved mules in a wretched harness, and altogether was a mockery of the pomp and pageantry of the grave.

The subject reminds me to mention the receipt by the last English mail, of a letter from the family of Ramsey, in whose fate you express an interest, from the account given of his sudden death, last October. It is in answer to one by which I communicated the bereavement. He was of a pious household, who were deeply afflicted by the intelligence sent, but consoled by the assurance, that every possible attention had been paid to him. The letter is from a young man, the only surviving son of the family. He says, " It is impossible to attempt a description of the scene exhibited, as I endeavored to read aloud the heartrending account of the death of one we loved so dearly. It can never be forgotten by any one present. The whole family were overwhelmed, and I myself entirely unmanned;" and adds in another part—" the night after we received the melancholy tidings, a most touching incident occurred: caused by my youngest sister Jessie, a child of six years, when preparing to retire to rest. She had not been told the sad news, and while on her knees by my mother's side praying aloud, her little hands resting upon her lap, she prayed, as was her custom, that God would keep and bless her dear brother at sea, and bring him in safety home to us. The scene that ensued was most afflicting; we all wept most bitterly, while the little one cried as if her heart would break, when told that the poor brother, for whom she prayed, was lost to her for ever in this world.

CHAPTER XVIII.

June 7th.—The tedium of the long stay of the Congress at Montevideo was relieved once, by a cruise of three weeks off the Plata. The chief object in this, was to exercise the crew at the sails and in working ship, and to give practice at sea with the great guns and small arms. The effect of the change was good, both morally and physically. The vicinity of a port, so free to dissipation as Montevideo, is demoralizing both to officers and men; and it is well, as Commodore McKeever remarked to me in speaking on the subject, occasionally at least to put the broad sea between the ship and the seductions of the shore.

On the 22d ult. we again set sail for this place. The island lies closely on the coast about midway between the Plata and Rio de Janeiro. It is twenty-eight miles long, from four to eight wide, and is separated from the main by a narrow and irregular strait, varying in breadth from one and two, to three and more miles. It was settled earlier than any part of the continent in this section, and gives name to the province on the main opposite, within whose boundaries it is included. Its harbor is one of the best in the Empire, and was once a great resort for shipping, especially for refreshment and repairs by those engaged in the whale fishery. The principal town, called Nossa Senhora do Desterro, or "Our Lady of Banishment or Exile," containing a population of eight or ten thousand inhabitants, is the capital of the province and the residence of its President.

On the morning of the 2d inst., the island, overtopped by the loftier mountains of the main, was in view at a distance of thirty miles; and coasting along it we entered the straits and came to anchor by nightfall. The land is broken and lofty, and beautifully verdant: the eastern shores next the sea presenting, as we sailed along them, alternate stretches of white sand beach and projecting promontories of rocks crowned with woods. There is not a sufficient depth of water for a frigate to pass through the channel, and the entrance for large ships is by the north end of the island. It is winding, and with the mountains of the island and the main on either side, presents the features of a magnificent harbor rather than the appearance of an arm of the sea. We were delighted with the varied outlines and general beauty of the whole, in contrast with the scenery of the Plata, though but few evidences of civilization are visible; a small habitation here and there along the shore, being the only indications of the presence of man.

The next morning the whole surface of the water, glassy as a mirror, was dotted two or three miles south of us with the canoes of fishermen; their white hats, shirts, and drawers contrasting strongly in the early sun with the black sides of their canoes. We were some miles from the customary anchorage, and the presence of so large a ship as the Congress even, attracted no attention from them, and brought no canoe with the milk and eggs and tropical fruits for which we were longing. Soon after breakfast we ran some miles further south to our present anchorage just inside of two forts, one—that of San José—on the island, and the other—that of Santa Cruz—on an islet of the same name near the main. The panorama surrounding us is truly beautiful—approaching, in some respects, even that of Rio de Janeiro, though less wild and sublime in outline. The lofty and massive mountains on the main, jutting down to the water in bold promontories, indent the shore with little white-beached coves whose overhanging cliffs are crested with palm-trees and festooned with creepers. The white dwellings of the inhabitants, sprinkled along the shore, and the checkered cultivation of the uplands behind, combine in furnishing attractive imagery to the eye and associations of rural comfort and simplicity to the heart. The symmetrical outlines of the old fortresses on either side, and their moss-covered and grass-tufted parapets and ramparts, give an air of antiquity to some points of the scene, while the primitive canoe of the aborigines, under paddle or rude sail on the water, tells us significantly of a state of semi-civilization only. With the brightly gleaming sun of the morning, there was a freshness and elasticity of atmosphere, welcome and most exhilarating.

The present acting American consul of St. Catherine resides at Santa Cruz, the name of the anchorage at which we are. His name is Cathcart, formerly the master of an American whale-ship, but now long a resident of this part of Brazil, where he married a native of the country, and has a family of children, and extensive possessions in lands and slaves.

His residence is nearly abreast of us on the main, a mile or more distant. It is situated on an elevated platform above the beach, in a beautiful little cove, with a glen in the rear: the whole overhung by a wooded mountain. I availed myself of the first opportunity of visiting the shore, and accompanied Purser W—— and Lieut. R—— who went on duty. Mr. Cathcart was on the beach to receive us and conduct us to his house. With the exception of this structure—which is of stone, stuccoed, and whitewashed, and roofed with tile—every thing here, in general aspect, is so like the South Seas, that I felt as if suddenly transported there, and again amidst the scenes and places so familiar and so dear to me twenty years ago. The palm-tree, tossing its plumed branches in the wind, the broad leaves of the banana rustling in the breeze, the perfume of the orange blossoms and cape jessamine, the sugar cane and coffee plant, the cotton bush, the palma christi and guava—the light canoe upon the water, and the rude huts dotting the shore—all hurried me in imagination to the Marquesas, the Society and the Sandwich Islands.

As the Consul proposed returning to the ship with us our stay was but short. I, however, accomplished my purpose of a ramble for half an hour. This I found quite sufficient for the time. The hills descend so abruptly at all points to the water, and are so furrowed with ravines, that one can proceed scarcely a hundred rods in any direction along the shore, without making ascents and descents of such steepness, as soon to induce fatigue, and make a short walk go far in point of exercise.

Large ships cannot approach nearer to the port and city of Desterro than the anchorage of Santa Cruz; a distance of twelve miles. The day after our arrival, a party of officers made a trip to that place in one of the ship's boats; and on the 4th inst. I joined another, by a similar conveyance. The morning was brilliant, with a cool and bracing air. There was no wind, but with ten stout and willing oarsmen we made good progress, though the tide, for a portion of the distance, was against us. Two beautiful wooded islets lie midway in the straits, or bay, as the water—twelve miles in length and from three to five in width—appears here to be. The largest of these has a battery planted on the north end, the site of which is scarped from the solid rock, about half the height from the water line to the summit of the islet. With the exception of this battery, and two or three buildings connected with it, the whole is one mass of foliage interspersed with boulders of granite. We rowed closely along its western side, and were charmed with the freshness of the verdure and the variety and richness of its growth; especially in the drapery and festooning of parasites and creepers. As we approached our destination we fancied a striking resemblance, in the formation and general aspect of the western side on the mainland, to the section of the Hudson lying between Tarrytown and the entrance to the Highlands. This led to a comparison of the scenery of the straits in general with that of the Hudson. Beautiful indeed as this St.

Catherine is, all who had seen both, admitted a close rivalry at least on the part of the other.

A promontory of the island projecting far eastward into the straits, cuts off the view of the town from the north—excepting a church tower or two over the land—and gives to the water the appearance of being land-locked. It is not till sweeping through a narrow channel past the bluff point, you find yourself in a horse-shoe bay,—a half mile perhaps in diameter, with the city encircling its sandy beach.

The view of the town is striking, as, on doubling the point, it opens thus abruptly to the sight. It contains eight thousand inhabitants. It is prettily situated on the widely curving shore, and, facing the straits southward, is flanked on the east by lofty, verdant, and overhanging hills. A double-towered church, rising from the centre of the city, and a spacious snow-white hospital, crowning a terrace on the eastern side, are the most conspicuous of the public buildings.

A small platform of plank on piles, forms the landing for the boats of the shipping; but the canoes of the country are generally run upon the beach. There was a cleanliness about this, and in the market-place adjoining, truly welcome in Brazil, and prepared us to be most pleasantly impressed with the general aspect of a spacious, unenclosed square—like the green, or common of a New England village—upon which we immediately entered. This lies close by the water and in the middle of the town. The principal church or cathedral, whose towers we had seen over the land, ornaments it on the north side. It stands upon a terrace platform, having circular enclosures on either side, filled with plants and shrubbery, and overtopped by two or three graceful palms, and an Australian pine. On the west side near this, is the palace or Governmental House, occupied by the President of the province; the dwellings of two or three wealthy citizens; and a hotel near the water. From the balconies of the last, the party, who had preceded us the day before, were beckoning to us a welcome. The establishment is in charge of an American from New

England, married to a native of the place. It is more homelike in general appearance and better kept than any public-house we have seen in South America, excepting the Hotel de Provence in Buenos Ayres.

As it was my purpose to return to the Congress the same evening, there was little time to search for objects of special interest, if indeed there were such; and I contented myself with a walk through and around the place. The streets are laid out with regularity, but are ungraded and pass over hill and through hollow, according to the original surface of the ground. The buildings stand upon them at irregular distances from each other; and many having gardens and yards about them, the whole has a village-like aspect, not indicative of the amount of population embraced within the boundaries of the town. The people seem kind and well disposed; are simple in their habits and courteous in manners. Though my dress furnished no badge of naval service, or distinctive mark of my profession, yet, recognized as a stranger, I was every where saluted as such with the greatest deference and respect. I had been told that a new cemetery, situated on a hill on the western side of the bay, commanded a fine general view of the city and surrounding country. Under the impression that I had reached this, I passed through a fine gateway, and by a flight of steps to a terrace walk, but at once perceived that I was in the grounds of a private residence, and was retreating to the road again, when invited by some attendants near to enter and stroll over the place at my pleasure. This I did. It was tastefully laid out in lawns and flower gardens, and abounded in fruit. On expressing thanks to the Portuguese gardener when taking leave, he added to my obligation by presenting a choice bouquet, with an offer of oranges and other fruit *ad libitum:* adding, that the signor, his master, would have been happy to receive me had he been at home, and would be pleased at any time with a visit from me.

The day was exceedingly fine, and my ramble of an hour and more in the suburbs, over smooth paths and through hedge-shaded and flower-scented lanes, was most grateful after the dreary monotony of the scenery in the Plata and the tedium of long confinement on board a ship.

The females of Desterro are celebrated for their skill in the manufacture of artificial flowers from feathers, beetle wings, fish scales, and sea shells; and an arrival of strangers in the place causes the doors, and halls, and rooms of the hotel to be thronged with negroes and negresses, bearing tray-loads and boxes of these articles for sale. Many of them are tasteful and ornamental; especially those formed from the polished wings of the beetle. Those of fish-scales wrought into necklaces, armlets, wreaths and bouquets are also pretty; and, were the material not known, would appear costly. The first of these I ever saw were worn by a bride at Montevideo; the effect by candle-light was much that of a set of pearls, which I at first supposed the ornaments to be. A coarse but serviceable thread lace, is also a manufacture of the place. The chief article of commerce is coffee, that of St. Catherine being of superior quality.

At 3 o'clock we sat down to a profusely spread table d'hôte, one of the most tempting public boards I have seen since leaving the United States, consisting of a variety of fish, oysters, lobster, different kinds of meats, chickens, turkey and birds, cooked and served in American style. The bread was excellent, and upon it alone, with the delicious fresh butter from the German settlement of San Pedro d'Alcantara, twenty miles distant in the mountains on the main, I could have made a most satisfactory repast. The interest of the feast was enhanced by some intelligence communicated in regard to the chief attendants on the table: the head waitress was no less a personage than a Princess Royal of Cabinda, eldest daughter of the monarch of that style, and niece of "King John," chief of the Kroomen. She is a fine intelligent-looking woman of thirty years, whose mien and general bearing were by no means unbecoming the rank she held in her native land. Another of the servants was a male slave of the same age, full of activity and spirit, and seemingly very cheerful and happy. By industry and economy, and the gratuities he has received, for civility and fidelity in his situation, he has laid up the amount of his purchase-money, with the exception of a small sum. He expects soon to be free; and, having caught a spirit of adventure and enterprise from the many of our compatriots, who of late years have touched at St. Catherine's for refreshment on their way to California, designs pushing his fortunes in that golden region—an example of adventure, in purpose at least, almost without parallel, I am told, among the Brazilians of Portuguese blood. While the whole world has been excited to enterprise by the modern discoveries of gold, not a vessel, I learn, has been fitted out from Brazil in quest of fortune in this way, and scarcely a Brazilian tempted to join the thousands who have touched here and at Rio on their way to California.

The next day I joined Commodore McKeever and his secretary in a stroll on shore at Santa Cruz. Captain Cathcart met us on the beach, and, becoming our cicerone, first led us up a romantic little glen in the rear of his dwelling, by a well kept pathway overshaded with orange trees and palms, and bordered by coffee-plants and bananas. It followed the course of a murmuring and babbling mountain stream, which fretted its way over a bed of rocks, and beneath and around massive boulders of granite. The pathway itself was sufficiently attractive to have induced us to take the walk, but there was, as we found, a special object for pursuing it. It leads to the graves of two sisters of the ages of fifteen and seventeen, daughters of Major Gaines, Governor of Oregon, who died here a year ago on their way to that territory, after a few days' illness with yellow fever, contracted during a brief stay at Rio. Their sudden death, within a day of each other, in the opening bloom of youth, and their burial by the wayside, as it were, in a strange and undesired land, with the many affecting incidents related to us connected with the event, threw a touching interest around the spot, and caused us to linger with deep sympathy near their graves. They lie side by side within a small, picketed enclosure, where the rose and willow and other appropriate growth, planted by the hand of the Consul, are already spreading in tropical luxuriance. They are said to have been intelligent and accomplished, and full of the buoyancy and hope of young life. The bereavement under the circumstances must have been desolating to the parents, and their burial on these strange shores a most affective trial.

After the examination of a mandioca and coffee plantation, and of a fruit yard, we strolled over a spur of the mountain to an adjoining cove in which Captain Cathcart formerly resided, and which is still his possession. His former dwelling is converted into a school-house for his own children and those of two or three of his neighbors. The tutor, a young Brazilian, is employed by the Consul at his individual expense. The books and school apparatus were most primitive, and limited to the merest elements of instruction; still, the scene presented by the assembled group of scholars and their young teacher, had more of promise in it for the future, than any thing before met in this region.

I spent yesterday morning in going over the same ground with Captain McIntosh, who had not previously been on shore. We extended our walk across two or three additional ridges of the hills, which feather down from the mountains to the water, and break up the shore, by their projecting points, into numerous little coves encircled by interval lands and bright glades. In these chiefly are nestled the humble cottages of the poor, in single dwellings or in hamlets of three and four. The views from the side-hills above are varied and beautiful, and ever bring with them to me strong associations of the South Seas.

In the afternoon, accompanied by Dr. C—— and one or two others, I took a walk northward from the consulate, first across a natural meadow running inland a half-mile from the beach, and afterwards, by a mule-path, over a steep and thickly-wooded hill of the primitive growth—the whole mountain of which this is a spur, densely covered with wood, presenting in many points masses of foliage of great richness and beauty. Our walk terminated at a clearing, where preparations were making for the erection of a shanty of small timber, wattled at the sides and ends, preparatory to being filled in with clay. The scene reminded me of parts of Otsego near Cooperstown in my boyhood, where the felling, and logging, and burning of trees by the first settlers were in progress. The timber here, however, is by no means so tall and heavy as the white pine and old hemlock of that region, and appears to be exclusively of hard wood. We saw, at too great a distance to admit of examination, two flowering trees with blossoms of most brilliant hues; and were afterwards shown at the consulate a branch of an azalia, loaded with flowers of the purest white variegated with bright cherry color.

I must not omit to mention the very unexpected recognition of each other, by Captain Cathcart and myself yesterday. After taking leave of him the evening before, I said to Dr. C——, "The oftener I see the Consul, the more I am persuaded I have met him before: it must have been at the Sandwich Islands." A similar impression it seems was on his mind; and he remarked to a party of officers, as the boat in which I was, shoved off, "I am sure I have known Mr. S—— somewhere; but I have not been out of Brazil for twenty years—it must have been when I was whaling." To this, one replied, "it may have been at the Sandwich Islands, when Mr. S—— was a missionary there." "A missionary! is it possible that this Mr. S—— is the same: now, I know all about him. I remember him well; the first time I was on shore he invited me to church, and though I was an entire stranger to him, only a boat-steerer, he took me afterwards to dine with him and his lady." This being repeated to me, gave identity to my own reminiscence, and led to a very cordial greeting the next morning as old friends.

My last walk, in this short visit of a week, was taken this afternoon, in company with Commodore McKeever and Dr. C——. It was on the island. We landed at one end of a long curving beach, beneath the rocky bluff which is surmounted by the dilapidated fortress of San José, now dismantled and abandoned. After enjoying the view from its parapets, we followed a path leading up the ridge of the hill, till we gained a lofty point of rock, commanding a wide stretch of country to the eastward not in view from the ship. A part of this, embracing a circuit of many miles, was level. It appeared to be well fitted for the culture of rice, much of which is grown in St. Catherine, but apparently is unredeemed; a vast jungle in a state of nature, without indication of an inhabitant. The evening was very fine, and the air so exhilarating, that we skipped and jumped from rock to rock, amidst bush and bramble, with a freedom we would not have ventured had we known what we afterwards learnt, that the spot is noted for the venomous reptiles with which it abounds. Of these we saw none, however, and indulged in our gymnastics without fear. Indeed, I have not seen a living serpent or reptile of any kind since I have been in Brazil: not a scorpion, and but one centipede, and that in a ship-chandler's in Rio de Janeiro. On our return we passed, near the beach, grove after grove of orange trees, so laden with fruit that the ground beneath was covered, as in an apple-orchard at home, after the trees have been shaken in the gathering season.

CHAPTER XIX.

RIO DE JANEIRO.

June 20th.—On entering this port on the 16th inst., we all felt anew the exciting influence of its wild and magnificent scenery, and were constrained again to pronounce it unrivalled, by any thing seen by us in any part of the world.

The last report of the health of the place which had reached us at Montevideo, was favorable. The yellow fever, after having prevailed a second season as an epidemic, was said to have disappeared. Our apprehensions on this point were excited for a time, however, as we came in, by perceiving the man-of-war anchorage to be entirely deserted. In place of three or four different squadrons, English, French, Brazilian, Portuguese and American, riding at their moorings, like a flock of water-fowl, not a solitary ship was discoverable: nor was there a sign of movement of any kind, on the whole bay. This we thought ominous of bad news, but happily without just cause. The first boat from the shore, assured us of the good health of the port. Whatever malaria may exist has lost its malignancy, and exhibits itself only in cases of imprudence and special exposure, in the milder types of intermittent fever. It is the winter season, or period at which the sun has reached its farthest remove in this latitude, and all nature is in double freshness and brilliancy. The coloring of the skies in the mornings and evenings is beautiful: this is especially the case after sunset, when at times a golden and vermilion glory has filled the west with a splendor I do not recollect to have seen surpassed. The effect of this upon the pinnacled rocks and precipices of the mountains—brought into bold relief by the shades of the hour—and upon the promontories and islets of the bay, the church and convent towers, and the leading architecture of the city, is gorgeous. This was particularly the case, an evening or two ago, while Dr. C—— and I were enjoying a stroll over Gloria Hill. Our progress was arrested by it: and after standing for some time in silent admiration of the picture presented, from the elevated terraces in front of the church, we joined in the exclamation, "no words in our own or any other language can describe such a scene: painting itself could do no justice to it!"

The temperature now, even at mid-day, is not too hot for exercise, the mean height of the thermometer being 73° Fahrenheit. The weather resembles that of the finest in June at home; the evenings and nights, however, are cooler. This is the general character of the weather from March to September; and nothing in climate can be finer. During the rest of the year, the heat, with the mercury at mid-day at 90°, is oppressive and debilitating.

We have renewed our acquaintance pleasantly with Don Juan and Doña M——, and are disposed to regard the simplicity of mind and heart, evidenced by them, the kindness of their manners, and the cordiality of their hospitality, as characteristic of the people of the country in general; and to believe that they would be manifested to all foreigners of respectability, as readily as to us, under circumstances to call them into exercise. Our friends of Praya Domingo, however, make no secret of the fact that our nationality is a strong recommendation to them. Both profess great admiration of the United States as a nation, not from what they have seen of its citizens—for we are the first and only Americans they have known—but from what they have heard and read of our history and condition, and the practical working of our institutions.

I have taken but one new walk: this was through the valley of the Larangeiras, in company with Captain McIntosh and Dr. C——. Much as I had often admired its general features, in passing through the open street of the Cateté, from which it branches westward to the mountains, the heat of the weather, and its distance from the ordinary landing, prevented a visit to it. It is a half mile, perhaps, in width at the entrance, but soon becomes only a narrow glen, terminating at the end of a couple or more miles, beneath the steep sides of the overhanging mountain. A fine carriage road winds through it, crossing and recrossing repeatedly a sparkling mountain stream, which brawls and babbles and murmurs, from side to side. It is charming throughout: so quiet and secluded, so embowered and rural, so fresh in atmosphere and luxuriant in growth, and so varied in the architecture of its dwellings, from the ornamented villa and sculptured palace, to the simplest and most humble of cottages. The orange and coffee tree, the banana and other broad-leaved vegetation of the tropics, cluster thickly around; and are overshadowed by the loftier growth of the magnificent mango, the towering palm, the feathery foliage of the tamarind and acacia, and here and there that of the thorny cotton-tree or Bombax, with its trunk and limbs well guarded by the defences which give to it a descriptive name.

Roses and jessamines, and brilliantly flowering creepers; the gay hybiscus, the thick-set bloom of the purple bignonia, and the gorgeous glare of the poinsetta, meet the eye at every turn, and fill the air with sweet perfumes. In contrast with our imprisonment on board ship at Montevideo, it was a luxury scarcely appreciable by others, to stroll amidst such imagery; with an occasional glimpse, through an open gateway or the ornamental railings of an enclosure, of the fountains and grottoes, the alcoves and bowers, the gravelled walks and tesselated pavements, the busts, the statues and statuettes, which embellish the grounds of those "rich in this world's goods."

Near the head of the valley, a winding pathway on one side

leads up the acclivity by steep ascent, to the line of the aqueduct, fifteen hundred feet above the level below. One section of this is peculiarly beautiful. It overhangs the valley, and embowered overhead, reminded me forcibly and pleasantly in many of its features—with the exception of the tropical growth—of the gravelled terrace of the old road at Cooperstown, which leads to the "Mount Vison" of Cooper's Pioneers. In a secluded nook near by, is the residence of the British minister: an irregular cottage, buried in shade, and vocal with the murmurings of water-courses. After passing this, as we gained height after height, and looked down with bird's-eye view, the Larangeiras and its surroundings seemed, in the lights and shades of the hour, like a sketch in fairy land.

The fatality in the city, of the late epidemic, has led to the construction, recently, of great numbers of residences along the spurs and sides of the mountains. One of these is just finished, near the point at which we reached the aqueduct. The site is superb; and, while resting from the fatigue of the sharp ascent, we greatly enjoyed the magnificent prospect of both land and sea which it commands. From this point, the descent of five miles along the aqueduct to the city is so gradual, for the greater part of the way, as to be almost imperceptible. For two miles the pathway is a lofty terrace, cut in the face of the mountain for the course of the aqueduct, from which, beneath overhanging trees, you look up on one side, upon steep rocks and wild woods, and down on the other, as from the parapets of a lofty castle, upon a succession of views of cultivated and surprising beauty. Indeed, the whole walk seemed to me like that through a picture-gallery of magnificently drawn, and gorgeously colored landscapes. The aqueduct does not follow a straight line, but runs zigzag, at long, obtuse angles. The pathway is beside it, and in following its course, new and varied vistas, both before and behind, are constantly presented. The massive masonry, and finished workmanship of the time-marked, and moss-covered old structure, contrast strongly in their aspect of civilization, with the wildness of the overhanging cliffs and forests, while in many places, the gay coloring of the endless variety of lichens and orchidæ which cover it, gives to the surface the appearance of richly variegated marble.

Before we reached the city, the shades of the evening had gathered around us, as deeply as the moon near her second quarter would allow. Many of the objects around and above us, were thus brought in bold outline against the sky. This effect was particularly beautiful, where the palm or cocoa-nut tree spread its long and graceful plumage, in dark masses upon the light beyond.

The last striking picture which met the eye as we descended the hill of Santa Theresa, was that of a family, grouped in an arbor of roses and honeysuckle, canopied with clustering bignonia, on the angle of a wall twenty feet above our heads, silently enjoying in the twilight the last fannings of the sea-breeze, while from the towers of the convent close by, the vesper bell sent forth its silvery sounds in invitations to prayer.

June 26th.—It is to the Romish Church that we are here chiefly indebted for every thing in the way of spectacle. Two principal feast days have occurred within the week past: that of Corpus Christi on the 19th, and that of St. John the Baptist on the 24th inst. The fête of Corpus Christi was observed with great display. It was instituted by Urban IV., six hundred years ago, in honor of the then newly adopted doctrine of transubstantiation, and consequent adoration of the host. Its legendary origin is traced to Juliana, a nun of Liege, who, while looking at the full moon, saw a gap in its orb, and by peculiar revelation from heaven, learned that the moon represented the Christian Church, and the gap the want of a festival for the adoration of the body of Christ, in the consecrated wafer. This she was to begin to celebrate, and to announce to the world. The authorization of the festival by papal bull, was induced by the following miraculous incident. While a priest, who did not believe in the change of the bread into the body of Christ, was going through the ceremony of benediction, drops of blood fell upon his surplice, which, when he endeavored to conceal them in the folds of his garment, were formed into bloody images of the host. His scepticism was thus overcome; and the bull of Urban, authorizing the adoration, was published. This occurred in 1264, and the bloody surplice is still shown at Civita Vecchia as a relic!

In Rio de Janeiro, as in all papal countries, Corpus Christi is a chief festival in the year. Its celebration was commenced at the dawn of day, by a general peal of the bells from every church and convent tower, by the booming of cannon along the shores, and the hissing and crackling of rockets in the sky. Flags were every where unfurled; draperies of silk and satin, of gold and silver tissue, of damask and velvet of every hue, were displayed, from the windows and balconies of the houses in the principal streets; and the windows of the palace ornamented on the outside with rich hangings of crimson damask. High mass was performed in the imperial chapel at 11 o'clock. This was now opened for the first time, after having been for a year undergoing a thorough renovation, by regilding and new painting in fresco. The effect is rich and chaste. On either side of the nave, between the entrance and the transept, are the shrines of the apostolic saints, above which hang paintings of each, with the accustomed emblems of their individuality. "The Supper," by a master, ornaments the altar of a side chapel at one end of the transept, and a beautifully executed and classically draped effigy of St. Julian in wax, in a sarcophagus of glass, adorns the other. The altar-piece of the grand altar covers the entire end of the chapel within the chancel. The subject is the assumption of the Virgin. The royal family of Portugal—at the time of the immigration—in attitudes of adoration, occupy the foreground: the Queen mother, John VI. and his wife, Carlota of Spain, and Don Pedro I., then a lad, being the chief figures.

The imperial body-guard in state dresses, with halberds at rest, early formed in lines on either side of the nave from the entrance to the transept. The intervening space, newly carpeted, was in reserve for the ministers of state, the officers of the household, and other dignitaries of the Empire. A procession of these soon made its appearance from a vesting-room communicating with the palace, and opened in file along the nave for the passage of the bishop and his ecclesiastical attendants to the chancel, and of the Emperor, who followed them, to a canopied throne near the high altar. The Empress and her ladies had already entered the imperial tribune facing the throne. The bishop was in full prelatic dress, wearing his mitre and bearing the gilded crosier emblematic of his office. When the chapel was thus filled, the coup d'œil presented a brilliant scene in the masses of rich embroideries in gold; the jewelled decorations of the dignitaries of state; and the court dresses of the different classes of the aristocracy. These last were chiefly of velvet in rich hues, lined with white silk—purple, maroon, mazarine and sky blue, light and dark green, and here and there a suit of the same of plain black.

The orchestra was full, and embraced the best performers of the opera company, both vocal and instrumental. As the service proceeded, the varied attitudes and groupings in the chancel and at the altar, of the officiating priests

"Glaring in gems and gay in woven gold;"

the floating incense; the harmony of the duo, the trio, and the quartette; the touching strains of the solo; and the burst of the full chorus, could scarcely fail to impress the senses. And when added to this general effect, at the elevation of the host each halberdier, with battle-axe reversed, dropped on his bended knee; every courtier bowed his forehead to the ground; the bishop humbled himself at the steps of the altar, and the Emperor kneeled on the platform of his throne; the whole tableau was one most striking in its dramatic show. Externally all was a profoundness of adoration, which, directed spiritually to the Godhead, would have been irresistibly impressive; but addressed to a mere wafer, and to be regarded as gross idolatry, it was both painful to the mind and saddening to the heart.

Long before the termination of the mass, a procession was marshalled in front of the chapel in the palace-square, awaiting the addition from the church of the ecclesiastics and the court, before moving through some of the principal streets. The leading group was unique; and apparently the most attractive part to the surrounding crowds. It consisted of a colossal effigy of St. George, in knightly armor, mounted upon a splendidly caparisoned charger from the Emperor's stud, led by a groom in oriental dress. An armor-bearer in black mail, and other attendants in characteristic costume, formed the suite; while a dozen led horses in housings of green cloth, stiff with the imperial arms in massive silver, completed the cortège of the pasteboard saint All else in the show was purely ecclesiastic, with a great display of the varied costumes and emblematic devices of the Romish Church. At the end of the religious service, the dignitaries, both of Church and State, fell into the line, and were followed by the host, borne by the bishop beneath a fringed and tasselled canopy of cloth of gold, one of the gilt supporters of which was held by the Emperor with uncovered head.

Don Pedro, wherever seen, bears inspection well; and carries with him as much of the impress of his station as any monarch I have seen.

There was no public procession on St. John's day, but its approach was heralded by a great setting off of rockets and other fireworks the night previous, and the glare of bonfires in different parts of the city. These were seen with fine effect from the ship; especially the rockets, with the dark mountains for a background. The evening following was observed in a similar manner: altogether like the night of the fourth of July at home. At every respectable-looking house, fireworks of more or less elaborate workmanship were displayed; rockets of all descriptions were shooting in brilliant corruscations through the air; and illuminated balloons sent up, while colored lamps, thickly clustered upon the convents crowning the hills, flashed through the darkness like diadems of diamonds.

July 2d.—On a former visit at Rio, I gave you some account of the Foundling Hospital and Female Orphan Asylum, in connection with the marriage of an éleve of the last. This is the second of July, the fête day of St. Elizabeth—that on which the asylum is open to visitors, and on which, usually, the marriages of such of the inmates as are under engagement take place. The Emperor and Empress were among the visitors today, and sanctioned by their presence the marriage of four couples in the chapel. The anniversary had been fixed upon, for throwing open to public inspection a new building for the Hospital of the Misericordia, of which both the Foundling Hospital and Orphan Asylum are appendages. I improved the opportunity to pass through the wards of the sick. These were in the most perfect order and neatness. Every possible provision seemed to be made for the care and comfort of the inmates; and the whole establishment gave evidence of fulfilling the benevolence of its design.

The practical benevolence of the Romish Church is exhibited in no form more general and commendable, than in the care which is taken of the poor and the sick. Rio abounds in hospitals for these. Some are connected with convents or monasteries, and others are separate and independent institutions. They are founded and sustained by incorporated societies, corresponding in their general features with the voluntary organizations with us at home for philanthropic and charitable purposes, but here called brotherhoods. These are of various names; that of the Misericordia or "House of Mercy," is the largest and most wealthy, and owes its origin, nearly three centuries ago, to the piety and benevolence of the celebrated Jesuit, Anchieta. The hospital is situated on the bay beneath Castle Hill. Its doors are open at all hours, night and day, to the sick of both sexes, of all religions and of every country and color, without any form or condition of admittance: all receive gratuitously the ablest medical attendance and the best nursing and care. The numbers of its patients amount to thousands yearly, the proportion of deaths occurring being about one-fifth of the whole received.

The original building is old, and has been long insufficient in its dimensions and convenience, for the numerous applicants for relief. A new structure has been for ten years and more in progress on an adjoining site. A large section of this, two-thirds of the whole plan, is now completed, and was opened to the public for the first time to-day. The edifice is a noble structure. The façade on the street of the part finished being four hundred feet. It is four stories in height, and is surmounted, in the centre, by a finely proportioned and symmetrical dome. The whole presents the finest architectural feature of the city, in the approach from the sea. The interior throughout is palace-like. The plan is admirably arranged for ventilation and light, and embraces every modern improvement for the insurance of cleanliness and purity. The structure is quadrangular. The parts already finished enclose two spacious courts, beautifully laid out in walks intermingled with flower-gardens and shrubberies, as places of exercise for the convalescent. Each is ornamented with a fountain; when the building shall be completed, corresponding courts on the new part are to be added. The perspective through the long corridors and the lofty wards, which communicate with each other the whole length by folding-doors, is exceedingly fine: indeed, the whole structure is a credit to the civilization of the age, and is a splendid monument of the munificence and benevolence of the Brotherhood of Mercy.

The institution embraces a department for the insane. For the separate accommodation of such patients, another imperial-like structure is in progress and nearly completed, on the beautiful bay of Botafogo. It already attracts the eye of the stranger entering the port, more than any other object in the surrounding panorama. Of this the Emperor has been a principal and munificent patron.

The possessions and funded capital of the Misericordia are

very great. The dying bequests of the charitable, in money and in real estate, for the long period of centuries, with the advance of value in property, make it one of the most richly endowed institutions of the Empire, and insure perpetuity to its worthy and Christ-like charities. Membership is secured by the payment of an initiation fee and an annual subscription: this guarantees the right to a support in sickness and in poverty, and to the religious services of the church in burial. Members to the brotherhoods are received at any age, even that of the merest childhood. On one occasion, I witnessed the ceremonies of an initiation to the fraternity of the Carmelites. It took place with much ceremony in the church of the order. A very large number were received, and included boys from the ages of five and six years to full manhood. Assembled in the sacristy, each placed over his ordinary dress a cape or mantle of silk, the badge of the order on occasions of ceremony, and each receiving from the appointed officers a consecrated amulet, a girdle of patent leather, and a rosary, walked in procession to the grand altar of the church. The whole building was in high decoration, with a superb display of gold and silver plate on the altar, and of reading desks of solid silver in the chancel. The dresses of the officiating priests, and the officers of the society, were new and rich; and the music of the first order. The ceremonies of the initiation consisted in verbal pledges on the part of the novitiates, anointings, crossings, sprinklings with holy water, and perfuming with incense, and were followed with showers of rose-leaves scattered widely from silver salvers, over the newly received.

July 22d.—The principal incident of the last few days has been a wedding, on the 20th, in the family of Mr. R——, the bride being Miss R——, his daughter. The marriage took place at the residence of Mr M——, the maternal grandfather of the lady, who holds a chief place among the merchant princes of Rio. It is situated seven or eight miles westward from the city, beyond the valley of Engenho Velho, beneath the mountains of Tejuca. Our commander-in-chief, to a seat with whom I had been invited, is a man of great simplicity in his habits of life, and averse to any thing like display in his movements. The appearance, therefore, of a showy equipage with four horses—as the carriage which he had directed to be in waiting at the landing—took him quite by surprise, and led to an order immediately for the dismissal of two of the animals; but to this the coachman objected so strongly, with the assurance from his master that the four would be found necessary before reaching our destination, and that no one ever drove to Mr. M——'s with a single pair, that the Commodore was obliged to submit. So, ordering his valet, who happened to be in attendance, to mount to his place—that there might be some keeping in the turn-out—we were off with a whirl, four-in-hand.

The drive, for the greater part of the way, was the same we had made in our visits to the country-seat of Mr. R——. While yet a couple of miles from our destination, we had full proof of the desirableness at least, of having four horses to the carriage. Though there has scarcely been any rain for a fortnight past, the road through the flat valley, in a soil of stiff clay, became so heavy that it was difficult for the four to save us from being fixed in the mire, in which the wheels at times were sunk to the hubs. In due time, however, we reached the stately gateway, by which the broad domain of Mr. M—— is entered. This is a semicircular structure of white marble, with massive gates and railing of cast iron in rich patterns: erected at a cost of more than seven thousand dollars. The drive from this to the house is a broad avenue of closely planted mango trees. The mango is one of the noblest of what may be called the civilized trees of the country, in contradistinction to the natives of the forest. In its loftiness, roundness of top, wide-spread limbs, and thickset foliage of deep green, it resembles the black ash of the Middle States, more than any tree familiar to you, which occurs to my recollection at the moment: the general outline is perhaps more spreading. It is the season of its blossoms, though these are not yet in full display. The flowers come out in spikes, like those of the horse chestnut, and rise thickly over the whole tree. Their color, while now yet in bud, varies from a light pea-green to a brownish red, the general effect being like that of the common chestnut when in bloom; when fully blown, however, the flowers are white. These, when close at hand, contrast beautifully with the dark green of the leaf; but, at a distance, present an almost indistinguishable mass of whiteness.

The want of neatness and good keeping in the grounds of Brazilian country-houses is observable, even in those of Mr. M——, though his residence is quite a palace, and his wealth estimated by millions. The mansion is of stone, massively built, and about eighty feet square. The general height is two stories, but a central section, having an ornamented pediment and entablature, rises to three. It is in the Italian style, with balustrades around the flat roof surmounted by marble vases filled with aloes. The façade in extent and in general effect reminds me of the President's house at Washington. A spacious portico with tesselated pavements, leads into a lofty hall, from which a staircase with a double flight of steps conducts to the drawing-rooms, on the second floor. The principal rooms of the ground floor are a dining-hall, ball-room, music-room, and chapel. The views are beautiful. That in front commands the entire plain, filled with the country-houses of the rich and their surroundings, the spires and towers of Rio, and the mountains across the bay, in the distance; and that in the rear, a great variety of wild mountain scenery, in primitive luxuriance and solitude, close at hand.

We were among the first to arrive, but were quickly followed by a large company, among whom were many richly attired ladies. Rich and fashionable dress is here peculiarly a passion with the sex; and I was told by a gentleman present, when speaking on the subject, that a lady would not think of moving in general society in Rio, without an allowance for the toilette of at least two thousand dollars a year.

The groom being an Englishman, the marriage as a civil contract had taken place early in the day, at the British Consulate:

he being a Protestant also, while the bride is a Roman Catholic, the religious rites were twofold—Romish and Protestant Episcopal. Contrary to the usage at home, the bridal party joined the general company in the drawing-rooms while the guests were assembling. When all expected had arrived, Mr. M——, the grandfather, who in the Romish ceremony was to give away the bride, approached, and taking her by the hand, led the long procession to the private chapel below. The service was performed by the priest of the Parish, who is also the family chaplain, in the sacerdotal robes of his grade.

It was in the Portuguese language, and much abreviated, we were told, from the fact that one of the parties was a Protestant. Immediately after the benediction, when the parties had been proclaimed man and wife, female servants in the rear of the chapel scattered from baskets of silver, over the bride and her party, as she turned from the altar to meet the embraces of her friends, handfuls of freshly gathered rose-leaves and orange-blossoms. The effect, as fluttering lightly through the air they fell in thick showers on the group and the whole company, was poetic and pretty.

The Protestant ceremony, conducted by the Rev. Mr. Graham, Rector of the British church in the city, took place immediately afterwards in the principal drawing-room, a magnificent apartment, with hangings and furniture of crimson damask and decorations of gold. The closing scene here, in place of the shower of rose-leaves and orange-flowers of the chapel, was the tableau presented by the bride kneeling on a rich footstool in the midst of her bridesmaids, receiving with bowed head and tearful eyes the touching blessing with which the Episcopal rite ends.

The marriage-feast, of sixty covers, was served in the ball-room, a lofty hall with decorations in white and gold. The entertainment, in the display of china, glass, and plate, and of flowers in vases of Sèvres manufacture; in ornamental confectionery, and the profusion of luxurious viands, was all that wealth in its liberality and taste in its artistic exercise could command.

On shipboard, two incidents of more than commonplace interest have occurred since my last date. One is the departure for the United States of Lieut. R—— in ill health from the effects of the climate. In this, the wardroom mess and the ship sustain a great loss. He is one of the most interesting young men I have known in the service. Firm in principle, cultivated in mind, clear in judgment, prudent in action, and accomplished in his profession, he exhibits great symmetry of character as an officer, while the frankness and polish of his manners, and the warmth of his affections, make him attractive as a companion and dear as a friend.

My last interview with him before he left the ship was most gratifying to me, from the assurance it gave, that to the many other attractions of his character there would be added, immediately on his arrival home, that of openly avowed membership with the Church of Christ. Nothing during our cruise has imparted to me such unfeigned satisfaction : indeed the result of our conversation on this subject, was a joy I cannot well express.

The other incident was of a painfully different nature : one of those outbreaks, which, so long as strong drink holds its sway over so many seamen, no precaution or vigilance can, at all times, effectually guard against on board a man-of-war. For a long time the Congress has been under the most favorable auspices in regard to discipline and general good conduct. Contentment, cheerfulness, and ready obedience, seemed to be the prevailing feelings of the crew. But, on the evening of the 18th inst., just as the last guests of a party—similar to that of which I gave an account in October, had left the ship, it became known that liquor in large quantities had been smuggled on board, and that many of the men were intoxicated. Sixty or seventy were soon beyond all self-control, and, maddened by rum, were most insolent and insubordinate to the officers who attempted to restrain them. In the darkness of the deck, it was difficult to distinguish the ringleaders ; and after these were secured in double irons, they made the rest of the night hideous, by their boisterous profanity and drunken ribaldry.

The investigation of the matter showed that the 'dinkey,' a small boat used as a tender by the messenger-boys and servants in communicating with the shore, had inadvertently been left afloat astern, in place of being hoisted from the water as usual, before dark. One or two of the crew made their way to this, and succeeded in bringing off from the shore, liquor sufficient to have intoxicated the whole ship's company. It was freely offered to all, but sixty or seventy only would partake of it; a fact speaking well for the mass in contradistinction to the few. Still, such an outbreak, though limited to a small number, and those the veriest vagabonds on board, is disheartening to those who believe in the practicability of maintaining the discipline and good order of a ship, by a rule of kindness.

The consequence of this conduct was a kind of quarantine of the ship the next day; no boats were allowed to leave for the shore, and both officers and men remained on board. It was Saturday, and I had not sufficiently recovered from the shock before the Sabbath, to throw off a despondency in regard to any high results from the preaching of the Gospel to such hearers, or to overcome a feeling that I was speaking but to the wind. There is never a want, however, of the listening ear; and I felt reproved for my unbelief by the first chapter of the Bible read at the service, in which occurs the declaration:

"As the rain cometh down, and the snow from heaven,
And returneth not thither,
But watereth the earth,
And maketh it bring forth and bud,
That it may give seed to the sower, and bread to the eater;
So shall my word be that goeth forth out of my mouth:
It shall not return unto me void,
But it shall accomplish that which I please,
And it shall prosper in the thing whereunto I send it.
Instead of the thorn—shall come up the fir tree,
And instead of the brier—shall come up the myrtle tree.
And it shall be to the Lord for a name,
For an everlasting sign, that shall not be cut off."

I was the more impressed with this reproof to my despondency, on returning to my room, by accidentally falling upon a paraphrase of the same truth, in the following verses:

"Ye who think the Truth ye sow
Lost beneath the winter's snow,
Doubt not Time's unerring law
Yet shall bring the genial thaw.
God in nature ye can trust:
Is the God of grace less just?

Workers on the barren soil,
Yours may seem a thankless toil;
Sick at heart with hope deferred,
Listen to the cheering word:
"Now the faithful sower grieves—
Soon he'll bind his golden sheaves."

If the Almighty have decreed—
Man may labor, yet the seed
Never in his life shall grow,
Shall the sower cease to sow?
The fairest fruit may yet be borne
On the resurrection morn!"

CHAPTER XX.

MONTEVIDEO.

September 30th.—New aspects in the political affairs of the La Plata, led to the return of the Congress to this place, early last month. Previous to our departure from Rio de Janeiro, the U. S. steamer Susquehanna, bearing the flag of Commodore Aulick, of the East Indian squadron, arrived there, bringing as passengers, the Hon. Mr. Schenck, chargé d'affaires at the court of Brazil, and the Hon. Mr. Pendleton, commissioned with the same office to the Argentine Confederation. This last gentleman came to Montevideo in the Congress, on his way to Buenos Ayres.

The French Government not having sanctioned the articles of pacification, agreed upon by Admiral Le Predour and General Oribe, a year and more ago, the armistice between the belligerent parties on shore is terminated. Hostilities are again commenced by the interchange of occasional shots between the outposts, and now and then a slight skirmish, in which a few persons on both sides are wounded, and sometimes one or two killed.

The change would be comparatively of little importance, as to the promise of any speedy issue, were it not for simultaneous movements connected with it, on the part of Brazil on the one side, and two of the principal States of the Argentine Confederacy —those of Entre-Rios and Corrientes—on the other. By reference to an atlas, it will be perceived that the chief rivers, whose confluent waters form the Rio de la Plata—the Uruguay, the Parana, and the Paraguay, corresponding in their extent and their importance to the broad valleys through which they flow with the Ohio, the Missouri, and the Mississippi of the Northern Continent—have their rise in Brazil, and, in their course, border her territories for long distances. The free navigation of these is essential to her interests. One chief object in the policy of Rosas, however, has been to keep them closed to all foreign commerce, that the trade of the confederacy might centre exclusively in Buenos Ayres; and thus to enrich and aggrandize her, at the sacrifice of the interest both of Brazil and of the sister republics of the confederation. All negotiation on the part of the court of Brazil, to secure free access to the interior of the Empire by the tributaries of the Plata, having proved abortive, that government has determined to try the effect of arms. General Urquiza, the President of the States of Entre-Rios and Corrientes, long the principal coadjutor of Rosas, and the most successful and distinguished of his soldiers, weary of his tyranny, and opposed to his narrow-minded and selfish policy, has entered into a compact with Brazil to aid in the accomplishment of her purpose. The first object to be attained is the overthrow of Oribe, and the consequent relief of Montevideo from siege; and thus to lay the basis for a joint attack on Buenos Ayres. Urquiza, with a force of fifteen or twenty thousand Entre-Rians and Corrientans, is approaching in one direction; and the Baron Caxias, having an equal force of Brazilian infantry and artillery, in another: while a squadron, consisting of a frigate, two sloops of war and three steamers, under the command of Admiral Grenfell, has arrived from Rio, and is at anchor near us.

This determination of Urquiza, as the governor of two of the principal Argentine States, and the public measure by which it was avowed, have led to a striking proof of the mendacity, by which it is charged that Rosas has hitherto sustained his despotic sway. It is said, and with no little show of truth, that his whole system of government—notwithstanding the boasted patriotism, disinterested and self-sacrificing toil in the public service, which the press and archives of the confederacy printed by his order and under his immediate personal control, attribute to him—is but a cunningly devised tissue of deception and falsity.

For years, it has been the custom of Rosas formally to tender to the representatives of the confederation, the resignation of his office as Minister for Foreign Affairs, pleading to be released from it, on the grounds of the great burden of the charge, his advancing age, broken constitution, and declining health. This is invariably followed by the most laudatory and fulsome panegyrics, from the leading members of the House, upon his character—the value of his past services, and the necessity of their continuance, and the unanimous resolution that he shall still fill the office: it being well known that not a member dare—even if he had the secret will—to move or second the acceptance of the proffered resignation. The Archivo Argentino, or Government Register, printed in English, and French, and Spanish, and sent widely over the civilized world, is filled with the record of these political farces. This year, however, Urquiza, as the President or Governor of Entre-Rios and Corrientes, promptly accepted the resignation; and by public proclamation, released Rosas from all further charge of the foreign relations of those States. The address of Rosas to the House of Representatives, in view of this defection, has just been issued. It is strikingly characteristic of the man, and is a curiosity, both as a literary production and a document of State. As such, I furnish it to you entire, though not responsible for the translation; that is by 'authority,' and is taken from the official print.

The first two lines of the motto it bears are the prescribed caption of every official paper, from the most important to the most trifling; and are stamped on the badges, hitherto universally worn by the Argentines. The third line is an addition just decreed. The terms "Unitarian" and "Federal," designate the original parties in the confederation; the first being applied to those who are in favor of a consolidated government, similar to that of the United States, and the last to those who advocate that of the compact at present existing. Under Rosas, the Unitarian party became outlawed and in effect exterminated.

LONG LIVE THE ARGENTINE CONFEDERATION!

DEATH TO THE RUTHLESS, LOATHSOME UNITARIANS!

DEATH TO THE INSANE TRAITOR, THE RUTHLESS UNITARIAN URQUIZA!

PALERMO DE SAN BENITO, Sept. 15th, 1851—

Year the 42d of Liberty, 36th of our Independence, and 22d of the Argentine Confederation—

To the Honorable House of Representatives—

MESSIEURS REPRESENTATIVES:—

To command the Republic during a long period of agitation and social disorder; to save the country from fratricidal war; to accompany it in the glorious defence of its liberties; and contribute to preserve it from the ambition of the destructive and treacherous band of ruthless unitarians, was the eminently honorable mission that the Argentine people imposed upon me, and which I gratefully accepted with the enthusiasm and love due to my country and to my fellow-citizens.

After a memorable epoch, in which was assigned to the Argentine Confederation the glory of consolidating its independence, overwhelming its enemies; and to the undersigned, the distinguished honor of presiding over it; after the Republic had suppressed internal anarchy and was in the enjoyment of peace, developing its elements of prosperity, I considered the moment had arrived to resign the supreme command, to which I had been exalted by the spontaneous, reiterated suffrage of my countrymen, —and I earnestly requested you to appoint another citizen as my successor.

You refused to admit my fervent prayer—the inhabitants of this province also opposed it with kind firmness, and exercising the right of petition, begged your honors to persist in not acceding to my repeated tenders of resignation; and the Provinces of the

Confederation, expressing their wishes through their Honorable Legislatures and Governments, likewise exacted, with generous interest, my continuation at the head of the national affairs, as the means of insuring the present happy condition of the Republic, and of preparing for it a glorious future.

Overpowered by such decision, and so much benevolence; oppressed by a deep-felt gratitude toward the Argentine Federals, yet destitute of words becomingly to express those feelings, I presented to your honors, to my fellow-citizens, and to the confederate provinces, the homage of my most ardent and profound acknowledgment—I recognized with veneration the immense debt which the magnanimous vote of the republic imposed upon me, but unwilling to sacrifice to grateful emotions the sacred interests of my country, I continued vehemently yet respectfully to demand from your honors and the confederate provinces a successor, who, unbiassed by the scruples arising from my republican views, could co-operate more efficaciously than myself, to the aggrandizement of our dearly beloved country.

The tranquillity which the Republic experienced, the union which prevailed throughout its provinces, the wisdom with which, ameliorating its institutions, it expanded the resources of its welfare, and the external peace which its loyal, upright and generous policy towards all nations foreshadowed, indicated to me that the moment had presented itself for resigning the command, without injury to the nation.

Animated by so cheering a conviction, I insisted in my fervid renunciation before your honors, and the confederate Provinces, believing that my prayer, the sincerity of my words, and the cogency of my reasons, would duly influence the minds of the Argentine people, and induce them to accede to my separation from the supreme authority.

But while I expected this, and the undisturbed state of the Republic warranted me to entertain such a hope; at this very moment, the insane traitor, the ruthless unitarian Urquiza, raised the standard of rebellion and anarchy. Aspiring to sever, with his degraded sword, the bonds that unite the people of Entre-Rios to the confederation, and to constitute himself the arbiter of the Argentines, he ignominiously sold himself to the Brazilian Government, that, persisting in its obstinate ambition, has invaded and attacked, with unprecedented treachery, the territory and the Independence of the Republics of the Plata.

In so solemn a crisis for the Argentine community, when its loyal sons, displaying, as at all times, their renowned valor, rise in arms to resist and chastise their enemies, avenging so many and such scandalous outrages; when they prepare themselves with sublime self-denial for the most honorable efforts, I have received a new declaration from the Confederate Provinces, that peremptorily demands my continuance in the supreme command, and of which you will be informed by the correspondence that I will have the honor of presenting.

And since the nation so demands it of me, in such critical moments for its tranquillity; since in the presence of violent foreign aggressions, and an unexampled rebellion, my compatriots request me to accompany them in the post I occupy, to defend our independence and national honor; since the Republic, exasperated by the audacious hostilities of the Brazilian Government, and the treason of the ruthless Unitarians, prepares to retaliate the war which they have precipitated; at so notable an epoch I cannot refuse, nor do I refuse, honorable Representatives, my continuance in the Government, provided your honors, my compatriots, and the Confederate Provinces consider that it may be useful and necessary to the national welfare.

Consistently with my principles, my obligations, and my reputation, I cheerfully defer to the call of the Republic in the actual circumstances, and thus continuing in the supreme command, I also will have the signal honor of accompanying my beloved federal compatriots, in their heroic resolution of vindicating the national independence and glory, attacked by the perfidious Brazilian Cabinet, by the ruthless, loathsome Unitarians, and by the despicable insane traitor, the ruthless unitarian Urquiza.

In accordance with this determination, I therefore present myself, in the same manner as the loyal Argentines, resolved to fulfil once more my reiterated pledge, of sacrificing all in defence of the order, the liberty, and the honor of the Confederation.

My fellow-citizens, who have always found me participating in their difficulties, will now find me the same, with sound and robust health, and always consistent with those principles. They will see that, if when the Republic enjoyed peace and tranquillity, I desired to withdraw from the supreme command, to continue my services in some other subaltern post, where I might have performed them to advantage, now that new enemies of the Confederation appear, and that the loathsome band of the ruthless Unitarians, headed by the insane traitor, ruthless unitarian Urquiza, dares to raise its bloody standard, here I am, ready at the call of the nation, and with energy equal to my duties, and to the hopes of the public, willing to contend in union with the virtuous Argentine Federals, till we have left triumphant and consolidated, the independence, the rights, the dignity, and the future fate of the nation.

This, Messrs. Representatives, is the resolution I have adopted in view of the present events and circumstances.

And desiring ere now to transmit it to your knowledge, I had the honor of announcing it verbally to the Honorable President, and to one of the deputy secretaries of your honorable Corporation, requesting the former, on reporting it to the Honorable Representatives, at the first session they might have, to reiterate to them my profound gratitude.

God preserve your honors for many years.

JUAN MANUEL DE ROSAS.

October 6th.—Affairs on shore are rapidly approaching a crisis. Oribe, who led his troops westward some days ago, to meet the advancing force of Urquiza, has been driven back into what has been so long his besieging camp; and, cut off both from the interior and the river, he is virtually the besieged instead of the besieger. Deserted already by some of his troops, who have joined the advancing enemy; limited in the supply of provisions for those who remain; and daily more and more closely encircled, he must speedily capitulate, or fall in an unequal conflict.

The external aspect of the region about the Mount is completely changed. Instead of the utter desertion which has hitherto marked it, without a sign of man or beast over its whole extent, it now exhibits every where the animation and activity of a bee-hive. A detachment of Urquiza's cavalry, in charge of vast herds of cattle for the subsistence of his army, has taken possession of the Mount; and their horses, tethered and grazing, are passing up and down its sides, from the beach to the little fortress on the summit, and run straying about in every direction. The intervening heights of the country, are crested with mounted videttes, almost within gun-shot of the encampment and batteries of Oribe, as if the force of which they are the advance guard was already in battle array; presenting, through a glass, picturesque and striking objects, as they stand with poised lances and fluttering pennons, in strong relief against the sky. It was confidently expected, from the general appearance of things, that an assault would take place last night; but it passed without any thing more than a random shot occasionally from a musket, and now and then the booming of a great gun.

During the long siege of nine years, a large town, numbering eight or ten thousand inhabitants, has grown up in the vicinity of the encampment of Oribe. It is called "Restoracion," in reference to the object of this chieftain—the restoration of himself to supreme power, or the restoration, as he may consider it, of peace and prosperity to the Republic. It is a port of entry, with an open roadstead, called the Buçeo, five miles east of Montevideo. The greatest consternation prevailed there at first, when Oribe, breaking up his encampment, marched forth to meet Urquiza, with orders for his whole force to follow: leaving Restoracion entirely unprotected. It was industriously rumored that the departure of his troops would be the signal for an attack by the soldiers of Montevideo, with liberty from their commanding officers of pillage and rapine. Representations of this were made to the various foreign squadrons here, and a vessel of war from each was despatched to the Buçeo, to afford protection to any of the inhabitants who might seek an asylum, by flying to them. The alarm, however, has in a great degree subsided, from the return of Oribe, and a proclamation by the Government of Montevideo, with orders under the severest penalties, against every act of aggression and violence by the soldiery in case of the occupation of the place by them.

The Mount being now, for the first time since our arrival in the Plata, free of access without an apprehension of risk or annoyance of any kind, Captain McIntosh gave Dr. C—— and me a row in his gig to visit it. It was a great treat to ramble freely over the hitherto forbidden ground, and from the summit to command, at a single glance, the topography of the whole country for miles, as if it were a map before us: all, too, robed in the fresh and bright green of the opening spring. The general surface of the region in view here, as indeed throughout the republic, is a rolling prairie. Covered now with vast herds of cattle and droves of horses, and the rude encampments of the liberating army, in bivouac here and there in the distance, it reminded me much of some of Catlin's pictures, illustrative of scenes and scenery in the Buffalo and Indian regions of the far West. Oribe's encampments and defences, with the town of Restoracion and its port, were in distinct view in the east, over and beyond Montevideo. There was less appearance of immediate hostilities, than on the day previous. An armistice of twenty-four hours for negotiation, had been agreed upon. The videttes and reconnoitring parties had been withdrawn, and the detachments of troops in sight were dismounted, and lounging about among their grazing horses and cattle. Some two or three hundred German troops, mercenaries in the employ of Brazil, who had arrived by water, were on the beach immediately beneath us, in entire readiness for marching—their baggage-carts and other appliances of war prepared for immediate movement. They are a fine-looking corps; young, healthful, and fresh, enlisted in Holstein with the expectation of remaining in the country as settlers. The day was bright and beautiful, and the excursion of an hour or two, exceedingly pleasant.

October 10th.—The pacification hoped for, has actually taken place, by the unconditional surrender of Oribe, with his entire force, amounting to some fifteen thousand men to Urquiza. This occurred on the 8th inst., and was officially proclaimed throughout the city the same evening. The ringing of all the bells of the place, the firing of cannon and musketry, the setting off of rockets and the glaring of bonfires, assured us on board ship of the reality. The next morning the whole city seemed but a floating mass of flags, thrown to the breeze from every pinnacle and housetop, exhibiting all the colors of the rainbow, in the devices of every civilized banner; English, French, and American, Austrian, Prussian and Sardinian, Peruvian and Chilian, Dutch, Montevidean and Brazilian. Captain McIntosh took me early on shore with him. A suspension of all business, and the general holiday of a week, had been proclaimed by the government; and the people both within the city and without, were half mad with joy. And well might they be, after nine years of non-intercourse—those within, pent up for that length of time in the narrow limits of their walls and fortified lines, and those without, cut off from all communication with the town. The consequence has been a general rush of men, women and children, from the town to the country, now in all the freshness and bright verdure of spring; while the outsiders, so long excluded, have hastened with like eagerness, if not in equal numbers, to the streets and squares of the city. The scene presented was one of great and sometimes touching excitement, in the meeting for the first time in years, of those bound to each other in the closest ties of relationship. Husbands and wives, parents and children, brothers and sisters, lovers and friends, who had been thus separated, rushed into each other's arms in the open streets. An American lady told me she could never have imagined such a spectacle; and could scarcely do any thing for the day, but stand in the balcony of her house, alternately in laughter and in tears, at the scenes, comic and tragic, taking place around her. The enjoyment of a pic-nic seemed the prevailing passion of the citizens. Whole families were met by us in numbers setting off on foot, with baskets of refreshments, attended, in some instances, by servants bearing side-saddles for the ladies; horses being procurable outside, not for the hire of a day only, but in full possession at a price of one or two dollars. Some of the riders, we were afterwards told, were placed in rather an awkward predicament, however, after having proceeded some distance on their new purchases, by having the animals reclaimed and seized by their true owners, the soldiers from whom they had been bought having stolen them.

It is a subject for devout thankfulness, that thus far this important change has taken place without an instance, so far as is known, of violence or outrage. Those, who, a week ago, were ready to cut each other's throats, are embracing as they meet, and rejoicing together, that for the time being at least, "the sword is turned into the ploughshare, and the spear into the pruning hook." There are, however, among those who have unconditionally capitulated, twenty or thirty officers who are trembling for their lives. One of these, who is particularly obnoxious to the Montevideans, as a deserter from their service to that of Oribe, reached the American consulate just as we entered. Partly in disguise, he had ridden at full speed through the streets, and dashing, without dismounting, through the open portal into the inner court, threw himself on the mercy of the consul for the protection of his life. He feared that to be recognized would be but to die by the hands of the first one of the citizens who could lay hold on him. He is a fine-looking fellow, and was splendidly mounted, but was in a tremor of agitation.

In the course of the morning, I took a stroll some distance beyond the city gates, and found abundant subjects for observation in the endless variety of costume, colors, and character exhibited by the outsiders—civilians and soldiers, men, women and children, who were thronging to the city in great numbers; all, of course, on horseback, for in this country even the beggars are mounted. In many instances, it is true, two persons rode the same horse; in some cases three; and in one even four—a man and his wife with each a child in their arms: the entire family, it is probable, thus seeking a glimpse of the city. The most amusing spectacle of the kind I noticed, was a cavalier quite dashingly equipped, with a goodly-sized live hog tied to the saddle behind him, in the manner of a valise in travelling. The head of the animal—quietly submissive to his destiny—hung down on one side, and the nether limbs on the other, while the equilibrium of the whole was preserved by a firm grasp of the captive's tail in the left hand of the rider!

CHAPTER XXI.

MONTEVIDEO.

October 18*th*.—Yesterday, in company with Lieut. T—— of the Congress, and Mr.Z——, Consul for the Hanseatic towns, I made a visit to Urquiza, the chieftain of the Plata, whose star is now so much in the ascendant. His head-quarters are at Pantanoso, where his troops are encamped three leagues westward from the city. By the raising of the siege, horses are once more to be obtained in Montevideo. Mr. Z—— was nobly mounted upon the fine animal, on which the officer from the outside, mentioned under the former date, dashed through the portal of the American consulate the first day of the pacification. Mr. Hamilton had succeeded in procuring a passport to Buenos Ayres for him; and, purchasing his charger, made a present of it to Mr. Z——, his son-in-law. Lieut. T—— and I were provided with animals at a livery stable, just opened, to which we walked to make our choice. The keeper, who, himself, acted as hostler and groom for us, is no less a personage than an authenticated Austrian baron, of an old family among the nobility of the empire; and who, reduced in fortune, is ashamed to beg, but not thus to occupy himself for an honest livelihood, in a foreign land. It was from him I now received my first lesson in the horsemanship of the country; being instructed to guide my Rosinante, not by pulling the rein of the bridle on the side I wished to turn

11*

him, as with us, but by keeping both reins of an equal length in the hand, and touching the neck of the animal with that opposite to the direction he is to go.

The weather was delightful. In the early morning the sun threatened to be hot; but afterwards a veil of gauze-like cloud, without shading too much the brilliancy of a day like June at home, prevented any discomfort from it. After clearing the line of the city walls, perceiving it to be low-water in the bay, we struck down from the ordinary road, to the hard sand of the beach, which sweeps in wide curvature in the direction of the Mount, and dashed off on a full gallop across it. Parties of native horsemen were scampering in both directions over the same ground, looking—with their ponchos and long hair streaming in the wind behind them—as wild and picturesque as so many Arabs of the desert.

At the end of a mile we turned up the bank into the highway. This is wide, level, hard and dry, with hedges of aloes and cacti on either side. There is scarcely a tree of any kind to be seen; but now and then a fruit tree, a row of trim poplars, or a clump of weeping willows just in full leaf, reminded us of home. This was especially the case with the willows, the first graceful wave of their fresh, long branches, setting me down at once beneath those at Riverside. The soil seemed to be of great richness, a black mould which bears every growth in exuberance. I never saw fig trees equal in height and spreading tops, to those passed in one enclosure. Evidences of the long civil war were every where seen in the ruins of houses, and in deserted grounds; but, occasionally, we came to a quinta or country-seat, still in good repair, whose massive gateways, tesselated courts, balustraded terraces, surmounted by vases filled with air-plants and gay flowers gave proof of the taste and elegance which once characterized the suburban residences of Montevideo.

We now came upon an open country, without hedge or enclosure of any kind. The whole surface was covered with rich verdure, brightly enamelled by ten thousand flowers of every hue, and fragrant with the perfumes of spring. As we caracoled gently along, or, again, following the custom of the land, dashed forward at full speed, groups of people, peasants and soldiers, on foot and on horseback, were passing and repassing; and not unfrequently clustered thickly around the dark and dirty entrances of the pulperias, or grog-shops, which here, as elsewhere where man is, are ever to be found—the whole presenting, in features and in form, in costume and in colors, a constant study for the sculptor and the painter.

The region of country around the bay—along the shores of which we still continued—is well watered; and we crossed two or three streams in the course of our ride. As we ascended from the bed of one of these to the general level, we came in view of another, along the gently rising banks of which, on either side, lay stretched in irregular detachments three or four thousand troops. This encampment, in all its appointments, had a most primitive and unscientific aspect. The tents, such as they were —very much of a gipsy character—did not appear sufficient for the shelter, in sleeping and in bad weather, of half the number of soldiers; and the whole equipage of the camp was as rude as that of so many Indians. The predominance of scarlet in the color of every thing appertaining to it, imparted, however, a gay and brilliant air to the whole. A park of artillery, planted on a gentle swell of ground, commanded the approaches, and had more the appearance of modern warfare than any thing else attracting the observation.

On inquiring for head-quarters, two or three tents were pointed out on a knoll, on the opposite side of the rivulet, quite separate from the general encampment. A company of lancers were clustered irregularly at no great distance in the rear of these—their long and effective-looking spears, with a scarlet pennon floating from the top of each, being staked in lines in front of them.

As we approached, we perceived the marquee of the commander-in-chief to be distinguished from the rest, by broad stripes of white and blue, and by the artistic manner in which it was pitched. Behind it stood an immense vehicle, more massive and ponderous in its structure than the heaviest omnibus ever seen at home—the travelling carriage of his excellency, evidently fitted for hard service, by such bracings with raw-hide ropes about the springs, whipple-trees and axles, and such bindings of green hide around the hubs and spokes and wheel-tires, as would create a sensation in a civilized country. Near by, stood a gigantic cart with wattled sides, and a roof fifteen or twenty feet in height: the baggage-wagon, doubtless, for the needful provender of the general-in-chief and suite.

When we drew up, we were approached by a noble-looking adjutant, tall and stalwart, with boots to his hips, a steel-scabbarded sword, which might have served for a Goliath, and spurs of massive silver, that—in want of marbled pavement or planked floor for the effect—caused the very ground beneath him to rattle. My companions, having made known their official character and our nationality, and the desire of paying our respects personally to the chieftain, we were politely requested to dismount, our horses delivered to the charge of the guard, and our cards taken, preparatory to an announcement. Immediately on the presentation of our names, we were conducted to the front of the tent and ushered into the presence of the general. He rose to receive us with courteous salutations, and a cordial shake of the hand. The tent was small, but exceedingly neat. Its poles were bamboo, that in the centre which raised the canvas to a peak, being surrounded by a square camp table, on which lay a round black hat with the scarlet band of the confederation, a pair of black kid gloves, a riding-whip, and a magnificent bouquet of fresh flowers—a propitiatory gift, probably, from some fair hand in the neighborhood. Three tent bedsteads—one on either side and one at the farther end—one or two camp stools, and a square of ingrain carpet on the grass, constituted the furniture.

We became seated on the bedsteads at the sides, while Urquiza took a position by the table in the centre. He was in a military dress coat of blue, the collar and cuffs being handsomely decorated with embroideries in gold of the oak leaf and acorn. A waistcoat of scarlet damask, pantaloons of blue with a red stripe down the seams, and well polished boots, completed his costume. He is of moderate height, but stout, broad-chested, and finely formed, and has a Spanish roundness of face and limb. He was smoothly shaved, and without the moustache usually worn here, both by military men, and by the people in general. In feature, he is decidedly handsome, with fine mouth and teeth, large, dark eyes full of vivacity, and a complexion clear and glowing with manly health, but bronzed by exposure.

His expression is open and frank—one that a physiognomist would trust for honesty and magnanimity; and his manners and address courteous and gentlemanly, without being courtier-like or artificial. I know not when I have been more favorably impressed on a first interview, with any one, either in public or private life. Personally, he is evidently one to be admired; and, if his character, morally and intellectually, is at all in harmony with his physical advantages, I can readily perceive how the popularity he has already won, in the part he is now acting, may run into enthusiasm. He must be nearly fifty years of age; but, were it not for the thinness of his hair on the top of the head, I should say he was not more than forty.

A favorite mastiff, a noble-looking animal, lay stretched at his ease on the carpet, and attracting our notice became the first subject of our conversation. He originally belonged to another officer; but, on meeting Urquiza, left his master and attached himself to him with a pertinacity which resisted every attempt to drive him away. He has constituted himself the especial guardian of his person, and has for years been his companion, night and day. Several remarkable anecdotes, of feats in the camp and on the battle-field, told of him, paved the way for a free and animated conversation on more important topics—embracing the present state of affairs in the Republics of the Plata—the results thus far, of Urquiza's own movements as a liberator, and purposes designed by him, yet unachieved. "It is time," he justly remarked, "that the contracted and narrow-minded policy, dictated by the selfish views of the rulers of the Plata, should be made to give way to measures more in unison with the spirit of the age; and that the wide rivers and rich plains of these magnificent countries, should be thrown open to the commerce, and be made free to the immigration of people from all nations."

The hope was expressed, that when he should reach Montevideo—where it was taken for granted he would make a public entry—he would visit the Congress; but, before the word Montevideo was well uttered, he hastily interrupted the sentence by exclaiming, "Montevideo!—No—no, I shall not go to Montevideo!" He, it seems, studiously avoids every appearance of courting popularity, and of making a display of himself unnecessarily; averring that the only object for which he comes into the country, is to free the Montevideans from the thraldom of the tyranny by which they have so long suffered. Having accomplished this, he says he has nothing further to ask or desire, except that they may be prosperous and happy, united and free. The early career of Urquiza as a partisan of Rosas, and as the victor over the Montevideans themselves, in the beginning of the invasion by the Argentines, is said to have been as bloodthirsty and cruel as that of any of his compeers, in the civil contentions of the States of the Plata. But great apparent humanity, as well as consummate policy, has thus far marked all his present measures and movements. In the beginning of his march against Oribe, he proclaimed the anxiety he felt to prevent all effusion of blood; that he came as a friend, not as a foe; that his mission was one of peace and of patriotism in a common cause. The consequence of this annunciation in advance, was a general gathering to his standard in his progress, and the desertion to him, at every opportunity, of whole detachments of the troops sent to oppose him. On expressing the surprise which we felt at being told by him, that the thousands of soldiers immediately around, and constituting his only guard, were exclusively those who, but a few days before, had laid down their arms to him, and, who till then were commissioned to cut his throat—he said—"We are all brothers now—one people and one blood: it only remains for us to free our common country from a common tyrant," referring of course to Rosas. The nearest detachment of the troops brought with him from Entre-Rios was quite two miles distant.

At the end of a half hour, we took leave, greatly interested in all we had seen and heard during the interview. As a rigid moralist, I am bound perhaps to qualify, in a degree, my admiration of this chieftain, from the knowledge I have gained of some of the particulars of his private history. An inquiry made by one of our party, led the General to say, that though he had no wife living he had a large family; and that the mother of some of his children, having recently died, he regarded himself as a widower. The truth is, he has never been married. It is by no means unusual for persons here to live long together without the marriage-tie, and often with entire fidelity to each other. It is to a relation of this kind he referred, and in which he had a numerous family born to him; but he admits the claims of paternity in a large number besides; and so justly, it is said, that the title of the novel, "A child of thirty-six fathers," may with a slight transposition, be applied with literal truthfulness to him, as "The father of thirty-six children"—the exact number, I am told, of his acknowledged offspring. So much for this chieftain for the present; we shall doubtless hear much of him, and perhaps meet him again, before taking a final leave of the Plata.

Oribe has been permitted, since the capitulation, to retire on parole to his country-seat, situated on the shore of the bay, in the neighborhood of his former encampment. Lieut T—— and I, as neutrals in the partisan conflicts of the country, felt some disposition to call upon him in his reverse of fortune; but the antipathies of Mr. Z——, arising from a knowledge of his history and character, and the long endurance of evil by the Montevideans at his hands, would not permit him to join us in a visit of the kind. As condolence under capitulation and overthrow would have been more difficult to present acceptably, than the felicitations we had just addressed to the fortunate rival, we did well, perhaps, to content ourselves with the view in the distance of the white walls of his dwelling, in the midst of extensive plantations of poplar and willow. If all that is said of his past acts of cruelty be true, he well merits the reverse he has suffered, and the contempt into which he has fallen.

The ride, on our return, was constantly enlivened as before, by passers by, both on foot and on horseback, forming a great variety of groupings, and an endless diversity of costume. One common mode of transporting burdens was of a most primitive kind: a hide spread on the ground, and attached to the saddle or person of the horseman by a long leathern rope. Whatever was to be carried was piled upon and made fast to this simple sledge, and thus dragged along.

At the end of a couple of miles from the head-quarters at Pantanoso, we turned inland for a short distance from the direct road, to inspect the fort of the "Cerrito" or little hill, so recently evacuated by Oribe. The rise of ground to it is very gentle on every side, and the central point of elevation two hundred and fifty or three hundred feet only, above the level of the bay. The little fort cresting the apex is abandoned, except by a single keeper. It is old and dilapidated; and defective in its original construction, in the leading principles of modern engineering. It appeared incapable of standing a salute by its own guns, much less the fire of artillery in an attack. The view from the parapets is extensive in all directions; and, in the freshness and verdure of the spring, peculiarly beautiful. It embraces a fine inland view, the Mount, the bay and shipping; the massive walls and towers of Montevideo; and the new town of Restoracion. At the base of the hill on the east, lay, in a quadrangular village, the little huts of mud, thatched with grass, which have for years been the quarters of the besieging soldiery. They must have been wretched enough in appearance at any time; but are doubly so, in their present state of desertion and half demolition.

The ride of a mile from this cantonment brought us to Restoracion. This, till the capitulation, was quite a thriving place, having attracted, by its port of entry at the Buçeo, the little produce the country, in its devastated condition, could furnish for exportation. But its vocation is now gone. The port is already closed by decree of the government, and the decline of Restoracion will be even more rapid than its rise. All business will necessarily flow into its old channels in the city; and the new town, at best, be only an impoverished suburb of the old.

It is well laid out: its streets very wide, regular, and well built. Its chief architectural feature is a very fine structure: a spacious quadrangle, enclosing double courts, and ornamented by a lofty tower. It is called "the college;" and was designed by Oribe for an institution of learning, but appears thus far to have been used only as a town hall, for the accommodation of the municipal officers and the police.

This brings me to the comical part of our excursion. Having dismounted for the observation of the place on foot, the inspection of the building just mentioned, and of a new church of some merit in its architecture, we again took horse to meet an appointment for dinner in Montevideo, three miles distant. We had scarcely reached the centre of the town, however, before my horse came suddenly to a dead stand. He had travelled beautifully all the morning, without the slightest evidence of a stubborn or vicious disposition, or any bad habit. It was in vain, however, that I now urged him forward. All the effect of doing so was to cause him to turn abruptly to the one side or the other, or completely around; and, when I resorted to the whip and spur, neither of which had before been required, he dashed upon the sidewalk to the right or to the left, and rushed headforemost into the shop-doors and windows, putting men, women, and children to flight in every direction. Of the crowd of boys soon gathered near, I heard some, by way of commiseration, exclaim, "What a wicked horse!" others less courteous, and with knowing looks as to the merits of the case, "What a poor rider!" till Lt. T——, a Virginia cavalier, insisted on an exchange of animals. This we made, but without securing a better issue. The horse he had ridden behaved in the same manner, or when started, persisted in dashing round the first corner come to, and in rushing into the first enclosure or stable-yard open to him. I kept him going, however, from point to point, as best I could—first down one street and then up another; around this corner and around that—with my friends in full gallop behind, till all three were brought to a stand by getting between two walls, which formed a kind of *cul de sac*. By this time we had fairly roused the whole place, without gaining the advance of a rod towards Montevideo, and Mr. Z—— proposed that I should make the further trial of his horse. The excitement of the chase after me, the hurraing of the boys, the shrieks of the women, and the general tumult, had fired the spirit of this fine animal, and the moment I had gained the saddle, headed in the direction we wished to go, he started at full speed through the principal street, while—

> "The dogs did bark, the children screamed,
> Up flew the windows all;
> And every soul cried out 'Well done!'
> As loud as he could bawl."

Finding myself thus well started, I was determined to allow my steed no chance of a halt in the gait he had chosen, at least till well in sight of the city, and kept him on the full spring. My friends were in close pursuit; and the nearer they came the faster I fled, till we well-nigh fell from our horses in convulsions of laughter, at the Gilpin-like appearance of the chase. Had I worn hat and wig, I should have lost them; and, as it was, doubtless presented a comical sight, in my efforts at once to retain my seat in the saddle, and to keep a naval cap on my head, and the spectacles on my nose. All the amusement, however, did not centre on me. Mr. Z—— is immensely tall and slender. The stirrups of the saddle exchanged with me for his own, were too short for him by at least a half length. He had not altered them; and in sitting on the horse, his knees were brought well up to his chin, making him, at the rate we were riding, far from the least comical figure of the party.

The cause of this incident in our adventures was ascertained to be the fact that, till the day previous, the only home of the two horses ridden by Lt. T—— and me, had been at Restoracion; and, on reaching their old haunts, they had no will, after a ride of fifteen miles, to leave them again, even for the more dignified quarters of the Baron, their new master in the city.

October 22d.—For two or three days past, the troops of Urquiza, in detachment after detachment, have been thickly clustering around the base and on the sides of the Mount—like the settling of flocks of pigeons on the ground, in the migrating season at home. The whole region in sight from our ship is now little else than a tented field, so covered with figures in glaring red as to remind me vividly, by the brilliant coloring thus thrown over the landscape, of the fields of scarlet poppies I have seen in some parts of Europe. The nearest of these encampments is by the water's edge, within a couple of miles of our anchorage. Yesterday morning Captain McIntosh invited Dr. C—— and myself, to accompany him and Captain Corey of the "Southampton" in a visit to it. The morning was beautiful in weather, and the opportunity for observation exceedingly interesting.

We landed at a point where, at the commencement of the civil war, there had been an extensive manufactory connected with the staple productions of the Republic—hides and tallow. Every thing here bore evidences of the devastation which has swept over the whole country in its industrial pursuits: roofless buildings and crumbling walls, uprooted pavements, overthrown furnaces, and rust-eaten boilers. Some of the stone enclosures still standing, presented a common but singular sight, in a capping, twelve or eighteen inches in depth, formed of the horns and the frontal bones of cattle, so arranged and interlocked, as to produce, in their regularity, and in the whiteness into which the whole is bleached by the weather, quite a striking and picturesque effect—as suggestive of taste and beauty in fence building, as the drooping leaves of the acanthus are said to have been in the finish of the Corinthian column. Beyond the curving sand-beach of a little cove, a quarter of a mile from this landing, the nearest encampment was spread over the bright verdure of a gently swelling knoll. The scene presented by it was novel, and strikingly picturesque. The snowy whiteness of the tents; the bright green of the grass; and the glowing red of the caps, mantles, and chiripas, or swaddling blankets, worn in place of trowsers by the soldiers, were brought out in brilliant contrast by the morning's sun; while the pennons of scarlet, fluttering from the tops of the lances, stuck in long lines and in thick clusters over the ground, gave an air of lively animation to the whole.

No check was placed on our movements, nor on the scrutiny of such observations as we chose to make. The uniforms of my companions led to constant military salutes from such as recognized their presence; and we were treated with unvarying civility. We were much struck with the physical aspect of these troops. They are an uncommonly fine race; large, muscular, and athletic: a powerful set of men, whom—perfect centaurs as they are on horseback—it would be a fearful thing to meet as lancers on full charge in battle. They are very dark and Indian-like in complexion; their faces covered with bushy whiskers and mustaches, and their long, black, uncombed hair flowing in the freedom of nature over their shoulders. Occupied in all the various employments of semi-civilized soldiery in camp, they furnished, individually and in groups, studies of which an artist would have rejoiced to avail himself. Some splitting billets of wood for cooking, some roasting meat, and some eating it at their fires; some washing their clothes in a rivulet, just by, and some bringing water from a spring; a few were lounging on the grass in conversation, and a few walking listlessly about; but the greater number—nine out of ten—were gambling with cards. Seated in numbers, from four to seven, around a poncho spread on the grass, with the money at stake upon it, they shuffled, dealt, and played, while groups of double the numbers, standing around and over them, threw down their dollars at hazard, and waited the issue of the game. So entirely were the players and betters absorbed in their games, that they took no notice whatever of us as strangers, nor of any thing occurring around them. The importance of the political struggle now commenced, insures good payment to the troops. A large distribution of cash has recently been made, and the soldiers seem very flush in pocket, and very free in the disposal of their funds. Card-playing is a chief amusement, and gambling a ruling passion among all classes of the people.

The subsistence of the soldiers consists solely of fresh beef: eaten without bread, or vegetables, or even salt. Morning, noon, and night, beef, and beef alone, furnishes their repast. The manner of cooking it is this. A small circular hole, three or four inches in depth, is made in the ground, and a fire kindled in it. A long, slender stick or wooden skewer, sharpened to a point at both ends, is run through a piece of meat, and one end of the stick so fastened in the ground on one side of the hole, that the meat hangs at a low angle over the flame and coals of the fire. The outside thus soon becomes scorched and burnt, and in a few minutes, one of the mess removes it from the fire, by taking hold of the upper end of the stick with the left hand, while his ever-ready knife is in the right. Seizing the meat with his teeth, as he holds it up before him, he cuts off a mouthful by a single quick stroke of his knife, and passes the skewer and its burden to his next messmate. Each of the group thus in turn takes his share of the part roasted. That which remains raw is again placed over the fire, and a similar process gone through with, till the hungry are all satisfied, or the supply consumed. We were very courteously invited by one group, to take seats upon the sheepskins spread for them, and to partake of their primitive meal; but excused ourselves from accepting such kind hospitality, by the plea of a want of appetite.

The encampment stretched, in greater or less regularity and compactness, from the point at which we were, three miles and more northward, to the head-quarters of the commander-in-chief; and from thence again westward by the banks of a stream, the like distance around the Mount to the Plata. The inspection of one portion gave us the characteristic and leading features of the whole; and, after an hour's stroll through the nearer sections, we ascended the Mount, to enjoy from the ramparts of the fortress, the wide landscape they command under its new aspects of animated life. This was exceedingly picturesque in the varied display of so large a force in camp and bivouac. The smoke of fires, in preparation for the noonday meal, rose in pearly columns on every side; and thousands of tethered horses, and unnumbered herds of cattle were grazing every where over the rich plains.

Immediately beneath the walls of the fort, on the northern side, within stone's throw beneath us, is a *corral*—an enclosure for the keeping of cattle, surrounded by high walls, with a barred entrance at one corner. It was now filled with hundreds of fine animals. As we stood looking down upon this, three horsemen, followed by three men on foot, entered it; and we unexpectedly became witnesses of the manner of butchering an animal here, whether taken wild on the open prairie, or, as at present, penned up in a corral. The uses of the *lasso* and *bolas*, and the dexterity of the South Americans in the management of them, are familiar to every school-boy. It was with the lasso the horsemen now operated. The animal designated for slaughter, was, in a few moments, artfully detached from the general herd, and made captive by the horns, with the unerring lasso, thrown at the same moment by two of the horsemen—the third having as readily entangled him by the hind legs as he ran. The three horses trained to the business, the moment the lassos were thrown, braced themselves firmly by their forefeet against the ground, bringing the lassos perfectly 'taut' in three different directions, and thus holding the beast as unmovable, as if staked by the head and heels. As he became thus fixed, with his hind legs drawn closely together, one of the men on foot sprang quickly behind him, and by a single sweep of his long and murderous knife, severed the hamstrings of both legs, bringing the hinder part of the animal to the ground, as if by a stroke of lightning. He still stood on his fore legs; but, in as quick time almost, the butcher was at his head, and by one plunge of the same instrument, sent his heart's blood gushing over the ground, and the fore legs staggering, gave way. By a skilful movement of the lassos by the horsemen he was jerked on his side as he fell, and the men on foot, seating themselves upon the quivering, and still living carcass, at once commenced their incisions, and the dissection of the skin. The whole process of this catching, killing, flaying and cutting up an animal, is often the work of less than ten minutes. The spectacle is barbarous and disgusting; yet the saledaros, or general slaughter-houses, are often visited by foreigners, for the purpose of witnessing it, as a matter of curiosity.

October 24th.—Early in September, Commodore McKeever was called to Buenos Ayres by official duty. He made the passage in the U. S. sloop Jamestown, to which his flag was transferred, and returned on the 22d in the American propeller "Manuelita de Rosas," now running as a packet between Buenos Ayres and Montevideo. Mr. Harris, late chargé d'affaires, on his way to the United States accompanied him; and it is officially announced, that the Congress will sail immediately for Rio de Janeiro, to carry him that far on his passage home.

The visit to Urquiza, and the stroll through the camp of his followers, it will thus be seen, were made in fortunate time. Had they been delayed longer, I should have had no opportunity for the observations they afforded. We are to return to the Plata; but not till the successful revolutionist and his troops will long have left the neighborhood of Montevideo. On the 22d he issued a proclamation to the inhabitants of the republic. I like its style and spirit much. In it he has thrown aside the accustomed verbosity and grandiloquence, characteristic of the state papers of this section of the world, and the barbarous vituperations of partisanship; and avows his principles and purposes in a manly and patriotic manner. I close this section of my record with a hasty translation.

"The Governor and Captain-general of the Province of Entre-Rios, General and Chief of its army, and General of the vanguard of the allied armies of operation, to the inhabitants of the oriental Republic of Uruguay:

"ORIENTALS! I promised to fight for your liberty and national independence, and I have fulfilled my word. The chains with which the tyrant of my country enslaved you are rent in pieces. It only remains for me to break those which bind the unhappy people of Buenos Ayres, where a hateful rule still oppresses the Argentines. For this the soldiers of liberty must still combat.

"I am about to leave you, but wherever destiny may carry me—whether to the field of battle, to the quietude of private life, or to the guardianship of the tranquillity and glory of my country, I shall ever pray for your prosperity, and for the perpetuity of those blessings which I have recovered for you, after the long and disastrous struggle which has desolated the rich plains of your country, and crimsoned them with the blood of your brothers. These precious blessings are your liberty and your independence.

"ORIENTALS! Be free, by submitting yourselves to the authority of that citizen whom constitutional suffrage shall elevate to the chair of the chief magistracy, and by upholding the laws which protect the lives and property of the people. Be independent by living unitedly beneath the glorious banner, which is the symbol of your nationality, that other governments observing it may respect you; and that you may merit the admiration of those who have sworn to exterminate a bloody tyranny, and firmly to establish an empire of liberty and law, in the Republics of the Plata.

"ORIENTALS! In union is strength; in peace prosperity; and in the oblivion of civil discord and the exercise of republican virtues, the happiness of your children and the perpetuity of your national institutions.

"ORIENTALS! Union, peace, and fraternity among all, is the charge to you from him who has the glory of having contributed to the restoration of your liberty and independence.

"JUSTO JUAN URQUIZA.

"Head-Quarters of Pantanoso, October 21st, 1851."

Thus closes the first act in the political drama now in performance on the banks of the Plata.

CHAPTER XXII.

RIO DE JANEIRO.

December 10th.—The Congress has been a month at moorings here. Nothing worthy of special notice has occurred on shore in the interval. The court and church, by the customary pageants on gala and fête days, have furnished the chief objects for sight-seeing, and varied walks by the water side and on the mountains, my principal sources of recreation. Our return to the metropolis was welcomed, socially, by Mr. Schenck, the new minister, and by Gov. Kent, the Consul, in elegant hospitalities to the officers of the Congress; and Admiral Reynolds, relieved after long service by Admiral Henderson, in the steam frigate Centaur, gave proof of his continued friendship by a farewell dinner to us before putting to sea, "homeward bound."

The unity of my record, however, requires the brief notice of one or two events on board ship. On the evening of the 25th ult. an outrage was perpetrated by two or three of the crew, calculated to bring a reproach upon our good name for order and discipline. I was on shore with Commodore McKeever, when it was reported to him, that a policeman of the city, who had taken a deserter on board, had been knocked down on the deck when crossing the gangway, and, it was feared, had been fatally injured. This seemed a daring outbreak against the discipline of the service, and a serious offence against the municipal authority of the city. Great excitement was produced by it, and an investigation of the affair at once instituted. Two chief offenders were discovered and confined in irons, in dark cells, till a formal trial of the case should take place. At first, the assault seemed so wanton, as to be inexplicable; and could only be resolved into an act of unmitigated villainy. I was not long, however, in gaining a clue to its solution, which, though it did not excuse, explained the grounds of provocation, and very greatly palliated the offence. The person attacked, instead of being a policeman, was only one of those who are too well known among sailors as land-sharks—a runner to a sailor boarding-house, who had been in the habit of entrapping the men on shore, and imposing upon them in various ways. On a recent occasion, he had decoyed one of our crew—under peculiarly aggravating circumstances, and with pretensions of kindness and friendship—into the hands of the police; and had been guilty of a cowardly and abusive attack upon him personally, afterwards, when he had no power to resent it. Great indignation against him had thus been excited; and his unexpected appearance on the deck of the Congress, led to a speedy determination among a few, to seize what might be their only opportunity for revenge. A crowd was quickly gathered at the gangway, as if in mere curiosity, by which the opportunity of tripping him up would be afforded, as he should leave the ship. This purpose was successfully accomplished, and so quickly, that there was no time for any one to interfere. The chief injury he sustained was from striking his head upon the combings of a hatchway; but nothing serious to him is likely to ensue; and the crew at least, much as they regret the reflection upon the character of the ship in connection with the affair, think he received only that which, according to the sailor's code of honor, was justly his due.

But this is a very trivial matter, in comparison with the chief event which has happened: the loss to us of Captain McIntosh, as commander of the Congress. The U. S. ship Falmouth, Captain Pearson, of the Pacific squadron, came into port recently, homeward bound. An exchange of commands took place; and

Captain McIntosh left in the Falmouth, on the 6th inst. To part with him thus unexpectedly, was to others of the Congress, as well as to me, a severe trial Every officer felt it; and there was a general lamentation among all hands of the crew. His reputation in the service is of the highest merit, not only as an accomplished officer, but as a finished gentleman; and, favored with his confidence—especially on the most important of all subjects—and intimately associated with him, I deeply feel his absence. Indeed, when his return to the United States was first announced, I could scarcely be reconciled to it. All things, however, are now going on promisingly under our new commander, who comes to us with favorable antecedents, and high professional character. The ship is in beautiful order; and general harmony and contentment prevail, with every promise of a continuance of the happy auspices which have hitherto marked our cruise.

One thing is very certain—that to me time flies with the velocity of the wind. Each day is too short for its allotted routine of duty; and Sabbath crowds upon Sabbath, as if the week were reduced to half its length of days. Do you ask how this can be in such long and distant exile? I answer, because I find varied occupation to interest and keep me employed from morning till night. I will give you the outline of a day on board. To begin at the beginning: while every thing is still enshrouded in darkness, three loud and measured beats upon a bass drum fall on the dead silence of the ship at the hour, like the heavy tread—according to romance writers of old—of a ghost in a haunted castle, at midnight. They are the signal for the firing of the morning gun of thirty-two pounds, which occurs simultaneously with the last stroke on the drum, and is followed by the beating of the reveillé. This, however, is not intended, and, in general has not the effect to waken the hundreds of sleepers on board from their repose, but only to proclaim the first approaches of the dawn in the east, or, in nautical phraseology, "to make daylight." It is not till half an hour afterwards that the boatswain's pipe, followed and joined by those of his mates, is heard to echo shrilly round the decks, preparatory to the clear and stentorian cry by him, "Up, all hands!" caught also by his mates and bawled by them about the ship, in varied tones of voice, but all very considerably above concert pitch. Then again in like manner, "Up all hammocks!" and should it be a washing-day, of which there are two or three each week, a third cry is heard, "All hands wash clothes!" or All hands wash hammocks!" as the case may be. Every one springs at once from his hammock; all on board is bustle and activity; and, for an hour or more, there is heard a universal rubbing, and scrubbing, and scouring on deck, till the clothes are all washed and hoisted fore and aft on lines in the rigging. Then comes a dashing and splashing of water, and a thumping and bumping, a pounding and grating of "holystones" over the sanded decks, that would effectually break the slumber of any one but a naval officer. By the inexperienced, all this would be thought an effectual substitute for the gong, in rousing one from his slumbers, and in hastening him to the deck to enjoy the balmy land-breeze, and the glorious coloring of the morning on the landscape. As to the morning gun and the reveillé, I neither heed nor hear the sound of either of them once in a month; and as to the beauty of the morning, and the fresh air of the deck, woe to him who seeks them, unless prepared to receive a shower-bath of dirty water, by the bucketfull, at every hatchway he attempts to ascend, and to wade ancle-deep, in search of some spot where he can stand for a moment, without being tripped up by a "squill-gee," or knocked off his feet by the thrashing about of huge "swabs."

This general ship-cleaning is not ordinarily finished till near 8 o'clock—the breakfast hour on board; when our flags are thrown to the wind with a salute to them by "Hail Columbia," or the "Star-spangled Banner," from the band. Breakfast is followed by a change of dress in the crew; and the ship thus in the nicest order, and the men in uniform clothes of pure white, with cuffs and collars of blue, we are ready for both the duty and the pleasure that the day may bring forth. Denied the fresh air and bright scenery of the early day, by the comfortless state of the deck, I give the first hour after breakfast to the enjoyment of these, and the rest of the morning to study.

The arrival of the long-expected library for the crew has given quite a literary aspect to their hours of leisure. I have voluntarily undertaken the office of librarian; and a half-day twice a week, is necessarily given to the record of the issue and return of the books. Evening classes, to which I also voluntarily give a general superintendence, have been formed among the adults for improvement in reading, writing, and arithmetic; and six or eight of the more ambitious and promising, receive occasionally from me in my room, lessons of an hour or two, in the higher branches of arithmetic and in navigation. Thus, with a couple of hours on shore for exercise, and daily visits to the sick and imprisoned on board, I find my time fully occupied. I say visits to the imprisoned; for, since the abolition of the lash by act of Congress, it has been found necessary to erect cells—as remote as can be from the ordinary resorts of the crew about the decks—for solitary confinement. The interviews which I am permitted to have with those under such punishment have proved to be salutary in their effect in the discipline of the ship; and I claim the liberty of access to them, as a privilege of my office.

American seamen, as a class, are fond of reading; and often, not only of reading such books as the Arabian Nights, trashy romances, tales of piracy and murder, and Munchausen stories, but books of history, biography, travels, and even poetry. Among the works ordered, is a set of Washington Irving's writings: no volumes are more called for—especially the lives of Columbus and Mahommed, the Conquest of Granada, and the Sketch Book.

The most remarkable reader among the crew is an old main-mast-man of most trustworthy character. Religious works exclusively are his choice. The Bible is his constant companion; and, besides an entire set of the Evangelical library of the American Tract Society, which I brought with me for the use of any who would receive them, he has carefully read almost every volume of a theological and practical nature in my own library—including portions of Horne's Introduction, the whole of Dwight's Theology, and the entire works of Archbishop Leighton. Of good countenance and personal appearance in general, sedate and quiet in his conduct, and scrupulously neat and particular in dress, he forms a study for an artist, as, seated near the main-mast, where he is stationed at sea, his knees spread with a piece of white duck—to keep all spots from his nicely covered volume—with spectacled nose, he pores over it hour after hour, so entirely absorbed by its contents as to lose all consciousness of the varied movements around him. He seems truly a good man, and sincerely interested in religious things; but when I question him in regard to personal faith and hope, he shakes his head negatively, as if he dare not presume to these; probably from the consciousness of an infirmity which he finds it difficult to overcome—the inability to resist indulgence in strong drink on shore. Aware of this he, for the most part, very wisely declines accepting the liberty of leaving the ship. There are other instances of like self-denial from the same cause, among some of our "best men," in sea phraseology.

December 12*th.*—I recollect having stated, that the first sight which arrests the eyes of the stranger on landing in Rio, is the number, varied employments, and garb of the negroes. The first, and chief human sounds that reach his ears, are also from this class. Their cries through the streets vary with the pursuits they follow. That of the vegetable and fruit venders is monotonous and singular; but so varied, that each kind of vegetable and fruit seems to have its own song. The coffee carriers, moving in gangs, have a tune of their own to which they keep time, in an Indian-like lope, with a bag of one hundred and sixty pounds' weight, poised on their heads. The bearers of furniture form a regular choir. One or two, with rattles of tin in their hands, resembling the nose of a watering-pot, perforated with holes and filled with shot, lead the way in a style truly African. To this is allied, with full strength of lungs, a kind of travelling chant, in which at times all join in chorus. It is full and sonorous, and rendered pleasant, if from no other cause, by the satisfaction from it visible, in the shining and sweating faces of the poor blacks. An effort was made by the authorities, some years ago, to put a stop to the unceasing vociferations and songs of the slaves; and a decree to that effect was issued. But on trial, it was found that the poor creatures drooped and faltered under their task, as they worked in forced silence; and soon moped in such melancholy and depression, that the attempt was abandoned. They now have full license to let out their musical voices; and the way some of them give utterance from their full chests, "to gigantic sounds, is a marvel to low-voiced humanity." This is in direct contrast to the habits of the Brazilians. The chief and only sound you hear in the street from them, is a singular kind of softened hiss, the nearest resemblance to which the unpractised American could make, would probably be, according to a suggestion of Gov. Kent, in the effort to pronounce the word "tissue" by a quick and single action of the lips and tongue. This can be heard at a considerable distance, and seldom fails to attract the attention of the person to whom it is directed. No loud call—no halloo! to stop or to stand—no rough salutation or boisterous recognition is here heard, but all is quiet and calm. A beckon of the hand, as if you wished the person to approach, accompanied by a play of each finger, is the salute to a passer-by in a carriage, or one at too great a distance for the ordinary low tone of voice. The motion would be taken by a stranger for a beckon to come near, but when this is intended, the action is reversed, the back of the hand being towards the body, and the motion of the fingers a scoop inwards.

This sparing of the voice and this quiet action, indicate the general indolence of the people, induced by the debilitating influence of a tropical climate, and is characteristic of all their habits. It is a principle with them to sit at rest as much as possible, and when forced to move, to do so slowly and gently—to be calm and composed, quiet and noiseless. With this view of life, they eat, sleep, keep their temper and grow fat.

Public conveyances here, as elsewhere, afford good opportunities for studying some of the manners and habits of the people. Lines of omnibuses run in various directions through the city, and far into the suburbs. Gov. Kent has found it convenient during his residence here, to make much use of them, and says, that in so doing, he has been led to remark among other traits, the marvellous patience of the natives, and their utter disregard for loss of time. No matter how long, or however unaccountable the delay in starting, there is no inquiry made, no remonstrance uttered, no English or American fretting and scolding and threatening. The Brazilian passengers on such occasions appear as if they would sit for the day and the night, without a look or question of impatience. On one occasion, he was making a passage in a steamboat from the port of Estrella, on the western side of the bay of Rio. In crossing a shoal she grounded in the mud and remained fast for an hour; not a native passenger manifested the least curiosity or anxiety in regard to the detention. No one asked the cause or went forward to make any investigation, or to ascertain whether the tide was rising or falling. There was nothing on board either to eat or drink, except water; yet no one inquired how long the delay might be, but each taking out his tablets, or a newspaper, began writing or reading as if all were going on well.

Another trait strikingly exhibited in the omnibus, is the remarkable politeness and civility of the citizens, in some respects. Every man that enters the vehicle raises his hat to his fellow-passengers, who return the salute in the same manner. Sometimes in doing this, if the ommnibus suddenly starts, there is an amusing struggle between politeness and the self-preservation which demands the use of both hands, ending at times in a stumble and fall, hat in hand, in the anxiety to do the accustomed honors. But no one thinks of yielding his seat after it is once taken, either to sex or age; and if the only unoccupied place should be at the furthest end of the carriage, the most delicate woman, on entering, must force her way to it as best she may. This is to be attributed to the national dislike to locomotion, and to the *vis inertiæ* incident to the climate. Men will often sit wedged together in a hot day, after vacancies on both sides have occurred, rather than move a foot for a more comfortable position.

The omnibuses are drawn by mules, and amusing scenes are often witnessed by the display of their characteristic obstinacy and ill-temper. As a friend remarks, in the language of some modern reformers, "from their unfortunate and misdirected organization, they exhibit, at times, great lightness of heel, and a savage desire to kick something." The drivers, however, manage them admirably, and guide them skilfully, at a rapid rate, through the narrow streets. The carriages are strongly built—as they need to be; for the pavements are very rough. To this, however, the drivers pay little heed, and generally drive the most rapidly over the worst sections. In one respect the rate at which they move is an inconvenience to those wishing to take passage. The drivers have nothing of the "wide-awake" qualities of the Yankee jehus of the same vehicles at home. They never look out for passengers in the cross streets, and never behind them, but wait to be hailed by the native "hiss." The foreigner may not be accomplished in the utterance of this; and when once the omnibus is well started, there is a farewell to all hope of a seat for the trip.

CHAPTER XXIII.

San Aliexo.

December 14*th.*—Where, or what, you will ask, is San Aliexo? It is a spot which reminds me more of my home than any place I have seen for eighteen months past, notwithstanding the existence of features in its scenery in the widest possible contrast with any found there. Even while I write, there is a rumbling and babbling of water near at hand, which tempts me to fancy that I am at the table of the little library so familiar to you, and that it is our own brook I hear, made unusually merry by the meltings of the spring, or the pourings of an autumnal rain. But this is not telling you what, and where, San Aliexo is.

It is a little valley at the foot of the Organ Mountains, thirty miles from Rio de Janiero. Mr. M——, in whose bride, brought to Brazil by him from the United States last summer, I recognized with so much surprise and pleasure, my young friend, M—— G——, daughter of Capt. G——, of the navy, resides in it; and a visit to her and her husband has led me here. My messmate, Captain T——, of the marine corps, is an uncle of Mrs. M——. He passed a fortnight recently at San Aliexo, and joined the ship again, three days ago. Mr. M—— accompanied him on board, and so earnestly urged an invitation from himself and my young friend to their place, that I returned with him, and have now, for two days, been enjoying their hospitality in the very perfection of rural life. The trip as far as Piedade, at the head of the bay, twenty miles from Rio, is made by water. Till within a year or two, the packets plying between this place and the city, were exclusively sharp-built and gracefully modelled lateen sail-boats; but now, a little steamer, scarcely larger than the smallest "tug" at New York, also makes a daily trip. We embarked on this at noon, and reached Piedade at 3 o'clock; having stopped to land and receive passengers at Paqueta, the most beautiful of the islands in the upper part of the bay.

The day was remarkably fine; neither too bright nor glaring for the enjoyment of the scenery, as is often the case in this, the midsummer of the year, nor too sombre from the thickness of the screening clouds. There was quite a number of passengers, male and female, and of a variety of nations—Brazilian, Portuguese, French, German, Swiss, Italians, Englishmen, Americans, and numerous Africans, both bond and free. The Italians were image venders, having with them the long board which they carry on their heads in their travels, filled with the plaster casts of saints and angels, dancing-girls and satyrs, and, for aught I observed to the contrary, statuettes of the Prince of Evil himself. The images of the saints led to conversation among some of the passengers, long resident in the country, on the superstition and superstitious practices of the common people. Some of the anecdotes related were quite amusing. San Antonio, or St. Anthony, is the patron saint of the Portuguese. It is upon him chiefly they rely for aid in various straits and difficulties—especially in the recovery of lost or stolen property. The highly glazed and gaudily painted effigies of this saint, represent him with an infant Saviour in his arms. This baby-image is not, however, part and parcel of the principal cast, but a separate piece attached to the arm of the saint by a long pin, which can be inserted in a hole in the plaster, and removed at pleasure. And for what purpose is this arrangement, do you imagine? I could scarcely have credited the statement, had not an examination of the images corroborated it: the purpose is, that the saint, when regardless of the prayers made to him for aid in any specific case, may be punished by having the child taken from him! This, I am assured, is often done. An additional infliction for hard-heartedness or contumacy on his part, is to put his image behind the door with its face to the wall, or to stand it on its head, up-side down! A gentleman present related the following fact, illustrative of a like degree of superstition. An old Portuguese, near whom he lived as a neighbor for a long time, and with whom he was familiar, said to him one day, "You Protestants do not believe in miracles?" "No, not in miracles of the present day—do you?" "Certainly." "And why?" "Because I have experienced them myself." "Indeed! and when was that?" "Oh! at different times: once in Portugal, when I was a young man. Like most young fellows, I was fond of dress then, and wore a pair of silver shoe-buckles, of which I was very vain. One Sunday having them on, I set off for chapel two or three miles distant, by a cross path, and when I got there, one of my buckles was gone. I was very much troubled; but staid to mass, vowing to San Antonio, if he would get back my buckle, I would give him a wax candle. On my way home, I kept looking along the path to see whether San Antonio would hear my prayer; and before I had gone half the way, there lay the buckle before me all right, on one side of the path. At another time I lost a favorite dog. I was very much grieved, and felt the loss so much, that one day, when walking along the road, I made a vow to San Antonio of a half pound of candles, if he would only bring him back; and I had scarcely said the words, before my dog came bouncing through the hedge to me as fast as he could run!" Such was the amount of the old man's experience in miracles.

While mentally classifying my fellow-passengers, as to their nationality and social position, my eye rested on one of them, apparently some sixty years of age, whose aspect was peculiarly intelligent and gentlemanlike. A round jacket of blue cloth, trowsers of cotton striped blue and white, long boots of the country of undressed leather, with spurs of like fashion, a broad-brimmed, low-crowned, white felt hat, and a whip in hand, told that he was prepared to ride after reaching the landing. Pointing him out to Mr. M——, I said, "That person, I presume, is a country gentleman of the first class." Looking in the direction indicated, he replied, "That is Admiral T——." This I at once perceived to be the fact; and, both of us having before met him, we approached with our salutations. He is an Englishman, who left the British naval service when a lieutenant, thirty years ago, for that of Brazil, and has been advanced in it to the rank of admiral. After much important naval service, he was appointed adjutant-general of the Empire, during the minority of the Emperor, an office which he held for many years; but is now off duty, and on the retired list of the navy. I first met him in Rio in 1829; and a second time since the Congress has been on this station, but in so different a dress, that I did not now recognize him. He was on his way to a coffee plantation in the Organ Mountains; his horses and servants being also on board the steamer. His reception of us was most cordial, and his conversation during the remainder of the passage, interesting and instructive, from a perfect knowledge of the country. No meals are served on board the packet, and he insisted upon our joining him in a Brazilian lunch, as he called it, of sausages, made partly of beef and partly of pork—with a strong mingling of garlic—stuffed in a large skin, in imitation of those of Bologna. Cheese, and bread in rolls, with oranges for dessert, made up the repast: all being served in most primitive style, on the wrappers of brown paper in which the articles had been purchased at the grocer's. Each of us used his own knife in helping himself, and all drank from a cup of silver, belonging to our host, which was as bruised and battered, as if it had done service for a whole mess in a dozen campaigns. We ate upon deck in the midst of our fellow-passengers; and were waited on by a slave in shirt and trowsers of coarse towcloth, without shoes or hat, but in a livery-jacket of blue turned up with red, and a red waistcoat. His master seemed most kindly attached to him, saying that, "in fidelity, honesty, and in every qualification for his business, he was worth any twenty ordinary servants 'at home' "—referring, I suppose, to England.

Piedade, the place to which the steamer plies, consists of one long range of buildings under a single roof, and comprises a warehouse, for the storage of coffee and other products on their way to the city, and the returns in foreign goods; a packet office; a shop for the retail of articles in general demand; and a small venda or tavern—the eating and sleeping-rooms of which communicate directly with the stables and mule-stalls in the rear. Room for this establishment — along the front and on one end of which the wharf extends—has been scooped from the base of an isolated, round-topped promontory, which rises from the bay, much in the manner, and with the general appearance of Stony Point, near the entrance of the Highlands on the Hudson. We had intended to dine here; but the luncheon of the admiral saved us from all temptation on landing, from the oily dishes of the dirty venda, which, rank with garlic, were spreading their perfume around, and we hastened to proceed on our way.

It was quite a pleasure to see a light and tasteful wagon of American manufacture, with seats for two and a caleche top, in readiness to receive us; and one still greater to move off in it, at a rapid rate, behind two fat, sleek, and spirited mules. These animals are much more serviceable than horses in this climate. I am becoming so much accustomed to their appearance, as almost to admire them. Some of those brought to the landing to meet the passengers in company with us, were beautiful; especially two that were milk-white, rivalling the drifted snow. The saddle-cloths and bridle-reins were also white, and in the most perfect keeping. In these animals, as well as some others, I could trace lines of beauty: particularly in their long and delicately shaped ears, their neatly shaven tails, and slender and symmetrically formed legs. On being mounted, they amble off, too, with their riders in such an easy and knowing way, that I am beginning to have quite a fancy for a well-trained beast of the kind.

Carriage roads are not common in Brazil. That on which we now were, is the principal among the few in this section of the empire, and leads across the mountains to the mining districts in the far interior. It is narrow, but well graded; having the earth thrown up in the centre with deep and wide trenches on either side. It is for the most part unfenced; enclosures by the wayside, wherever there are any, are formed by hedges of the thorny acacia, of mimosa, the running rose, the wild orange tree, or the hybiscus.

The road presented a lively scene for some distance, in the movements on it of the passengers from the boat—some in clumsy carriages, but chiefly on horse and mule-back, and the poorer class and negroes on foot. These last, with trunks and portmanteaus, boxes, bundles, and different kinds of packages of greater or less weight on their heads, walked erectly and with firm and rapid stride. The country between the waters of the bay and the foot of the mountains, a space of ten or twelve miles, is alluvial, low and wet,—a sandy and marshy plain, overspread with brushwood and jungle, from which numerous rounded hills rise abruptly on every side. These, well-wooded, and partially cultivated, are the sites of the few dwellings seen. The first part of the way presents the aspect of a region abounding in miasma and mosquitoes, with few attractions as a place of residence. At the end of four miles is the town of Majé, situated on a small river of the same name. It is the head of boat navigation, and counts a population of three or four thousand: but seems a dull and inactive place, and may be summarily described as a shabby and dirty Portuguese town.

Beyond Majé the country improved in appearance. The hills were more numerous and more swelling in outline, and their sides and summits more richly tufted with foliage. Here the chief animation of the scene consisted in long "troupes" of heavily laden mules with their muleteers, on their way from the interior, or returning from Piedade with panniers less heavily laden or entirely empty. Some were *en route;* others, grouped under the shade of immense open sheds or *ranchos*,—places built at distances of a few miles by the wayside, for the accommodation of these troupes—were resting for a brief time; and others again, relieved from their burdens for a longer stop, were seen eagerly seeking food, wherever they could find it by the wayside.

The enterprise which brought Mr. M—— to Brazil, and has made him a resident here, is the establishment of a cotton manufactory; and the road into which we turned from the great turnpike, as it is called, at the end of three miles from Majé, is of his own construction, to facilitate the transportation of the raw material and manufactured goods, to and from his establishment, five miles distant. It is not so wide or so well graded as the public road, but most creditable as a private work, and a great advance upon the mule-track and bridle-path of former days. The last four miles of the drive along the rich bottom-land of the Majé, and afterwards of its tributary, the Peak River, was beautiful. The narrow, lane-like road is lined closely on either side with green hedges, in some places of mallows covered with purple flowers, three or four feet only in height, and in others of the wild orange tree, rising to twenty and thirty. The loftier ranges of the mountains in front of us were hidden in clouds; still the wildness and beauty of the shafts which buttress them, and of the hills which form their bases, were more and more impressive the further we advanced. At length, as we turned the shoulder of a projecting hill, the little valley, three miles long, and half a mile wide, hemmed in and overhung by the wildest and loftiest peaks of the Organ Mountains, opened suddenly to view. To my eyes it was fascinating in its secluded beauty, and the wild sublimity of its surroundings. I can scarcely describe the effect, from association, of the unexpected sight of an "American Factory," with its modest belfry, rising loftily and in snowy whiteness from the midst of green groves and bright streams; the cottages of the operatives being clustered around it; and, in a grove of acacias, a quarter of a mile distant, the "American" dwelling of the proprietor. I use the word "American" not in reference to fashion merely, but to material and constrution, the whole having been fitted for use in the United States. There was not an image, in all that gave animation to the picture, to break the illusion of having been suddenly transported from Brazil, and set down in some manufacturing glen at home.

Mr. M——'s house is situated on a natural terrace, twenty feet above the level of a beautiful meadow of *alfalfa* or Peruvian grass, which lies between it and the factory. A road on the bank of the river runs beside this, in front of the house and lawn; and is a perfect specimen of the "green lane," in the English landscape. Smooth, straight, and turf-covered, with a hedge of mimosa on the meadow side, and embowering thickets of bushes and trees overhanging the river on the other, it forms a striking object in the scene: one harmonizing well with the rural quietude and simplicity of the whole. In the lawn, which is on a level with the meadow and lane, there is a fountain and fine jet d'eau, and upon the terrace above, another between the drawing-room windows and the grove of acacias. A garden of fruit and flowers on the opposite side of the house, is separated from it by an artificial stream, whose bed is so paved with rough stones as to produce a constant murmur of soft sounds, as the water glides over and around them. Every thing in sight, indeed, though the place is new, presents a picture of taste and rural beauty, that makes me think of the "happy valley" in Rasselas.

It is unnecessary to say that I was most cordially received by my friend, whom I found in all the freshness and bloom of American beauty, and that I felt at once at home in her neat and tasteful abode.

Dec. 16*th*.—At the end of three days even, I cannot resist a feeling of having been transported from Brazil to some mountain region at home. There is nothing in the general foliage, except here and there the tufted top of a palm, or the broad leaf of the banana, to forbid the illusion. The place, in its quietude, its bright meadow and green lane, edged with hedges, its river whispering over a stony bed, beneath thicket-covered and tree-embowered banks, reminds me of Landsdown; while the house, an importation in all its parts from the United States; the factory, of which the same is true; and the distant hum of its busy looms and spindles, present a picture as strikingly characteristic of New England.

The weather is charming: clear and bright, with an occasional cloud of snowy whiteness floating against the deep blue of the sky, while breezes of grateful elasticity fan down from the mountain tops in the mornings and evenings, and sweep back through the valley with coolness from the distant sea at noonday. The nights, in their utter silence, are in wide contrast with those to which I have of late been accustomed: not a sound is heard but the plashings of the fountains and the murmurings of many waters.

The Sabbath was a day of rest indeed. I officiated at a service held in the hall at 11 o'clock, and would most gladly have attempted to make the day one of spiritual good to the operatives of the factory, and the numerous dependants of the establishment, by public worship with them. With the exception of the foreman and one or two assistants, however, all these are foreigners—Portuguese and Germans, whose languages I do not speak, and who, moreover, are chiefly Romanists, not accessible to a Protestant by preaching. The greatest number of those who are employed in the factory are females—Germans from the Imperial colony of Petropolis: the male portion are Portuguese from Oporto and the islands of Madeira and Terceira. The house-servants, the waiter, coachman, gardener and under-gardener, are Portuguese; the chambermaid, cook, and laundress, free negresses.

There is a Romish chapel within three miles of the valley; but it is closed for the most of the year, and is not frequented by the work-people here. The parish priest, like most others in the country, is living in a state of open concubinage, and is in other ways unpopular as to his morals. In passing through Majé, we met a fine-looking young man, handsomely mounted, followed by two negroes on mules. I was struck with his appearance, and, remarking it, learned that he was a son of the padre of the place, the eldest of a large family. We saw the father shortly afterwards, and received a bow from him at a door, as he was about to mount his mule. This animal I observed to be one of the finest of the kind I had seen; and I was struck with the peculiar fashion of the stirrups of the saddle; they were of polished brass, richly wrought, and in the form of a Turkish slipper.

December 18th.—On Tuesday I took a ride of two miles or more on horseback, to the head of the little valley. This presents a most wild and romantic scene: making one feel, in gazing upon it,—while mountain piled upon mountain, and pinnacled rock rising above pinnacled rock, tower, almost perpendicularly, thousands of feet overhead,—as if you had not only passed beyond civilization, but had arrived at the outer edge of the world itself, where, by the inaccessible barriers in front and on either hand, it is more impressively said than even by the waves of the sea-shore, "Hitherto shalt thou come, but no further."

After passing Mr. M——'s place, the only road is a mule-path, wide enough for a single animal, and in all respects, excepting the tracks of repeated use, in the state in which nature formed it—not a stone removed, and not an ascent or descent, however abrupt and precipitous, smoothed or graded. A few scattered habitations formed of wattled sticks, plastered with mud, and thatched with grass, are seen here and there; but less comfortable, apparently, and less attractive as dwellings, than the meanest log cabins on the outskirts of pioneer life in the United States. A few patches of mandioca, and one or two of Indian corn, alone indicated any cultivation of the soil, or gave evidence of a pursuit of industry.

The course of the principal stream is a broad bed of wild and massive rocks, from one to another of which, ordinarily, you may step dry-shod; but, in rains, these are covered by rushing and foaming torrents, and the stream is impassable. The next morning Mr. M—— accompanied me in a second ride, up a valley branching to the west from this, called the Peak Valley, from a remarkable peak of granite, which rises at its head: one of those sugar-loaf shafts, so common in the geological formation of this region. This valley, too, is exceedingly wild, in its chief features; and is watered by a rapid stream called the Peak River, tributary to that on which the factory stands.

The only drawback to the entire satisfaction of my visit, for the first three days, was the concealment by thick clouds, of the pikes or fingers as named by some, and all the higher ranges of the Organ Mountains which immediately overhang San Aliexo. These had so often been the object of admiration at a distance, when visible from Rio, that I was impatient to behold them close at hand; but had been tantalized only, by an occasional, indistinct, and momentary glimpse, through the mist of an opening cloud, of a fantastic peak or shelving precipice, standing high in the heavens above us. Just at nightfall, last evening, however, the veil was entirely lifted, and I charmed beyond expectation by the scene thus disclosed: and not without reason, as even the imperfect sketch accompanying this will show.

I was up with the dawn this morning, and, finding the whole range to be still uncovered, hastened to a part of the lawn which commands the best view of it. The rising sun was just beginning to illuminate the loftiest peaks with a bright and golden light; and I stood for an hour riveted to the spot, in the study and untiring admiration of a scene, gorgeous in coloring, and of unrivalled sublimity in its outlines. By nine o'clock the mists from the valleys had again enshrouded the whole in clouds.

Though the present is the rainy season of the year, till yesterday the weather was bright as that of June at home: but then, while we were at dinner, it began suddenly to pour down in torrents; presenting every thing out of doors in a new phase. At the end of a couple of hours the rain ceased; and the paths in the lawn and the road soon became sufficiently dry to allow our taking a walk. Mr. M—— and I went to observe the effect upon the river. This was surprising. From a bed of rocks, among which a shallow stream was lazily flowing, it had become a swollen and irresistible torrent: wide and deep, roaring like a tornado, and foaming like the sea. As we approached a venda, or retail store and grocery, a quarter of a mile up the valley, there was a shout and call for us, by several persons collected there, to hurry on, as if something unusual was to be seen. These, at the same time, set off on a run towards a point near by them, which commands an unobstructed view of the river above. Mr. M—— told me, as we hastened forward, that the sight was the approach of an additional flood of water from the mountain. This, though not now so remarkable in its appearance as it sometimes is, was very singular. The mass of water tumbled by such showers down the precipices which hedge in the little valley, is so great, and rushes so suddenly into the bed of the river, as in itself to exhibit the appearance from bank to bank, of passing over a dam. The perpendicular elevation of this new body of water above that previously forming the surface of the stream, was a couple or more feet.

We were standing at the time, near a rude mill for grinding the root of the mandioca, and the conversion of it into farina—the "staff of life" in Brazil; it was in operation, and the process in the manufacture going on, under the management of a half-dozen nearly naked negroes. The mandioca is every where seen growing in plantations of greater or less extent, in all the tropical parts of Brazil. It resembles the palma christi, or castor oil plant, in its general appearance, more than any other growth that occurs to me. The leaves, though smaller and of a darker green, are in like manner digitated or finger-shaped, and the stem and branches irregular and scraggy. It grows to the height of four and five feet, and attains maturity at the end of eighteen or twenty months after being planted. The roots produce the farina. These, at full growth, are of the size and general appearance of a large irregularly-formed parsnip. After being brought from the field in wide, shallow baskets, carried by the negroes on their heads, the first operation is to scrape off the outer skin with a knife. In this state the root is very white and pure in looks, bnt poisonous in acrid juices. A rasp or coarse grater is so arranged as to be turned by a water-wheel; against this the root is held, and becoming finely grated, falls into a trough or tub of water, prepared to receive it, and is reduced to a pulp. In this state, it is placed in baskets and pressed with heavy weights, till freed from the water and its own juices. It is then dried, broken up or powdered, sifted through a coarse sieve, and placed in a very large flat iron pan, having a furnace with slow heat beneath. In this it is thoroughly dried, without being allowed to scorch or burn. It is then put in bags for use or sale.

One of the effects of the rain, was the appearance of numerous cascades and temporary waterfalls on the tops and sides of the mountains. I dare not venture to guess even, at the extent of some of these. They foam down their courses, white as drifting snow, and look beautiful, amid the deep green of the forests, and the dark precipices over which they pour.

The history of Mr. M——'s enterprise in the introduction of cotton-spinning and weaving, here, is quite interesting, and has caused me to look upon him as a pioneer in such business, well worthy the reputation of our countrymen for energy, invention, and indomitable perseverance; and an instructive example of the importance of a fixed purpose for the accomplishment of an end. He met, at first, with a succession of disappointments and unexpected obstacles, which would have utterly disheartened and broken down a spirit less determined, and less elastic than his own. Brought up in mercantile pursuits without practical knowledge in mechanics or manufacture, he determined, in 1846, to attempt the establishment of a cotton factory in Brazil. A gentleman from Rio, then in New York, encouraged him in the project, by the assurance that the vicinity of Rio furnished ample water-power for the object; that, abounding in hills and mountains, streams of water in sufficient volume, were in various places poured down. The Brazilian minister at Washington, also expressed great interest in the subject, and by way of encouragement to Mr. M——, gave him a copy of an act, passed by the

Imperial Legislature in 1842, by which all machinery for manufacturing purposes of the kind, was exempted from duty. Under these auspices, he expended capital to a large amount, in the necessary machinery, in materials for the large structure in which it was to be put up, and in the freight of both to Rio. Mr. M—— hastened in advance to Brazil, to make choice of a site for the establishment, and secure it by purchase: but only to meet a first disappointment. The streams on which his Brazilian friend had relied, as abundantly ample in water-power, would have scarcely sufficed, as Mr. M—— expressed it, to water the mules necessary in the work. An exploration of the entire region within thirty miles of Rio became necessary, for the discovery of an unfailing stream, with water sufficient to turn a large wheel, and in a situation to be available. He could gain no information on the point upon which he could rely, and was obliged to make the search in person, through woods and wilds, and over marshes and moors, and in ignorance, at the time, of the language of the country. A month thus occupied, brought to his knowledge two supplies of water only, that would answer his purpose: one at Tejuca, nine or ten miles from Rio, and another in the direction of Petropolis, a colony of Germans in the mountains. That at Tejuca, besides being already leased for other purposes, was inaccessible except by mules as means of transportation, and therefore, not to be thought of; the other was the private property of the Emperor, and not obtainable in any way.

Such were the prospects of Mr. M——, with fifty thousand dollars worth of material on its way to Rio, accompanied by several workmen under high pay, for the erection of the necessary buildings, and to put the machinery into an available condition. After all other search had proved in vain, he was accidentally led to this valley, and unexpectedly here found much, if not all, he was looking for. About the same time, the shipment from the United States arrived; but, notwithstanding the decree furnished him by the Brazilian minister, declaring such articles free, the officials at the Custom House pertinaciously demanded the duty upon them. This, according to the tariff, like most of the imposts here on any thing foreign, was high, and would have materially increased his expenditure. The only alternative was an application for relief in the case, to the minister having cognizance of such affairs. Those in official position in Brazil, from the Minister of State to the most insignificant employé of a bureau, hold the dignity conferred in high estimation, and are inaccessible in proportion to their rank. Three months elapsed before Mr. M—— could gain the audience sought; and then, only to be told, that the exemption referred to in the decree of the Imperial legislature, was exclusively for the benefit of persons who had already established factories and needed additional machinery; not for those who were introducing machinery for a new establishment. The decision, therefore, was that the duties must be paid; but, for the law in the case, he was referred to the attorney-general of the empire. This dignitary condescended to grant Mr. M—— an audience at the end of an additional six weeks; but decided with the minister, that the duties must be paid, or at least, deposited with the collector of customs till the factory should be in operation. Thus, though the enterprise was one of great importance to the interests of the country, and such as should at once have secured the favor and aid of the government, the entire material necessary for carrying it into execution, was kept for nine months in the hands of the custom-house officers, greatly exposed to rust and injury, and only released on the payment of several thousands of dollars. It would occupy too much time to pursue the history of the enterprise in detail: in the construction of a dam across the river at a great outlay of money and labor, only to have it swept away by a flood from the mountains; in the consequent necessity of digging a long raceway along the base of the hills, without the possibility of securing the adequate number of laborers, white or black; and also, of making the road of five miles to the turnpike. Over this last work, when finished, the whole of the material for the factory building and the machinery, among which a single piece—the shaft of the great wheel—weighed 7000 lbs., was to be transported, without any of the facilities, so common with us, for accomplishing it.

The mechanics and artisans, brought from the United States for the erection of the building, were found to be incompetent in many respects; and the result was, that Mr. M—— was obliged himself to perform much of the manual labor even, and instead of planning, devising, and superintending only, to become practically a carpenter, mason, machinist; and even freightmaster and carter, as no one around him, whose aid he could secure, knew what course to pursue in an emergency, or even in any common difficulty that might occur: he was obliged first to discover how a thing was to be done, and then do it himself. Still he persevered through every discouragement and disaster, till his efforts were crowned with full success, and the factory was early in operation.

Though it is only in the more common fabrics in cotton that the manufacturer here can yet compete with British and American goods; and the article chiefly produced, thus far, is a coarse cloth for coffee bagging and the clothes of slaves, he deserves a medal of honor from the government, and the patronage of the empire, not only for the establishment of the manufactory, but for the living example set before a whole Province of the indolent and sluggish natives, of Yankee energy, ingenuity, indefatigable industry, and unyielding perseverance.

CHAPTER XXIV.

RIO DE JANEIRO.

December 30th.—It was quite a trial to bid adieu to the charms of San Aliexo. My kind host and hostess were earnest in their persuasions to detain me through the holidays; and I would most readily have yielded, but for an engagement to officiate, on Christmas morning, at the marriage of Miss K——, the daughter of the American consul, to Mr. R—— of the family of that name, already so often mentioned. The groom, though a native of Brazil, claims, through his father, the rights of a British subject; and the civil contract took place, in conformity with an act of parliament, in the presence of the British consul, at his office, at an early hour of the day. The marriage was afterwards solemnized by me, according to the Protestant service, in the drawing-room of the American consulate; and, Mr. R—— being a Romanist, a third ceremony occurred, as at the wedding of Miss R——, his sister, last August, in the private chapel of the country house of Mr. M——, his maternal grandfather.

The company assembled at the consulate was large, and the retinue of carriages by which it was conveyed the long drive to Mr. M——'s, quite imposing. Four-in-hand is the usual turnout here, for such a distance, and Mr. Schenck, the American minister, led the way, next after the bride and groom, in an elegant chariot drawn by four beautiful white horses. Commodore

McKeever's carriage had four fine mules. I was of his party. The sky was slightly overcast with fleecy clouds, and the coachman's box being so lofty as to overlook the walls and hedges, which screen so much of the taste and beauty of the suburbs from view on the level of the street, in defiance of every Brazilian idea of dignity, I perched myself upon it, for the greater enjoyment of the drive. The day being a general festival, the whole population of the city was in the streets in holiday dress; and in the extended suburbs through which we skirted our way, the inhabitants—by whole families—were everywhere seen in the verandahs and lawns and door-yards of the houses, in the cheerful and quiet enjoyment of the fiesta. A fondness for splendor and display of every kind—in dress, furniture and equipage—is strikingly a characteristic of the people here; and the showy procession, recognized as a bridal cortège, created quite a sensation as it dashed onward—manifestly exciting the admiration and lively sympathies of the observers.

From my elevated and unconfined position, I enjoyed the whole much; and feasted, the entire distance, on the gorgeous display of flowers, exhibited in the succession of tasteful gardens and pleasure-grounds which I overlooked.

The mansion and grounds of Mr. M—— I described to you in connection with the previous wedding. The religious ceremony now, was the same in every particular, from the scattering of the rose leaves and orange buds before the bride in the procession from the drawing-room to the chapel, to the showering of the same over her and the whole company, with the closing benedictions at the altar. A concert in the music-room immediately succeeded the ceremony, and continued till the banquet was served at six o'clock. This was more luxurious, if possible, in the variety and costliness of its delicacies, native and foreign, in season and out of season, than on the former occasion; and superb in its table-service and plate. The decorations in flowers alone, would, in a less favored climate, have formed no inconsiderable item of expense; while the fruits, in the perfection of their kinds

—all freshly gathered—pines, figs, oranges, sweet-lemons, grapes in clusters like those of Eshcol, bananas, mangoes, and melons, were most artistically arranged. After coffee in the drawing-room, dancing was commenced; and, taking our leave, we were safely on board ship shortly after ten o'clock.

Thus passed my Christmas, and thus is our compatriot, Miss K——, married; and, in the language of the world, "well married." But alas! married in Brazil: away from an American home; away from the intelligence and high cultivation of American life; away from the pure morals, spiritual aspirations, and religious privileges of American Christianity; away from almost every thing that I would wish an American girl to hold most dear!

January 7th, 1852.—This festive period of the year presents constant opportunities of witnessing the slave and negro population in holiday aspects. For many nights past, Gloria Hill, at which the Commodore's barge usually lands in our evening visits to the shore, has echoed till a late hour with the songs, the wild music, and the tread of the dance in their favorite amusements; and yesterday afternoon, I accidentally became a spectator of a grand gathering of the kind. It was "Twelfth" or "King's day," as sometimes called,—being that commemorative of the adoration of the Magi in the stable of Bethlehem; and is a chief festival with the negroes.

I left the ship with the intention of taking, once more, the long walk through the valley of the Larangeiras to the aqueduct, and thence to the city by the hill of Santa Theresa. When about half way up the Larangeiras, however, my attention was arrested by a large gathering of negroes within an enclosure by the wayside, engaged in their native, heathen dances, accompanied by the wild and rude music brought with them from Africa. I stopped to witness the scene: a counterpart, in most respects, to those which, during the first period of my residence at the Sandwich Islands, attended the orgies of pagan revelry there. Many of the principal performers, both among the dancers and musicians, were dressed in the most wild and grotesque manner—some, as if in impersonation of the Prince of Evil himself, as pictured with hoof and horns and demoniac mien. Many of the dances surpassed in revolting licentiousness, any thing I recollect to have witnessed in the South Seas; and filled my mind with melancholy disgust: the more so, from the fact, that a majority, if not all the performers, as was manifest from the crosses and amulets they wore, were baptized members of the Romish Church—Christians in name, but in habits and in heart heathens still. Exhibitions of this kind are far from being limited here to extraordinary holidays, or to the seclusion of by-places. I have seen them in open daylight, in the most public corners of the city, while young females even, of apparent respectability and modesty, hung over the surrounding balconies as spectators.

I know not how long the revelry had now been going on; but either from the free use of *cacha*, the vile rum of the country, or from nervous excitement, many seemed fairly beside themselves. These danced till ready to drop from exhaustion; while shouts of encouragement and applause followed the persevering efforts of those who were most enduring and most frantic in muscular exertion. The performers on the African drums and other rude instruments, who accompanied the monotonous beating and thrumming upon these with loud songs, in solo and chorus, of similar character, seemed especially to enter into the spirit of the revelry, and labored with hands and voice and a vehemence of action in their whole bodies, that caused the sweat to roll down their naked limbs as if they had just stepped from a bath of oil.

By the time I had finished these observations, the evening was too far advanced for the walk upon which I had started, and I retraced my steps to the Catete, the principal street, connecting the city with the bay and suburbs of Botefogo. In it, towards evening, the wealth and fashion of the city, especially in the diplomatic and foreign circles, is generally met in carriages and on horseback for the daily afternoon drive. Many of the equipages equal in elegance those in New York and other of our chief cities; while well-mounted riders, liveried coachmen, footmen, and grooms, give to the whole quite the air of a metropolis. That, however, which most struck me on the present occasion, was an amusing side-scene. Though less generally the custom than formerly, it is still the habit of some of the *bourgeoisie* of Rio, at least on Sundays and great holidays, to promenade to and from church, by whole families, parents and children, from adults to infants, with a retinue of servants—in their best dresses, and in formal procession of two and two. The sight thus presented is interesting, and often amusing, from the formality and stately solemnity with which they move along. The servants bring up the rear, and, whether male or female, are usually as elaborately, if not as expensively dressed as the rest of the family: and often, in the case of the women, with an equal display of laces, muslins, and showy jewelry. Apparently in imitation of this usage of the white population—or rather of the Portuguese and Brazilian, for there are no whites among the native born here—two jet black African women, richly and fashionably attired, came sauntering along with the most conscious air of high-bred self-possession. They were followed by a black female servant, also in full dress, carrying a black baby three or four months old, and decked out in all the finery of an aristocratic heir—an elaborately wrought, lace-frilled and rosetted cap, and long flowing robe of thin muslin beautifully embroidered, and ornamented with lace. Every one seemed struck with this display; and I was at a loss to determine whether it was a bona fide exhibition of the pride of life, or only in burlesque of it, with the design of "shooting folly as it flies." The common blacks, crowding the doors and gateways, burst into shouts of laughter as they passed; while the nurse, at least, of the party showed evidence of a like disposition. Indeed, I think I did not mistake, while looking back upon the group, in seeing the fat sides and shoulders of the black ladies themselves, notwithstanding their lofty bearing and stately step, shake with merriment, under the slight drapery of their fashionable and elegantly finished mantillas.

These may have been persons of wealth, and of respectable and even fashionable position in society; for color does not fix the social position here, as with us at home. It is a striking fact, that in a country where slavery exists in its most stringent form, there is little of the Anglo-Saxon prejudice in this respect, so universal in the United States. Condition, not color, regulates the grades in social life. A slave is a menial, not because he is black, but because he is a slave. In Brazil, all the avenues to wealth and office are open to the free man of color, if he has character and talents, and the ability to advance in them. As I recollect to have stated before, the officers of the standing army and of the municipal guards and militia, exhibit every shade of color as they stand side by side in their ranks; and I learn from Gov. Kent, that the leading lawyer of Rio is a mulatto. Some of the members of Congress, too, bear evidence of negro blood; and the Governor says, that he has met at the Imperial balls in the palace the "true ebony and topaz" in "ladies and gentlemen black as jet," yet glittering, like the rest, with diamonds.

As to the general treatment of slaves by their owners, it probably does not differ in Brazil from that exhibited wherever there is irresponsible power. House-servants in Rio are said to have easy times, and to do very much as they please; but to judge by the instances I have seen of field laborers, I fear such have but a sad and wearisome life.

The eventual effect of the abolition of the slave trade, will doubtless be to ameliorate the treatment of the slaves, and particularly that of their children. In former years, when the price of a slave was only a hundred and twenty milreis, or about sixty dollars, it seemed to have passed into a settled principle, as a mere matter of profit and pecuniary calculation, that it was cheaper to "use up" the blacks by constant hard labor, and by extorting from them the utmost profit, and when they sunk under it to make new purchases, than to raise children or to extend the term of service by more moderate labor; but now, when the price of a slave has advanced to six and seven hundred dollars, the estimates in the economy of the case will be different; and both parents and children will fare better.

The incidental mention of the annoyance experienced by Mr. M—— of San Aliexo, in getting admittance into the country of the machinery requisite for the establishment of his factory, except by the payment of enormous duties, reminds me of noting some facts connected with the regulations of the Custom House here, derived from authority on the subject so reliable as my friend, the American Consul. These are a source of continual disgust to foreigners, particularly to masters of vessels, and those engaged in maritime matters. They are fifty years behind the age: reach to every minute particular, and seem to be framed with especial reference to fines and penalties. Indeed, one of the items in the annual estimates of expected receipts by the government, is fines on foreign vessels; and to seize and fine, appears to be a fixed purpose of the officials. A few pounds of tea, a pig, cups and saucers, and other small articles of the kind, not on the list of stores, or in the judgment of the visiting inspector an extra number for the size of the vessel, are at once seized and sold at auction at the Custom House door, to swell the receipts of the Imperial treasury. It is said that nothing but a metallic substance, held before the eyes, or placed in the palm of the hands, will prevent these petty seizures. Sometimes the articles seized are of considerable worth, and, in addition to the loss of their value, would lead to the imposition of a heavy fine. No discrimination or distinction seems to be made between cases of accident, ignorance, good faith and honest intentions, and those of designed and evident attempts to smuggle or to evade the law.

It makes no difference whether there is more or less in the shipment than the manifest calls for; if too much, then it is evidence of a design to smuggle the excess—if too little, it is evidence of fraud on the other side. The bed they make is that of Procrustes. If there is a barrel of flour—or any other article—more or less in the cargo than in the manifest, a forfeiture and fine follow with unyielding certainty. One regulation is,

13*

that a master shall give in a list of his stores within twenty-four hours after his arrival. This, it is expected, will include every thing. But it is impossible to know to what extent at times the regulation will be carried. In one instance, recently, a hawser—which had been used, and was in a long coil on deck, ready for immediate use again, and was necessary for the safe navigation of the ship,—was seized, on the ground that it was not in the list rendered. The master remonstrated, and set forth the facts—protesting that he should as soon have included his masts and boats, his anchors and cables, as this hawser; but all the authorities of the Custom House refused to give it up, and the vessel sailed without it. It was only after the question had been pending a long time before the higher authorities, on the strong representation of the American Minister, that restoration to the proper owners was made.

No person is allowed to go on board any vessel, before the discharge of the cargo, without a custom house permit. A poor sailor, a Greek by birth, who came here in an American vessel, and was discharged at his own request, was passing an English vessel in a boat a few days afterwards, and being thirsty, asked for a drink of water: the man on board told him to come up the side and get it. He did so, and after drinking the water returned to his boat. A guard-boat saw and arrested him. He pleaded entire ignorance of the regulation of the port, but in vain: he was fined a hundred milreis, and being unable to pay, was sentenced to be imprisoned one hundred days, or at the rate of a day for each milreis of the fine. He was eventually released, however, through the intervention of Gov. Kent.

Even the consul of a foreign nation must obtain a written permit before he can visit a vessel of his own nation, till she is discharged. The permit in any case is in force only for a single day. It must, too, be stamped at a cost of eight cents. Indeed, every paper of an official nature must be stamped. No note or bill of exchange is valid, unless stamped within thirty days of its date: the duty or the stamp being proportioned to the amount of the note or bill. The revenue derived by the government from this source, is, of course, large.

The want of confidence, indicated by the minuteness and rigid exactment of these custom-house regulations, is said to be a characteristic trait of the people. There is great external civility towards each other; many bows are exchanged, and frequent pinches of snuff, and there is an abundance of polite and complimentary speech; but, full and frank confidence in the intentions, purposes and words of those with whom they deal, seems to be greatly wanting. Some light may be gained upon this point from the fact that by public opinion, by the criminal code, and by the actual administration of the law, offences against the person are looked upon as of a higher grade than the *crimen falsi*. To strike a man in the street with the open palm, and even under extreme provocation, is the great crime next to murder; and so of all offences against the person. An assault is considered an insult and an indignity, as well as a breach of the peace.

Direct stealing is visited with condign punishment; but all the crimes coming under the charge of obtaining money or goods under false pretences, and those involving forgery, lying, deception and fraud of all kinds, seem to meet with more lenient treatment. Convictions in cases of such crimes are not often obtained, and when they are, the sentences are very light. A short time ago, a very congratulatory article was inserted in the newspapers intended in perfect seriousness as a warning to evil doers, which called public attention to the gratifying fact, that two men had been convicted of gross perjury in swearing in court, and had each been sentenced to imprisonment for one month!

It is but just, however, to say, that in no country is there greater security for person and property. Though petty theft is not uncommon, robbery is almost unknown; and offences involving violence, daring, and courage of a reckless kind, are very infrequent.

The recent trial of a foreigner on a charge of murder, gave

me an opportunity of observing the process in the criminal court. The preliminary measures after an arrest for crime, are somewhat similar to those which are taken in like cases, before a magistrate at home. The party is arraigned and verbally examined by the *subdelegado*, or justice of the district in which the crime charged has been commited. This examination is reduced to writing. The accused is asked his age, his business, and other questions, more or less varied and minute, at the discretion and pleasure of the justice. He is not compelled to answer, but his silence may lead to unfavorable inferences against him. After the examination of the prisoner himself, witnesses are examined. If these are foreigners, the official translator of the government attends, to translate the answers, all of which are written down by the clerk. The witnesses are sworn on the Evangelists, the open hand being placed on the book, but this is not kissed as with us One custom struck me favorably, in comparison with the business-like and mere matter of form mode of administering an oath in courts at home. In every instance here, all rise—court, officers, bar and spectators, and stand during the ceremony. All rise, too, and stand while the jury retires.

After the preliminary examination is completed, the magistrate decides whether or not the accused shall be held for trial; and submits the papers with his decision to a superior officer, who usually confirms it, and the accused is imprisoned, or released on bail.

It is only in criminal cases that a jury forms a part of the judicial administration. As with us, it consists of twelve men. Forty-eight are summoned for the term; and the panel for each trial is selected by lot, the names being drawn by a boy, who hands the paper to the presiding judge. In capital cases, challenges are allowed, without the demand of cause. The jury being sworn and empanelled, the prisoner is again examined by the judge, sometimes at great length and with great minuteness, not only as to his acts, but to his motives. The record of the former proceedings, including all the testimony, is then read. If either party desire, the witnesses may be again examined, if present, but they are not bound over, as with us, to appear at the trial. Hence the examination of the accused and of the witnesses at the preliminary process, is very important and material. In many instances, the case is tried and determined entirely upon the record, as it comes up.

After reading the record, the government introduces such witnesses as it sees fit, and the prosecuting officer addresses the jury. The defendant then introduces his witnesses, and his advocate addresses the jury, sometimes at considerable length. The prosecuting attorney, if he desires it again, speaks in reply; and sometimes the argument becomes rather colloquial and tart, the questions and answers being bandied rather sharply.

The judge charges the jury briefly, and gives them a series of questions in writing, to be answered on the return of the verdict. The decision of the case is by majority—unanimity not being required, even in criminal cases. The questions put by the judge relate not merely to acts, but to motives, character, and other things, which may extenuate or aggravate the offence and sentence, and cover usually the whole case in all direct and remote accessories. A case begun, is always finished without an adjournment of the court, though it should continue through the day and entire night.

In the arrangement of the court-room, the judge with his clerk sits on one side, and the prosecuting officer on the other; the jury at semi-circular tables on either side. Two tribunes are erected, one at the end of each table, for the lawyers engaged in the case; these usually address the jury sitting. The lawyers not engaged in the suit in hand, are accommodated in a kind of pew, under the gallery, which a stranger would be likely, at first, to take for the criminal's box or bar.

Public executions very seldom occur. There seems to be a repugnance to the taking of human life, if there is any possible chance to substitute imprisonment for life, or a term of years. Every point of excuse or mitigation is seized upon. One cannot wonder at this, when he regards the mode of capital punishment, the barbarous and revolting one of Portugal and Spain—a relic of barbarism, in which the condemned is ordered up a ladder under the gallows, and then forced to jump off, when another man immediately ascending, mounts the shoulders of the poor wretch, and jumps up and down upon him, with his hand over his mouth till he is dead. Those who have witnessed it, represent it as a most awful and revolting spectacle. This executioner is usually a criminal condemned himself to death, who is allowed to live by agreeing to perform the savage act when required. The old Portuguese custom of gratifying every wish of the condemned, as to food and clothing, is still retained; and for the twenty-four hours preceding his execution, the poorest black slave can order whatever in these respects his fancy dictates: segars, and wine, and luxuries of every kind are at his command.

MONTEVIDEO.

January 30th.—Intelligence from the Plata led to the return of the Congress to this place, on the 24th inst. Mr. Schenck, American Minister at the court of Brazil, came passenger with us, as the guest of Commodore McKeever.

During the three months of our absence, public interest, in political and military affairs, has been gradually centering at Buenos Ayres. The siege of Montevideo being raised, and the Argentine troops which had so long invested her having become part and parcel of the army of Urquiza, and been withdrawn by him to the territory of which he is captain-general, preparations have been in gradual process for a demonstration against Rosas, by the combined forces of Entre Rios and Brazil. Aware of this, every effort has been made by the wary Dictator, to rally his partisans, to give fresh force to the prestige of his name, and to excite the popular feeling in his favor. To aid in this, all the winning power of his accomplished daughter, has been brought forward. To afford better room for its exercise, a public ball of great magnificence was given at the new opera-house in Buenos Ayres.

At this, Dona Manuelita held a kind of court; and, after having received throughout its course the homage of a queen, was, at its close, drawn in a triumphal car, by the young men of the city, to the governmental mansion. New levies of troops had been raised and drilled, and the whole city and country placed under martial law.

A fortnight ago, Urquiza and the allied army of thirty thousand, crossed the Parana without opposition; and, invading the province of Buenos Ayres, advanced within twenty miles of the city. It is now a week since Rosas, leaving Palermo at the head of twenty thousand soldiers, took the field in person, to oppose his further progress. It is said that previous to the march, Dona Manuelita, attired in a riding-dress of scarlet velvet embroidered with gold, and splendidly mounted, reviewed the troops; and, like Queen Elizabeth on the approach of the Spanish Armada, delivered to them an animated and inspiriting address.

A crisis, it is evident, is not far distant; and all is intense expectation. The universal impression is, that Rosas must fall. It is believed that there is treachery around him. An advance guard, in command of Pachecho, one of his best generals, has been defeated under circumstances which leads to the belief that, like Oribe at Montevideo, this officer had a secret understanding with Urquiza; and that the issue at Buenos Ayres will speedily be the same as that which occurred here four months ago—the triumph of Urquiza, through the desertion to him of the opposing soldiery.

This state of affairs led Mr. Schenck and Commodore McKeever, with Secretary G——, to proceed at once to Buenos Ayres. Captain Taylor of the marines was of the party, a company from the guard of the Congress under his command having, with Lieut. Holmes, been ordered to Buenos Ayres by the Commodore for the protection of American citizens and their property, in case of the overthrow of the existing power. As the crew are to have general liberty on shore here, during the passing fortnight—a time when my vocation for good seems to be suspended, and which, both on shipboard and on shore, is to me ever one of trial—I was urged much to accompany the party. Two reasons, however, forbade this—one, the still precarious state of a lad, who, the day we entered the river, fell from a height of ninety-six feet to the deck, without being killed outright; and the other, an engagement to officiate at the marriage of Dr. W——, one of the assistant surgeons of the Congress, to my friend, G—— H——, a daughter of the American Consul. This is appointed for the 5th of February, till when, at least, I must remain at Montevideo.

I have been twice only on shore—once with Captain Pearson, to accompany him in an official call; and again, one afternoon for a short walk. I had not intended being away from the ship more than an hour; but, shortly after attempting to return, when not a half mile from the shore, a furious tempest came rushing upon us. There was no alternative but to return to the landing before it. It was so sudden and so violent, that before the boat could well be secured within the mole by the crew, the whole bay was in a foam, and a heavy sea rolling over it. It was impossible to communicate with the ship the next day; and the following night was still more tempestuous. The hotels of the city afford but indifferent accommodations; and I availed myself in the detention of the ever free hospitality of Mr. F——. I improved the opportunity, too, by calling on the various families of the British Church before I should meet them again at the services of the chapel on the Sabbath. The last day, however, was taken up wholly in reading with absorbing and affecting interest, a manuscript loaned me by Mr. Lafone, and recently received by him from Terra del Fuego. I mentioned, under a date at Rio six months or nine ago, the arrival there of H. B. M. ship Dido, on her way to the Pacific, with orders from the admiralty to visit Terra del Fuego and the adjacent small islands, in search of a company of missionaries who had gone from England the year previous, but from whom nothing had been heard. A schooner chartered by Mr. Lafone, and sent by him about that time with the same object, anticipated the errand of the man-of-war, with melancholy result. The whole party, consisting of Captain Gardiner of the Royal Navy, Mr. Williams, a physician, Mr. Maidenant, a catechist, and four boatmen, perished from hunger and exposure, in the inclemency of the last winter there. The graves of some were found, and the unburied bodies of the rest. Among the effects is the full journal of Mr. Williams, from the time of his departure from England, till within a few days, as is supposed, of the death of the whole.*

Their object was the conversion and civilization of the poor degraded savages of those dreary and forbidding regions. Though Captain Gardiner, the projector and leader of the enterprise, had navigated the waters of Cape Horn, and become familiar with the region while on service in the navy, he was ignorant of the language of the natives, and was without an interpreter. Failing to establish friendly relations with the brutish people, the whole party became impressed with the idea, either with or without sufficient cause, that their lives were in jeopardy from them; and, abandoning the shore, in a great measure, they took to the water in frail and ill-appointed boats. In these they fled from bay to bay, and from islet to islet, till worn out with fatigue and exhausted from want of food, they fell victims to sickness, starvation, and death. Mr. Williams, to whose journal the remark I first made refers, abandoned, at very short notice, a handsome practice in his profession, a choice circle of friends, and a happy home in England, for the enterprise of philanthropy in which he so soon perished. From the record he has left it is evident that he was a deeply experienced and devout Christian: simple-minded, frank, and pure in heart. In this faithful diary, every thought and feeling of his inmost soul seems fully unbosomed. His faith never failed him, under the most afflictive and dispiriting trials; and his soul continued to be triumphantly joyous amidst the most grievous destitution and suffering of the body. I read the

* See Memoir of Richard Williams, published by the Messrs. Carter.

details of the journal as penned in the original manuscript by such a man with intense interest; and came off to the ship, deeply impressed in mind and heart, with the sadness of the tragedy which put an end to the record.

CHAPTER XXV.

BUENOS AYRES.

February 12th.—Public events here, for the last few days, have been more exciting in their progress, and more important in their issues, than any that have occurred on the Plata for many years. On the evening of the 4th inst., the Hon. Mr. Schenck arrived from Buenos Ayres on his return to Brazil. He boarded the Congress from the steamer in which he came, announcing, as he crossed the gangway, the utter overthrow of Rosas by Urquiza, "foot, horse and dragoons!" as he expressed it. This had occurred on the morning of the preceding day. He left the city the same evening, when thousands of mounted troops were pouring through it in rapid flight, before the victorious pursuers. It was not yet known whether Rosas had fallen in battle, was a prisoner, or had made a safe escape.

Before the arrival in Buenos Ayres of Mr. Schenck and Commodore McKeever, he had left for the camp, ten miles distant; and they did not see him. They were twice at Palermo, however, on visits to Dona Manuelita; once before any collision between the hostile forces had taken place; and again on the evening of the 1st inst., when it was known that an advanced guard of six thousand Buenos Ayrean troops, under General Pachecho, had been routed the day previous, and the general made prisoner · a foreboding shadow of the coming event. Till then, Manuelita had sustained her position with great spirit and energy; receiving all visitors—official, diplomatic, and private—as usual, in the saloons of the Quinta, and conducting with ability and despatch the affairs of the Home Department of the government. Toward the close of the last named evening, however, when surrounded by those only who were in her immediate confidence, tears might occasionally be seen trembling in her eye, or stealing down her cheek; but only to be dashed away on the approach of any from whom she would conceal the weakness. It was now well known to her that a general and decisive battle might at any hour take place; and that Palermo, immediately in the line of march from the point of contest to the city, was no longer a place of safety for her. The night was one of splendid moonlight in midsummer, and among others, Commodore McKeever and Mr. Schenck remained with her till a late hour of the evening. Before they left, a walk in the flower-garden was proposed by her; and, taking the arm of Mr. Schenck, she led the way to the rose-covered arbor mentioned in my visit last year. Standing within it in silence for a few moments, she said—"This is my choicest retreat at Palermo; it is here that I come alone, to be alone; and I am here now for the last time, perhaps forever!" adding, as the tears fell rapidly down her face, upturned to the moon, as if in appeal to Heaven for her sincerity, "I leave Palermo to-night! Whatever the issue of the morrow is to be, I know our cause to be just, and believe that God will give to it success!" In this, however, she was mistaken. That cause, the next day but one, was utterly defeated; and the following midnight witnessed her flight with her father disguised as an English marine, and she in the dress of a sailor boy—not from Palermo only, but from her city and country, without even a change of clothes, to find safety and a conveyance to distant exile, under the protection of the British flag.

But this is anticipating the order of events. Rumors of the defeat, on the 1st instant, of the vanguard of the army of Rosas, or some disaster of the kind, reached the city on Sunday evening, the 2d inst.—the night on which Manuelita forsook Palermo. It produced little impression on the public mind, however; and on Monday the shops were open, and general business transacted as usual. At daybreak on Tuesday, heavy cannonading was heard for several hours in the direction of the opposing armies. Early afterwards, whispers of a defeat were afloat; and a straggling cavalry soldier here and there, soon followed by others, in groups of three and four, began to enter the city. The excitement spread rapidly, till three guns from the citadel—the signal for martial law—confirmed the report of the overthrow, and led at once to the shutting up of every shop, and the closing of every door. The retreating cavalry now rushed through the town by hundreds, and soon by thousands, hastening from harm's way to their homes in the pampas of the South. General Mancilla, the brother-in-law of Rosas, and governor of the city, despatched messengers to the foreign ambassadors, reporting the place to be defenceless, and soliciting their intervention with the approaching conqueror, for a halt in his march, till terms of capitulation could be presented. Permission was at the same time granted by him, for the landing of the marines attached to the different foreign squadrons in the harbor, to protect the lives and property of residents from their respective countries—British, American, French, and Sardinian. Forty American marines, including those from the Congress, were disembarked from the Jamestown, under the command of Captain Taylor and Lieut. Tatnall, and the crew of the captain's gig, in charge of Midshipman Walker. These were distributed in the central and richest part of the town—at the Embassy and Consulate of the United States; at the residence of Mr. Carlisle of the house of Zimmerman, Frazer & Co., the head-quarters of Commodore McKeever; and one or two other principal American mercantile establishments. At the same time, a hasty consultation of the diplomatic corps led to the sending of a deputation from their number to the head-quarters of Urquiza, in behalf of the city. The chief member of this was Mr. Pendleton. Mr.

Glover, the secretary of our commander-in-chief, an accomplished young man, well fitted for the service by his talents, and the facility with which he speaks the principal modern languages, formed one of the mission. The special object was to solicit from the victorious chieftain an order to restrain his troops from entering the city, till the authorities could make a formal surrender to him, and thus spare the inhabitants the violence and rapine they had reason to fear. Happily the exhaustion of the victors rendered such an order, for the time, unnecessary. The whole force of thirty thousand men had been without refreshment of any kind, except, perhaps, a little water, for forty-eight hours; and, after having put their opponents to flight, they found it absolutely necessary to come to a rest themselves, not far from the scene of the principal conflict.

It was not till noon of the following day, that Urquiza reached Palermo, and established his head-quarters there. Here the deputation first met him, and readily secured the interposition of his authority in the point of mercy craved. Notwithstanding this, early the same morning—that immediately succeeding the battle—before any thing had been heard from the deputation, the sack of the city in one quarter was reported to have commenced; and, in confirmation of the rumor, the alarm-bell of the Cabildo, or town hall, sent forth an incessant peal. It appeared that a large number of the routed cavalry of Rosas, finding the pursuit by the victors given over, remained in the outskirts of the town during the night; and at the dawn of the next day, commenced breaking open the shops and houses in the more remote parts, and stripping them of their contents, bore off the plunder; alleging the authority of Mancilla himself, the governor of the city, for the outrage. The dress of the troops of both armies is the same; red flannel shirts, caps, and cheripas or swaddling cloths. Those of Urquiza, that they might be distinguished by each other in battle, had chosen for a badge a square piece of white cotton cloth, placed on the shoulders by thrusting the head through a hole in the centre, in the manner of a poncho.

This badge these marauders assumed that they might be mistaken for the invading soldiery. Emboldened by success in the outskirts, they began to penetrate the central parts of the place. The terrified inhabitants believing them to be the invaders, submitted unresistingly to rapine and spoliation, lest they should lose their lives; and consternation spread every where with the increasing violence and robbery. Many of the largest and most valuable plate and jewelry shops had already been sacked; and the spirit of plunder grew in proportion to the success.

At this juncture, while a party of twenty or thirty of these mounted pillagers was engaged in bursting off the door-locks of a rich jeweller's shop with powder, a company of American marines and sailors, in charge of Midshipman Walker, accompanied by Mr. Graham, the American Consul, on their way to the chief scene of pillage—turned into the street near them. The robbers at once fired upon them, happily without injury to any one. Our fellows, under the authority of their officers, were not slow in returning the salute; bringing to the ground, by one volley, four of the leading brigands. Two were killed outright, and two mortally wounded. The rest wheeled instantly in flight, and were seen no more. This first example of the manner by which to check the pillage, led at once to a rally by the citizens. They immediately commenced arming themselves, and a stay was put to the progress of what, in a short time, would have become a general sack of the town.

Mr. Glover arrived the same moment, at the consulate near which the above scene took place, to report the success of the mission on which he had accompanied Mr. Pendleton. He had passed a sleepless night, and been in the saddle many hours; but, as there was reason to fear that the check which had been put by our marines upon the pillage, would be but temporary, and that the marauders would soon return in augmented numbers to avenge the death of their comrades, as well as to load themselves with fresh booty, he was requested by Commodore McKeever to return immediately to Palermo, and solicit from Urquiza a force sufficient to control the disorder and robbery existing. The Chief of Police, at the same time made his appearance, to urge the same measure. Accompanied by this functionary, Mr. Glover, therefore, again hastened as an express to the Quinta. He was admitted immediately to the chieftain, though his companion, the Chief of Police, was forbidden his presence. The object of his visit was accorded, by an instant order for the entrance to the city of a body of troops sufficient for its protection. Informed of the result of the rencontre with the American marines and sailors, he gave full sanction to the interference, and authorized its continuance. The report of this interview was quickly spread through the city; and the patrol of the foreign marines and armed sailors, and the speedy arrival of the forces promised by Urquiza, allayed the panic of the inhabitants.

The troops of Urquiza brought with them orders to shoot down all persons implicated in the robbery and disorder. This was reiterated by the Provisional Government appointed by him upon receiving, as soon as he had taken up his quarters at Palermo, the deputation from the city, empowered to surrender it to his mercy. Under the orders thus issued, three or four hundred persons, both men and women, were summarily put to death, within twenty-four hours; and a scene of such frightful carnage was taking place, with the liberty of its continuance for eight days, that the humanity of Mr. Pendleton led him, accompanied by Mr. Glover, to hasten once more to head-quarters, to beseech that an immediate stop might be put to a slaughter in which it was so apparent that the innocent, through false accusations of robbery, might become the victims of their political and even private enemies. The good sense of Urquiza led him at once to appreciate the justice of this appeal to his humanity, and to countermand the order first issued. The alarm was thus quieted, and a general feeling of safety restored.

It is quite a matter of congratulation with us, that the marines and sailors of the Congress and Jamestown, should have been so eminently the means, by their prompt and gallant conduct, of staying a frightful evil; and, that the prestige of the American name, through the frank and philanthropic agency of Mr. Pendleton and Mr. Glover, should have had such ready and such important influence with the victor, now invested by right of conquest with all power here.

These particulars I learned before leaving Montevideo, from my friend Lieut. Turner. This officer was despatched to Buenos Ayres by Captain Pearson, immediately after the report made by Mr. Schenck of the overthrow of the Dictator. He went in charge of the American propeller, "Manuelita de Rosas," which the emergency of affairs and the absence of every suitable tender of the kind in the squadron, led Commodore McKeever to charter for the time being. He arrived in the midst of the excitement and consternation of the second day after the battle, when the pillage was at its height, and the summary execution of the perpetrators by the troops of Urquiza was begun. Being a fellow Virginian and a friend of Mr. Pendleton, he was invited to a seat in a carriage with him and Mr. Glover, on their last mission of humanity to Palermo; and thus was a spectator in the city and its environs, and at the Quinta itself, of a succession of scenes of alarm and confusion, of bloodshed and affecting tragedy in various forms, which it is not often the lot even of a naval officer to witness. The city, containing more than a hundred thousand inhabitants, was under pillage and in panic; the wide suburbs were thronged with ten thousand savage troops, dashing to and fro in various directions; the bodies of dead men were scattered about, after having been shot down, or having their throats cut, not in the conflict of battle, but in wanton pursuit, or by order of a drum-head court-martial; women in common life were rushing here and there in terror, and ladies of wealth and rank hastening in their carriages through these scenes, in agitation and affright, to the centre of power, to throw themselves at the feet of the conqueror, in supplication for the lives and fortunes of those dearest to them.

It was in the carriage of Madame E——, a sister of the fallen

Dictator, that the party made the excursion. This lady herself made one of their number; and, under the favoring auspices of the American minister, sought the presence of the chief, who now occupies the palace, and wields the power, so long and so recently in the undisputed possession of her brother. The avenues and corridors of Palermo were crowded with mothers, sisters, and daughters, pressing for audience, on like errands of mercy. The suits of many of whom, I am happy to add, were not in vain, but most promptly and generously accorded. Such were the scenes amidst which Mr. Turner passed his first day here. Those of the second, in a ride of fifteen miles, to the battle-field, under the guidance of an adjutant and the protection of a guard furnished by Urquiza, were, if possible, more exciting and more revolting to the feelings, and scarcely bearable in the disgust created. The whole way was marked with evidences of the completeness of the overthrow; and the scene of the conflict, strewn for miles with the bodies of the slain lying still unburied. The whole atmosphere was tainted with the effluvia of the dead, both of man and beast, and sad demonstration given on every side of the horrors of war.

It was his representation of the state of affairs that led me—the marriage of my friends Miss H—— and Dr. R—— having been duly celebrated, and the crew of the Congress still in the process of a general liberty—to the determination of making the visit of a few days. I came up in the propeller, still bearing a naval pennant: embarking on the evening of the 10th, and arriving the next morning.

On landing, I found every hotel and lodging-house crowded to overflowing, with officers, naval and military, both natives and foreigners, and with strangers from various quarters, who had hastened to the capital on hearing the result of the conflict. After long search, I was able to secure a small sleeping-room only, in a public house of very inferior order; and suffered so much during the night from the oppressive heat, fleas, and musquitos, as to have made up my mind by morning, to return to the

Congress the same day. During my former visit, I had made the acquaintance of the Rev. Mr. Lore and Mrs. Lore, of the Wesleyan Methodist mission here, and had been so much interested in them by the brief intercourse, as to be unwilling to take my departure now without a call at the parsonage, of a few minutes at least. Here I was most cordially welcomed; and the cause of my intended return becoming known, they at once laid an interdict upon my purpose, and constrained me to accept a room in the parsonage, in their power to offer, and the kind hospitality of their house.

I had brought with me from the Congress, with the purpose of affording him a peep at Buenos Ayres, one of the lads of the ship, who had been commended to my special care by an excellent widowed mother at home, and who had merited this indulgence by long-continued good conduct in his position on board ship. His leave of absence extended to the passing day only; and, knowing that he was especially anxious to visit Palermo, I applied to Mr. Lore, as soon as it had been determined that I should remain, for aid in securing a vehicle to take the drive with him. This he at once gave; but in place of a carriage from a livery stable, as I intended, he soon appeared with the handsome equipage of one of his parishioners, and accompanied us in the excursion.

The morning was excessively hot—the character of the weather for the last fortnight. No rain had fallen in that time, and the road was one continued bed of deep dust, kept in constant motion by the thousand and ten thousands of horses and cattle, which the large force in bivouac in the environs of the city had brought together. It is computed that on the day of the battle, and for some days succeeding it, there were not less than three hundred thousand horses, within the circuit of a few miles, around the city. The number of cattle may be estimated by the allowance granted to the troops for subsistence—one animal a day for every hundred men: the number of men in both armies, the conquering and the conquered; amounts to more than fifty thousand, and the daily consumption, therefore, is at least five hundred. It would require pages to describe the novelty and wild romance of the scenes witnessed in our short drive. The riding at full tilt, to and fro, of unnumbered Indian-like horsemen in the picturesque and fiery costume of the native cavalry; the flying past of carriages in one direction or another, through the thick dust of the road; the lassoing of cattle amidst the herds crowding the open plain; the butchering them when entangled, wherever that might be—even in the middle of the highway; and flaying them while still alive, and scarcely well brought to the ground; the masses of hides, and horns, and offal scattered about every where; some freshly stripped from the carcasses and others in a shocking state of putrefaction; the hundreds of loose horses scampering about amid clouds of dust; and unnumbered savage men, in all attitudes, and in every kInd of grouping, presented sights beyond the power of description.

As we approached the Quinta, such objects became, if possible, more varied and more crowded: while dead horses and dead cattle lined the road-side, and in some places dotted the ornamental canals of the domain with their bloated carcasses. The white shell-dust of that, which was once the private drive, covered every thing so thickly, that the iron railings, now bent and broken down, the orange trees and willows, once kept so neatly washed and so green, appeared as if just powdered with meal. Indeed, the aspect of every thing in this respect, was very much that of a landscape at home after a fall of snow, while the trees and their branches are still in leaf. The house itself—though surrounded, as when last seen by me, with guards and soldiery, and in the same dress; and by a long line of carriages and led horses awaiting the visitors within—had a closed and forsaken air. The reception rooms occupied by Urquiza, are not in the front. Those there, in which we had been received, with blinds drawn, and shutters closed, appeared as though death, as well as desertion, was there. It was not our purpose to alight; and, after a general survey of the establishment as we drove by, we returned to the city amidst the same scenes through which we had arrived.

The next evening I joined a large party of American ladies and gentlemen, residents of Buenos Ayres, in a visit of ceremony to Urquiza at Palermo. Notwithstanding the pressure of military and state affairs in the disposition of his troops, and the appointment of a provisional government for the city and province, he has been constrained to hold an almost uninterrupted levee, for the reception of the crowds whose interest it is to pay court to him. Many of the most servile of the partisans of Rosas have done this in the most sycophantic manner; and many of them, I have rejoiced to hear, only to meet his ill-concealed contempt and pointed rebuke, by a refusal to recognize their presence in some instances, and by prompt and stern dismissal from the audience-room in others. One incident which occurred interested me much. Col. Maximo Terero, the favorite aide-de-camp of Rosas, and the affianced husband of Doña Manuelita, was made prisoner on the day of the battle. It was believed by many—judging of the course Urquiza would pursue in the case, by the sanguinary precedents of Rosas and other successful aspirants in the past history of the country—that he, and such others of the immediate partisans of the Dictator as had fallen into his hands, would be severely dealt with, if not summarily shot. Contrary to all expectation, Col. Terero was at once set at liberty on parole. Touched by this magnanimity, Gen. Terero the father, a confidential friend of Rosas, and long his partner in extensive financial operations, hastened to Palermo to wait upon the commander-in-chief, and to thank him for the clemency and kindness he had shown to his son. He approached him with the following words, "Gen. Urquiza, I have come to Palermo to tender to you the unfeigned thanks of a father, for sparing the life of a son, whose life and liberty were in your power. You have, sir, my most sincere and heartfelt gratitude. I thank you from the bottom of my heart. I am known to you as the friend of General Rosas. He long since won my confidence, has long had my warm friendship, and I have never seen cause for withdrawing these from him." The frankness and independence of this address met an appreciating spirit in Urquiza; and seizing him cordially by the hand, he exclaimed, "Gen. Terero, I am most happy to see you. I am glad to hear you express yourself as you have. I believe what you say—yours is the first honest speech I have heard in Palermo; and I honor you for it."

At the time of our presentation by Mr. Pendleton the saloons and corridors were crowded; and the audience was brief, and, on the part of the General, unavoidably constrained. He wore a dress-coat of black, with white waistcoat; and, though polite and gentlemanly, appeared to much less advantage and less at home in the drawing-room, than on the tented field of Pantanoso. He appeared, too, to be jaded and exhausted; which he indeed must be, after the fatigue and excitement without intermission of the last fortnight. At the end of fifteen minutes we took leave; and after a turn along the parterres of the flower-garden, drove rapidly to the city, to escape a gust of wind and rain which was seen to be gathering with great blackness, in a threatening quarter.

On Friday, I made a visit to the hospital, in which most of the wounded of both parties are now collected, to the number of five or six hundred. The accommodations, in ordinary times, are limited and indifferent, and are now altogether inadequate. The surgeons and physicians are too few for the duty, and the services of Dr. Foltz, of the U. S. sloop Jamestown, have been gratefully accepted. The wounds of many of the poor creatures are frightful; especially those caused by grape and round shot. From the heat of the weather, and the length of time that elapsed after the battle before they could be properly attended to, such are now in a dreadful condition. Those made by lances are chiefly from behind, and show frightful thrusts on the part of the pursuers. Many of the wounded have died daily; and the state of many more is hopeless. The edifice appropriated as a hospital is itself spacious and massive, and is of special interest, from having been the residencia or palace of the viceroys of Buenos Ayres. Mr. Lore took me a ride also, the same morning, through the suburbs, in a semicircular sweep from one end of the city to the other—the base-line of the circuit being the river. There is little to interest one in the scenery, the whole is so flat; and the road was but a succession of dry and dirty lanes, lined by mean and shabby huts. We called in the eastern suburbs upon an English family, parishioners of Mr. Lore, who occupy and cultivate as a fruit and vegetable garden, the grounds of what appears once to have been a tasteful and luxurious country-seat. We were most kindly received, and refreshed with some very fine peaches and grapes, the former the last gatherings of the season. The situation is an exposed one in times of public commotion and disorder; and we were shown a cavern, screened and hidden almost beyond discovery, where the females of the household were to have been concealed, had the city, in the overthrow of Rosas, been given over to pillage and rapine. In one part of the enclosure, a natural terrace attains a height of about twenty feet above the general level. To this I was led as one of the finest points of view in the neighborhood. The extent of the landscape commanded from it was less than a mile, across a flat meadow, bounded at that distance by a range of tree-tops, above which rose the masts of some small craft at anchor in a stream, whose banks the trees line. I could scarcely avoid a smile in hearing this called a "fine view," while in imagination my eye swept, in comparison, over that spread before you in such wide expanse at Riverside. In the course of our ride, we visited the English Protestant burial-ground; a rural cemetery on the south-side of the city. It embraces several acres, surrounded by a substantial wall, entered by a handsome gateway of iron; and has a lodge for the keeper, and a small, well-built chapel for the funeral service. Besides a variety of prettily-arranged shrubberies, it is ornamented with two or three avenues of the Pride of China, which grows here in great perfection: the whole forming an attractive and rural resting-place for the dead.

The observations of the day were completed by the inspection, under the guidance of Mr. Graham, of the new city residence of

Rosas. It is already in possession of the provisional government appointed by Urquiza, and its elegant saloons are converted into offices for the various public bureaus. It is an extensive and finely-constructed edifice, one story in height, enclosing several quadrangles, and covering half a square; the front extends the length of a "block" on a principal street near the centre of the city. The middle section of this contains the suite of private rooms of the late owner. From these the furniture had been removed, preparatory to the sale of all his effects. The structure, though of one story only on the streets, rises to two in some of the inner sections. The whole is well built, and, for this part of the world, beautifully finished. One of the inner courts is filled with orange trees, and another contains a garden of choice flowers. A lofty tower or mirador rises from the centre. This is ascended by a spiral staircase of mahogany. The view from it comprises, as on a map, the city, river, roadstead and shipping; and the country in every direction as far as its flatness allows the vision to reach. It conveys a strong impression of the size, good order, and architecture of the city. Every prominent building is in conspicuous view: all the old Spanish churches—the Cathedral, the Merced, the collegiate, or former Jesuit College, that of San Francisco, San Domingo and San Miguel; and the Residencia or vice-regal palace, now the general hospital. All these are of dark stone, and are time-stained and moss-covered: massive and enduring piles, with many attractive features in the varied taste and symmetry of their architecture, and in the well-defined proportions of dome and tower, pediment and belfry. The lantern top of this look-out is furnished with a fine telescope, by which every object is subjected to near inspection; and it was a favorite resort of the Dictator, during his hours of seclusion in town. One story of the tower leading to this observatory, is a handsomely proportioned apartment, paved with tessellated marble of red and white. It is said to have been the favorite sleeping-room of Rosas, when he remained in the city over night, being secure from approach except by the spiral stairs, which could be easily defended. A fixture in one of the galleries of an open court into which the chief suites of rooms open, particularly struck me as a novelty : it is a fireplace with a grate and handsomely finished marble mantle, so that, if one choose, he may sit by a fireside in the open air, when the temperature makes it desirable.

As I looked around upon the spacious and well-appointed establishment, through which Doña Manuelita, a few days since, moved a princess, surrounded by luxury, and oppressed with the adulations of courtiers and admirers, I could not but anew deeply sympathize with her, in her flight and exile, with scarce a change of apparel, or a friend to cheer her under her reverse of fortune.

On leaving, we made an effort to gain admission to the Sala, or hall of Representatives near by, and to the public library of the city; but without success, from the absence of the persons having possession of the keys. A *Porteno*—a name by which the Buenos Ayreans pride themselves in being called—of intelligent and gentlemanlike appearance, on overhearing our application for admittance to the library and the cause of its failure, said pleasantly to us, " It is well for the credit of the city that the key cannot be found; we are thus saved a just reproach in the eyes of intelligent visitors."

CHAPTER XXVI.

BUENOS AYRES.

February 24th.—On Saturday, I accompanied a large party of ladies and gentlemen, Americans and English, in a visit to the scene of the late battle. It is called indiscriminately, "Monte Caseros," from the name of the country-house at which Rosas took position in meeting the enemy, and "Moron," from that of the nearest hamlet, a mile or two distant.

We were off at an early hour. The morning was brilliant, and delightful in its freshness: almost too cool, in contrast with the excessive heat of the first few days after my arrival. The road we took led past several country-seats in the suburbs, at which the victorious troops were still quartered. Their horses and camp-fires had made sad havoc with the shrubberies and plantations of these; many of the trees being terribly barked by the former, while their limbs had been stripped off and cut up for fuel by the latter. Bivouac after bivouac, and rude encampment after encampment, extended miles beyond Palermo; while the road on either side, and often in its centre, presented the aspect of a continued slaughter house—the hoofs, horns, hides and entrails of the animals daily slain for the subsistence of the soldiery, being scattered about every where, and polluting the air with their offensive effluvia. The whole distance of fifteen miles, gave evidence of the desolating effects of the retreat of the vanquished, and of the marauding presence of the victors.

At the end of twelve miles, we came upon the military village of Santos Lugares, composed of brick huts, the regular cantonment of the army, from which Rosas had led his force of twenty thousand to Monte Caseros, on the evening of the 1st instant. This seemed now, literally, a " deserted village : " every building being vacant, with the appearance of having suffered utter pillage. It has its church, and an extensive common, or green, ornamented at one point by a clump of ombu, a species of gum-tree—the chief emblem of the country. Shortly after passing this, we caught view in the distance of the white tower of Monte Caseros, the head-quarters of Rosas at the commencement of the battle. Its mirador, or observatory, commands a view of the surrounding region; and from it he watched the advance of Urquiza, and for a time, the progress of the engagement. He then descended to the field, and took part in the fight, till it was evident the day was lost. Persuaded of this, he seized a cartridge from the box of a common soldier; breaking it in pieces, he blackened his face with the powder, and mounting a magnificent horse, in readiness near by, succeeded in making his escape amid the dust and uproar of the general rout. He made his way without being recognized, to the residence of the British minister in the city. There his daughter joined him, and under the guidance of that gentleman both sought refuge at midnight, in the disguise before mentioned, on board the flag-ship of Admiral Henderson.

Evidences of the conflict, or rather of the flight and pursuit, now began rapidly to multiply, in tattered portions of clothing and in accoutrements—caps, sword-belts, cartridge-boxes, bayonet-sheaths, cuirasses, and broken musical instruments, and drums. What seemed the most singular part of this camp equipage, was the quantity of letters and manuscript papers, scattered widely and for great distances over the ground. Soon the more revolting spectacle of a dead body presented itself here and there, naked and ghastly, blackening in the sun, in a frightful state of decomposition, and tainting the whole atmosphere by its impurity. These multiplied rapidly as we advanced; none of the slain of either party having yet been buried, excepting such as have been sought for and discovered by personal friends. The brick walls of the country-house and those of a large circular dove-cote, of the same material, whitewashed, are a good deal marked and shattered by balls both of cannon and musketry. After Rosas had left the observatory and the house, a strong party of his officers kept possession of them. When the battle seemed to be given up, it was supposed by the victors that these, like others outside, had surrendered; but on attempting to enter, they were met by a volley of musketry, with the cry of "Viva Rosas!" This led to an immediate onslaught by the assailants; and every man within, amounting to thirty or forty, was at once put to the sword. Till within a day or two past, their bodies lay piled upon each other as they had thus fallen, upon the stairs and platforms of the tower; and since having been dragged out, still lie scattered over the lawn in nakedness and putrefaction. Two or three bodies are stretched on the roof of the dove-house also, as they fell on being shot down in its defence.

Though the engagement commenced at daybreak and continued three or four hours, the number of the slain is thought not to exceed three hundred; and the wounded, not more than six. Still these numbers are quite sufficient, where father met son and brother met brother, in deadly fight. While we were on the tower, two brothers happened there, and pointed out to us the positions of the two forces, at different times during the engagement. Both were in the battle, one with the troops of Rosas, and the other with those of Urquiza.

With the exception of the objects mentioned, there was little to interest; and, after strolling around for an hour or two, we returned to the shade of the ombu trees of Santos Lugares, to partake of an ample lunch, provided by the ladies of the party. One result of the excursion, was the opportunity it afforded me of gaining my first sight of what is here termed the 'camp;' the flat open country of the pampas, or plains, which extend hundreds of leagues, with a surface more level and less wooded than that of the prairies of the West with us: a vast sea of grass and thistles, without roads or enclosures, and without a habitation, except at long intervals. Nothing breaks the unvarying outline, unless it be now and then an ombu, rising on the distant horizon, like a ship at sea. Travellers upon these plains, whether on horseback or in carriages, like voyagers on the ocean, direct their course over the trackless expanse, by compass.

The 19th was appointed for the public entry of Urquiza into the capital, with the entire allied force, cavalry, infantry, and artillery, to the number of twenty thousand. Rain during the preceding night, laid the dust and freshened the air. The morning was pure, cool and pleasant, somewhat obscured by clouds till noon, but after that hour, clear and brilliant. Every street and every house was gay with fluttering flags and the banners of all civilized nations, and the whole city in gala dress. I had invitations to the balconies of several private houses in different streets through which the procession would pass; but preferred a roving commission, with the advantage of being able to change at pleasure my point of view. I chose a stand at an angle of the Plaza Victoria, or place of victory, the principal square in the city, near a triumphal arch thrown over the street through which the procession would *débouche* upon the Plaza. It was the best point for observation; giving a near view of the chief officers and troops, and commanding in coup d'œil the masses of people in the open square; the decorations of the monument of victory in its centre; and of the public buildings facing it, as well as of the crowded balconies and flat-topped roofs of the surrounding houses, thronged with spectators of all ages and both sexes in holiday attire.

Urquiza as captain-general and commander-in-chief, with his staff, headed the columns. These had formed at Palermo, the cavalry being eight, and the infantry and artillery twelve abreast. The chieftain's dress and that of his staff was not full uniform.

With a military coat, he wore a round beaver hat and scarlet hatband, and held a riding-whip in his hand as if on a hunt. The red hatband, besides its demi-savage look, gave offence, it is said, to the Buenos Ayreans, by reminding them of the thraldom of which it had been made a badge under Rosas; and which, with the waistcoat and every thing of the same color, they had indignantly and with abhorrence thrown off, the moment they found themselves free to do so. It is also said that every demonstration of popular feeling, by shouts and vivas, had been interdicted; and there was little enthusiasm manifested in this way. Bouquets, however, were showered upon the conqueror in great abundance, and his hands and those of his immediate suite were filled with such as had been picked up and handed to them. It struck me, notwithstanding, that there was nothing very gracious in the expression of countenance or manner of the hero: that something had gone amiss, and he was only tolerating with decent civility the courtesies shown him. He declined to dismount in the city, and continued the ride in circuit to Palermo again. The cavalry, constituting the principal body of the troops, in the Guacho dress of red flannel shirts and cheripas, white cotton pantalets, and red caps worn *à la brigand*, had all the appearance of so many wild Arabs, clothed in red in place of white. They were barefooted, and unshaven and unshorn; and varied in complexion, from the red and white of the Saxon, here and there, to the jet of Congo. Four hours were occupied by the procession in passing a single point; though the cavalry, towards the close, rode at full charge, when, especially, they bore an aspect as wild as that of the desert itself. General Lopez, the Governor or President of the Province of Corrientes, second to Urquiza in command, appeared in full military costume, as did Baron Caxias, chief of the Brazilian division. Both were magnificently mounted.

The booming of cannon from various points was heard during this triumphal march through the city; and a stationary band in front of the cathedral played at intervals, as the regimental bands, one after another, passed beyond hearing. In the evening, the arcades surrounding the eastern and southern sides of the Plaza, the cabildo or town hall fronting it on one side, the cathedral at one corner, and the monument of victory in the centre, were illuminated; and for an hour and more, there was a good display of fireworks. The remaining days of the week were proclaimed holidays, and the decorations in flags, the illuminations, and music at night were continued.

Two days ago, a grand Te Deum, in commemoration of the overthrow of Rosas, was celebrated in the cathedral, in presence of Urquiza and of the newly appointed provisional government; the officers of the allied armies; and of all the dignitaries of the church. An immense crowd was brought together by the interest of the occasion itself, and by the spectacle presented in so large an assemblage of persons of official rank and power. The ordinary services were accompanied by a rhapsody in the form of a sermon, delivered by a young ecclesiastic, who, from having been chosen for orator on such an occasion, must have some pretension to talent and eloquence. I have seen a copy of his discourse in Spanish, and will give a hasty translation of some of its passages which throw light upon the popular view of the public character and government of Rosas; and give proof also of the adulations showered upon the Conqueror. The address occupied more than an hour in the delivery, and is at least a curiosity as a sermon. The text from the Vulgate, was announced in Latin, and was the opening verse of the song of Moses after the destruction of the Egyptians in the Red Sea:

> "Let us sing unto the Lord, for he hath triumphed gloriously:
> The horse and his rider hath he thrown into the sea."

The introduction, written in Dellacruscan style, and delivered with the action of the stage, consists of all manner of apostrophes—to the Plata, to Liberty, to Peace, to the Argentines, and to the Virgin Mary, for aid in the office of his ministry. Two general points are then presented,—one the duty of thanksgiving for a deliverance from evil; the other of thanksgiving for blessings conferred. Under the first he institutes a parallel between the rejoicings of Rome on the fall of Nero, and of those due from Buenos Ayreans on the overthrow of Rosas: thus—"Tell me, was it right for the Romans, adorning themselves with garlands of flowers and clothed with gladness, to hail with hallelujahs the jubilee of their deliverance; to throw open their temples and offer incense to their gods in testimony of their gratitude, when they saw the dead body of the most barbarous of their sovereigns—that monster, whose cruelty was not satiated with the blood even of his own mother, and whose corruption made him regardless of the most sacred obligations of the marriage tie? Was it not right, I say, that the Roman people should hymn songs of thankfulness before the altars of their gods, in view of the still palpitating remains of Nero, that impersonation of cruelty, who, seated on a mount, instead of weeping like the prophets over the destruction of the capital set on fire by himself, rejoiced in the death-shrieks of its inhabitants? I do not believe, gentlemen, that any of you condemn this conduct of the Romans—do I say condemn? I know that you justify, you praise, you applaud it; and if it was right, if it was laudable, if it was praiseworthy in the Romans gratefully to acknowledge, and joyfully to give thanks to their gods for a deliverance from the tyranny of Nero, is it not equally so in us Argentines to offer to the true God the incense of our praise for liberating us from the despotism of Rosas—that tyrant, that wild beast, that scandal of our nation, that shame upon humanity, that scourge of society and of religion, that minotaur, more thirsty for blood than him of Crete who fed on human victims? Yes! all of you will confess that it is just—and the more just as he was more cruel than even Nero. How more so? Can it be possible that there ever was a man as cruel as he, much less more so? Sirs, the lengthened series of eighteen hundred years did not, indeed, produce such a man: but the epoch of the barbarous Dictator of the Argentine Republic had not yet arrived. The nineteenth century, great in all its aspects in the annals of ages, was to be conspicuous by the production of this monster of cruelty. Yes, gentlemen, he was not only as cruel, but more cruel than the oppressor of the Romans.

"Let us make the comparison. But first, Argentines, rise from the places you occupy—rise, and make haste to close the temple doors that no foreigner come in; and if any such should already have entered, supplicate them to retire, that they hear not of the horrors perpetrated by a son of our soil. Yes! rise, hasten quick, fly! But why? Alas! oh sorrow!—stay! stay! it is too late: the clamorous echo of the cry raised by his cruelty has resounded to the ends of the earth. I retract my call, and beg you, Argentines, to fly—yes, fly to the portals of the temple: but let it be to open them widely from side to side, that entrance may be given to the inhabitants of the whole world—if it were possible, of the entire universe—to be witnesses of our reclamation, and hear the protest we solemnly make in the presence of the heavens and of the earth, before the altars of our God: Neighboring Republics! Foreign nations! all ye people of the earth! know, and transmit to your descendants from age to age that the children of the Plata repudiate this monster; we despoil him of the prerogatives of an Argentine; we banish him from our fatherland; and by the unanimous vote of the entire Republic, sentence him to wander from place to place, and from land to land; and, like Cain the fratricide, to carry the mark of his crime branded on his brow, that his own ignominy may be the expiation of his transgressions.

"Yes! I again say, Rosas was more cruel than Nero. Let us analyze the facts in the case. Why is Nero represented in history as the greatest tyrant among sovereigns? Hear Tacitus: 'He was,' says the historian, 'the assassin of his mother, of his brother, of his tutor, and of an immense number of Christians. He set Rome on fire.' What horrors! and the tyrant of the Argentines, did he perpetrate such enormities? Some of them he did—others he did not. But the credit of omitting to perpetrate those which he did not commit is to be attributed to a dissimilarity of circumstances, not to a difference in moral principle Rosas did not sacrifice his mother, but it was because she did not threaten to deprive him of his power. He did not sacrifice his brothers, because none of them attempted to snatch from him the reins of government: or if they did, they fled beyond his reach. He did not sacrifice his tutor, because he never had one; but he had an instructor in political economy and a patron in his early public career, and him he did assassinate. Oh! sad remembrance! Sirs, you all know the horrible death of Maza, President of the House of Representatives,—that noble patriot and good man, who was murdered in the very temple of the laws: not in its vestibule, but in the very sanctum sanctorum!

"And did Rosas sacrifice a large number of Christians? Alas! would I were not under the necessity of answering this question. Well then—I will not do it; but answer for me, ye numerous auditors who listen to me. Speak, ye many widows, whose hearts, as ye listen to my words, are broken with sorrow—let the tears speak with which you have been fed till the present day. Speak, ye fathers, who still pour out your grief in sighs upon your children's tombs. Speak, ye numerous orphans, who, while embracing with kisses the fathers of your love, have suddenly beheld them expire beneath the point of the dagger! Do thou, O city of Buenos Ayres—do thou speak: and speak every province, speak every town, speak every family of the Republic! Oh, thou year of 1840! O fatal epoch! What days of darkness, what days of mourning, what days of tears! your memory will forever embitter our existence. Ah! yes—in every street, in every house, in every room, we then stumbled over some victim—innocent victim, for, to be innocent was, in the eyes of that wicked one, the greatest of crimes. Humanity is horrified by the frightful truth! The story seems like a fable, but we ourselves are witnesses to the facts. Had the blood which was then shed, been mingled with the waters of the mighty river rolling beside us, they would have reddened to crimson. Death itself seemed exhausted in the execution of such cruelty; and the dead themselves, could they speak, would exclaim, 'How horrible!'

"And were they Christians only that he immolated? Nero did not slay his priests; at least, history does not say that he attempted it. And Rosas, did he? Ah! that tyrant not only attempted it, but placed the seal upon the record of his impieties in the blood of the anointed of the Lord. That blood still cries to Heaven for vengeance, and like the infernal furies, will follow and torment the guilty criminal.

"And Rosas? did he burn the city? Would he had destroyed it rather than have prolonged our martyrdom. But in this there would have been too much humanity for him. His object was to protract our agony the better to enjoy the misery.

"Finally, what were the articles of Nero's religious faith? You all know that he was a Pagan—how then could it be strange that he should persecute his adversaries? And Rosas, was he likewise a Pagan? Would that he had been!—that he had been so openly! His wickedness was not so great that he did not call himself a Catholic. Ah! unhappy man, thou art accountable for the abuses introduced to the church; for thou, like another Henry VIII. of England, didst constitute thyself the priest, and the bishop, and the Pope of the Republic. If there has been demoralization in society, thou art accountable to the Great Judge for it; for thou hast interfered with the most sacred rights of religion, education, and laws; and for twenty years hast set back the civilization of the Republic, and made the relentless knife the only inducement to excel. But, it is enough! Thanks to the valiant, the all-powerful Urquiza! the country now reposes in tranquillity: we are free from the despotism of the odious tyrant.

"And is it not right that we should be thankful to the Almighty for the benefits received at his hands? We have attained our liberty. Oh! incomparable good! Oh! gift of inestimable value! And to whom shall we give our thanks, if not to Thee, O Father of mercies?—to whom if not to Thee, O Giver of all joy. To Thee, therefore, O Fountain of all felicity, we give thanks! But likewise to thy name, O great Urquiza! to thee, whose name will be immortal; to thee our gratitude will be eternal, and the echo of our acknowledgments will be heard, even to the ends of the earth. The heart of every Argentine will be a temple from which thou wilt receive the sweet incense of our affection; and tradition will for ever transmit to our descendants the name of him who has restored to us our liberties. Most excellent sir, we salute thee as the morning star of the happy day of freedom that has dawned upon our country. We acclaim thee as our Washington! The Washington of the Argentine Republic! What a glory for you, sir! Argentines! I call your attention to your deliverer: fix your gaze on that bold champion. Let your modesty, sir, suffer me in the transports of my gratitude to express the sentiments of my heart. Yes, Argentines, fix again, I say, your gaze on that brave warrior. See you those scintillating eyes beaming with humanity? they have suffered prolonged vigils for your liberty. Behold that capacious brow—even yet bronzed by the suns of the camp! it has been absorbed in the profoundest meditations for your liberty! Do you perceive those features full of expressions of goodness? they have suffered the rigors of heat and the inclemencies of the seasons for your liberty. Witness ye that elevated and finely modelled breast, the temple of a magnanimous heart? It has been exposed to the bullet and the lance of the tyrant, for your liberty. Do you observe the nervous arm and powerful hand, so well known in battle? they have wielded the sword valiantly for your liberty: yes, for our liberty, he voluntarily renounced his sleep, to give his mind, day and night, to deep thought; for our liberty, he sacrificed his own comfort and well-being; for our liberty he hazarded his life! For our liberty he has suffered hunger, thirst, and conflicts; and to achieve it, impetuous rivers have appeared to him but smooth rivulets, enormous deserts like populous plains, the longest marches but short excursions, and the greatest obstacles the merest trifles. What courage! what heroism! what patriotism!

"What fortune is ours, Argentines, to have a man of so much excellence, in him whom Providence has sent to liberate us, and give to us the guarantee of a constitutional government. Eternal Father, God of all goodness, what thanksgiving shall we render to Thee for this evidence of Thy mercy?"

With this fulsome rhapsody, terminates the second act of the political drama of the Plata.

CHAPTER XXVII.

MONTEVIDEO.

March 30th.—While in Buenos Ayres, we were indebted for repeated hospitality, at dinners and other entertainments, to the American Minister and other fellow-citizens from the United States, including my kind friends of the Methodist parsonage, where I was a constant guest.

We left on the 25th ult. The Montevideans exult greatly in the overthrow of Rosas; and, on our return, we found the citizens in the midst of public rejoicing, and various festivities. The 12th inst. was a grand gala for the reception of the troops of the Republic, which had been engaged in the battle of Monte Caseros. Among the most gallant of these was the negro regiment. A few days afterwards, I witnessed a religious ceremony of thanksgiving, at the cathedral, characteristic of the services of the church here, in which this composed the audience. Marching into the public square in two detachments, each led by a band, they formed in line, in front of the church, and entering it in military procession, filled its spacious nave. The bands took a stand on either side near the chancel. The soldiers, at the word of command, knelt with their arms reversed; the priest approaching the altar, opened the books and commenced the service, not by reading, at least not so as to be heard, but in pantomime. One of the bands, at the same time, began the performance of an opera, in which it was relieved at intervals by the other; while the bell of the priest gave signal, from time to time, to the soldiers, for the requisite smitings on the breast, crossings of the forehead, lips and chest, and bowings of the head. The music of the opera was continued without intermission for half an hour, till the performance at the altar was brought to a close; and then changed to a lively quick-step, to the gay movements of which, the troops again marched to their quarters.

The French Admiral, Lepredour, and the Brazilian Admiral, Grenfell, both received official intelligence from their respective governments by the last mail-packet, of their advancement from the rank of rear to that of vice-admiral, in acknowledgment of the importance of their services here. The 21st inst. was made a festival in the squadrons of both, as the day on which their new flags were first hoisted, when they received a salute from the vessels of their respective squadrons, from those of other nations here, and from the batteries on shore.

Admiral Grenfell, an Englishman by birth, and originally an officer in the Royal Navy, is greatly distinguished for his gallantry, and for many brilliant acts in the naval history of the South American States: first, under Lord Cochrane,—the present admiral, Earl Dundonald—in the Chilian Navy; and afterwards under the same officer in that of Brazil on the Atlantic coast. For twenty years past he has rendered most important service in the Imperial Navy; has had chief command on occasions of distinction and honor; and, still in the confidence of the Emperor, was called from the civil appointment of consul-general in England, to take command of the squadron sent to facilitate the operations of the allied forces of Entre-Rios and Brazil, against Rosas. This he successfully did, rendering abortive the defences which Rosas planned to prevent Urquiza and Caxias from crossing the Parana—thus removing the only obstacle in their march to Buenos Ayres. For this service, to the order of the Southern Cross, previously conferred on him, that of the Grand Cross of the Imperial Order of the Rose is added, and he promoted to the highest rank in the Brazilian Navy. He has been a regular attendant on the Sabbath in the chapel, in which I officiate on shore; and apparently is one of the most devout of the worshippers there, and one of the most attentive of my hearers.

Shortly after my return from Buenos Ayres, it was intimated to me that some appropriate notice of the important political events which had occurred, not only in the relief of Montevideo from siege, but in the overthrow of its most powerful enemy, would give satisfaction to the church and congregation. On the succeeding Sabbath, therefore, my discourse, in addition to such allusions as I thought proper to make—in regard to the affairs of the Republic of which this place is the capital—embraced the duty of Protestant Christians, resident in it, though not themselves citizens, towards the people and their rulers. The general tenor of my subject may be inferred from the text, "I exhort, therefore, first of all, that supplication, and prayers, intercessions and giving of thanks be made for all men: for kings, and for all that are in authority; that we may lead a quiet and peacable life in all godliness and honesty." The practical application which I attempted to enforce will be most readily condensed by a quotation from a familiar hymn:

"So let our lips and lives express
The holy Gospel, we profess,
So let our works and virtues shine,
To prove the doctrine all divine.

Thus shall we best proclaim abroad
The honors of our Saviour God;
When His salvation reigns within,
And grace subdues the power of sin."

Admiral Grenfell was present. I was in doubt as to the light in which he, a monarchist by birth and an imperialist by commission, might view the subject as illustrated, in some portions, by the history and experience in faith and prayer, of the fathers of our own Republic; and was gratified to hear that he had expressed himself in terms of unqualified satisfaction with the entire discourse.

April 20th.—Since my last date, we have made a cruise of three weeks off the Plata. In addition to the various exercises, nautical and military, for which chiefly we put to sea, several interesting experiments were made under the direction of Mr. Parker, the flag-lieutenant of our ship, in deep sea soundings. The first result of much interest was obtained on the 3d inst., in S. Lat. 35° 25′ W. Long. 45° 10′. It was during a dead calm; the surface of the ocean being every where glassy as a newly-frozen lake. Not a ripple at any point met the eye. At 9 o'clock in the morning, a reel, on which had been arranged ten thousand fathoms of line, furnished by the Hydrographical Bureau and brought to the Congress by the sloop St. Mary, was fitted to one of the quarter-boats, in which Lieut. Parker and Mr. Glover left the ship to try the depth of the sea. They had expected to be absent a few hours only, and took no refreshments, not even a breaker of water with them: but the calm continued, and interested in the duty in which they were engaged, they remained with the boat's crew the whole day in voluntary fast. The sinker was a thirty-two pound shot. Eight thousand five hundred fathoms were expended, and at sunset the line was still slowly running off the reel. The true depth gained was believed to be only about three thousand five hundred fathoms; the remainder being stray line carred away by a strong submarine current. The existence of this was conclusively ascertained: its rate being nearly two miles the hour, in a direction opposite to the surface current, which had a force of about one mile per hour. The determination of this fact was an abundant reward for the labor of a wearisome day in the glaring sun. Nine miles of the line were lost. Upon attempting to haul it in, the tension became so great that five men could obtain a few fathoms only per minute; and greater force being applied, it parted a few hundred yards from the boat. Different soundings were afterwards satisfactorily secured, at the various depths of 950, 1500, 1780, 2000, 2100, and 2200 fathoms, the particulars of which are prepared for transmission to Lieutenant Maury. Fifteen thousand fathoms of line were furnished by the Congress when in Rio, to the commander of H. B. M. Frigate Herald, whom we met there; and it is reported that soundings were obtained by him on his way to the Pacific, at a depth of more than seven thousand fathoms.

The calm which enabled us to make our first deep sounding continued for three days, with a temperature like the finest autumnal weather at home. The sky during the time, was clear and brilliant, both by day and night: for a full moon, in a state of the atmosphere peculiarly translucent, afforded us a splendor of light that enabled the crew to occupy themselves in reading. During this time, I saw men at their stations reading books, even of small print, in the mid-watch. Immediately afterwards, however, we experienced the heaviest gale, with the wildest and most tumultuous sea we have known since leaving the United States. In a small vessel it would have been fearful; but the Congress is so large, and so perfect a sea-bird in her motions, that she rides and sports among the billows with an ease and triumph that call forth admiration only. She dashes from her bows and lofty bulwarks, in seeming playfulness, seas which would sweep the decks of a small craft, or bury them beneath an avalanche of water. Though the gale was heavy, the sky was bright; and in the afternoon, especially when the rays of the sun fell obliquely upon

"The restless, seething, stormy sea!"

the scene was magnificent. As sea after sea rose high against the sun, it would change in hue from the blue of indigo to emerald green. Then cresting into snowy whiteness, would scatter itself far and wide, in beds of sparkling diamonds. The tumultuous rushing and roaring of mighty waters in endless forms around us; the deep roll of the frigate to the leeward; and then, the rapid plunge headforemost down a mountain, as it were, into a yawning gulf below, made the afternoon to me one of admiration and delight.

Below decks, it is true, every thing was uncomfortable enough. The ward-room was dark and dreary; and the gun-deck all afloat. Still, as is generally the case with the sailor in such rough weather, all hands were in high spirits, and the deeper the roll of the ship—though by it, one half the crew should be pitched across the ship; and the heavier the plunge downward, though followed by rivers of water taken in at the hawser-holes and bridle-ports—especially, if those on deck were at the same time drenched by the breaking on board of a sea, or by being thrown into the floods rushing along the water-ways, the louder was the laughter and the greater the glee.

The poop-deck, from its elevation and the command it gives of every thing far and near, is a favorite resort of the officers. It is also, in ordinary circumstances, a place of etiquette. To sit while there, is not allowable, at least in the day-time, except to the Commodore and Captain, or such as they may invite beside them; much less is it etiquette to lie there. But now, the wind was too strong and withal too cold to stand, or even to sit; and going up after dinner, and finding it abandoned except by a sailor at the main-halliards, wrapping myself in a pea-jacket, I stretched myself in a corner to the windward, flat upon the deck, with my face partially protected by the hammock-nettings, turned to the sea. The position gave me an unobstructed view of the raging and roaring deep; and for an hour and more, I exulted in the contortions of the storm and the ever varying beauty and sublimity of the scene. Towards evening, the appearance of the Commodore and Captain brought me to my feet; and we together enjoyed the spectacle till the setting sun and gathering night dropped a curtain of darkness over it.

DESTERRO.

May 22*d*.—The Congress is again at the island of St. Catherine. We came to anchor at Santa Cruz, on Saturday the 15th inst.; and on the following Monday morning, I came to this place in company with our Master S—— and Secretary G——. When here last, the principal hotel was admirably kept by an American. He has since died, and his place is well supplied by a Mahonese, named Salvador. After having engaged rooms for the night and ordered our dinner, we sallied forth for a walk in the suburbs of the town. It is so long since we have been within reach of any thing like rural beauty, that, surrounded by it here, we were like school-boys turned loose for play; and in the brilliancy of the morning and elasticity of a bracing air, felt, as one of us expressed it, ready to fly. The south wind blew freshly over the hills and through the trees, and, at one point in our walk, with novel and charming effect upon the widespread branches of a couple of Australian pines. Under its breathings these became perfect Eolian harps, sending forth as we stood beneath them, the most touching strains of melody; swelling at times into the fulness of the organ, and then dying away in cadences, so soft, as to make the

"Listener hold his breath to hear;"

while the nerves thrilled under the expiring tones. I never heard "a voice of nature" more charming.

We were again struck with the great civility of every one we met, from the well-dressed gentleman to the humblest slave. As we stood near the enclosure of a poor cabin, admiring the peculiar beauty of a rose in the perfection of its bloom, a negro came to the door, and with pleasant salutations, begged us to pull it, though it was the only one in flower; at the same time cutting a cluster of buds from the bush himself, and adding sprigs of geranium for a bouquet.

After an excellent dinner served by Salvador, we towards evening took a walk along the beach and the eastern shore of the bay, to one of the finest points of view. The picture presented in the glowing light of the setting sun was very fine. Our walk led us past the general hospital. It is finely situated on a commanding terrace, and has recently been enlarged and refitted, through the liberality of the Emperor and Empress, by donations made by them in their visit to St. Catherine's in 1845:

the one having given ten thousand dollars for this purpose, and the other two. It is a foundling hospital, as well as an infirmary. The window containing the roda or turning-box for the reception of the infants left, was open, though shaded by a screen of green cloth, embroidered in the centre with the Imperial arms, and with the motto in Portuguese—"Meus pais me desemparao a Divina Providencia me protege." "My parent deserts me, but Divine Providence protects me."

I rose early the next morning and took a stroll through the market. It is a new and neatly kept structure, immediately adjoining the beach. I say beach, for there are no wharves. This was now filled with canoes run up on the sand, and laden with vegetables, fruit, wood, and various articles of traffic, in which a brisk barter was going on. On the grass of the open square in front, groups of mules were clustered with pack-saddles and panniers burdened with similar articles, brought for a like purpose from the interior; and near by, negro women in all kinds of costume and of every color, were seated frying fish, and boiling black beans into a kind of soup, and preparing other edibles for the breakfast of the muleteers and passers by. Here, too, were collected, according to daily custom, two or three dozen boys, from eight to twelve years of age, each having a bamboo stick across the shoulder, from one end of which was suspended a tin can capable of containing three or four quarts, with a small tin cup attached as a measure. These are the milkmen of the place, belonging to the small farms in the adjoining valleys, to a distance of seven or eight miles.

Our breakfast at the hotel was à l'Americain: such an one as Salvador boastingly said "a Brazilian would not know how to get up." Immediately after despatching it G——, S—— and I set off in a boat for the village of San José on the mainland, nine miles across the straits in a south-easterly direction from Desterro. This was in prosecution of a purpose we had formed of visiting the German colony of San Pedro d'Alcantara in the mountains, some twenty-five or thirty miles inland from San José;

partly to observe the progress made by the immigrants after a settlement of twenty-five years; and partly for the effect upon our health and spirits of a ride for a couple of days on horseback. There was no wind, and we were rowed over by a Brazilian, the owner of the boat, and a young negro, his slave. The views from the water in every direction are beautifully lakelike. The points and bluff headlands projecting into the water, are in many instances peculiarly striking in their terminations: consisting of columnar shafts, piked splinters, and immense boulders of granite, so arranged as to have the appearance of the ruins of Cyclopean fortresses, even to the remains of seeming embrasures. In other instances they might pass for fragments of a Giant's causeway.

We were an hour and a half in making the distance. We had been directed for information and aid in accomplishing our purpose to a German named Adams, residing at a beach called the Praya Compreda, in the immediate vicinity of San José, He is a kind of chieftain among his countrymen of the colony, and could be of more service to us than any other person. We landed near his house, a substantial and comfortable edifice of stone, appropriated in its lower apartments to the varied business of a commission merchant, grocer, and tavernkeeper. It was here we were to procure horses and a guide for the excursion. At first the prospect of success was rather unpromising. Though kindly received by Adams, he said it was impossible for him to furnish horses—that all his were entirely used up by a hard ride from which they had just returned, and he knew of no others that could be obtained: nor was there any one in the place who could act as a guide. However, upon setting forth our entire dependence upon him, at the recommendation of his friend; the anxiety we felt to make the trip; our nationality, and the ship at Santa Cruz to which we were attached, he so far relented in his first decision as to say he would see what could be done; and at the end of a few minutes it was determined, that after a good feed, his two horses, with the addition of a couple of mules, should be at our service, and that Adams himself should become our companion and guide.

Matters being thus satisfactorily arranged, we employed the time for the requisite preparations, in looking around us, and in learning a little of the character and history of our host. He is a stout, thickset, square, iron-framed man of forty-five, with a good-natured, but most determined and inflexible face. He has been twenty-four years in the country, having been one of the pioneer colonists of Alcantara, and resident in the mountains till within a few years past. He is now well to do in the world, and has a wife and family of six children. A daughter of eighteen soon became an object of unfeigned admiration to some of our party. She is very pretty in face, fresh and blooming in complexion, with a refined and intelligent expression, and perfect in the proportion and symmetry of her figure. There was a fitting of the head and neck to the bust, and an air and bearing in her walk, that would have become a princess. It is so long since we have seen in common life one who would be called at home a truly pretty girl, that we were quite charmed with the neat and modest air of this Christianlike and civilized beauty. A brother, too, some two years older, tall, stout, and well modelled, moved about with the straightness and the elastic step of an Indian.

As we were strolling through the little hamlet, a straggling suburb of the village of San José, we were told by a passer-by that an American was living close at hand—pointing out to us his residence. We found this to be a cobbler's shop, and our compatriot in it a cobbler: a scapegrace, as we soon learned, from no less noted a place of apprenticeship than the "Mammoth" boot-store in Chatham Square, New York. He is about twenty-eight years of age, has been eleven years at St. Catharine's, and is married here; but notwithstanding, is confessedly still much of a "Bowery boy," and no great honor to his country. A Bible in English, lying on the counter, was the only evidence of good we discovered during our interview, in which he did a small job in his line for one of us. His boast of Protestantism, and of his defences of the truth amid the superstition and idolatry, as he termed it, in which he lives, did not pass for much in our estimation, interlarded as his conversation was, with oaths and other proofs of moral degradation.

At two o'clock we were mounted for San Pedro d'Alcantara; Adams and S—— on horses, G—— and I on mules. Adams, wearing a low-crowned, broad-brimmed, black felt hat, seemed to be literally stuffed into the drab cotton shooting-jacket, which he had added to the shirt in which we first met him. The other most conspicuous article of his dress was a pair of tan-colored boots, reaching to his knees, with saddle-bag tops, put to the use here of a portmanteau. G—— and S—— each wore over their coats a gaily striped Buenos Ayres poncho; whilst I was provided with a boat-cloak, as a defence against sun, wind, and rain. We set off with fine weather and in high spirits. We had long become so weary of the monotony of life on board ship at Montevideo, and the confinement of our passage hither, that the change was most welcome; and we ambled off through a sandy lane leading directly inland from the water, as cheerily as if just escaping from prison.

On gaining the height of the first ridge, we had an extensive view over a wide valley covered with wood. It surprised me to see so wide an extent of level and seemingly rich land, immediately on the coast, unredeemed; but we learned that beneath the wood it is a mere swamp. The rising grounds skirting it, present abundant evidence of the productiveness of the soil: plantations of coffee, sugar-cane, mandioca, cotton, Indian corn, and the castor oil plant, were spread widely around, while the orange groves were so laden with fruit, as to appear in the sun like masses of gold. The road for many miles was broad and smooth, lined with hedges of mimosa and wild orange, and ornamented here and there by clusters of roses and jessamine. By degrees, however, as we advanced in the mountains, especially in the ascent and descent of spurs of hills, it became narrow and rough, and little more than a bridle-path. The country became proportionally new and uncultivated; still in many places it was homelike, from the meadows and rich bottom lands which here and there bordered the mountain stream, which we began now closely to follow towards its sources. A thousand beautiful pictures in outline and foliage were presented during the ride of the afternoon, enlivened and varied by the windings of the small river beside us—flowing at times through lawnlike banks as smoothly as the waters of a lake, and then again rushing, and leaping, and foaming amidst gigantic boulders of granite, down rapids and over cascades, with the tumult and uproar of a cataract.

We had constant evidence along the road, in the new dwellings and outbuildings of the inhabitants, of their improving circumstances and advancing civilization. This was conspicuous in more than one instance in three successive specimens of architecture in a single habitation, by the additions made at different times. First, there was the little cabin, composed of small sapling-like timbers, wattled and filled in with mud and coarsely and rudely thatched, now rickety and ready to tumble down, the original shanty of a settler in the wilderness; next, and joined to it some years later, another more spacious in its area, and of more substantial frame, more smoothly plastered and more elaborately thatched—more neat in the finish of its door and window frames, and entire workmanship; and lastly, the recently constructed cottage of stone, stuccoed and whitewashed, and roofed with tile—bearing testimony of the prosperity and the improved domestic accommodations of its owner. This is descriptive of the Brazilian section of the country, before we came in the neighborhood of the German colony; though the same fact was observable in a more marked degree among the European immigrants.

Night overtook us when yet a league from our destination. Most of this distance was made in such darkness that we could not distinguish an object around us; not even the road we were travelling. We could only follow the lead of our guide, trusting to the eyesight and sagacity of our beasts, for security in mounting sharp hills and in making steep descents beside the roaring waters and shelving precipices. The way thus began to be tedious and we to feel weary. A bright light from a large and cheerful dwelling near the road side, before which our guide halted, led to the hope that we had reached the end of our day's journey. This Adams was desirous of making it; but, after an animated parlance in German, in which the whole of a large family, men, women and children, who had crowded to the door, joined, while we, wayworn riders, looked wistfully at the brightness and seeming comfort within, he was told that we could not be accommodated, and must push our way through the darkness and chill mists of the mountains, a mile further. Slight showers of rain now began to fall from the heavy clouds overhead. When at last we did come to a halt, and were invited to dismount, the only object discernible was the dim light of a lamp amidst the bottles of a little grog-shop and grocery, six feet by ten. We found, however, that it opened on one side into a room of somewhat greater dimensions; and this again in the rear into a kennel-like hole, filled with children of all ages, from one to eight and ten years, most of them very primitively clad, and some so much so as to be entirely naked.

It was at once very evident that this barnlike room, open overhead to the rafters, and furnished only with a coarse heavy table and two or three rude wooden benches, was to be both our supper room and dormitory: the grog-shop on one corner and the kennel behind, constituting the rest of the dwelling. Hungry and weary we gladly made ourselves at home in it. The civility of the landlord, and his manifest desire to do honor to guests under the protection of so distinguished a patron as Mynheer Adams, but especially the early appearance of a trim and active little German girl of eighteen, with neatly arranged hair and blooming complexion, moving about with the self-possession and dignity of an heiress, though without stockings, and for shoes the clumsy sabots or wooden slippers of the country, began to raise our hopes as to fare and accommodations.

Soon the savory fumes and musical hissing of ham and eggs, in a frying-pan in the adjoining penthouse, and the aroma of coffee, gave further encouragement to our empty stomachs. A snowwhite cloth was at the same time spread over one end of the bar-room table; and it was not long before we were seated at a very palatable meal, which the personal cleanliness of the little cook and waiting-maid encouraged us to dispatch without any very close inspection of the plates on which it was served, or the particular condition of the black knives and five-pronged German silver forks with which it was eaten. In the mean time we had become somewhat enlightened as to the domestic condition of the household. The lady of the mansion had given birth the day before to a sixth son, and was lying in a little dark recess on one side of the rear shanty: mother and son doing well. The maid-of-all-work was a sister in charge of the household during the confinement.

Shortly after our arrival a new character was introduced, in the person of a German doctor, in attendance on the mother and child: a man of talent and education, we were told, but now, from habits of drunkenness, a poor degraded wretch, shabby in dress, and filthy in person. He soon rendered himself utterly disgusting to us, by the profaneness and vulgarity of the broken English by which he attempted to commend himself to us, as travellers. He came from the fatherland somewhat more than a year ago, with the German legion furnished by Brazil, in the allied armies of the Plata, for the overthrow of Rosas. In this, he was a surgeon, but forfeited his commission through intemperance. He was disposed at first to be very friendly, and to address us as "hail fellow well met." The advances were received so very coldly, however, especially on the point of most interest to him, the participation of a glass of grog, that after a word to the sick, he took his departure in the darkness and rain for another grog-shop, as we were told, to meet more congenial companions.

The cravings of hunger relieved, we began to cast a look around as to the promise of rest for the night, after the weariness of a rough and rapid ride of twenty-five miles. The bare and dirty floors, and narrow and hard benches along the walls, seemed to furnish the only choice of couches. We had made up our minds to this alternative; and, so far as my companions were concerned, with a half shiver as to the degree of comfort held out. The mountain air was not only damp, but positively cold. In addition to my saddle for a pillow, I had a thick cloak in which to wrap myself, but G—— and S——, with nothing to cover them but their light ponchos, had the prospect of half freezing. A shrug of the shoulders, however, chiefly indicated the nature of their thoughts on the subject. To our relief, a large rush mat was early spread in one corner of the room, and immediately afterwards, with triumphant looks of gratulation to one another, we beheld our host with his little sister-in-law lugging in from the adjoining apartment an immense straw bed, of dimensions sufficient for the accommodation of half a dozen persons. Spread out to its largest extent, and furnished with bolsters, clean sheets and blankets, it looked so tempting, that, arranging the cloak and ponchos for additional covering, and laying aside our coats, boots, and cravats, we were soon in the indulgence of the rest to which it invited us. We were constrained by Christian civility to offer to our guide a fourth part of the couch. In anticipation of his acceptance, I had chosen for myself an outside berth, where I supposed I should be the farthest removed from him. He declined the place offered, however, and spreading a sheepskin saddlecloth and other gear on the floor, took up his quarters beside me. Thus my selfish manœuvre was in vain, and the big German was my next bedfellow. It was well for my repose that I was right weary; for he soon began puffing and snorting in his sleep with the labor and noise of a high-pressure steam-engine, which otherwise would have effectually kept me awake. We were four in a row; but there was no lack, as I soon discovered, of numerous other bedfellows. Flattering myself that they were nothing worse than fleas in clean and polished armor, I did not allow myself to be disturbed by them; but leaving them to skip, hop, and jump as they pleased without hindrance, I slept soundly till morning, and rose without a vestige of fatigue.

I was all impatience to know what kind of a place, under the disclosures of daylight, San Pedro d'Alcantara would prove to be. On hastening to the door, for the windows without sash or glass were closed by board shutters, the first object that met my eyes was the little rustic chapel of the settlement, perched on the top of a beautifully wooded and round-topped hill. It is picturesque and rural, and the most conspicuous and ornamental object in the landscape. The place itself is a hamlet of a dozen dwellings, most of them mere huts. Half the number are plastered and whitewashed, and in place of thatch have roofs of red tile. The mountain stream, whose course we had followed from the bay at San Josè, here a small rivulet, flows through its centre. The little valley in which the hamlet is embosomed, is encircled by hills of more or less steepness, most of them still covered with trees and underwood, and presents all the features of a new and frontier settlement at home. After breakfast, accompanied by Adams and our host, who adds to his occupation of publican the office of sexton to the church, we ascended the hill to the chapel. It is most rude in its architecture both within and without, and is furnished with several frightful daubs, of what are intended for saints and angels. A cemetery surrounds the chapel. It contains a few graves, and is encircled by a broad path for the convenience of religious processions. There is no parish priest; but an itinerant ecclesiastic makes a quarterly visit for confession and absolution, and the celebration of mass. In answer to my inquiries on the subject, our host said, "We come up to the chapel every Sunday morning and every saint's day, and make a procession, and do what we can, and then go down and drink, dance, and sing, and enjoy ourselves the rest of the day!"

It had rained heavily in showers during the night, and the weather was still drizzling and unsettled. Still we felt disposed before returning, to push our observations a little further in the interior. To this Adams offered no objection, and we again mounted. Shortly after leaving the hamlet westward, we came to a very steep and long hill—quite a mountain. The soil is an adhesive oily clay, and the ascent was difficult and amusing. It was almost impossible for our animals to obtain a sure foothold; and they constantly slipped and floundered, and slid backwards in a manner that at first was startling. The view from the top, of the little valley and hamlet, the stream meandering through it, and of the rude chapel and its surmounting cross, was picturesque and quite Alpine.

The descent on the opposite side was as steep, and more hazardous than the ascent had been: our beasts, with their fore-legs stiffly outstretched, often made involuntary slides of eight, ten, and fifteen feet, till "brought up all standing," as the phrase is, by a cross gully or a large stone. As the whole ride was but the constant ascent and descent of a succession of spurs of hills, running down into the little valley through which the mountain stream flowed, it proved a regular morning's sport of "coursing down hill" after a new fashion. At first it was a little startling; for when the slide began, whether backwards, in a precipitous ascent, or headforemost down a breakneck descent, there was no calculating where one would fetch up; a little experience, however, begot such confidence in the self-management of the animals—especially the mules, to one of which I still adhered—that I soon began to enjoy it, and rather to look out for and encourage a good long slide upon the well-braced limbs of my beast. This was particularly the case on our return, in the descent of the long hill immediately overhanging San Pedro. This is quite precipitous, and for nearly half a mile we slipped, slipped, and slipped, one after another, first in one direction in the road, and then in another, zigzagging here and zigzagging there, but bringing up at every successive point safely, till we were constrained to laugh outright, as we looked from one animal and his rider to another, and felt that each of us presented the same comical figure.

The general features of the scenery were much the same as those passed over the preceding evening. Steep hills, well-wooded, rose abruptly on either side from the little valley. In this lay rich bottomlands, some in long peninsulas, and others in horse-shoe form, according to the varied windings of the stream flowing through them. Many beautiful pictures, some of nature in her wildness, and others with intermingled cultivation and improvement met the eye, with evidences in the dwellings and farms of the settlers of increasing comfort and progressive civilization. At the end of three miles, our guide proposed that instead of following the public mule-track further, we should turn aside by a gateway upon the more level valley. This we did, and soon entered upon a section more like farming-land at home than any thing before met. After passing two or three comfortable-looking dwellings, we came in view of an extensive plantation of comparatively level and well improved ground, with a cluster of buildings a half mile in the distance, superior to any we had yet seen. It proved to be the residence of a cousin of our guide, at which he wished to give us an introduction. Widespread, meadow-like fields lay before us, and on one side upon an open lawn stood a neatly-finished little 'chapelet,' if I may coin a word. This looked pretty in the landscape, from its whiteness in contrast with the green of an encircling hedge. It was not more than twelve feet square, open in front, and probably intended to be scarcely more than a canopy over a shrine of the Virgin or some favorite saint.

From the time of entering the German colony the day previous, salutations of good will and pleasure were addressed to our guide from the habitations we passed far and near—often at distances as great as the voice could well carry them; now, as soon as he was recognized among the party approaching, the demonstration was most cordial and prolonged; while before we could alight, father, mother, daughters, and sons gathered around the cavalcade with the most cheerful welcome. Every thing indicated that we had arrived at the mansion of a magnate in the colony, if it were not that of the lord of the manor himself. It must not be inferred from this, however, that we met any very impressive display of aristocratic life, either in costume, manners, or dwelling. The proprietor was unshaven and unshorn. His dress, though clean, was very thoroughly patched, and included neither coat, stockings, hat, nor cravat. The costume of the lady consisted principally, of a single essential garment, made and arranged so inartistically as to give to her figure very much the outline of a bean-pole. The forms of two strapping daughters of sixteen and eighteen were much more after the German model; but their toilette was little more elaborate than that of the mother, and the skirt of the single robe worn by them, scarcely the length of that of a Bloomer without the pantalets. The sinew and muscle thus displayed in bare arms and bare ankles and feet, would have justified the belief that they had spent their lives in tree-chopping or log-rolling, and led one of our party in his astonishment to exclaim, with the favorite expletive of 'by George,' "either of them would thrash any one of us in a minute!"

It was beginning to rain quite smartly as we dismounted, and whilst the sons took charge of our horses, we were hastily ushered into a good-sized room, which, though exhibiting a combination of hall and parlor, bedroom and kitchen, took us quite by surprise in its style and finish. It presented a neatly panelled wainscot, of the handsome cedar of the country, extending from the floor to the cornice; the ceiling also being panelled with the same material. A long table and benches beside it, a sofa of mahogany with cane seat, and half a dozen chairs to match, an old eight-day clock in a straight black case, and a high dresser with drawers of the same color and material—both manifestly brought from the 'faderland'—constituted, with the accustomed display of delf and china, the principal furniture of the room.

In the early morning, at San Pedro, the first indoor object that arrested my attention, was the thickset and burly figure of our guide, beside the counter of the little grog-shop and grocery, stirring with a spoon the contents of a shallow earthen pan, on the surface of which played the blue flames of burning spirits.

The interest with which he watched the operation was not limited, it was very evident, to the beauty of the flashing and leaping flame, as he stirred and stirred the liquid. Half suspicious of the reply that would be given, I asked him, "what he was making?" And received for answer, with a smack of his lips, "Oh, something very good for the stomach in these damp mornings in the mountains—very necessary against the fogs! it is cachasa,"—the common rum of the country—"and sugar," of which, at the end of fifteen minutes' preparation, he would fain have persuaded us to partake, with the assurance "that all the bad of it was burned up." And now, at the farm-house, we had scarcely become seated, before our host made his appearance with a tumbler of the same, with a regret that he could not in its place offer us wine. On declining this, bowls of milk were presented. And such milk! The like of it I have not seen since leaving the banks of the Hudson. An excellent loaf of bread, a mixture of wheat and Indian meal, was added, with the sweetest of butter and equally good cheese. A plate of the farina of mandioca being also placed upon the table, I made my lunch chiefly on a bowl of milk thickened with it; and found the diet a capital substitute for the hasty pudding of New England and the Dutch *suppawn* of the Middle States.

In the mean time, a feat of agility performed by the younger of the two daughters mentioned, came near proving too much for the gravity of some of our number. She had not entered the room when we did, having received an order at the time, of some kind, from her mother. This obeyed, she was unwilling, probably, to lose the interest of so unusual a visit; and perceiving at the door that but one seat in the room was vacant—the farther end of the sofa, ten or twelve feet off—and suspicious of the undue exposure before strangers of her nether limbs, in a deliberate movement over the intervening space, she measured well the distance, and with a gathered momentum, by a single lofty hop, skip, and jump, came down *à la Turque* upon it, with feet and ankles entirely concealed beneath her scanty skirt, but with a snapping of the bamboo that threatened to be fatal to the bottom of the sofa.

After luncheon, we sallied forth for the inspection of a mandioca and a sugar mill in an adjoining building, and a view of the piggery and gardens—the entire household forming our suite. We had already discovered the wife to be very decidedly the head of the family. Her will and word, doubtless, were law in the domain, outdoors as well as within. The husband seemed a meek, good-natured but inefficient person, while his better half was full of energy and enterprise; and, probably, besides the exercise of better judgment, had accomplished more hard work, in the field as well as in the kitchen, than any other person on the place. She at once took the lead in showing off the premises, and in giving all the information desired in regard to them. Her husband and herself were so poor at the time of their immigration, twenty-four years ago, as to be necessarily indebted to their cousin, Adams, for their passage-money. Their plantation was a gratuity from the government, as an encouragement to colonists. It is a mile in length, by half a mile in width, and was then in a state of nature, and of little value. It is now reclaimed and well cultivated; and could not be purchased, as we were informed, for less than ten thousand milreis or five thousand dollars. In addition to this fine property and comfortable home, with good buildings and a stock of all necessary animals, Mr. S—— the proprietor, is a capitalist, and has money at interest. Mrs. S—— has been handsome, and still has a finely chiselled face and good expression. The daughters, too, are pretty: at least they appeared so to us. It is so long since we have seen the fair skin and the fair complexion of the Northern woman, or met the energy, activity, and elastic movement of the fair Yankee, that we are scarcely competent to the exercise of unprejudiced judgment in the case.

At the end of an hour we took our leave, pleased with the visit, which evidently had also been a pleasure to our hosts. The wetness of the morning had increased, and before we had accomplished a mile on our return, the rain began to pour in torrents. We sought the shelter of an orange-grove till the shower should pass; but finding it inadequate to the emergency, Adams, exclaiming, "This will not do!" pushed ahead a short distance, and dashed, all mounted, into a mandioca mill at one end of a dwelling near by. We of course followed, and found ourselves with our beasts snug and dry in the kitchen as well as mill of the proprietor. Here, during the delay of half an hour, we had an opportunity of witnessing again the whole process of converting the root of the mandioca into farina; while Adams, having, through an open door, spied the family of the house at their noonday meal, alighted, and notwithstanding his previous hearty luncheon an hour before, of bread, butter, cheese and milk, sat down and made a full dinner: and this, only as was afterwards proved, by way of stimulating his appetite for the repast we had ordered to be in readiness on our return, at San Pedro, and to which he did as ample justice as if he had not broken his fast before for a day.

While waiting for this meal to be served, a very pretty and modest-looking German girl of fifteen rode up to the door of the little inn. She wore a neatly fitting dress of pink calico, a pocket-handkerchief tied under the chin as a covering for the head, and French gaiter boots, and sat her horse à la cabellero. She was on her way to San José under the escort of a friend, without whose protection, the Germans told us, she could not possibly make the trip with safety, such was the villainy and licentiousness of the Brazilians of the country. In the state in which the roads are, her attitude as a rider was unquestionably the most secure.

When ready to set off ourselves, rain had again began to pour; and for a time the prospect of being able to start was unpromising. The drunken doctor, once more in attendance, persisted in assuring us that it would rain thus all the afternoon; and said it would be madness to think of leaving. His urgency for our stay was an additional motive for us to be off; and as soon as there was a slight improvement in the weather we mounted, and after making up a purse, much to the delight of our host, as a gratuity to the sixth-born son, bade adieu to San Pedro d'Alcantara. It was now four o'clock, and Adams said we could not reach San José at the earliest before nine. We started notwithstanding, with the will and purpose of making the shortest possible work of the intervening distance; and certain of our road, left our guide to gossip by the way as he chose, with the many friends hailing him from the heights above or the valleys below, as far as the voice could be carried, while we rode pell-mell, up hill and down dale, often slipping and sliding for long distances, at the seeming hazard of both limbs and neck. In this way, we accomplished half the distance before nightfall, and reached a lower region of country, where there had been little or no rain.

During the ride, we met several troupes of mules, and their muleteers, returning with empty pack-saddles from the bay. Among others, one belonging to our host of San Pedro, which we had seen setting off in the early morning with articles for the market of Desterro. Occasionally, too, we overtook, and, after riding for a time side by side, passed horsemen and mule riders going the same way with ourselves. Just as darkness was beginning to fall rapidly around, we thus fell in with a well-mounted, fine-looking Brazilian, having the appearance of a respectable planter. Adams was far behind, and S—— had the lead of our party, his horse being a tolerably good traveller. My mule, a sure-footed beast, came next, and then G——'s. The Brazilian, after riding side by side with each of us in turn, by degrees got in advance of all three. As he was evidently well acquainted with the road, S—— and I made up our minds to follow him closely, as the pioneer in the darkness for any unsafe spot ahead. As both man and horse appeared fresh, however, this required pretty brisk riding. With the thickening of the night, our new friend accelerated his speed; and the faster he led, the faster we followed. Presently it was impossible to discern a trace of the road, or to discover whether it were smooth or rough, tending up hill or down. The white Guayaquil hat of the Brazilian, was all that was left visible to S—— of horse, or rider, and a line of deeper darkness hastening from me ahead, was all that I, with the most fixed gaze, could perceive of S——. I lashed my mule to keep up in the chase, S—— kept snapping his riding whip in the fashion of a French postilion, while the Brazilian seemed to be spurring on his steed at full tilt. Away we thus went, S—— managing to keep before him the vision of a white hat, which threatened each moment to be lost in the darkness, and I at an equal remove from him, with all the powers of sight intently fixed, to follow a moving speck of concentrated blackness. To make sure of the identity of the phantom of my own chase, I occasionally called out, "S——, do you still see him?" to which the reply would come, "Yes! but I tell you he is going it: but I'll take good care not to lose him,—there can be but one road, and I'll make sure of so good a lead."

It was amusing, though it might have proved no joke, to be thus trotting at full speed in impenetrable night, and that on a hard-motioned animal at the end of a thirty-miles' ride. We had kept the gait for an hour perhaps, without venturing to slacken its pace for a moment, or to take our eyes from the respective points, white and black, before us, when all at once, that on which mine were fixed was gone: urging my mule forward, in the attempt to regain it, I perceived him begin to stumble, and found that he was off the path. Reining him up, I called out for S——. He, I discovered, was at a stand also at no great distance, and in answer to the question, "Have you lost your guide?" answered, "He has just vanished like a veritable ghost—he disappeared in a moment in a mass of blackness, and but for the creaking of a gate, I should have been headforemost into a hedge after him." The darkness was so great that it was impossible to move with safety without some indication of the direction in which we ought to go, and we had patiently to wait the approach of G—— and Adams to relieve us from our dilemma.

Soon the whip of the former, urging on his little mule, and the jingling of the stirrups and heavy iron spurs of the latter were heard at no great distance; and giving place in the lead to Adams, at the end of a half hour we alighted safely at the point from which we started. I was too much fagged to care for any refreshment but that of sleep; and, while S—— and G—— sat down to a supper of "pain perdu" and green tea, made my way to a clean and comfortable cot beneath the tiled roof of the garret, and was soon lost in a repose—

"above
The luxury of common sleep."

CHAPTER XXVIII.

May 24th.—Mr. Wells, an American gentleman of wealth, long resident in Desterro, is a person of leading influence in the commerce and society of the place. For many years he held the office of American consul with honor and popularity; but was superseded two or three years ago, through the political influence of a partisan office-seeker at home. The new incumbent, disappointed in the profits expected from the office, soon resigned it. Through private pique against Mr. Wells, he left the papers of the consulate and an acting appointment to the office with Captain Cathcart, though he is in no way qualified for the duties or honor of the situation.

Among others to whom Mr. Wells, as the only representative of the United States here, has at different times extended his hospitality, are the present Emperor and Empress. Their majesties and suite were entertained by him at a magnificent fête, in their progress through this section of the Empire in 1845. I was furnished with letters to him by Dr. C——, an old friend, and by F—— of the Congress. These I delivered before making the excursion to San Pedro; and on my return, became a guest beneath his roof. His house is on the palace square, in the immediate neighborhood of the residence of the President of the Province. It is one of the finest dwellings in the place, and commands from the windows and balconies of the drawing-room, an extensive view of the town, bay, and surrounding mountains. It has been my lot to occupy a great variety of sleeping rooms, from those of the palace to the wigwam, but I think the bed assigned to me here must have precedence, in its dimensions at least, above all I have before met. It is truly regal, taking even that of his majesty of Bashan in the days of his overthrow, as a model. I have not measured it, and its area may not quite be, as his was, "nine cubits by four;" but its elevation I suspect is quite as great; the upper mattress, as I stand beside it, being nearly on a level with my shoulders, and accessible only by a flight of mahogany steps. The canopy is of proportionate altitude. The dignified feeling with which one ascends to this place of rest, is not a little increased by the remembrance that it was by these very steps their Imperial Majesties, when in St. Catherine's, mounted to their couch.

Mr. Wells has been bereft of a wife and child, and is left alone; but has borne his afflictions with the resignation of a Christian. It was pleasing to discover, that though so long a resident of a place "wholly given to idolatry," and cut off from all the public means of grace, he maintains the regular worship of God, morning and evening, with his household of African servants.

The quietude and comforts of such an establishment are a great luxury after the weariness of long confinement on shipboard; and I feel that the visit at Desterro will constitute quite an episode in the tedium of our cruise. The town itself presents every where a pleasing mingling of city and country, giving to the whole a village-like simplicity. The walks, in every direction, are varied and beautifully rural; and whatever Desterro may be as a permanent residence, it is certainly delightful for a sojourn of a few days.

Yesterday afternoon my attention was attracted by the sounds of music in the Matriz, or mother church, at the head of the square; and walking over, I discovered it to be that of a funeral service in a mass for the dead. A beautiful catafalque, with richly festooned draperies of pink satin and gold and silver tissue, occupied the centre of the nave. Upon this, in a straight coffin of pink velvet, trimmed with gold lace—so formed as when thrown open to expose the entire figure—upon a satin mattress lay the corpse of a little girl of three years, most tastefully and expensively arrayed in what may be concisely described as a full ball-dress of pink and blue gauze, with edgings of gold and silver fringe over a white satin robe: the whole being wreathed with garlands of exquisitely finished artificial flowers. The feet were in silk stockings and satin shoes, and the head crowned with fresh roses. Death had evidently done his work quickly and gently. There was no emaciation; no traces of suffering; the face was full and perfect in its contour; and the limbs round and symmetrical. A placid and smiling expression, in place of the ghastly look of death, led to the impression of its being only a deep and quiet sleep that we gazed on—an illusion strengthened by the delicate tinge of rouge that had been given to the cheeks and lips.

On all former occasions, when I have seen the corpse of a child thus decked out—according to the usage here—I have felt as if it were a mockery of death and the grave, thus to mingle the tinsel and vanities of the world with the sad lesson they teach. But now, however incongruous with the solemnity of such an occasion these fanciful adornments may seem to us, there was nothing repulsive in the spectacle presented. Indeed, I found myself insensibly impressed with the extreme beauty of the child, and the exquisite taste and artistic effect of the drapery in which she was laid out. Ingeniously constructed wings of gauze are often appended to the other adornments of an infant corpse, emblematic of the truth that,

"With soul enlarged to angel's size,"

the spirit has taken its flight to a station of blessedness near the throne of the Redeemer. All persons of wealth and position in society, are thus, in Brazil, borne to the grave in full dress—the soldier in his uniform, the judge in his robes, the bishop in his mitre, and the monk in his cowl.

On this occasion, the officiating priest with the bearers of the crucifix and censers, and other attendants, stood in the midst of the blaze of wax lights by which the bier was encircled; while the walls of the church were lined by hundreds of gentlemen of the first respectability, in full black, and each supporting a candle of wax of the length and size of an ordinary walking-stick. The child was of the family of Andrada; a name pre-eminent in the Province and Empire for patriotism, scientific attainment, and political distinction.

Towards evening I took a long walk with Mr. Wells. The suburbs in every direction are full of rural imagery and picturesque beauty. The rising grounds command extensive views of undulating land, of water and of mountains; and the roads and lanes are so walled in by luxuriant hedges of the flowering mimosa, running rose, orange-tree, and coffee bush, as to embower one, even within a stone's throw of the town, as if in the heart of the country. The flowers of the mimosa hanging in thick pendants, cover the hedges with a mass of whiteness, more entire and more beautiful than that of the hawthorne, while those of the running rose, clustering closely like the multiflora, make the roadside they border one bed of bloom. There is too a repose and tranquillity in the evenings, and a delicacy in the tintings of the colors at sunset, that make a stroll at that time of the day peculiarly delightful.

After a circuit of two miles by an inland route, we approached the town again by a suburb which constitutes the west end, both in the topography and the fashion of the place; and exhibits a succession of pleasant residences surrounded by tastefully arranged flower-gardens. Just as we were passing the grounds of one of the most attractive of these, a vehicle, the first I have seen, except a Roman ox-cart, since I have been here, overtook us and drove through an iron gateway into a court, beyond which appeared long vistas of gravelled walks and embowering shade. The carriage was a calóche, or old-fashioned chaise, of rather rude construction, painted pea-green, with orange-colored wheels and shafts. It was drawn by a single horse guided by a postilion, and contained a very stout gray-headed gentleman of sixty, who entirely filled up a seat designed for the accommodation of two. It was no less a personage than Lieut. Gen. Bento Manuel, the highest military officer of the southern section of the Empire, recently from Rio Grande, where he was long chief in command, and where he did efficient service for the government during great political agitation and threatened revolution. He is so stout as to be readily excused from walking or riding, and possesses, with a single exception, the only wheeled carriage in the Island of St. Catherine's.

The ringing of a cracked bell at the Matriz, and the gathering of the population in that direction on the evening of the 21st, led me to it again as a point of observation. It was the beginning of a Novena, or daily service, of nine days' continuance, in commemoration of the descent of the Holy Ghost—the following Sabbath being Whit-Sunday. This celebration is universal in city and country; and is distinguished by an observance, the origin and specific meaning of which I have been unable to trace, that of the choice and induction into office for a year, of a lad under the blasphemous title of Emperor of the Holy Ghost. He presides in mock majesty at the festival, and is regarded with special honor at all others during his continuance in office. The selection is usually from a family of wealth, as the expenses attendant upon the honor involve an outlay amounting at Rio and other chief places to five hundred, a thousand, and fifteen hundred dollars. This is appropriated to the furnishing of dress, music, lights, and refreshments during the celebration. The empire over which he sways the sceptre comprises the apartments of the church, in which the gifts brought to him by the people in the name of the Holy Ghost are deposited, and an enclosure adjoining, where auctions are held for the disposal of these to the highest bidder. On this occasion, two rooms opening from the church were gayly fitted up, one—a side-chapel with altar and crucifix—as a throne-room for the Emperor, and the other for the temporary deposit of the gifts. In front of these, and communicating directly with them, a large auction-room was erected, screened by canvas over head, and furnished with benches for the accommodation of spectators and purchasers. The gifts are brought gratuitously by the people, and the proceeds of the sales go to the treasury of the brotherhood of the Holy Ghost for purposes of charity.

As I arrived a procession was just approaching. It was led by a negro, in a dirty coarse shirt and pantaloons, the common dress of a slave, bareheaded and barefooted, who bore a large flag of red silk, with a dove embroidered on one corner, and long streamers of ribbons flowing from the top of the staff on which it was suspended. It was the sacred banner of the Holy Ghost, a kiss of which, or the burying of the face in its folds, insures all needed blessing. A little fellow, eight or ten years of age, followed, beating a small drum with all his might, then came a man in ordinary dress, thrumming on a guitar the accompaniment of a monotonous ditty, sung at the top of his voice as loud as he could bawl; the complement of the music being made up by a fiddle on which a round-shouldered old Portuguese was sawing and laboring, with fingers, elbow, and head, with an earnestness, to give full effect to the squeaking and screeching sounds he was sending forth, as if life itself depended on the zeal he should display.

The Emperor elect now made his appearance, a lad of eleven or twelve years, neatly dressed in the fashion of a man, as the usage with boys here is, having a broad red ribbon across his shoulders, from which was suspended on the breast a large silver star stamped with a dove, emblematic of the Holy Ghost. Six or eight men robed in short cloaks or mantles of red silk, the dress of the brotherhood, bareheaded and carrying lighted wax tapers, followed him. A rabble of noisy and excited boys and men, white, black, and yellow, made up the cortège. They had been to escort the Emperor from his residence with becoming honor, to open the festival.

Previous to his arrival the church had become densely filled, principally with females, seated closely together on the floor—mistress and slave, lady and beggar, without distinction of rank or name, black, white, and every intermediate hue, the whole number amounting to six or eight hundred. Through this crowd the procession made its way up the nave, the musicians still drumming and thrumming and scraping on their instruments, and bawling out their song louder than ever. A priest met it at the high altar; and the whole returned through the church to the depository in which were the gifts. These he consecrated by prayer, the sprinkling of holy water and fumigations with incense, after which, escorted in like manner, he again entered the church. Hundreds of men in addition to the women, now lined the walls and stood closely packed together along the entrance to the church, and the service of the Novena commenced. It was chanted throughout to the accompaniment of a lively, and to me any thing but a devotional air. The whole sounded very much like that of a song I recollect to have heard in childhood, beginning with the line "Marlbro' has gone to the war," as a theme, followed with variations. At different points in the chanting the whole audience joined pleasantly in a lively chorus. At the end of an hour this service closed. The Emperor made his way in the manner in which he had arrived, to the throne-room, while the audience hastened to fill to suffocation that for the auction-room in front of it. Bonfires were kindled, rockets sent up, a general illumination outside displayed, while any number of negroes and negresses, venders of refreshments in cakes, candies, and orgeat, rivalled one another in bawling out the superior qualities of their individual stores, the whole scene much like that of a Fourth of July night at home. A band of music struck up in an orchestra near the throne-room, and the auctioneer issuing from the depository, bearing a bouquet of crystallized sugar, began the sale by a solicitation for bids, setting off the value of the article with the merriment and sallies of humor which give reputation to the office. A passage through the centre of the place was kept clear; in this he walked backwards and forwards, giving exercise to his wit, as he exhibited the article under the hammer. Most of the gifts, this first evening, consisted of cakes and confectionery. Some of the bouquets of sugar flowers were most artistically manufactured; and one sold for ninety milreis, or forty-five dollars.

Additional gifts were constantly brought in. They were generally borne in trays on the heads or in the hands of servants, accompanied by the giver. Children too were often the bearers; and one of the prettiest sights of the evening was that of a beautiful little girl in the arms of her father, carrying in her bosom two young doves, white as drifted snow, and as gentle and innocent in look as they were white.

Each offering was made to the young Emperor on the bended knee, and to each one thus kneeling before him, he extended a silver dove, forming the end of his sceptre, to be kissed, and gave in return a small roll of bread. At ten o'clock the auction closed for the night, and the Emperor was escorted to his home by torchlight as he had arrived, but with an additional rabble for his court, and a higher effort in noise and screeching from his band.

May 29th.—Commodore McKeever and Dr. C—— have been fellow guests with me at the residence of Mr. Wells for some days. Previous to their arrival I had taken two or three pleasant rides with our host, and this afternoon our whole party enjoyed another. The Commodore and I were particularly well mounted; our animals were at once so spirited and willing, so playful and gentle, with a gait as easy to the riders as if swaying on the springs of a well-poised carriage. The weather too was charming; and our route after the first half mile being one which we had not before taken, had the additional attraction of novelty. It led southward along the curve of the beach, and was thickly bordered on one side with the American aloe, now in full flower, and on the other by a succession of neat cottages embowered in orange groves, overtopped by palm trees, with dooryards gay in the bloom of the scarlet geranium and the dazzling brilliancy of the poinsetta. The road for a mile was a continued hamlet, with greater evidences of thrift and general prosperity than any suburb we had passed through. On leaving the water we struck into a narrow valley, lying between two ranges of hills; and were delighted with the homelike appearance of the well-cultivated fields and rich pasture lands of the small farms scattered through it. But for the tell-tale palm tree, the rustling banana, and the golden orange, we might have fancied ourselves in some prosperous and well-cultivated little valley in New England. There was nothing to remind us of being in a slave country. All the labor in cultivating the small plantations is done by the owners of the soil. The district is well peopled, and the inhabitants are healthful, prosperous, and seemingly light-hearted. We met and passed many groups of men and boys, engaged in various rural employments. They were invariably bright and cheerful in looks, and most civil and courteous in manners. In general, they are light and slender in figure, and elastic in movement; but apparently without much stamina, and are far from good looking in feature. The females in early youth are passably good looking, and having fine eyes and teeth, might in some instances, be called pretty; but as mothers, they soon become haggard and homely. The climate is salubrious and not excessively hot, yet the complexions of the mass are like those with us who are under the influence of the ague, or just recovering from a bilious fever. This is true of the pure-blooded natives, if any such there be, as well as of those who clearly are a mixed race.

The special object of our ride was to gain a point of view, on the top of a mountain, said to be the finest on the island; and, after a ride of two miles in the valley, we turned into a side road for the ascent. We followed the meanderings of a stream as it babbled along its course, and soon came among the cabins of the dwellers among the hills, perched like birdsnests on terraced points, on either hand above us, in the midst of groves of orange trees and coffee plants. The road gradually changed into a mere bridle-path, till at the end of an additional two miles it suddenly terminated altogether, at a barn near which two men were standing. To these Mr. Wells mentioned the object of our ride, and made an inquiry of them as to the best way to reach it; when, for the first time since I have been in Brazil, I heard a reply of ill-nature and incivility. The elder of the two, in a most gruff and surly manner, said there was no way to go up, and if there were, there was nothing to go for—wishing to know what business we had there at all. Without regarding his mood and manner, Mr. Wells again said, "Is there not a fine prospect from the top of the mountain, and a path by which we may reach it?" to which the man again said, "No! there is nothing but rocks, and I don't know what you can want with them!" Fortunately, at this juncture, a third person made his appearance, whom our friend at once recognized as a regular customer in the sale to him of coffee. From him we readily learned that there was a fine prospect, at a short distance further, but that the ascent to it would not be easily made on horseback; and, volunteering to lead our animals to his cottage close by, he said he would accompany us the rest of the distance on foot. We soon discovered our conductor to differ as widely from his boorish neighbor in taste for scenery as in disposition. He was not only aware of the magnificence of the prospect to which he was leading us, but said he very often went up to the point commanding it, for the mere enjoyment of so fine a scene. Its elevation we judged to be two thousand feet; and we were well repaid for the ascent by the grand picture spread before us. This embraced the greater part of the entire island; its mountains and valleys, rivers and bays, bold promontories, low points and curving beaches, with the whole of the straits, and the coasts along the continent as far as the eye could reach.

On descending to the cottage of our guide, he urged us to

partake of a cup of coffee before leaving; and we entered his cabin, more for the purpose of a peep at the domestic economy of the establishment than with a view to the refreshment. If this home, in its aspects of comfort, may be taken as a fair specimen of its class, it indicates a very low state of civilization among the rural population. It consisted of a single room with a floor of earth. The few articles of furniture visible were of the rudest kind, the whole interior exhibiting little more cleanliness and order than the wigwam of an Indian. A slatternly-looking wife, surrounded by two or three dirty children, did not promise much for the nicety of the coffee she might prepare; and we availed ourselves of the near approach of night and the length of the ride to the town, as excuse for declining the proffered hospitality.

The habits of life among the people are simple, and their diet unvarying and frugal. A cup of coffee and a biscuit made of the farina of mandioca, are the only food of the morning, and there is but one set meal during the day, served at noon. Preparation for it, however, is the first duty of the household, in the morning; and consists in putting a kettle of water over the fire. In this a small piece of *carne seche*, or jerked beef, and black beans, in proportion to the size of the family, are placed, and kept boiling till the middle of the day.

The leisure of the evening had begun, as we made our way down the mountain; and the inhabitants were seen in groups around their doors. Every cabin had its crowd of children, the ring of whose joyous laughter in their varied sports and play, echoing from side to side of the little valley, added fresh impressions of pleasure to the scene. The ignorance in which they are brought up, however, is lamentable. Ignorance not only of letters and books, but of almost every thing. A bright-looking and handsome lad of twelve years, the son of our civil guide, on being asked his age, said he did not know, and seemed equally uninstructed in other commonplace matters. Yet he was evidently as full of natural intelligence in mind as he was active in body. He is one of the little milkmen I have mentioned, who crowd the market square in the morning, and who, with his can of milk on his shoulder, leaves his mountain home every day before the dawn, for the walk of four miles at least, by the most direct path: he is home again to his breakfast of coffee and farina, by eight o'clock.

The Indians and the snakes of this section of the Empire have been among our topics of conversation with Mr. Wells. The settlement of the white man extends but a short distance inland from the coast: not more than fifty or sixty miles at farthest. The interior is still a wilderness in the possession of wandering bands of the Aborigines. These cherish a deadly hatred against the whites; and, prowling along the frontiers in small companies, rob and murder them whenever they find opportunity. Sometimes they venture within twenty and thirty miles of the coast. A party of seven, not long since, made an attack at daybreak upon the shanty of an American, who has put up a saw-mill on the borders of the forest. Though single-handed, he hazarded a shower of their arrows, and afterwards put them to flight by the show of a musket, that, from the dampness of the priming-powder, missed fire.

Venomous snakes are said to be numerous on the island, and some are found occasionally even in the town. Not long since, a German lady, in returning from a party in the evening with her husband, trod upon one whose bite is considered to be death. Fortunately, her foot was placed near its head, and she escaped its fangs; and though it coiled itself about her ankle, she succeeded in throwing it off without injury. A remedy said to be a specific for the most virulent poison of these reptiles is kept at the apothecary's; and families in the country make it a point to have a supply on hand. The mixture consists of six drachms of the oil of amber, two of the spirits of ammonia, and one of alcohol. The dose is twenty-four drops in a wine-glass of brandy, or other spirit, three or four times a day; the wound being also washed and kept wet with it. The ammonia is the active agent in the cure; and should be given freely till a profuse perspiration is induced. If the theory of some be true, that the virus of all snakes is but a modified form of prussic acid, the volatile alkali, ammonia, is the antidote, as that is known to neutralize the fatal acid. Alcohol alone is thought to have effected cures. A young German here was bitten not long since in the country, and being without the prescribed antidote, and unable to obtain it, unwilling to meet in consciousness the doom which he believed to await him, he swallowed a whole bottle of the common rum of the country, that he might be thrown into a state of insensibility. This was soon the case, and remaining dead drunk for twenty-four hours, on recovering his consciousness he was free from all effects of the bite. Here too, there may have been philosophy in the cure. The poison of a serpent being a powerful sedative, its effects may be best counteracted by a powerful stimulant.

A sad case occurred some three weeks ago at Santa Cruz. A fine young man of twenty, the proprietor of a small plantation, was at work with his slaves preparing a piece of ground for a plantation of sugar-cane. Coming to a spot in which the bushes and undergrowth were particularly thick, he cautioned the negroes against working in it with their naked feet and legs, as it had the appearance of a piece that might be infested with snakes. Protected himself by boots, he entered to open a way in advance, but had scarcely done so before the fangs of a *jacaraca*, one of the most poisonous of reptiles, were fastened in an unprotected part of his leg. Neglecting to apply immediate remedies, he was in a short time a corpse.

May 29th.—I have been complying here with the injunction recently received to "make hundreds of sketches;" and this morning, while taking one, of the lower parts of the square and market-house, from the balcony of the drawing-room, had an opportunity of introducing the Commodore as a conspicuous figure. In a stroll in the square before breakfast, he stopped for a little observation near the groupings of men, donkeys, and milk-boys in front of the market. Espying among them the bright little fellow we had seen at his father's cabin on the mountain, with the benevolence and good-will of his nature, he bought the whole stock of boiled beans and farina of an old negro woman seated on the grass near by, and gave the boys in general a breakfast. They all seemed delighted, especially the old negress in receiving the pay, and had quite a frolic. The gratuity of a penny also fell to each boy. With characteristic improvidence and a development of the national passion, the little fellows, after having their stomachs well filled, set to and gambled with each other for the next hour, till every penny they had thus received had made its way to one pocket.

May 21st.—The Novena and subsequent auction was in regular continuance every evening of the last week. On Thursday our party again attended the former to hear the music, and the latter to catch the manners of the people. All the chief dignitaries of the place were present, the President of the Province, the Chief Justice, the Treasurer, and the Captain of the Port. To the residence of the last we were invited to a supper at the close of the auction, and the next morning waited on the President at the palace, or Government House. This is a spacious and lofty building, the ground-floor in front serving both as the entrance-hall and as a guard-room for a company of soldiers, and the corresponding rooms above being divided into a cabinet for official business on one side of the staircase, and a grand sala for reception on the other, with an intervening ante-room common to both. When our visit was announced, the President was engaged with official visitors in his cabinet, but soon made his appearance. He is a small, black-eyed, intelligent-looking man, careless and slovenly in dress, and most simple and republican in his manners. As he spoke Portuguese only, the conversation was necessarily carried on through interpretation by Mr. Wells, and the interview was more brief than it otherwise would have been.

The Presidents of the Provinces are appointed by the Emperor, and their salaries paid from the Imperial treasury. These vary in amount, in proportion to the extent and importance of the Province. That of the President of St. Catherine is four thousand milreis, or two thousand dollars. The selection for the office is usually from persons who are strangers in the Province for which the appointment is made, that the influence of family connections and personal friendships may not prove temptations to partiality in the distribution of the gifts and emoluments under his control.

An anecdote related of a former incumbent of the office, throws light upon the spirit sometimes induced by party politics here, and shows the despotism in small matters which a high official may exercise with impunity. The public square had been lined, at great care and expense, with a closely planted row of date palms. Uniform in height and size, in the course of a few years they became sufficiently grown to furnish by their plumed tops a beautiful screen against the sun, and were a great ornament to the place. The individual referred to, whose name—Pariero Pinto—like that of Erostratus, deserves for a similar reason to be perpetuated, was unpopular as President. Ambitious, however, of becoming at the expiration of his term the Deputy of the Province in the Imperial Legislature, he offered himself to the people as a candidate. An opponent was elected by acclamation. To avenge himself for the slight manifested by his utter defeat, he deliberately set the soldiers under his command at work in felling the palms; and in the course of a single day, the stately trunks and graceful foliage of the whole were laid in the dust.

May 31*st*.—On Saturday the 29th, great preparation was seen to be making around the principal church for the festival of Whit-Sunday, which occurred yesterday. A row of palm trees were planted in front; the verandah, in which the auction during the Novena had been held, was draped and festooned anew with wreaths of evergreen and gay flowers; and tar-barrels, filled with combustible materials, were placed on the square for bonfires at night, though the moon is now in her full. The dawn of

the next day was ushered in with the ringing of bells, the setting off of rockets, the beating of drums, and the playing of bands of music. On looking out, every thing in the vicinity of the church was seen to indicate a grand festival. The temporary palm grove looked as if it had sprung up by magic. Gay flags and streamers of all colors floated from their plumed heads, from the roof of the church and its verandahs, and from various other points. After a service of worship in the drawing-room of Mr. Wells, Dr. C—— and I walked over to witness the scene. The congregation, consisting chiefly of females, had just begun to assemble. There are no seats or pews in the churches here, the whole interior being an open area in which all seat themselves, or kneel upon the bare pavement or floor, without the mat or rug which I have seen elsewhere. Soon the whole space became closely crowded. Most of the women were in full dress; the predominating materials being black silks, satins, and velvets, with short sleeves and low necks, and a half handkerchief of fancy-colored silk fastened round the throat by a brooch. A black lace mantilla upon the head, and the indispensable fan, completed the costume. The variety of garb, however, was considerable; and varied according to the circumstances and position in life of the wearer. Some, as penitents, were draped in mantillas of black cloth, so folded over the head as to reach to the eyes, and fall on either side over the whole figure to the feet. Two or three colored women, whether veritable Arabs or not, wore the thick white cotton veil of the women of the East, so arranged as to leave little of the face except the eyes and nose exposed, while long cloth cloaks reaching to the floor, enveloped their persons. Many of the most expensively and most tastefully dressed persons were negresses. These entered with a self-possession in air and movement, if not with a stateliness and grace, rivalling those of the most aristocratic of the whites; and were followed, like them, by one or more well-dressed servants. We were told that they were the wives, and in some instances the mistresses, of some of the most wealthy of the citizens. A few were in colored silks and dress bonnets of Parisian make, but the black lace veil, with or without the addition of a simple flower, either natural or artificial in the hair, was the general head-dress. All the children were arrayed as if for a dress party. By degrees there was a perfect jam on the floor; the greatest order and propriety however prevailed, each person sitting quietly with the face turned reverently towards the high altar.

At length a movement and bustle in the crowd without—the whizzing and explosion of rockets; the pealing of bells, the heathenish beating of drums, the tinkling of a guitar, and scraping of a fiddle, with the bawlings of the accompanying songs indicated the approach of the young Emperor. He soon entered the church with the cortège before described, and forced his way through the dense mass of women up the nave to the chancel, where seats were in reserve for his mock court and for the officiating priests. The boy was now robed in imperial dress—white small-clothes, silk stockings, and gold-buckled pumps; a flowing mantle of state of crimson velvet and gold, lined with white satin, a ruff of broad lace around the neck; and over all, the ribbon and decoration of the Holy Ghost before-mentioned. A crown of silver of the imperial pattern richly wrought, and a silver sceptre were carried before him on a cushion of velvet. A little girl of five or six years, apparently his sister, followed him. She was in full dress as an Empress, in tissues of silver and gold over pink satin, with a train of green and gold, and head-dress of ostrich feathers. The lad was seated on a throne, at the right of the high altar, the mock Empress on a chair of state beside him; the twenty or thirty gentlemen in attendance stood on the left opposite, while the vicar and his assistants in the richest of their priestly adornments, took their stations in the centre at the altar. All this was done with the most perfect stage effect. As if to give full opportunity to impress the imagination with this, a kind of interlude was introduced in the form of a procession from the vesting-room or sacristy, into a side chapel near the chancel, from which the vicar, under a canopy of crimson velvet, supported on four gilt staves by an equal number of attendants, fetched some seemingly precious thing, the consecrated wafer, a relic, or the anointing oil, and placed it on the altar where the crown and sceptre were already laid. The full coronation service was now commenced and performed in all its parts, including the consecration, the anointing, the crowning, and the enthronement, followed by the obeisance and kissing of hands, and ending with the coronation anthem; the whole was gone through with, seriously and solemnly, as it could have been at the coronation of Don Pedro himself. Mass was then chanted, after which the vicar was escorted through a side chapel to a concealed staircase; and making his appearance in a pulpit projecting overhead from the wall, proceeded to deliver a sermon of fifteen or twenty minutes' length. It was for the most part legendary and fabulous in matter; but throughout impressive and eloquent in voice and manner. The eager and solemn attention which was given, and the fixedness of every eye and every ear upon the speaker, proved the readiness of the people to hear and receive instruction; and I could but think with deep feeling of the effect which the preaching of the Gospel in its simplicity might produce, in speedily substituting the sacrifices of the heart for the crossings and bowings, the genuflexions and prostrations, with which the pantomime of the priests at the altar is now accompanied. I was never before so deeply impressed with a sense of the profanity and idolatry of what is here called religion, as while contrasting in my mind this evidence of a "hearing ear," among the people, with the puerilities and impiety of the childish show which preceded the discourse. It is seldom that a sermon is preached, and more seldom still one that is calculated to edify or produce any practical effects upon the morals, or true devotion in the heart. The people are not bigoted, and are desirous of religious instruction; so much so that, I am told, instances are known in which individuals have sent fifty miles for a tract; and, it is thought that they would here readily attend Protestant preaching in their own language.

The vicars of the churches are appointed by the Emperor, and paid by the state. The salary of the incumbent at the Matriz is fifteen hundred milreis, or about seven hundred and fifty dollars; a living which, with the perquisites of marriage, burial, and baptism, amounts to about two thousand dollars a year. In general the character of these pastors is dissolute. Their vows of celibacy are openly disregarded; they live almost without exception in a state of concubinage. One of the priests here has a family of ten mulatto children; and another, a former confessor in the royal family of Portugal and long resident at St. Catherine, who recently died of yellow fever at Rio, left also a large family. The Jesuits are more exemplary in regard to their vows of celibacy, and the bishop of Rio is among those who are above reproach in this respect.

After the sermon the young Emperor and Empress, attended by the sacred banner, the noisy musicians, and the usual cortège of dignitaries, proceeded to their stations in the auction-room, where the sales, we were told, continued with increased animation and mirthfulness till 10 o'clock at night.

To-day is a fête also, and an auction day. During it we made a call at the residence of the Captain of the Port, in acknowledgment of the civilty of the supper-party to which we had been invited. This dignitary was at the church. He was sent for, and apologized when we took our leave, for not joining us in a walk, by saying that duty required his attendance upon the Emperor.

The variety and the quantity of the confectionery made, presented, and sold at these festivals is surprising. Every device of ingenuity is put in requisition for the production of it in new forms. The lady of the Captain of the Port showed us a very large tray of work in sugar and flour, most elaborately wrought in its forms, and tastefully finished in coloring and gilding. It had been purchased at the auction for forty-two dollars, and presented to her by a friend. The whole was the workmanship of an old lady of more than three-score years and ten, who had given four months' time to its manufacture. The chief object seemed to have been to furnish the greatest variety in man, beast and bird. Every article was true to nature in figure and coloring; cottages and groves, fruits, flowers, and vegetables, specimens in conchology, entomology, and the whole range of natural history, with a wide margin in the catalogue for what was purely imaginative. The whole presented a striking evidence of the ingenuity, taste, and unwearying industry of the aged devotee.

And now, you will say, "Why give so much time to the observation and to the description of such puerilities, to say the least of them, as constituted the chief services of the church here on Sunday?" I answer, that I may certainly know by the "seeing of the eye," as well as by the "hearing of the ear," the distance to which this people are removed from the simplicity and purity of the Gospel; and that you may judge of the causes of their ignorance and superstition. These plays are acted, and these festivals prolonged and varied for the amusement of the populace, and to keep the masses content under the control of their spiritual guides. Lights and music, dress and flowers, form and ceremonies, the waving of banners and swinging of censers—the glare and glitter of the stage, are thus made to excite the imagination, and satisfy the thoughtless and ignorant mind with fleeting shadows, in place of enduring good. The whole system of Romanism as exhibited here, is little else than Paganism in disguise; a system in which old idols are presented under new names, and heathen processions and ceremonies substituted for that worship which is "in spirit and in truth."

June 18th.—We took leave of Mr. Wells and of Desterro the day following my last date; and two days ago made an attempt to get to sea; but a head wind set in and still prevents our departure. All hands are pleased with the delay; we cannot soon weary of such a place, the scenery is so beautiful, the climate so fine, the walks and rides so picturesque and rural, and the supplies for the refreshment of all hands are so abundant and so cheap. In addition to the fresh beef furnished to the ship's company, any quantity of pigs, turkeys, chickens, eggs, vegetables, and fruit is offered alongside in canoes, for private trade with the different messes and with individuals of the crew.

In the attempt to get to sea, we changed our anchorage two or three miles northward from the forts, and were brought into the immediate neighborhood of two beautiful little bays, encircled by gracefully curving beaches of white sand. Both abound in picturesque and wild scenery; and are in many places filled with orange groves overburdened with fruit, now in full season. Far from any grog-shop or means of dissipation to the crews, the boats ply backwards and forwards from the ship to the shore at all hours of the day, filled with officers and men in the enjoyment of a kind of saturnalia, in search of fruits, and flowers, and every thing rare and curious in nature. Some of the cacti, air plants, and parasites now in full bloom, are superb in their beauty. A hundred delicious oranges can be purchased for a penny; and, but for the presence of our ship, would not be worth to their owners the shaking from the trees. It is, too, the season of sugar-making. The apparatus and entire process are most rude and simple: each small plantation being furnished with a primitive mill of two rollers of timber to extract the juice, and a rough trough or two to conduct it to a boiler. The eating of the cane, and an occasional dip into the troughs and into the half crystallized contents of the cooling-pans, offer to all quite a tempting pastime. St. Catherine seems to be a province of small proprietors, whose productions, derived from their own labors, exceed but little the supply of their private wants. Each carries to the market a few hundred pounds only of coffee and of sugar annually—brought to the purchaser in small quantities, at different times, when some foreign article is needed.

The coffee of the island is of a superior quality, and the chief of its products: as it also is of the whole empire, though introduced into the country by the Franciscan Friar Villaso so recently as the year 1774. The first bush was planted by him in that year in the garden of the convent of San Antonio, at Rio de Janiero.

It was not till the revolt of St. Domingo that its price became such as to lead to its general culture here. In 1809, when coffee was first imported into the United States from Brazil, the whole produce of the empire amounted only to 30,000 bags; this year it is estimated that it will amount to 2,000,000, or a value of more than $16,000,000. The plants blossom in August, September, and October; and the crops are gathered in March, April, and May.

My last ride at Santa Cruz was with Captain Cathcart, in a visit to an estate called "Las Palmas," or the palms, recently purchased by him. It lies on the coast, ten miles north of his present residence. Mr. W——, Captain Pearson's clerk, accompanied us, for the purpose of making some correction in the "plot" of the plantation, drawn by a surveyor. We were to have started at an early hour of the day, but a pouring rain prevented. This state of the weather, however, changed afterwards into occasional heavy showers; and, at the risk of being drenched by these, we ventured to set off at eleven o'clock. The road is a mule-track, and at places, for long distances, consists of the hard sand of the beach. The frequent streams flowing into the sea from the interior are so swollen by late rains, that we found difficulty in fording them in safety. A second heavy shower after we started, came hastening upon us just as we were entering upon the longest stretch of beach on the route. This was smooth and hard, and afforded us a good opportunity of trying to outstrip the storm, till we could reach some place of shelter. Captain Cathcart is an exceedingly stout and heavy man—fairly stuffed into his clothes, and weighing 250 or 280 pounds. Mr. W—— is very long and very lean, with legs and neck like a crane, and arms to correspond. My own *physique* is familiar to you; and you would have been amused at the sight, could you have witnessed the manner in which we three scampered over this part of the road, with the pelting rain and rushing wind in full pursuit. A cotton umbrella and an overcoat kept me from the wet: but it was the last of the old umbrella—before the wind had well reached us, the outside had become the in, the top the bottom, and the whole structure of whalebone, steel, and muslin, an irremediable ruin.

About midway of the distance we came to a hamlet of two or three miserable huts, the remains of a settlement of poor Germans, who had been tempted from their distant homes by the flattering inducements to immigration held out by the government of Brazil, but to whom, on their arrival, the poorest sections of land in the region had been allotted as the promised gratuity. These, the settlers had no means of making profitable; and they are now left to disappointment and neglect. They are wretchedly poor; and those of them whom we saw looked pale and thin, care-worn and ill. Immediately beside the steep and worn-out lands assigned to them, there is a wide tract of level country belonging to the government, upon which these poor foreigners, had it been appropriated to them, would not only have gained a living, but in all probability acquired an independence.

On leaving these cabins, at which we halted a moment for a cup of water, we began to ascend the spur of a mountain which forms a headland on the coast, separating the bay along the beach of which we had come, from that on the opposite side, where the estate we were to visit is situated. The hill is un-wooded and steep, the path was very slippery, and the ascent difficult; but we accomplished it slowly, with fine views on our right over a widespread alluvial plain covered with thick set forests:

"A habitation sober and demure
For ruminating creatures: a domain
For quiet things to wander in; a haunt
In which the heron should delight to feed
By the shy rivers, and the pelican
Upon the cypress and the pine in lonely thought,
Might sit and sun himself."

In place of the heron and the pelican, however, we had the *Urapongo*—a large bird of the parrot tribe, which, like

"A flaky weight of winter's purest snow,"

was clearly seen at a long distance in brilliant whiteness amid the dark green of a tree-top—sending forth its peculiar and solitary song, in notes as shrill and metallic as the gratings of a coarse file upon steel, of which they forcibly reminded me.

Cathcart, from his Anglo-Saxon enterprise and energy, and consequent thrift and increasing wealth, has become quite the great man of the region; and seems to be in favor and on most familiar terms with all the inhabitants, black and white. He gave to every dwelling we passed by, whether near at hand or afar off, a hail of good will in one form or another, calling forth a quick response from the unseen occupants, and the speedy appearance of master, mistress, or slave. After gaining the level of the mountain, we came upon a cluster of mud houses surrounded by an orange grove, situated upon an elevation on one side of the road, the owner of which, an old Portuguese, we were told was worth a hundred thousand milreis, or more than fifty thousand dollars. As he will be the next neighbor of our host on his new estate, we turned aside for a moment to interchange salutations with the family. The whole aspect of things, in huts and negroes, in the mistress and an only child, a boy of ten or twelve years, was very slovenly, very slip-shod, and very filthy. The wife is a lively, black-eyed, chatty woman, scarcely yet in middle life; but the husband a gray-headed and withered old man of more than three-score years and ten. He is a great miser; and had on an old jacket of many colors, with patch upon patch, till it appeared to be of treble thickness. This he always wears both at home and abroad, and never by any chance lays aside. It is said to be inlaid with gold. The captain began at once to banter with him for the purchase of it, offering a very large sum, and causing by his jests in regard to it, great laughter among the negroes, and one or two white laborers near by; but the owner seemed to have no notion to close a bargain in the case. We did not dismount; but accepted the offer of a drink of fresh cane-juice from a sugar mill near by. It was brought to us in an old calabash, and tasted neither sweet nor clean.

Before reaching this place, we had entered into a wood, and were charmed with the variety and brilliancy of the bloom—scarlet and yellow, pink, purple, and white—exhibited in air-plants and parasites, creepers and flowery trees. Besides a great variety of the palm, there were wild figs, laurels, myrtles, cassias, and a kind of silk cotton tree—*chorisia speciosa*—with large rose-colored blossoms. The climbers are superb; and give to the trees they overrun an air of great magnificence. This is particularly the case in the *Solandra grandiflora*, with its large trumpet-shaped flowers; and a species of fuschia—*fuschia integrifolia*, which, running up to the tops of the loftiest trees, falls down in graceful festoons of crimson flowers. Among the undergrowth the scarlet blossom of the *cana speciosa* glared brightly on the eye. The forest did not appear to be primitive; but here and there a monarch of the wood was seen, which could have attained its height and widespread dimensions only by the growth of centuries.

While yet high on the mountain's side, we opened a full and magnificent view of the new purchase of Captain Cathcart. It embraces the entire superficies of a rich valley, ten miles at least in circumference, encircled on three sides by lofty timber-covered mountains, whose tops are the boundaries of the possession. These terminate on either hand in bold promontories, jutting into the sea, while between them sweeps a curving sand-beach, a mile and more in extent. A fine stream meanders through this domain. A rocky islet, in the centre of the bay formed by the projecting headlands, is tufted with palm-trees, and gives name to the estate. Though but partially reclaimed from its primitive condition, and for the most part a luxuriant mass of woodland only, in its wide expanse, manifest richness of soil, and evident capabilities of improvement under the axe and the plough, it seemed to the eye as thus pointed out to us, to be quite a principality. As an isolated possession I have seen nothing like it in Brazil. The history of the property may have added, perhaps, to the interest with which I looked upon it now in the hands of a new possessor. The late proprietor, Señor De L——, a man of good family, good education and good breeding, had been reduced by his imprudence, mismanagement, indolence, and I may add vice, to the necessity of disposing of it at a ruinous sacrifice. I had seen him the day before on board the Congress, bearing the air and address of a gentleman, mingled with the dejection of a confessed bankrupt: one not able to work, and too proud to beg. In the morning before setting off from the consulate, I had met, too, a daughter of his, of eighteen, decidedly the finest-looking and most attractive native female I have seen in Brazil: lovely, not only from positive beauty, but from evident amiability and feminine gentleness. And now, when I saw the exulting eye with which the new purchaser, the rough and uneducated whaleman, surveyed the lordly domain, I could not but think of the dispossessed and impoverished gentleman and his children, and sympathise with them in the loss of such an estate.

Shortly after commencing the gradual descent of the mountain, a rustic gate was pointed out as the entrance to " the Palms." The distance from this to the house is about two miles; and a little taste and labor would convert it into a parklike and lovely drive—first through interlacing woods down the declivity, and then over the green sward of a natural meadow, belted and dotted for a mile with groves, and clumps, and single trees of natural growth. The house is a substantial old mansion of brick stuccoed, with tiled roof and encircling verandahs. It stands in the midst of a lawn fronting the small river, which here empties with a serpentine sweep into the sea. It commands the entire view of the valley and encircling mountains, of the bay, its promontories and islets, and the distant sea. These lands have been a seigniory from the earliest settlement of the country; and the house was built a hundred years ago, when the proprietor was in office under government. It is most substantially constructed; and the window frames, door-posts and doors, and the columns of the verandahs, though never painted, are yet in perfect preservation; the close-grained wood of which they are formed, on being slightly scraped, exhibits the soundness and brightness of mahogany. In all things more perishable the establishment is in a most neglected and dilapidated state. The furniture has been removed, excepting that of a lofty and spacious dining-room, where a long and heavy old table—a fixture, with benches along each side, of corresponding fashion, still remains: all else is the perfect picture of ruined fortunes and deserted halls.

A servant had preceded us on foot with a basket of refreshments. To the contents of this was added an abundance of fine oysters from the mouth of the river, into which a heavy surf and daily tides pour floods of salt-water over the oyster-beds. When called to this repast, I was quite surprised to see, lying open on one end of the table, a large mahogany case with lining of crimson velvet, filled with a full dinner-set of heavy old plate of rich and massive patterns—including knives, forks, and spoons, of all sizes. In explanation, the captain told us it was the property of Señor De L——, left here on his removal from the house; and now brought forward in the hope of having it bought by him, adding, "but I was born with an iron spoon in my mouth, and am used to one still; and I have made up my mind, unless I can get the set for——," naming a sum not one third of its value, even as old silver, "I will never take it." Conscious, probably, from the knowledge he had of the necessities of the poor señor, that they were sure to be eventually his at his own price.

But why, you will ask, these details in a matter of no moment? I answer, because I know not when my feelings have been more interested, or my sympathy more excited than by an incident of the day, directly associated with them. Every thing without was so wet after the heavy rain, that we were confined on our arrival very much to the house and verandahs. Knowing that the family of De L—— had removed, and that a few slaves only of Captain Cathcart were in charge of the place, I was surprised to see a fine-looking, and strikingly handsome young man approach from a thicket near by. His only dress was a white cotton shirt, open at the throat, and a pair of pantaloons of blue nankeen, old and faded, but both perfectly clean and neat. Though bareheaded and barefooted, he moved with the self-possessed air and manner of a gentleman. Before I could ask, I was told he was a son of the late proprietor; brother of the young lady I had met at the consul's in the morning, and between whom there is a very strong attachment, as well as a very striking resemblance. The father, like too many others in this country, was never married; but as is extensively the custom here, he has several sets of children by different women—the secret of his wasted fortune. After an introduction to the young man, struck with his Adonis-like beauty both in figure and face—so like his sister as to lead to the supposition that they were twins, I felt some curiosity to know his age, and after a little conversation asked him in Portuguese how old he was? Though evidently bright and intelligent by nature, his reply was, "I do not know—my father can tell!" The captain immediately said to me in English, "There you have a sample of the utter ignorance in which these people are brought up; they know nothing, and are taught nothing worth knowing. This is a very nice young man as you see; but his father has given him no education. Poor boy! I felt very sorry for him the day I closed the purchase of this place and 'clinched' the bargain. He knew I had been some time in negotiation for it; was present at the moment, and seemed very anxious about the result; and when he saw that the whole was sold without any reservation, and the case settled, the tears started to his eyes, and he said—'So, father, you have sold all your property, and I am left to be like a negro! You always told me I should have a part of this land. Had you done any thing for me, had you given me any education, or taught me to do any thing, the case would have been different, and I would not have cared. But you have done nothing for me, and have not taught me to do any thing for myself; and now have sold all your land, and left me to work like a negro!' The father could only reply with tears, 'I know it, my son, but I cannot help it: I am in debt eleven thousand milreis, and have nothing to meet it but the two thousand five hundred which Captain Cathcart pays me for this property.'" I thus became acquainted with the terms of the purchase—about twelve hundred and fifty dollars for two or three miles square of the finest land in the region, parts of which at least have been long under cultivation! Antonio, the name of the young man, had himself, previously to the sale, planted a piece of the land with cane and mandioca, and asked the consul afterwards whether he might still work upon it, and gather the crops. He says his reply was, "Yes, my son, and call upon my negroes here to help you, and bid them work for you as if they were your own." He is now there with a single remaining slave of his father, for this purpose. Captain Cathcart invited him to join us at luncheon. He seems interested in him, and says that as soon as he removes from Santa Cruz himself, which he intends to do almost immediately, he will take the lad to live with him, and will be his friend. I trust he will be true to his word, and faithful to the promise in the case which I exacted from him. He is evidently greatly elated by the purchase, as well he may be, if he can reconcile his conscience to the price which the necessities of the seller forced him to accept for it. While looking over and pointing to a very small section of it, he said to me, "Mr. S——, if, when, as a boat-steerer on board a whale-ship I first met you at the Sandwich Islands, I had thought I should ever have been the owner of such a hillside as that, I would have felt amazing proud!" the continuation of the sentiment being of course—"judge then how I feel now, as the lord of this wide-spread manor, and the monarch of all I survey!" Wherever he turns his eyes, he sees and speaks of its varied capabilities for sugar, mandioca, rice, corn, cotton, coffee, cattle, hogs, timber—and if spared in life and health a few years, it is probable his present visions of the wealth to be derived from it, will be fully realized. While he was speaking thus, I again begged him to befriend Antonio, whose sad and dejected looks during our whole stay were in such strong contrast with the self-satisfied air and high spirits of his dispossessor. The deep pensiveness spread over the manly and handsome face of the young man as we bade him adieu, and his attitude—till we lost sight of him in the distance—leaning his head and shoulders against a pillar of the verandah with folded arms, as if lost in sad abstraction, still haunt me.

BUENOS AYRES.

June 30th.—For a third time I date from Buenos Ayres. The continued prevalence of the yellow fever at Rio de Janiero forbade a visit of the Congress there, on leaving St. Catherine; and the alternate was a return to Montevideo. On arriving at that place, general liberty on shore was accorded to the crew; and a bearer of despatches to the American minister here being required, I gladly availed myself of the Commodore's kindness in appointing me to the duty.

When I left Buenos Ayres in February, the town and province were under the rule of the Provisional Governor, appointed by Urquiza. As speedily afterwards as possible, a constitutional election was held for that office, and the same person was chosen by the people. Since then, a Congress of the Governors of the Provinces has been held at San Nicolas de Aroya, a city two hundred miles from Buenos Ayres up the Parana. This was preparatory to a general convention of delegates, for the formation and adoption of a federal constitution for the United Provinces, after the model of that of the United States; Urquiza being appointed for the interval Provisional Director of the Argentine Confederation. The result of the deliberations of the Governors has just been proclaimed, and the articles of agreement have been published. These, though seemingly wise and just, are unsatisfactory to the Portenos or Buenos Ayrians. Claiming, from their larger population, greater wealth, and higher civilization, a preponderating vote and influence among the States, they are unwilling to confirm the act of the Governors, which will limit them in the proposed general Congress, to the same number of representatives or delegates, with each of the other Provinces. The House of Representatives of Buenos Ayres, or Sala, as the body is here styled, immediately denounced the proceeding by strong resolutions; and great public excitement took place. On learning this, Urquiza, who has returned from St. Nicolas, withdrew his troops from their quarters in the city, planted a battery of guns on the parade ground near the cavalry barracks, which commands the town, and despatched a messenger to the President of the Chambers, with orders for the immediate dissolution of that body under the alternative of having it dispersed by his guns. The announcement of this led each member quietly to take his hat and leave the hall, notwithstanding the valorous resolution of the previous day, in which the determination had been avowed of sacrificing their lives rather than their liberty.

Two thousand or more of the citizens not long since organized themselves into a national guard; each individual having equipped himself at his own outlay, in a showy and expensive uniform. During the agitation of the Chamber, under the action of the Congress of San Nicolas, these sent a messenger to the house to assure the representatives that they would repair to their sittings and stand by them to the death. They were, however, at the time, much in need of percussion caps for their muskets. Urquiza hearing of this, and that diligent search was being made in the city for a supply, sent his own orderly to their barracks, with a couple of packages; and, it is said, called himself in the afternoon of the same day to inquire whether they had been received, and to say he would be happy to furnish them with a larger quantity if needed! Thus showing his utter contempt for the bravado of the 'shop-keepers,' as he calls them. On the dissolution of the Chamber this brave guard very speedily disbanded; and the next day small parties of the soldiers of Urquiza, in command of subalterns, went from house to house throughout the city, and took possession, without resistance, of all the arms they could find. Urquiza proclaimed himself Provisional Chief, but continued in office under him the Governor who had been elected by the people. All things are going on quietly under this coup d'état.

The general judgment of those who have had the best opportunity of knowing the people, is, that they are incapable of enlightened and stable self-government. Urquiza is regarded by these as greatly in advance of other chieftains of the Plata, in enlarged and patriotic views and principles. Full confidence is placed in his integrity of purpose, as well as in his firmness and daring of will.

His personal bravery at all events cannot be doubted. During the height of the excitement of the last week, while execrations loud and long were poured upon him by designing partisans and their followers, he rode fearlessly about the city attended by a single officer; and is resolved, at all personal hazard, to carry out the measures and policy which he thinks needful for the best interests, not only of Buenos Ayres, as a city and province, but of all the Argentine States. He believes the consolidation of the whole under a constitutionally appointed chief executive, indispensable to their permanent prosperity; and this it is his purpose to achieve.

July 20th.—It is seldom that the Rev. Mr. Lore of the Wesleyan Mission can avail himself of the assistance of a brother clergyman; and I have cheerfully taken upon myself, at his solicitation, on each Sabbath of my several visits here, two of the three services held in the chapel on that day and evening. The ordinary number of worshippers amounts to about four hundred, of whom fifty are church members. The established religion of the State being that of the Roman Church, and the civil regulations of the country not permitting Protestant preaching to the natives in their own language, the congregation and church consist exclusively of foreign residents—American, English, Scotch and Irish: of these, the greatest number are English. An interesting and flourishing Sunday school of two hundred and fifty scholars, is attached to the church, and in addition to the public services of the Sabbath, a weekly lecture and prayer-meeting are held in the chapel. The Sabbath after my arrival was that of the Communion. On the Thursday evening previous, Mr. Lore preached a preparatory sermon, and on the Sunday six new members were received into the church. They were all young persons, and of both sexes. A more than ordinary proportion of the church members are in their youth. It is a cheering sight to perceive among them so many young men, thus openly and decidedly choosing a life of piety in the midst of a city of general indulgence in worldliness and pleasure, and almost universal moral dereliction. In the full toleration of Protestant worship thus allowed, and in the open example seen and acknowledged by all—even of a few consistent and truly spiritual Christians, there is hope for this land: there is light shed abroad which cannot be hid, and seed sown which has already sprung up and borne fruit. Many things seem to indicate that, in the providence of God, the ignorant, superstitious and benighted population, is destined in the progress of time to give place by immigration from foreign lands, to those better fitted in mind and education, in energy and enterprise, and in enlightened principles, political, moral and religious, to mould the destinies of the nation and build up a free and prosperous empire. One cannot fail in passing along the streets, to be forcibly struck with the prevalence of the English language. You can scarcely move a square in any direction without overhearing it; while French, German, Portuguese and Italian—the patois of the Basques and the Gaelic dialect of the Scotch and Irish, are liberally intermingled.

Mr. Lore is deservedly popular in his position, both as a man and as a minister. He is an able and interesting preacher, and a faithful and affectionate pastor: ready to every good work—the comforter of the sick and afflicted, and the friend and benefactor of the poor and destitute. Mrs. Lore too, is admirably fitted for her station, and, full of gentleness and amiability, is universally beloved. The history of Protestant worship in Buenos Ayres may be briefly given. Its origin dates as far back as the year 1820. On Sunday, the 18th of November in that year, Protestant religious worship was first held here in a private house. The assembly numbered nine persons, the worship being led by Mr. Thompson, a Scotch Presbyterian, who had arrived in the city under the auspices of the "British and Foreign School Society," with the purpose of establishing schools on the Lancastrian system; and had so far succeeded in his object as to be then employed by the government as superintendent of a school of this description. This lay worship was continued till the year 1822.

In 1823 the Rev. Dr. Brigham, now long the secretary of the American Bible Society, and the Rev. Mr. Parvin, an associate, arrived as agents of the Bible and Missionary Societies, and by them preaching was established in a private house. Dr. Brigham, after a time, carried his agency to Chili and Peru, and returned to the United States; while Mr. Parvin continued resident here, as a preacher and teacher, till the year 1827. In this year he was joined by the Rev. Mr. Torrey, first as an assistant, and soon as successor, both in teaching and preaching. Mr. Torrey continued in Buenos Ayres till the year 1836; when relinquishing his position and returning to the United States, worship according to the Presbyterian form ceased, without any attempt having been made to organize a church.

The field was thus left open to the labors of the Methodist Episcopal Church; the Rev. Mr. Pitts, a missionary of this denomination, having arrived at Buenos Ayres about the time Mr. Torrey left. He preached, however, but a short time, and returning to the United States, was succeeded in the year 1837 by the Rev. Mr. Dempster. Public worship was continued by him in the same house in which Mr. Torrey had held his services; and his preaching was soon followed with such success as to demand an enlarged place for the congregation. In the ensuing year a lot in a very eligible situation was purchased for the erec tion of a church and mission house; the funds being provided for the purpose, partly by subscription in Buenos Ayres, and partly by an appropriation from the Methodist Missionary Society at home. The buildings subsequently erected are the present chapel and parsonage, on the principal street of the city, immediately opposite the stately church of the Merced. The chapel, a neat and simple structure, sixty feet in length by forty in width, with a façade in Grecian architecture, fronts upon the street; while the mission house or parsonage, approached by a passage on one side of the chapel, occupies the rear of the lot. A court, ornamented with shrubbery and trellised grape-vines, separates the two, giving to the premises a retired and rural aspect, attractive, and appropriate to the character of the occupants. The Rev. Mr. Dempster was succeeded in 1843, by the Rev. Mr. Norris; and this gentleman again in 1848, by Mr. Lore. The church and congregation are now not only self-sustaining, as to the support of the pastor and all the incidental expenses of the mission, but contribute liberally, according to their means, to the general societies at home for the promotion of the cause of Christ.

Besides the Wesleyan congregation and church, there are now in Buenos Ayres three of other Protestant denominations: one British Episcopalian, one Scotch Presbyterian, and one Reformed German. All these have much larger and finer buildings for worship, and much larger and more wealthy congregations. The salary of the Rev. Mr. Falkner of the British Church, amounts to $4000. The Scotch congregation, under the pastoral charge of Rev. Mr. Smith, is of the Established Church of Scotland, and also partly under governmental support. The German Church, whose pastor is the Rev. Mr. Seigle, has just completed a new place of worship; a beautiful specimen of Gothic architecture, and an ornament to the city. These congregations have each a large and flourishing day school under its supervision and patronage, beside Sunday schools.

I have renewed my intercourse most agreeably with several families here—particularly with that of Mr. H——, who is a fellow-Jerseyman. Mrs. H—— is also from Jersey; and I have a standing invitation to breakfast with them on buckwheat cakes, so favorite an article of diet there. The L——s and the Z——s of Montevideo, too, are now here. Among the acquaintances newly made, and to whom I am indebted for hospitality, are the J——s; Mrs. J—— being the daughter of an old friend, Captain M—— of the Navy. They occupy a tasteful and pleasantly situated quinta in the eastern suburbs of the city, where they entertain their friends with elegance; adding to a generous hospitality, the charm of fine music, in which, both vocal and instrumental, Mrs. J—— excels.

I have been desirous for some time, of making an excursion into the "Camp," as the flat country of the Pampas south of the city is called, in a visit to the estancia, or cattle farm of an American of respectability, but have not yet had it in my power to accomplish the purpose. My opportunities for sight-seeing have consequently been limited to the city. The room I occupy is on the second floor of a house finely situated on the edge of the bluff upon which the town lies. Its windows on one side overlook the quadrangular court communicating with the street. In this there are some magnificent specimens of cacti; among which are a prickly pear twenty feet in height, with a trunk like a tree, now covered with primrose-colored blossoms; and an octagonal plant of the same genus nearly as tall, filled with those that are of brilliant crimson. There is in it also a magnificent specimen of the "Uca Gloriosa." The view from the other side commands the whole length of the alameda or public walk, the river, with the inner and the outer anchorage, and all the movements of the roadstead and landing. When the tide is out, the sands to the east, for a mile or more, are nearly or quite bare. At all times, except when the water is at flood, the landing of passengers and freight is by cart. Familiarity with the sight does not take from its interest. Sometimes both horses and carts are seen half submerged in the water—intermingled with boats, some under sail and others pulled by oars,—the drivers, to keep themselves from being wet, standing on the shoulders of their beasts, in the manner of circus-riders. It is amusing to see them start from the shore on the approach of a boat or boats with passengers. They rush off under the shouts and lashings of the drivers, plunging and ploughing through the water, over the rocks and into holes in the rough bottom, in utter disregard of every thing except a first chance at a customer. The horses are so well trained to the business, that the carts are as readily turned and backed up to a boat on reaching it, as a fish is moved in the water by its fins. The whole performance is so droll and amphibious, that I never cease to be amused in witnessing it. When the water is low, freight and passengers are often taken on board these carts from small vessels at their anchorage. At such times too, horsemen and dogs, and various other animals, are seen scampering over the sands in the shoal water, as if the mirror-like surface were the ice of a frozen river.

When the wind is fresh, a heavy sea rolls over the sands. Then the vocation of the carts is at an end, and they seek the security of the shore. The boats too, securely anchored outside the rocks, are left to toss upon the water by themselves, and for the time-being, a non-intercourse occurs between the shipping and the shore.

The construction of a mole to extend beyond the sands is entirely practicable, and would be of immense importance, and a great saving of expense in the trade of the place. So essential a work should have been accomplished a century ago. Had the amount lavished by Rosas in redeeming the marshes of Palermo, and in rearing upon them his country palace, been thus appropriated, it would long since have secured a convenient and safe landing both for goods and passengers, and have been a lasting and honorable monument of his public spirit and patriotism. A day or two since a detachment of the troops of Urquiza embarked from this landing on their return to Entre-Rios. It is the winter season; the weather was wet, cold, and piercing, and the whole number, amounting to some hundreds, were kept for hours, shivering in the exposure incident to the slow means of getting off to the transports in which they were to sail; first in squads of eight or ten in a cart, and then in equal numbers in small boats.

The *lecheros* and *panderos*—the milkmen and bakers—form striking features in the scenes of the street in the early morning. Both grades are invariably mounted on shabby, rough-coated little horses or mules. They seat themselves very longitudinally on the shoulder-blades of the beasts, their legs being stretched out almost at full length; while the supplies they carry for distribution are balanced on either side from neck to tail—the milk in long tin cans of different sizes, stowed in different compartments of leather fixtures, something in the form of old-fashioned saddle-bags. The bread is distributed from immense panniers of ox-hide, cured with the hair on, made oval, in band-box form, burying the animal beneath their ponderous shapes, and half blocking up the street as they pass. There is nothing especially peculiar in the dress of the bakers, they being dwellers in the city, and generally French, German, or Spanish by birth and in costume; but the milkmen from the country, at distances from five to fifteen miles, furnish illustrations of the grotesque and comical worthy of the pencil of a Cruikshank or Wilkie. None but an artist could do justice to their slouched hats of every form, the cotton handkerchief of divers figures and colors in which their necks and faces are bundled up, their ponchos of every hue—their cheripas of various materials from scarlet broadcloth and gayly-figured merinos, to horse-blankets, and fire-rugs; while half-yard wide pantalets of white cotton tamboured and fringed and worn over heavy boots or leggings of calfskin, make up the sketch.

On entering the plaza about seven o'clock a few mornings ago, I saw some hundreds or more of these figures, with their horses and milk-cans, grouped before the police office at the Cabildo or town hall. The spectacle was one of the most singular I have met, and led to an inquiry as to the cause of the unusual gathering. In answer, I learned that the extent to which the watering of the milk had been carried had led to the interference of the police. On that morning, every milkman as he entered the city found himself unexpectedly under arrest, and was hurried to the office of the chief, to have the product of his cows put to a test. All were now busy lugging their cans into the town hall to be thus cleared from the imputation of defrauding their customers, or, if found guilty, to pay the fine imposed by the laws of the municipality. I did not wait to learn the result, but believe few escaped the penalty.

To one informed of the extent of vexation and labor required in securing the milk, it is scarcely a wonder that it should be well watered before being brought to market. The cows of the native breed are impracticable to all domestic training or discipline. They not only require to be lassoed every time they are milked, but must be also tied head and foot, and during the operation have their calves by their sides. These must be permitted to draw the milk alternately with the use of the hand by the milkman, or nothing can be obtained from the animal. Much time is thus taken up in the operation; and the result is only about a quart of milk a day from each cow, and a pound of butter a week. The consequence is that milk commands from twelve to fifteen cents a quart; and butter from sixty-two to seventy-five cents a pound. The supply is furnished chiefly by the German and Basque settlers. The natives are for the most part too indolent to take so much trouble for the returns made, either for their own use or for sale.

RIO DE JANEIRO.

September 20th.—We returned to this port on the 13th inst: bringing passengers with us, Mr. Schenck, Chargé d'Affaires at the Court of Brazil, and a nephew, his private secretary. In addition to the diplomatic office he holds here, he was recently appointed by our government Envoy Extraordinary to the Republics of the Plata, for the purpose of negotiating, in conjunction with Mr. Pendleton, treaties of friendship and commerce. The unsettled state of affairs in the Argentine Provinces, however, interfered with the completion of this mission, and he has returned for a time to Rio de Janeiro.

Mr. Pendleton accompanied him as far as Montevideo; and during a brief sojourn there, the two diplomatists, with the aid of

Mr. Glover as interpreter and secretary, formed a treaty with the Republic of Uruguay, by which the United States are placed here upon a footing with the most favored nations. The promptitude, industry, and despatch of the ambassadors in the negotiation quite astonished the ceremonious, indolent, and procrastinating ministers of Spanish-American blood. After it was once initiated, they allowed themselves scarcely the relaxation of an hour till the parchments were engrossed; and the ink in their signatures was not well dry before the Chief Envoy was on his way with us to this place.

I will let an incident occurring at Buenos Ayres speak his general character. While last there, I occupied furnished rooms in the establishment of a shrewd, sharp-eyed, talkative Englishwoman. The window of her private apartment commanded the well-guarded portal, opening from the street into the pateo or quadrangle of the house; and from it she kept a watchful lookout on the movements of her lodgers and their visitors. A short time after I had taken up my quarters there, Mr. Schenck called upon me. My landlady soon became informed, by some means, of his name and position; and with the notions of rank common among those in humble life in her own country, was quite excited by the distinction conferred upon her lodger, and seizing the first chance afterwards of waylaying me, gave vent to her feelings on the subject by the exclamation—" And indeed, sir! so you have had the honor of a visit from your minister, the new ambassador! La me! I said to myself as I saw him come in, ' Why who can that very genteel, delicate-looking, strange gentleman be?' But I knew him at once for a diplomat. I can always tell them. I have had a great deal to do with them—Sir Charles Hotham, Sir William Ousely—and I know them at once, they are so clever—so very, very clever! Oh! rely upon it, sir! your ambassador is a very clever man: I could see it in his eye, sir! and then it was so kind in him to call. I knew him for a diplomat—so very genteel, and so clever," adding, " Clever, sir, clever—very, very clever!" as she bowed herself backwards into her little room, as if retreating after a presentation at court. And clever, indeed, Mr. Schenck is, both in the English and American use of the term. In regard to the last, he has given very decided proof in his great kindness to the Rev. Mr. Fletcher, seamen's chaplain here, who with Mrs. Fletcher arrived from the United States shortly after the Congress left, eight months ago. They early became settled in a hired cottage, but when Mr. Schenck received the diplomatic appointment to the Plata, he constrained them to leave it, and with their family to take possession during his absence, of the embassy and all its appointments, in furniture, servants, carriages and horses; and as it will be necessary for him to return to Buenos Ayres at the end of two or three months, wrote to them before leaving the river, that he came now only to be their guest till he should be recalled there by duty for an indefinite time. They are thus permanently at home with him.

Mr. Fletcher on his arrival, entered at once zealously upon the discharge of the duties of his position; and, while the yellow fever has again raged for months as an epedemic among the shipping and on shore, has been indefatigable in preaching the Gospel to the well, in nursing and comforting the sick and dying, and in consoling the afflicted, of whom there have been many among American and English shipmasters, who have had members of their families in greater or less numbers on board their ships with them, some of whom have died under very affecting circumstances.

The Rev. Mr. Graham, rector of the English Episcopal Church, has service in a neat chapel in the city on the morning of the Sabbath; Mr. Fletcher at the same time preaches to the seamen in port, on board some ship in the harbor, and in the afternoon holds worship in the drawing-room of the American Consulate. I have assisted him in this service since our arrival, and have felt it a privilege and a blessing to join the "two or three," who assemble there for praise and prayer, and to hear the preached word. The music is led by Mrs. Fletcher at the piano; and she is assisted vocally by Mrs. K——. This excellent person is a good representative abroad of her fellow-countrywomen of New England at home—sensible, intelligent, practical: ever decided in her expression of moral principle, and ever constant in the exhibition of her religious character. She has been greatly afflicted by the bereavements which have befallen her here in a strange land; but resigned in spirit, seems by them to be the better fitted for the duties of a Christian in this life, as well as for the inheritance which is to be the reward of such in the life to come. Mrs. F—— is not less strikingly the type of her class in Europe. She is a daughter of the distinguished and apostolic minister of Geneva, Cæsar Malan; and highly educated and accomplished, seems fitted alike

> "to shine in courts,
> Or grace the humbler walks of life."

CHAPTER XXIX.

CONSTANTIA.

November 22d.—A few days at "Boa Esperenza" in the mountains of Tejuca, ten miles from Rio, proved so interesting to my friend Dr. C—— and myself, that we determined to make a more distant excursion of the kind to this place, in the midst of the Organ Mountains, fifty miles from the city. The route to it passes near San Aliexo, and on our way we made an agreeable visit of three days to our friends there.

Constantia is the estate of Mr. Heath, an Englishman, which has become a favorite resort of the citizens of the metropolis in the summer season as a watering-place, for the enjoyment of pure and invigorating air, and the luxury of fresh and wholesome diet in the country. By previous arrangement, mules and a guide were sent for us two days ago to San Aliexo by the proprietor; and taking leave of Mr. and Mrs. M——, we were off for our destination after an early breakfast this morning. The day was splendid in its coloring, and full of freshness. Our guide, a bright, intelligent little negro of twelve, was all activity and good-nature; and mounted on a mule scarcely larger than himself, with a carpet-bag slung on each side of him in the manner of a pair of saddle-bags, went on his way whistling and singing as if he knew neither sorrow nor care. Instead of leading us, however, he rode behind in the fashion of a groom; but not so much for appearance, as we soon discovered, as to give a poke with the pointed end of his whip to one or the other of the animals ridden by me and my friend, when they became disposed to lag in their gait, or to start them forward by a sharp cut across their rumps with its lash.

The first stage of eight miles northward was to Freischal, an inland venda, or store, where the turnpike begins the ascent of the "Sierra." For that distance, the plain is very similar in its general features to the country between Piedade and San Aliexo, before described. The mountain scenery to the west, close upon the left, was, however, very fine; and was marked now, after heavy rains, by numerous watercourses and cascades, which foamed down from the heights above, in single shoots of hundreds of feet. Most travellers from Rio make Freischal a stopping-place for the first night; but the "Barriera," or toll gate, midway up the ascent, four miles further, is a much more picturesque and attractive spot; and we pushed on to this for luncheon, without alighting at the other. The road after passing Freischal winds at first in gradual ascent along the broad bases of the mountains. It is wide, smooth, and well graded; and paved at intervals for long distances with large cubes of granite, like a Roman highway. It was enlivened by troupe after troupe of mules passing in both directions, with heavy loads of produce from the interior, and of merchandise from the capital: each company of seven animals being under charge of a troupiero, or muleteer, though frequently moving by hundreds together, and sometimes crowding the road thickly for a half mile in succession. As thus seen *en masse* in the distance, either in meeting or overtaking them, they present an odd spectacle. The mules with heads bending to the ground beneath their burdens, are themselves for the most part completely hidden by the bulky loads they carry. The tips of their long ears, bobbing up and down with the motion of their step; the cross ends of the clumsy wooden saddle or frame, to which the panniers or other burdens on either side are affixed—something like the buck of a woodsawyer—sticking out above their shoulders; and the dried ox-hides surmounting the whole, to protect the articles transported from the weather, flapping like wings up and down in the irregular tread of the beasts, are alone seen: and to one unacquainted with the sight, would present objects in natural history difficult to be guessed at. There is a leading mule to each troupe, whose bridle and head-stall are gayly ornamented with tufts of scarlet and blue worsted, and often with showy plumes of the same material, and also strung with bells of varied sizes and tones—the whole a matter of rivalry in the taste and vanity of the respective troupieros. The leaders are so well trained as to allow no one of their own troupe, under any circumstances, to pass ahead of them on the road; so that the muleteers have to look out only for such as lag behind or stray by the wayside. These men themselves are black, and white, and of every shade of complexion; are of all ages, and in an endless variety of costume, as to the material and condition of old shirts and old jackets, old trowsers and old drawers, old hats and various head-gear—from the well clothed, to those almost in a state *puris naturalibus.*

The Barriera is as wild and romantic a spot as can be well imagined. I recollect nothing on a public road surpassing it, in these respects, unless it be the site of Alhama, in the sierra of the Alpuxares. It is a narrow ravine high upon the mountain's side, above which the fantastic pinnacles called the "Pipes of the Organ," bristle thousands of feet. From these a mountain torrent, foaming and roaring over and around gigantic boulders of granite, comes rushing down, and divided into two streams by an islet over which the road crosses, plunges headlong into a gulf below. In the midst of this islet, to which a bridge from either side is thrown, a neat little chapel, surmounted by a cross, rises upon the sight with pleasing effect, in contrast with the savage wildness of every thing around. At a neat venda just beyond, to which we had been directed by Mr. M——, we were served with a luncheon of boiled eggs and bread and butter. Our host was a civil young Portuguese, and the neatly whitewashed walls of the room in which we ate, were ornamented with a set of colored engravings, illustrative of the fate of Inez de Castro in the hands of Peter the Cruel. For the first time in my rambles in Brazil, I here saw a book in the hands of any one—it was a copy of the "Complete Letter Writer" in Portuguese, which the keeper of the shop was reading behind the counter when we went in.

We were now more than a thousand feet above the level of the plain. For some time before reaching this point, a beautifully shaped and luxuriantly-clothed mountain in front of us, had particularly attracted our attention. It here stood directly beside us on the right. Nothing of the kind can surpass the beauty of its foliage in varied forms and tints of green—interspersed with masses of white and of yellow, of purple and of scarlet. The white in many instances is not a blossom, but the leaves of the sloth tree—*cecropia peltata*. The under sides of these are covered with a white down; the leaves curl upward under the hot rays of the sun, and give to the whole tree-top, amid masses of verdure, a whiteness almost as pure, and more silvery, than that of the snowball. The yellow blossoms are chiefly of the acacia; the purple and the scarlet those of climbers—bignonias and fuschias. An American forest in October can scarcely compare in gorgeousness with these gay woods, in the seasons of their bloom.

From the Barriera the ascent becomes increasingly steep, and the road is formed by zigzag cuts in the sides of the mountains, and, at places, around their projecting shoulders. The angles at the turns are very sharp, and the road rises in terrace above terrace—at some points edging upon precipitous ravines and deep chasms, hundreds of feet in perpendicular descent. In these sections, the long lines of mules, as seen both above and below, struggling up or moving cautiously down, are particularly striking. In several places the way was wet and miry, and many a poor beast was down in the mud with his burden upon him, but lying quietly and patiently, as if accustomed to such accidents, waiting for the coming up of his troupiero to relieve him of his load, and thus enable him to rise. As we mounted higher and higher, the landscape became more and more extensive. By degrees the northern end of the Bay of Rio opened to view, followed rapidly by the islands which cluster in it; the mountain-ranges of its eastern coast; the Sugar Loaf, Raza and Round Islands in the offing; the Corcovado, Gavia and peak of Tejuca—embracing a panorama more than a hundred miles in circuit, in the midst of which the imperial city, though forty miles distant, was distinctly seen gleaming in the afternoon's sun. Such was the scene on one side of us, while on the other the pikes of the Sierra close at hand, rose in savage nakedness three thousand feet above our heads. The world boasts many pictures in nature, in which loveliness and sublimity are combined, but I doubt whether this "Boa Vista"—"Fine View," of the Organ Mountain does not rival any single combination of mountain, valley, and water, that man ever beheld. I can remember nothing in my own experience equal in interest to this day's ride; unless it may be the travel through the mountains of Granada, followed by the first view of the "Vega," with the city, the walls and towers of the Alhambra, and the snow-covered heights of the Nevada above, all gloriously lighted by the glowing hues of the setting sun.

Though uncertain of the length of time it would require to reach our destination before nightfall, we lingered long in silent admiration of the picture; and at last, found it difficult to make up our minds to turn the point of a projecting rock marking the highest elevation of the road, and which shuts it from view. From this point the descent on the north commences. It is gradual, and unmarked by any striking features, except the jagged peaks on the left. Thick mist and clouds soon enveloped these, and for a time the way became comparatively tame and uninteresting.

H—— Hall, the mountain home of Mr. H——, an English merchant of Rio, whom we had been invited to visit, is situated a short distance from the sierra. We called upon the family for a short time; but, anxious to reach Constantia, resisted their persuasions to remain over night, or at least to dinner, and hastened on our way. At the end of six miles, we turned from the public road into a bridle-path leading through thick woods, filled with the music of birds. Many of the trees overhanging us were magnificent in size—monarchs of the primeval forest, stately and venerable with the growth of centuries. One, whose branches entirely overarched the road, at an elevation of more than a hundred feet, particularly excited our admiration. Though its limbs were gnarled and distorted, and in themselves leafless, they were so fantastic in shape as well as gigantic in dimensions, and so adorned and draped with parasites and creepers, and festoons of gray moss, as to be a fit study for an artist.

At the end of three additional miles, we came suddenly upon a fine field of luxuriant Indian corn enclosed by a hedge. Into this a rustic gate led, which our guide threw open without dismounting, and uttered the announcement, apparently with as much pleasure as it gave us to hear it, "Esta Constantia!" "This is Constantia!" We were at the entrance of a little valley, two miles in length by a half mile in width, encircled by high hills, in the midst of which the buildings of the establishment of Mr. Heath are clustered. These consist of a principal house of two stories, plastered and whitewashed, and having a steep shingled roof; four cottages of one story in the same style, in front of this; and various out-buildings and offices in the rear, with quarters for the negroes—the whole having the general appearance of a Swiss or German hamlet. The approach is by a well-made drive, half a mile in length. Trees of natural growth have been left here and there near this and in the adjoining grounds; giving to the whole somewhat the aspect of a park.

Our host met us at the gate of an inner enclosure which protects the gardens and shrubbery. He is six feet and more in height, of a portliness in full proportion, and frank, open-hearted and cordial in manner. He had been expecting us for two days, and dinner was now a third time waiting our arrival. We had heard of his facetiousness, and that his anecdotes were irresistible; and had determined before meeting him, to maintain a becoming dignity. Before the dinner was half through, however, we found all our precaution vain; and under the rehearsal of some of his personal adventures in Brazil, were obliged to give way to fits of laughter, which made the tears run down our cheeks.

November 24th.—The estate of Constantia is two miles square. Its first owner was a Swiss, who gave it the name it bears, with the intention of cultivating the grape on its hill-sides, in the hope of producing a wine that should rival that of Constantia, at the Cape of Good Hope. But his expectations in regard to the production of wine were disappointed; and an experiment with coffee succeeded no better. The soil is too cold and too poor to produce the best qualities of either; and Mr. Heath purchased the whole property for a small sum. The house and adjoining cottages are situated in the midst of flower-gardens, which indicate by their growth any thing but poverty of soil; and are fragrant with the perfume of the tuberose and heliotrope, cape jessamine and white lily, and beautiful in moss-roses and camellias, the most splendid carnations, beds of violets and mignonette, and an endless variety of choice flowers. The stems of the tuberose exhibit eighteen inches of closely-clustered blossoms, and while the white lily at home seldom produces, I believe, more than six or seven flowers on one stock, I have here counted thirteen. The vegetable gardens and fruit-yards present a like display of exuberant growth, in peas, beans, potatoes, artichokes, cabbages, beets, cauliflowers, strawberries, raspberries, limes, lemons, peaches, pears, apples, quinces and grapes. These in constant succession bring a rich return to the proprietor from the market at Rio, to which, distant as it is, troupes of mules carry cargoes as far as Piedade, twice every week.

The work of the estate is performed by slaves, of whom, including women and children, there are thirty-three on the premises. They are well-fed, well-clothed, and well-treated, and seem to be contented and happy. Their master is a humane and kind man, and intends to give to all their freedom: in earnest of which he has already manumitted several, who still continue with him, and to whom he pays regular wages. The children come round him at his call with laughter and gambols, and scramble playfully for the biscuit and cakes and the other niceties which he carries with him from the dining-hall, for the purpose of distributing among them. The gardens are under the care of females exclusively: the superintendent, of the same sex, being thoroughly skilled in the business. Every thing in that department is under her sole direction, from the turning over of the earth for planting, to the gathering of the produce, and the arrangement of it in panniers for the market.

All hands are turned out for work at daybreak; are mustered by name, and receive orders from their master at a window of his room. A custom is observed here, and I am told in all well-regulated families in Brazil, which, were it any thing more than an unmeaning form, would be interesting. It is the asking of a blessing from the master every morning and every evening at the close of the day's work by all the slaves, of both sexes and of every age. The full form of words is the following: "I beseech your blessing, or grant me a blessing, in the name of our Lord and Saviour Jesus Christ!" To which the master replies, "Jesus Christ bless you for ever!" But it is the usage to epitomize these expressions by the interchange of the shortest possible abbreviations of them, and in words rather startling at first to the ear uninformed of the designed object; the slaves as they present themselves merely exclaiming, in all manner of intonations of voice and in every mood of humor—"Jesus Christ!" While the master, be he talking or laughing, eating or drinking, or in whatever way employed, without any interruption and seemingly without any regard to the import of the salutation, as abruptly replies, "Siempre!" "Forever!" The effect last night was quite ludicrous, as fifteen or twenty men and women came in from labor in the fields—probably weary and hungry and impatient of any delay—and thrust their heads rapidly, one after another, into the windows and doors of the verandah as we were at the tea-table, with the above exclamation of two words only;

followed instantly by the single one from the master, much in the manner of a *feu de joie.*

No bell, nor similar means of summoning the outdoor servants is used; but the clear, trumpet-like voice of the master is often heard far and wide, sending forth with a distinctness not to be mistaken, the names of those needed. While listening to these stentorian calls, I have been struck with the euphony and romance of many of the names, especially those of the females—Theresa and Rosa, Justina and Juliana, Januaria and Theodora: a list fit for the court calendar.

Within a few hundred yards of the houses on either side, sharp hills rise to the height of several hundred feet, partially covered on their sides and crowned on their tops with intermingled woods and cliffs. That on the south is marked in its whole length by the broad channel of a watercourse; this, at times, becomes a foaming cascade, compared with which, the artificial shoot down the hill at Chatsworth, would appear but the plaything of a child. At present the quantity of water, though flowing with great swiftness, is small, but furnishes an abundant supply for plunging-baths at the foot of the hill, and for keeping a corn-mill near by, in operation day and night. This mill is a curiosity in one respect—it is self-tending; so far, at least, as to cease working when the hopper becomes empty. The contrivance is very simple, and consists of a fixture at the bottom of the hopper, which, acting through a spring, shuts off the water from the wheel when the weight of the grain is removed.

The day after our arrival was one of rain, and we were kept for the most part indoors. This, however, we scarcely regretted. Indeed, we were more than content with confinement in the midst of such verdure and bloom; and were satisfied for the time, in the freshness, quietude, and rural repose of this secluded spot, with the companionship, through the windows and from the verandah, of the mules and cattle, the sheep and pigs, geese, ducks and chickens, turkeys and guinea-fowl, with which the pasture-grounds and enclosures are filled; and not less with that of our intelligent host in his hours of leisure, in listening to his anecdotes and reminiscences of life in Brazil. He has pre-eminently the talent of making one forget that he is a stranger in his house and a boarder at his table. You feel yourself rather to be the welcome guest of friendship under the hospitable roof of the lord of the manor, on whom you are conferring a personal favor by your visit. His sporting stories are very amusing and somewhat marvellous. There is no end to the rehearsal of the adventures of twenty years, in hunts after the leopard and ounce, the tapir and deer, the peccary and other game of the forests. He has, too, often been the guide and companion in this region, of the most distinguished travellers who have visited Brazil in that period. He ascended the loftiest peaks of the Organ Mountains with Dr. Gardiner; and gives details of privations and hair-breadth escapes in wildernesses before untracked by man, and upon cliffs and precipices previously unscaled, not found in the published records of the accomplished naturalist.

Yesterday and to-day the weather has been clear and fine, and delightfully bracing and elastic: the mercury varying from 65° to 70° Fahrenheit. The elevation of Constantia above the bay of Rio, is about 3000 feet. The highest point of the intervening range of mountains is 6000. The site of the houses does not command a view of the Organ chain: but, from the hill-side on the north, it is distinctly seen. We walked a short distance up this last evening, just before nightfall, and found the entire range magnificently clothed in the gorgeous colorings of the setting sun. Though at the distance of fifteen miles in an air-line, the sight was sublime. The serrated part presents aspects on this side altogether new; and more wild and fantastic, if possible, than those on the other. I secured the outline of a sketch, which, when seen by you, may lead you to suppose me sporting with your credulity.

We have rambled with delight at different times through the little valley in the rear of the establishment. It is two miles in length; is prettily watered by a winding stream and diversified by glade and dell—pastoral in its herds of cattle and flocks of sheep, and vocal with the murmuring of water and the music of birds. I do not include in the melody of these, however, the noisy chatter of flocks of parroquets; though the beauty of their gay plumage, added to the attractiveness of our walks, as, fluttering through the air, it flashed upon the eye in the bright rays of the sun, like masses of emeralds and gold. We made the attempt to ascend some of the hills for more commanding points of view; but found, even those which were without wood, and which appeared at a distance to be almost as smooth as the turf of a lawn, to be altogether impracticable, from the thickness and rankness of the growth of ferns with which they are covered. On a near approach, these were seen to rise far above our heads in impenetrable thickets. We undertook to advance a short distance among them; but, though Dr. C—— is of no contemptible height —six feet four inches—and not without proportionate strength of muscle, we were very willing, at the end of a few minutes, to give over the effort. Progress can be made through them only with a sharp bramble-scythe, or a sickle in hand. They are so thick-set, and so even in height, that the negroes, Mr. Heath tells us, in returning from labor on the hills, often make short work of the descent by projecting themselves headforemost for long distances, in steep places, over the compact surface of their tops.

PETROPOLIS.

November 30th.—We bade adieu to Constantia on the morning of the 26th inst. It was not yet sunrise when we took leave of our host for the ride of forty miles through the mountains to this place. We set off in the following order; first, a sumpter-mule, with our luggage and provender for the day, led by a negro on foot; then a courier, the counterpart in age, size, and blackness, of our guide from San Aliexo, but a perfect dandy in comparison, in his costume—being dressed in a trimly-fitted jacket and trowsers of new nankeen, a highly polished castor hat with velvet band and broad rim, beneath which was worn, in Brazilian style, a scarlet silk handkerchief, floating loosely down the shoulders behind; leggings of untanned leather, so wide at the top as to serve for the reception and safe carriage of all kinds of small packages and parcels, but terminating in bare feet well-spurred; the Padre, as I am styled, and his mule came next; while the fleet-surgeon, last in position, but first in height and dignity, brought up the rear. I was quite impressed with the appearance of respectability in our departure, by the long line thus formed, till, at the outer gate, it was suddenly shorn of its "proportions" by the loss of our footman, who, tying the halter of the beast he was leading, firmly into the long hair of the tail of our little courier's mule, gave us his benediction and returned to the house.

The morning was beautiful, the air fresh as the breath of June, and the light, fleecy clouds floating in the sky, tinted with bright hues. Our way for some miles was a grass-edged and dewy path through the woods. From these, unnumbered birds poured forth their matin songs as if

"every sense and every pulse were joy."

There is an untiring charm in the woodland scenery here; the growth is often so majestic and widespreading, and the foliage so varied in form and coloring. We were gratified by the near view, in two or three instances, of a fine, lofty, forest-tree, which had at other times attracted our attention at a distance, by the flowers of mingled pink and lilac with which it was thickly studded. These grow singly, and not in clusters; but the general effect, from the intermingling of strongly contrasted shades of one color in the same flowers, is that of the apple blossom. The lowest branches, however, were too lofty to allow a satisfactory examination of them. Among the most graceful of the growth, which in some places fringed and overarched our way, was the bamboo, shooting up in thick clusters to the height of fifty, and even a hundred feet. The tree-ferns, too, were conspicuous, their umbrella-like tops giving them in the distance the appearance of palm trees in miniature. Parasites and creepers entangled the whole woods, while the former, mounting to the tops of the loftiest branches, descended low again towards the ground in gracefully sweeping pendants. Surrounded by such imagery and breathing such air, with the golden sun flickering through the tree-tops upon our path, or gleaming brightly over a glade on its side, I felt as buoyant in spirit as when a boy I roved over the pine-covered hills of Otsego.

At one place the road merely skirted the woods and commanded a broad expanse of cleared land in a valley. A striking feature here, was the number of stately old trees which still studded the landscape. They were leafless and lifeless, however, and so blanched from top to bottom as to seem whitewashed. Masses of gray moss hanging in long pendants from the skeleton limbs, gave to them, in contrast with the vigor of life by which they were surrounded, a melancholy and funereal aspect. Just as we were emerging from a thick wood on a side hill which overlooked the trees below, my friend said to me, "All that is needed to make our ride perfect in its kind, is a sight of some of the wild animals of the country." I replied, "Yes, any thing but a tiger or a leopard." I had scarcely finished the sentence, when a succession of fierce and angry shrieks and screams burst forth beneath us; and looking in the direction, we saw a whole tree-top filled with black, long-tailed monkeys—they were in terrible commotion—a regular family quarrel. Every branch of the tree swayed to and fro, as they leaped about and swung themselves by their tails from the end of one limb to that of another. The tread of our mules or the sound of our voices, however, suddenly put an end to their squabble, and in an instant, the whole troop in affright disappeared in the thick wood.

At the end of a few miles we came to the turnpike by which we had mounted the Sierra, and followed it northward a short distance. It was crowded with troupes of mules, just setting off from the ranchos at which they had passed the night. The muleteers at one point, were engaged in replacing the burdens on their animals. Their occupation is far from being a sinecure. Besides making the journey of hundreds of leagues on foot, they have daily, and sometimes repeatedly each day, to load and unload their beasts, and to readjust the many straps by which the freight they transport is kept well-balanced, and secure from damage. The ordinary load of a mule is from six to eight "*arobas*" of thirty-two pounds each, and the usual distance travelled in a day, from twelve to sixteen miles.

The middle section of the journey was marked by a succession of pyramidal hills of bare granite, a thousand and more feet in height, rising from the bosoms of the valleys which encircle their bases like so many gigantic sugar-loaves. They appeared to be utterly inaccessible, and presented cliffs on some of their sides hundreds of feet in almost perpendicular descent. About noon, surrounded by parroquets in flocks and other birds of gay plumage, we gained the highest point of land on the route. It commanded sublime views of the mountains, both before and behind us; and, among other objects, one of special interest to us personally in the cabin of a free negro a short distance ahead, to which we had been directed as a good place to refresh our animals and to take our luncheon. We had accomplished fifteen miles of the journey. The next fifteen were less interesting in every respect; the general surface of the country was bare, and the mountains sterile and naked. The glare of the sun was oppressive, and by the time we had finished that additional distance, we began to be fagged and weary. And this, you will ask, while still surrounded by much that was strikingly novel and magnificent? I will refer you for our vindication in the case, to any one who has been ten hours in succession on muleback, riding up hill and down dale, over a scarcely practicable mountain road. A mule is a very nice animal for the ride of an hour over smooth ground, and one that is full-blooded and wellbroken, very passable perhaps for the ride of a day; but to be mounted from sunrise to sunset on such beasts as we had, and to travel for a whole day over such a road, are enough to make any one who has suffered the experience groan afresh at the remembrance of it. I was not aware before that there was such entire antagonism in the peculiar, short, broken, and half-finished motions of the brute; causing one to feel at the end of a day's journey very much as it might be supposed he would, if subjected in rapid succession for the same length of time, to a constant simultaneous jerk of the shoulders, twist of the hips, rap on the ankles, and thump in the back; while the head has been kept incessantly bobbing up and down in involuntary motion, like that of a Chinese image when once set going. I know nothing like it in travel for weariness, at least to the unpractised rider.

Late in the afternoon, we came upon the other great highway from the metropolis to the mines in the far interior, and following it, found the last ten miles, through the valley and beside the rippling waters of the Rio Piabanha, to be beautiful, not only in natural scenery, but from cultivation and long settlement. I must confess, however, that it required an after ride over it fully to persuade us of this. At the time, we were too much done over for high admiration of any thing; and were chiefly occupied in straining our vision for some indications of being near our place of rest. At length, the little guide, a short distance in advance of us, reining in his mule at the top of an ascent in a gorge of the hills, exclaimed to us in Portuguese—"Come see Petropolis!" We doubted whether it might not be still miles distant; but pushing on, were well pleased to catch sight of the town, pictured in beauty before us, not a quarter of a mile off, at the bottom of the hill. We were glad to see our little courier ride to the door of the first house at the entrance of the place, as the hotel which Mr. Heath had recommended to us as the best: had it been the worst, scarcely any inducement could have led us a hundred yards further in search of any other. We were barely able to dismount.

I never saw a place of which the common phrase "nestled among hills," is so descriptive as Petropolis—in fact, it is doubly "nestled." First, by a half-dozen beautiful hills which rise abruptly around it to the height of two or three hundred feet, and then again by mountains which tower to an elevation of as many thousands. The central part of the town lies in a little triangular basin, a half-mile in extent each way. From this, glens filled with cottages and pleasant residences, diverge in various directions. Each has a mountain-stream running through it, two of the principal of which, flowing from opposite directions, meet in the centre of the place. The surrounding country is the private property of the Emperor, by the purchase of his father Pedro I. It was the design of this sovereign to colonize it at the time with Germans, but his abdication prevented the accomplishment of this. His son carried it out, by offering, ten years ago, such inducements to immigrants in gratuities of land, that the colony now numbers six thousand inhabitants, chiefly Germans. The Emperor early built a cottage for himself in the centre of the village, with the view of making an occasional visit to the place. The appearance of the yellow fever in Rio as an epidemic, has since led to the construction of a palace on the same site, which is to be a regular summer residence of the Imperial family; and Petropolis, from the sickliness of the city and the example of the Emperor, has become the favorite resort, as a watering-place, of the rich and fashionable.

Though it is not yet the "season," there are many visitors here at present, among whom we were happy to meet our friend Lieut. F—— of the Congress, and a party of his English friends, residents of Rio. The whole place has the air of an enterprising, thrifty, and prosperous new settlement at home, attributable to the fact that instead of enervated and indolent Portuguese and Brazilians, the inhabitants are industrious, managing, and hard-working Germans. The walks and drives in the vicinity, for miles in every direction, are varied and beautiful. It is only a mile and a half from the "Alto do Sierra," the point at which the great highway from Rio to the mining districts gains the height of the chain; the view from which is thought by many to outrival that of "Boa Vista" in the Organ Mountains: we have enjoyed it under great advantages of light and shade, and think if there is a difference, it is that the latter has more wildness and sublimity of foreground, and the former more softness and beauty in the general panorama. The road by which the passage of the mountain is here made, is, in its grading and construction, an exceedingly fine work, equal to most of those found in the similar passes of Europe. The first railroad projected in Brazil is now in construction, from the bay of Rio to the foot of the mountains. Its line, clearly traceable from the "Alto," is a new and most hopeful feature in a landscape of this Empire. Among the most interesting of our fellow-guests at the hotel here, are the Chief Engineer, an Englishman—Mr. Bragge—and his family, and his assistant, Col. Golfredo, a Neapolitan exile.

The German population is about equally divided as to religious creeds; about three thousand being Protestants and three thousand Romanists. On the Sabbath Dr. C—— and I attended worship in the Protestant chapel. Places for Protestant worship are prohibited the external architecture of a church building; and but for the assemblage of people at the door, we should not have been able to distinguish the chapel from the row of houses under one roof, among which it stands. The interior is simple and rude, and sufficient only to accommodate three or four hundred worshippers. About that number were present. They are just now without a pastor, and the schoolmaster of the town officiated. The order of the services, including the reading of a sermon, was that of the Lutheran Church. The worshippers seemed serious and devout; and though the whole was to us in an unknown tongue, we endeavored—not in vain we trust—to make "melody in our hearts," with their singing, and with their prayers to pray "with the spirit and with the understanding."

CHAPTER XXX.

Buenos Ayres.

January 18th, 1853.—I am again in Buenos Ayres, and find it for the fourth time within the two years past, in an entirely new aspect. The contrast between its present condition and that in which I first saw it, is peculiarly striking. Then, all that met the eye gave evidence of peace, quietude, public order, safety, and seeming prosperity. There was the bustle of active business every where—at the crowded landing in boats and lighters plying rapidly between the shipping and the shore, and in the thronged thoroughfares in the trucks of the warehouses, and the ponderous carts with their long lines of oxen from the interior. Pleasure, too, was heard and seen on every side, in the gay chat of the promenaders on the sidewalks, the dashing by of equipages through the streets, and in the laugh and gallop of riders, both male and female, coursing along the shore. Now, in place of peace, there is war; in place of quietude and order, anarchy and confusion; in place of safety, danger; and of seeming prosperity, apprehended ruin! All business, foreign and domestic, is suspended; the mole is like a place of the dead, the shops and houses are all closed, the street deserted; every native male inhabitant, between the years of sixteen and sixty, under arms and on daily duty, and the city begirt, within a dozen squares of its centre, by hostile troops composed of its own people. By these, all intercourse between the city and the country is prevented, and all supplies of provision cut off; while they daily direct the murderous fire of their muskets and cannon down the streets occupied by their neighbors, relatives, and friends. And what, it will be asked, is the cause of this state of things, and what the origin of the civil war? Even the best informed on the subject here, whose feelings and judgment have not been perverted by partisanship, reply by saying, "Who can tell?" One thing is clear, the cause is not a spirit of patriotism excited by oppression, or the origin a sense of right under the pressure of wrong; nor are either traceable to the conflicting policy of contending parties in regard to the public good: patriotism, right, and public good, are but empty words here. The highest principle seems to be that of personal ambition, in a few military aspirants, sustained by ignorant and mercenary followers; and the ruling motive the attainment of power—power over "the receipt of customs," and power over the "Paper Bank," with the opportunity of robbing the public, under the name of office and the form of law. This may be thought a harsh and summary judgment in the case, but it is sustained by facts.

The history of public affairs at Buenos Ayres for the last six months may be briefly told. After Urquiza had found it necessary to dissolve the House of Representatives in the manner described during my last visit, and to assume the supreme authority, he gave full evidence of the enlightened and public-spirited policy of the government he purposed to exercise. His first measure was the establishment of the public schools which Rosas had suppressed; and the introduction into them of the Bible as the text-book of morals and religion. Another project was the building of a breakwater and mole, for the protection of ships and the benefit of the commerce of the port; and a third the construction of a railroad into the interior. This policy, in acts and purposes, begat confidence in him among capitalists and the friends of progress; and high hopes were entertained of future prosperity to the city and state. In September, however, he was called from Buenos Ayres to the Congress appointed by the diferent States, to convene at the city of Santa Fé on the Parana, for the formation of a general constitution and the consolidation of the Republics into one government. He left a small body only of his own troops at Buenos Ayres, and embarked on his mission. But the smoke of the steamer which carried him to his destination had scarcely faded on the horizon before a revolution was effected by his enemies, and a new government organized. The first measure adopted by it, was a resolution to invade Entre-Rios, the State of Urquiza. For this a force was despatched both by water and by land: that by water was summarily defeated and dispersed by the Entre-Rians, and that marching by land, informed of the disaster, halted on the frontiers. Money was of course necessary for the subsistence of the troops on this expedition; and the new minister of war obtained the issue of a large amount of paper money by the bank for this purpose. He forwarded it to the disbursing officer, however, with instructions to keep it in safety till he could arrive himself to attend the distribution of it among the soldiers. He left the capital professedly on this errand, proceeded to the camp, obtained possession of the money, crossed the frontier, exchanged the paper for gold, and emigrated beyond the jurisdiction of the government of which he was a member! The soldiers, disappointed in their pay, were conducted by their leaders to Buenos Ayres, to obtain redress by a new issue from the bank; but before they reached their destination a second revolution took place. The government which had enlisted and promised to pay them had been overturned; and that now in power refused their demands. In consequence of this the troops invested the city; and hence the civil war—the parties being the 'insiders' and the 'outsiders.' Those without are not in sufficient force to take the city by assault; and those within have no power by which to drive the besiegers from the suburbs. It is said that Urquiza has furnished material aid to the outsiders, and on the adjournment of the Congress of Santa Fé will join them in person with his Entre-Rian troops.

One can scarcely give credit to the atrocities committed in the guerillas, which almost daily take place—atrocities which would disgrace a horde of savages. What think you of the execution of prisoners by stretching them on the ground, making their wrists and ankles fast with thongs of raw hide to four horses faced in four different directions, and then, by starting these on the gallop, at a single spring, to tear them into quarters! Yet this has been done within a few days in public, and in the presence of an officer, from whom, an eye-witness, Mr. Lore received the account. A few mornings since the coachman of Mrs. Z——, coming into the town from a quinta or country-house near the lines, which the family had been obliged suddenly to abandon, perceiving two horsemen of the outside party riding furiously down the street towards him, stepped on one side to let them pass; and in doing so he observed something attached to a rope dragging behind them. A second look as they flew by, showed it to be the body of a man, in the uniform of the national guard, who had been either just lassoed or shot by them. At a short distance these fellows met three or four of their comrades; and drawing up to speak to one another, the whole party amused themselves by beating the head of the dead victim with the butts of their carbines!

For an hour or two, almost every morning and every evening, sharp-shooting is heard in various directions around the city. A party of twenty or thirty outsiders, will, at such times, dash up to the barricades at the ends of the streets, or a party of the same number of insiders will rush out beyond them—without any object in either case, but that of having a shot at each other —and blaze away till tired of the sport; fortunately, for the most part, without much bloodshed or a loss of life. Occasionally, one or two on either side fall, or an innocent spectator or passer-by receives a fatal shot. The people along the lines have now become so used to this, as not to regard these skirmishes. Last evening Commodore McKeever, Dr. C—— and I, went to the quinta of Mr. K—— to take tea. This is in the midst of the battle-ground between the lines. As we arrived, a sharp skirmish had just ended, during which musket-balls had struck the house, and one, the drawing-room window, near which Mr. and Mrs. K—— were sitting. A few evenings ago we were at the parade-ground, at the north end of the city, witnessing the evening drill. A skirmish was at the time taking place about half a mile distant, along the flat towards Palermo; and it was notable to see the perfect coolness with which one and another—some singly and others two and three in company—would catch up their muskets and walk or lope towards the scene of the guerilla, laughing and chatting as they arranged their arms for firing, as if it were a shooting-match for goose or turkey they were about to try a hand at, in place of the life of a fellow-being. The whole contest is boyish in its mode of operation, as well as murderous in its motive and end. I am told by those who have witnessed it at the lines, that the manner in which the parties challenge each other to these skirmishes—their taunts and ribaldry, shoutings and insults, are both amusing and ridiculous. Every two or three days a sortie is made by a body of three or four hundred from the inside, on a forage for grass. These generally lead to the loss of lives on both sides. A few mornings ago, on such an occasion, an officer from the inside performed quite a feat of valor and presence of mind. He suddenly found himself cut off from the party he was commanding by a mounted band, who had awaited him in ambush. The first intimation he had of danger was in finding a lasso around his neck. He freed himself expertly from this with his knife, just in time to receive one of the attacking party, coming at full charge upon him with a lance: this he not only parried, but wresting it from the grasp of its owner, unhorsed and pierced him through with it. By this time another lancer was upon him, but only to be run through with the same weapon. He then drew a revolver, with which he brought a third to the ground; and by wounding a fourth in another shot, effected a return to his own party.

March 12th.—The chief interest in public affairs still centres in the civil war. The presence of Commodore McKeever continues to be important and essential for the interest and safety of American residents and their property. His flag is borne by the "Jamestown," on board which a detachment of marines from the Congress, under Lieut. Holmes, is quartered, in addition to the guard belonging to that vessel. The quarters of the Commodore and his suite are on shore.

No important change in the attitude of the conflicting parties has occurred; though the arrival of a deputation appointed by the general Congress of the Provinces at Santa Fé, with proposals of mediation on the part of Urquiza, has given rise to some hope of an amicable adjustment of the difficulties. A corresponding deputation has been appointed by the government of the city; an armistice proclaimed; and a conference on neutral ground is now being held.

April 30th.—All overtures for reconciliation between the belligerent parties have failed, and guerillas are again taking place, with the usual loss of blood and life to both parties. A rigid blockade has been added to the investment of the city by land; and the consequence is a limited supply of provisions among the rich, and suffering and starvation among the poor. The skirmishes of the last two or three mornings have been very heavy; but such creatures of habit are we, that with cannon roaring all around us, and constant volleys of musketry at the distance of a mile or two only, bringing death with each discharge to some fellow-mortal, we now hear the sounds for hours without scarcely a thought of the fatal reslts. This morning as we sat down to breakfast at Mr. H——'s, two or three gentlemen descended from the flat roof of the house, where they had been watching with a glass the progress of a guerilla. They reported that they had just seen many on both sides fall from their horses, as the parties fired upon each other; but no one present seemed to feel that it was a matter of more moment than the issue of any common sporting-match. The besiegers have no mortars or bombs; but frequently send cannon balls far into the city. Two mornings ago, one of these took off the head of a poor woman a short distance only from the neighborhood in which we were, just as she had risen from her bed and was combing her hair. It is thus that they scatter firebrands, arrows, and death, and say, are we not in sport? My views of the reign of Rosas are much modified by passing events, and the knowledge they give of the people. In the various revolutions and counter-revolutions of years which preceded his accession to power, thirty thousand of them perished from bloodshed and violence at the hands of each other; and more lives have been sacrificed here, in the same manner, within the last three months, than during the whole of his despotic rule. His policy was to put summarily to death, those whom he regarded as factionists and dangerous citizens, and thus, by inspiring terror, to secure peace, order, and safety to the mass. How far was he in error?

Commodore McKeever, after the detention here of four months by the exigency of public affairs, during which he has rendered most important public service, is obliged by duty elsewhere, to leave the further protection of our countrymen and their interests to the commander of the "Jamestown;" and will bid adieu to-morrow to Buenos Ayres for the last time. We must therefore let the curtain drop on the tragedy in performance here; and be content to learn its uncertain issues in our own distant and blessed land. The last mail-packet brought to us the welcome intelligence that the Congress would return to the United States without waiting the arrival of 'a relief;' and on taking our anchors at Montevideo in a few days we shall be HOMEWARD BOUND!

POSTSCRIPT.

THIS volume has already been enlarged beyond the intended number of pages. In closing it, I would very briefly state that the experiment in naval discipline, with which the cruise of the Congress was commenced, previously to the abolition of the lash by law, was carried out with marked and satisfactory success. This is mainly to be attributed to the unwearied efforts, and the indefatigable devotion to duty, of the officers most interested—equally from motives of philanthropy towards the sailor, and a jealous regard for the honor of the navy—in the result. This is especially true, in regard to Mr. Turner the first lieutenant. During the last eighteen months of the cruise, good order, activity in duty, quickness and skill in the military exercises and naval evolutions of a man-of-war, and a general spirit of contentment were characteristic of the crew, in an extraordinary degree. The frigate entered the port of New York under the happiest auspices; and the conduct of the men at the time the manner in which they left her, and their deportment afterwards, were such as to challenge the admiration of those most familiar with such scenes. Intelligence which from time to time has since reached me, in regard to individuals of their number, has been most gratifying; while there has not been wanting proof, in the cases of some, of the highest results of the preaching of the Gospel, in a life of professed and consistent piety.

In regard to the countries to which so much of the preceding record refers, little of material importance has occurred since it was closed. Thirteen of the States of the Plata, bordering on the rivers Parana and Paraguay and their tributaries, have become consolidated under a constitutional government, to the Presidency of which General Urquiza is elevated. Buenos Ayres has pertinaciously refused to enter into this union; and left to pursue her own course, has fallen into a state of anarchy, to which there appears at present to be little prospect of a speedy termination. The same is the case with the Republic of Uraguay.

The condition and prospects of the Empire of Brazil are in wide contrast with these republics of the South. Political quietude and order pervade her widespread dominions, and a striking proof is presented by the stability of her government and her consequent prosperity, of the advantage she possesses in a well-balanced constitutional monarchy. Till the half-civilized people of South America become more enlightened, intellectually and morally, and better instructed in the true principles and right exercise of republicanism, a fixed and hereditary Executive in government is the only safeguard against the evils to which the struggles, among ambitious and unscrupulous military aspirants, constantly give rise.

The few years past have witnessed extraordinary progress in the material wealth, prosperity, and power of this Empire; a progress attributable to the stability of her government; to the necessities of commerce; and to the advancing and controlling civilization of the times. The greatly increased demand for her principal staple, coffee, as well as for many of her other important products—India-rubber, sugar, cotton, tobacco, dye-woods, and minerals—has led to a wise, liberal, and widespread system of internal improvements and inland and ocean steam navigation, for the development of the varied and vast physical resources of the empire. Don Pedro II. has imbibed and obeyed the spirit of the times as fully, during the few years of his actual reign, and advanced the material and social prosperity of his country as safely and rapidly, as any ruler living.

The importance to the United States of the trade of Brazil will hardly be credited by those not particularly informed on the subject. We derive from that empire a large number of articles of commerce indispensable to us; and send to it many of the most staple and valuable products of our agriculture and manufactures. We receive from Brazil our largest supply of coffee, India-rubber, hides, cocoa for chocolate, sarsaparilla, and other articles; and in exchange supply her with nearly all her breadstuffs—with beef, pork, lard, and butter; with corn, cotton fabrics, the implements of agriculture and the arts, with machinery, and the manufactures of iron and wood. This trade amounts to nearly nineteen millions of dollars annually; the balance against the United States being six millions paid in cash. It is believed by those best informed on the subject, that the establishment of a regular line of mail steamers to Brazil, with a suitable subsidy from the government for postal service, would be the means of doubling the amount of trade in the course of five years; and by the increased demand for our productions arising from the facility of communication and correspondence, would equalize the exchange, if not turn the balance in our favor. It is a reproach to us, that for the want of direct communication by steam, our correspondence, both commercial and diplomatic, with Eastern South America, is carried by English mail steamers, by the way of England, a distance of near eight thousand miles. From the same cause the disbursements of our government to its public agents there, are made only at a heavy percentage. To place the salary of nine thousand dollars in the hands of a chargé d'affaires at Rio, costs the government at home usually one thousand dollars, and the naval disbursements on that station are made at a corresponding loss.

Aware of the vast public and commercial interests to us as a nation of this matter, it is with great satisfaction I have learned that an association of capitalists of the city of New York, bearing the name of the "North and South American Steamship Company," has brought the subject before Congress in a memorial for aid, in consideration of mail service, in the establishment of a line of steamers between New York and Para. It is proposed to intersect the several European lines running to Brazil at the Island of St. Thomas, and to form a junction at Para, with the Brazilian mail and passage steamers which now regularly coast the empire a distance of four thousand miles, from the mouth of the Amazon to the Rio La Plata. Dr. Rainey, one of the gentlemen engaged in this enterprise, has by personal research informed himself fully of the practicability, under the suitable patronage of the government, of making this initiatory line of steam communication with Brazil and with the Plata, through the intervention of the Imperial lines, of incalculable value to the commerce and general interest of the United States. The committee to whom the memorial was referred, have reported unanimously in favor of granting the subsidy solicited; and there is reason to hope, that by the early action of Congress on the report, an abiding channel of friendship, commerce, and reciprocal good, will be opened directly between the United States and BRAZIL AND LA PLATA.

THE END.

G. P. PUTNAM & CO.'S PUBLICATIONS.

ADDISON'S WHOLE WORKS.

THE WORKS OF JOSEPH ADDISON: Including the whole Contents of Bishop Hurd's Edition; with Letters and other Pieces not found in any previous collection; and Macaulay's Essay on his Life and Works. Edited, with Critical and Explanatory Notes, by George Washington Greene.

"No whiter page than Addison's remains,
He from the taste obscene reclaims our youth,
And sets the passions on the side of truth;
Forms the soft bosom with the gentlest art,
And pours each human virtue through the heart."—POPE.

Complete in 6 vols. 12mo., cloth, price $7 50

half calf extra, price	$13 50	calf extra, "	17 50
half calf antiq. "	13 50	calf antiq. "	18 50

CONTENTS.

Vol. I.—MACAULAY'S Essay on Addison. Bp. HURD'S Notices, Prefaces, &c. Translations. Poems. Dramas.

Vol. II.—Dialogues on Medals (illustrated). Discourse on Ancient and Modern Learning. Letters. Political Writings.

Vol. III.—The FREEHOLDER, a Series of Essays. The PLEBEIAN, by STEELE, with the OLD WHIG (in reply) by ADDISON.

Vol. IV.—The TATLER, 64 Essays. The GUARDIAN, 53 Essays. The LOVER.

Vol. V.—The SPECTATOR, 128 Essays.

Vol. VI.—The SPECTATOR, (continued,) 145 Essays.

*** These volumes contain the FIRST COMPLETE COLLECTION ever made on either side of the Atlantic, of the works of this great model of English prose writing. That Addison's works are eminently worthy of an early place in every well-selected library, public and private, and especially in those established for the benefit of students in English literature, the following brief extracts from competent authorities will be considered as sufficient proof. The NOTES in this edition add greatly to its value.

"Whoever wishes to attain an English style, familiar but not coarse, and elegant but not ostentatious, must give his days and nights to the volumes of Addison."—*Dr. Johnson.*

"Never had the English language been written with such sweetness, grace, and facility. But this was the smallest part of Addison's praise. * * * As a moral satirist he stands unrivalled."—*T. B. Macaulay.*

"The entire works of Addison are now for the first time published in an American edition." *N. Y. Evening Post.*

"The form, size, print, and arrangement of the work are admirable."—*Boston Transcript.*

"The best, because the purest of the English classics. What a literary treasure do these volumes offer to the young men of our times!"—*American Courier, Phila.*

"No library is complete without this work, and no literary man will hesitate to give this a preference over all other editions yet published"—*Pittsburg Post.*

GOLDSMITH'S WORKS, BY PRIOR.

THE WORKS OF OLIVER GOLDSMITH: comprising a variety of Pieces now first collected. With Copious Notes. By JAMES PRIOR. 4 vols. 12mo., uniform with Addison and Irving; with steel vignettes. Cloth, $5; half calf, $8; half calf extra, $9; half morocco, $9; calf extra, $10; calf antique, $11.

CONTENTS.

Vol. I.—Frontispiece, (*Lissoy.*) The BEE, a Series of Essays. ESSAYS. An Enquiry into the Present State of Polite Learning. Prefaces and Introductions.

Vol. II.—Frontispiece, (*Edgeworthstown.*) Letters from a Citizen of the World to his Friend in the East. A Familiar Introduction to the Study of Natural History.

Vol. III.—Frontispiece, (*Ardagh.*) THE VICAR OF WAKEFIELD. BIOGRAPHIES—of Voltaire, Beau Nash, Parnell, Lord Bolingbroke. Miscellaneous Criticism.

Vol. IV.—Frontispiece, (*The Scheld.*) Poems. Miscellaneous Pieces. Dramas. Criticism relating to Poetry and Belles-Lettres.

*** Goldsmith is a universal favorite. The old and the young—the learned and the mere seeker of amusement—are alike fascinated by his varied and always charming pages. The purity both of his sentiments and his style, renders his works admirably adapted to the family library and to the rising generation.

"Can any author—can Sir Walter Scott, be compared with Goldsmith, for the variety, beauty, and power of his compositions? His works constitute the most precious wells of English undefiled."—*Quarterly Review.*

"You may take him, and 'cut him out in little stars,' so many lights does he present to the imagination."—*Athenæum.*

"This is the only complete edition, containing additions made to previous collections, of hitherto undiscovered productions of Goldsmith, which perhaps it would be safe to say constitute nearly one half of the collection in the present edition. This edition is the only one having any just claim to place, as embodying the full performances of Goldsmith, and as the fair exponent of his genius."—*London Quarterly Review.*

"A man of such variety of powers and such felicity of performance, that he always seemed to do best that which he was doing; a man who had the art of being minute without tediousness, and general without confusion; whose language was copious without exuberance, exact without constraint, and easy without weakness."—*Dr. Johnson.*

"The pieces now collected for the first time are numerous, * * * and both the old and new materials are accompanied with brief notes, clearing up the local and temporary allusions in which they abound, but which the lapse of another generation would have rendered it impossible for any diligence to explain."—*Editor's Preface.*

THE WORKS OF WASHINGTON IRVING. Author's Revised Edition, handsomely printed in 15 vols. 12mo., comprising the following works, viz.:

KNICKERBOCKER, . .	1 vol.	CRAYON MISCELLANY, .	1 vol.
SKETCH BOOK, ...	1 "	CAPT. BONNEVILLE, . .	1 "
COLUMBUS, ...	3 "	OLIVER GOLDSMITH, .	1 "
BRACEBRIDGE HALL, .	1 "	MAHOMET AND HIS SUCCESSORS,	2 "
TRAVELLER, . . .	1 "	CONQUEST OF GRENADA, .	1 "
ASTORIA, ...	1 "	ALHAMBRA, . . .	1 "

*** *Sets of the above may be had in the following bindings, viz.:*

cloth,	$19 00	sheep,	$20 00	half calf,	$30 00
half calf ext.,	33 00	half calf antiq.	33 00	calf extra,	37 50
calf antique,	40 00	mor. ext. gt. ed.	48 00		

THE SECOND SERIES OF IRVING'S WORKS will comprise the following, printed uniformly with the above, but numbered and bound separately, viz.:

THE LIFE OF WASHINGTON. (*In the Spring.*)

WOLFERT'S ROOST. (*Now ready.*) 12mo., cloth, $1 25.

New volumes. (*Preparing*).

THE LIBRARY EDITION, IN 8VO., OF

THE LIFE OF WASHINGTON, with portraits and plans, is published only by subscription. Vols. 1 and 2 now ready, price $2 per vol. This work may be had of the agents, or (by subscription) *through any bookseller.*

General Comments on Irving's Writings.

"The publication of this volume* may prompt many readers to brush up their acquaintance with our oldest and most charming American essayist. A new race of writers has appeared on the stage since his merits have been crowned with the most beautiful guerdon of authorship—a place in the memory and in the hearts of the wise, the thoughtful, the mirthful, the pure, the gentle, and the refined—but who has approached the revered veteran in the lambent brilliancy of his wit, the fascinating charm of his gayety, the youthful playfulness with which he hits off the humerous and whimsical in character, the facile grace of his pictures of nature, or the tranquil amenity with which he moralizes on the aims of life, alluring the reader to modest wisdom and chastened emotions, amid the feverous heats and dazzling glares of our every-day pursuits! Long will it be before the literature of this country will produce the rival of Washington Irving, and

* Wolfert's Roost.

WASHINGTON IRVING'S WORKS—*continued.*

long may he live to enjoy the happy pre-eminence which he so gracefully adorns."—*New York Tribune.*

"Few among the present readers of light literature—those 'omnivorous swallowers,' who bolt every thing warm and reeking from the press—have enjoyed the privilege of reading a new work from the pen of Washington Irving. For, to tell the truth, since that worthy gentleman has laid aside the pen with which so much that is memorable in American literature was conjured into being, a new and rabid class of readers has sprung into existence. Instead of the genial humor, the wholesome satire, the finished style of that distinguished author, we have pruriency, sarcasm, cant, flippancy, and commonplace. Readers, forty thousand to a book, have been found to batten on this unctuous melange, and the supply has continued with unabated malignancy. Imagination and fancy are alike unknown; they are dead, buried, and not likely to rise again. The potency of a literature is infallibly tested by the reminiscences it provokes. An author who can people a little world of his own, with such beings as man can attach himself to, lives in the commonplace suggestiveness of the hour."—*N. Y. Daily Times.*

"The other writings of Irving have been re-published and re-issued over and over again, in all sorts of editions, and still the demand for them flows on in a steady stream. A library is incomplete without them. The name of Irving has given lustre to American letters. He first, like the sun, dissipated the mists of prejudice which blinded and obscured the vision of foreigners, and his warm and genial rays first lighted up the pages of our national literature, and illustrated the answer to the sneering inquiry, 'Who reads an American book?' He, chief of all, has an English and Continental fame, while, to his own countrymen, his name is as a household word. He has equally the love and respect of all his fellow citizens.

"Mr. Irving publishes this work at the ripe age of 72. His literary life has occupied more than half a century. It will make the old young again to read this volume, carrying them back, as it does, to the early promise of the gifted writer, and leading them along over the many years during which they have been beguiled by his genius, instructed by his wisdom, and charmed by his sunny spirit and his hearty geniality." * * * —*Rochester American.*

"The golden prose of Irving has long since sunk into the heart of every reader of the English language. He is one of the rare few anticipating the verdict of posterity, and wearing, while living, the laurels of a classic. And no wonder, for his pure, genial sentiment, his clear thought, his musical sentences, his graphic words, form a combination of qualities that the whole range of English literature has never excelled. His style is transparent as a brook, showing the ideas as clearly as the crystal element does its pebbles."—*Albany Knickerbocker.*

"Do we really appreciate his works? The many pages that he has written, each binding man more nearly to his fellow; the many sketches that have caused Nature to become doubly endeared to us; that have made the Alhambra live again in all its early glory; that have revealed to us the workings of Columbus' yearning mind; that have cast an eternal spring over the whole region of the Hudson; that have destroyed more prejudices than Political Reformers have revived, and have purified the every-day existence of this *dollarous* age, we cannot willingly pass unrecognized."—*New Orleans Delta.*

"The library which does not contain these writings is indeed deficient."—*Cam. Chronicle.*

"Great Britain, France, Northern and Southern Europe, are alike familiar with his delightful and most healthful writings, and doubtless his own good standing abroad has done more than any other single cause to introduce the names and works of others of our countrymen. There is a charm about his writings to which old and young, the educated and the simple, bear cheerful witness."—*Christian Inquirer.*

"What Johnson and Addison have become as authors to the students of all countries, Washington Irving will follow to mould and correct the literary taste of future generations."—*Highland Eagle.*

WASHINGTON IRVING'S WORKS—*continued.*

Separate Volumes of Irving's Works.

KNICKERBOCKER'S HISTORY OF NEW YORK, from the Creation of the World to the End of the Dutch Dynasty; containing, among many Surprising and Curious Matters, the Unutterable Ponderings of Walter the Doubter, the Disastrous Projects of William the Testy, and the Chivalric Achievements of Peter the Headstrong, the Three Dutch Governors of New Amsterdam, being the only authentic History of the Times that ever hath been, or ever will be published. 12mo., cloth, $1 25.

——— The Same, with Darley's Illustrations, gilt extra, $2; half calf, $2 50; morocco extra, $3 50.

A few copies remain of the fine edition in 8vo., with the Illustrations by Heath, of the entrance of Peter Stuyvesant's army into New Amsterdam, and a fac-simile of the following letter from Sir Walter Scott, price $3 50 in cloth, $4 in gilt extra, $6 in morocco extra.

SIR WALTER SCOTT *to* HENRY BREVOORT, Esq., *of New York.*

"MY DEAR SIR,—I beg you to accept my best thanks for the uncommon degree of entertainment which I have received from the most excellently jocose history of New York. I am sensible that as a stranger to American parties and politics, I must lose much of the concealed satire of the piece, but I must own, that looking at the simple and obvious meaning only, I have never read anything so closely resembling the style of Dean Swift as the annals of Diedrich Knickerbocker. I have been employed these few evenings in reading them aloud to Mrs. S. and two ladies who are our guests, and our sides have been absolutely sore with laughing. I think, too, there are passages which indicate that the author possesses powers of a different kind, and has some touches which remind me much of STERNE. I beg you will have the kindness to let me know when Mr. Irving takes pen in hand again, for assuredly I shall expect a very great treat.

"Believe me, dear sir, your obliged humble servt.,

"WALTER SCOTT"

"ABBOTSFORD, April 23, 1813."

LIFE AND VOYAGES OF CHRISTOPHER COLUMBUS, TO WHICH ARE ADDED THOSE OF HIS COMPANIONS. By WASHINGTON IRVING. In 3 vols. 12mo., with Maps, &c., price $4 in cloth.

*** The subject of this work of course forms the very ground-work of all American history. No other work can possibly be its substitute. The author, during his residence in Spain, enjoyed extraordinary facilities for access to original materials, and he has presented the narrative (so intensely interesting in its very nature) in a shape eminently reliable for its conscientious accuracy, and at the same time as highly attractive to the general reader as the most skilful romance.

WASHINGTON IRVING'S WORKS—*continued.*

THE SKETCH BOOK OF GEOFFREY CRAYON, GENT[N].

"I have no wife nor children, good or bad to provide for. A mere spectator of other men's fortunes and adventures, and how they play their parts; which, methinks, are diversely presented to me, as from a common theatre or scene."—*Burton.*

CONTENTS.

Author's Account of Himself—The Voyage—Roscoe—The Wife—Rip Van Winkle—English Writers on America—Rural Life in England—The Broken Heart—Art of Book-Making—A Royal Poet—The Country Church—The Widow and her Son—A Sunday in London—The Boar's Head Tavern—The Mutability of Literature—Rural Funerals—The Inn Kitchen—The Spectre Bridegroom—Westminster Abbey—Christmas—The Stage Coach—Christmas Eve—Christmas Day—Christmas Dinner—London Antiques—Little Britain—Stratford-on-Avon—Traits of Indian Character—Philip of Pokanoket—John Bull—The Pride of the Village—The Angler—The Legend of Sleepy Hollow—L'Envoi.

THE AUTHOR'S REVISED EDITION, complete in one vol. 12mo., cloth, $1 25; gilt extra, with illustrations by Darley, $2 25; the same, half calf extra, $2 50; the same, morocco extra, $3 50.

*** A few copies remain of the larger edition, with fine portrait on steel, royal 8vo., price, cloth, $3 50; gilt ext., $4; Turkey mor. ext., $6.

BRACEBRIDGE HALL; OR, THE HUMORISTS. A Medley. 12mo., cloth, $1 25.

*** Descriptive of rural life and holiday customs in England, and adorned with entertaining narratives.

TALES OF A TRAVELLER. 12mo., cloth, $1 25.

——— The Same, with Darley's Illustrations, gilt extra, $2 25; half calf extra, $2 50; morocco extra, $3 50.

A few copies remain of the larger edition, illustrated, royal 8vo., cloth, $3 50; gilt extra, $4; morocco extra, $4.

ASTORIA; OR, ANECDOTES OF AN ENTERPRISE BEYOND THE ROCKY MOUNTAINS. By WASHINGTON IRVING. With a Map. 2 vols. complete in 1 vol., 12mo., $1 50.

*** This volume contains a narrative of the exciting adventures connected with the first exploration of the wilderness of Oregon, and the first settlements on the Pacific.

WASHINGTON IRVING'S WORKS—*continued.*

THE CRAYON MISCELLANY.

*** This volume comprises the TOUR ON THE PRAIRIES, and the VISITS TO ABBOTSFORD and NEWSTEAD ABBEY. 12mo., cloth, $1 25.

THE ADVENTURES OF CAPT. BONNEVILLE IN THE ROCKY MOUNTAINS AND THE FAR WEST.

Digested from his Journal, and illustrated from various other Sources. Author's revised edition, complete in 1 vol. With a Map. $1 25.

OLIVER GOLDSMITH: A BIOGRAPHY.

Complete in 1 vol. 12mo., $1 25.

——— The Same, gilt ext., with illustrations, $2; half calf, $2 50; mor. ext., $3 50.

A few copies remain of the large edition, 8vo., cloth, $2 50; gilt extra, $3; mor. ext., $5.

MAHOMET AND HIS SUCCESSORS.

Complete in 2 vols 12mo., $2 50.

——— The Same, half calf, $4.

"The aim of the writer has been to digest into an easy, perspicuous, and flowing narrative, the admitted facts concerning Mahomet, together with such legends and traditions as have been wrought into the whole system of oriental literature, and at the same time to give such a summary of his faith as might be sufficient for the general reader."—*Extract from Preface.*

"Those who read the life of Mahomet will find in the following pages most of their old acquaintances again engaged, but in a vastly grander field of action; leading armies, subjugating empires, and dictating from the palaces and thrones of deposed monarchs."—*Ext. Preface to "Mahomet's Successors."*

CHRONICLE OF THE CONQUEST OF GRENADA.

From the MSS. of FRAY ANTONIO AGAPIDA. 12mo., cloth, $1 25.

"He has availed himself of all the picturesque and animating movements of this romantic era. * * * * The fictitious and romantic dress of the work has enabled him to make it the medium of reflecting more vividly the floating opinions and chimerical fancies of the age, while he has illuminated the picture with the dramatic brilliancy of coloring denied to sober history." —PRESCOTT'S *Ferdinand and Isabella.*

THE ALHAMBRA.

12mo., $1 25.

——— The Same, with Darley's Illustrations, gilt ext., $2; half calf, $2 50; morocco extra, $3 50.

WASHINGTON IRVING'S WORKS—*continued.*

THE LIFE OF GEORGE WASHINGTON. By WASHINGTON IRVING. Of the *Octavo Edition*, (published by subscription only), Three volumes are now ready, each containing about 500 pages, elegantly printed with new pica type, on fine paper. Subscription price per vol. in cloth, $2; sheep extra, $2 50; half calf extra, $3 25; calf extra, $4.

The first volume contains a fine portrait from an original picture by Wertmüller (now first engraved), and three maps and plans.

The second volume contains PEALE's portrait of Washington (the earliest), at the age of 40, with maps and plans.

The third volume contains an engraving from HOUDON's statue of Washington at Richmond, and a splendid engraving carefully copied from STUART's original picture of Washington, in the Boston Athenæum.

LIFE OF WASHINGTON. *Duodecimo Edition.* 3 vols. published, uniform with his other works, with Portrait. Price $1 50 per vol.

"A work which will take its place in American households side by side with the Bible."—*Express.*

"It was peculiarly fitting that the brightest name in history should have put in requisition, for its commemoration, one of the most gifted and accomplished sons of literature. Washington Irving, whose literary fame scarcely knows a bound, has, for many years, been occupied upon this work, the first volume of which we have now the pleasure to announce. It has been elaborated with great patience and care; and is not more remarkable for its exquisite grace and beauty of style, than for the richness of its biographical and historical details. The present volume relates to that portion of his life which preceded the period of the Revolution, and during which he may be considered as having had his training for that great enterprise which at once rendered his name immortal, and marked a new and glorious epoch in the history of the race. It contains much that has not found its way into any previous life of Washington; and even if it had been nothing more than the old material, moulded over by that graceful mind that lends enchantment to every thing it touches, it would still have been justly regarded as a bright gem in our literature."—*Puritan Recorder.*

"Before making any extracts from the work, we cannot but express our satisfaction at its final completion. Its publication will form an important epoch in American literature. The life-long labors of its illustrious author could not have been crowned with a more appropriate termination. His name will henceforth be indissolubly connected with that of Washington, not only by his baptismal appellation, but by the noble monument which he has reared to his memory. It was a befitting task that the writer who has left such a brilliant impress of his genius on the nascent literature of his country—whose fame is devoutly cherished in the hearts of the American people—held in equally affectionate remembrance in the rude cabins of the frontier, the halls of universities, and the saloons of fashionable life—whose successes in the varied walks of classical composition have done as much to illustrate the character of America in the eye of the world as the eloquence of her senators or her prowess in arms—should create a permanent memorial of Washington in a style worthy the dignity of the subject and the reputation of the author."—*Gazette, Reading, Pa.*

"It is evident that the author has not only carefully investigated a vast amount of original

WASHINGTON IRVING'S WORKS—*continued.*

materials to which few persons could have had access, but that he also has devoted many years to a most congenial subject. In justice to the publishers we may state, that the work has been got up in a style well worthy of its subject."—*Evening Bulletin, Phila.*

"The time for representing Washington as a statue or a man of iron has gone by. He begins to be known as a man of immense passion, of the tenderest as well as strongest family affections, and of the most unaffected domesticity of taste. . . . All that patient and comprehensive research can do, Mr. Irving has done."—*Christian Inquirer.*

"This may be said to be the only life of Washington ever written. Irving has thrown around his story the graces of his brilliant style, and imparted a variety to his pages which never suffers the interest of his readers to flag. His work is a real, solid acquisition to the living literature of the age, and will take its place among those favored few which will go down to posterity."—*Pittsburgh Gazette.*

"This is the life of Washington that will be *read*, others hereafter will only be referred to."—*N. Y. Courier & Enquirer.*

"Every sentence is stamped with the individuality of genius."—*Ballou's Pictorial.*

"It is, in short, a model biography, and will meet with a hearty welcome from all classes."—*N. E. Farmer.*

New Series of Irving's Works.

WOLFERT'S ROOST, AND OTHER PAPERS. Now first collected. By WASHINGTON IRVING. 12mo., $1 25; gilt extra, $1 75.

"Washington Irving, dear, kind-hearted, clever Washington Irving, 'the idol of my youth, the darling of my manhood,' he, who under many names Geoffrey Crayon, Diedrich Knickerbocker, &c.—has 'tickled the town,' as Byron said of Moore, is once more before us; and his new volume, 'Wolfert's Roost,' and other papers, bear evidence of all that sweetness of mind and versatility of talent which have captivated thousands of readers."—*London Chronicle.*

"In leaving this attractive volume, we cordially recommend it to the lovers of pure, elevated, and warm-hearted literature. To the literati it commends itself for the completeness, closeness, and elegance of its style."—*N. Y. Daily Times.*

"There is as much elegance of diction, as graceful a description of natural scenery, as grotesque an earnestness in diablerie, and as quiet but as telling a satiric humor, as when Geoffrey Crayon first came before the world nearly forty years ago."—*London Spectator.*

"It would not be easy to overpraise this volume."—*London Athenæum.*

THE CRAYON READING BOOK, Comprising Selections from the various writings of Washington Irving, for the use of Schools. 12mo., half bound, 75 cents.

"A book to make the young observant and kind-hearted."—*Lit. World.*

The selections are admirable models of a lucid, chaste, and elegant style. We are grateful, by means of this volume, to be able to place in the hands of our young readers the gems of the most popular and gifted author of the day."—*From the Misses Sedgwick.*

TALES OF THE HUDSON: Comprising Rip Van Winkle—Legend of Sleepy Hollow—Guests from Gibbet Island—Dolph Heyliger—Wolfert Webber—Peter Stuyvesant's Voyage up the Hudson, &c. 16mo., plates, price 50 cents.

"One of the most delightful works in the language."—*Boston Transcript.*

"Summer tourists on the Hudson can find no pleasanter companion than this.

"The man is to be envied who, with a summer day before him, embarks on one of the floating palaces of the river, with this choice volume for his companion, as he is borne along the ample breadth of the Tappan Sea, by the walls of the Palisades, or threads the grand defiles of the Highlands, he will be put in a mood for the most exquisite enjoyment of book and landscape, as he glances from one to the other."—*Lit. World.*

FENIMORE COOPER.

THE NOVELS AND TALES OF J. FENIMORE COOPER.

New Library Edition, complete.

Embracing,

Last of the Mohicans,
Pioneers,
Deerslayer,
Path-Finder,
Prairie,
The Oak Openings,
Wept of Wish-ton-Wish,
Ned Myers,
Spy,
Redskins,
Pilot,
Mercedes of Castile,
Wing and Wing,
Monikins,
Lionel Lincoln,
Bravo,
Precaution,
Homeward Bound,
The Chain-Bearer,
Afloat and Ashore,
Miles Wallingford,
Home as Found,
The Crater,
Two Admirals,
Headsman,
Satanstoe,
Heidenmauer,
Water Witch,
Jack Tier,
Red Rover,
The Sea Lions,
Wyandotte,
Travelling Bachelor,
Ways of the Hour.

Complete in 34 vols. 12mo., neatly bound in embossed muslin, $34; sheep, library style, marble edges, $37 50; half roan, $28; half calf, $50; half Turkey, $50; half calf, gilt backs, $55; half calf antique, $55.

*** Each of the above may be had separately price $1 in cloth.

"The enduring monuments of Fenimore Cooper are his works. While the love of country continues to prevail, his memory will exist in the hearts of the people. * * * So truly patriotic and American throughout, they should find a place in every American's library."—Daniel Webster.

"No one has succeeded like Cooper in the portraiture of American character, or has given such glowing and truthful pictures of American scenery."—W. H. Prescott.

"He wrote for mankind at large; hence it is that he has earned a fame wider than any author of modern times. The creations of his genius shall survive through centuries to come, and only perish with our language."—W. C. Bryant.

"His surpassing ability has made his own name, and the names of the creations of his fancy, 'household words' throughout the civilized world."—Geo. Bancroft.

"The works of our great novelist have adorned and elevated our literature."—Edw. Everett.

"Cooper emphatically belongs to the nation. He has left a space in our literature which will not easily be supplied."—Washington Irving.

THE LEATHER-STOCKING TALES. Comprising Last of the Mohicans, Pioneers, Deerslayer, Pathfinder, Prairie. In uniform binding, containing extra title-pages, printed in red and black, on superior paper, in five elegant volumes. Neatly bound in embossed cloth, $5; in half Turkey or half calf, $7 50.

THE SEA TALES. Comprising The Pilot, The Red Rover, The Two Admirals, Wing and Wing, Water Witch. Uniform with the Leather-Stocking Series, containing extra title-pages, printed in red and black, on superior paper, in five elegant volumes. Neatly bound in embossed cloth, $5; in half Turkey or half calf, $7 50.

A NEW LIBRARY EDITION OF COOPER'S CHOICE WORKS.

CHOICE WORKS OF J. FENIMORE COOPER,

In Twenty Duodecimo Volumes, extra size.

In newly stereotyping this Edition, extraordinary pains have been taken to produce a most perfect specimen of typography, and the most scrupulous care has been observed in the reproduction of the text, which has the Author's latest additions and corrections, besides his new Introductions, Notes, &c.

*** The Works of COOPER, while their illustrious author was alive, were acknowledged, in other countries, to be the finest examples of American genius, and the noblest as well as the truest exhibitions of American intellect and feeling. At home, personal and partisan influences prevented the universal recognition of their extraordinary and peculiar merits. But all prejudices and asperities being buried in the grave, the people have dispassionately examined the claims of "our great national novelist," and their applause is awarded in acclamations. Never, in the proudest day of his life, was he so popular. Not a month has passed since the close of his splendid career, in which the general demand for his writings has not increased; and now, through all the Union it is as well understood that the works of Cooper should constitute a portion of the Family Library, as in Spain, that every reader should possess Cervantes; or in Germany, that Goethe, or in England, that Shakspeare, should be familiar in every cultivated household. Although much of this popularity is undoubtedly owing to their decided and intelligent nationality; yet, perhaps as much results from the just conviction that no other author, so eminent in his department, has ever before been so uniformly pure in morals and elevated in sentiment. No other body of romance, in any language, is so healthful and invigorating. This collection comprises—

1. THE SPY,
2. THE DEERSLAYER,
3. LAST OF THE MOHICANS,
4. THE PATHFINDER,
5. THE PIONEERS,
6. THE PRAIRIE,
7. THE PILOT,
8. LIONEL LINCOLN,
9. RED ROVER,
10. THE WEPT OF WISH-TON-WISH,
11. THE WATER-WITCH,
12. THE BRAVO,
13. THE HEADSMAN.
14. HOMEWARD BOUND,
15. HOME AS FOUND,
16. THE TWO ADMIRALS,
17. WING AND WING,
18. WYANDOTTE,
19. JACK TIER,
20. THE SEA LIONS.

N. B. This Edition will only be furnished in uniform Complete Sets; in no case will the Sets be broken.

The above twenty volumes, comprising the FINE EDITION OF COOPER'S CHOICE WORKS, are bound with great care, in a superior manner, after patterns of elegance and neatness, in the following popular and attractive styles:

Embossed muslin, the set, 20 volumes,	$25 00	Full Calf,	$50 00
Sheep, best Library style, marble edge,	30 00	Full Calf, extra, gilt backs,	54 00
Half Turkey,	40 00	Full Calf, antique,	54 00
Half Calf,	40 00	Full Turkey, gilt tops,	56 00
Half Calf, full gilt backs,	44 00	Super Calf, extra, gilt edges,	60 00
Half Calf, antique,	44 00	Super Turkey, extra, gilt edges,	60 00

THEODORE IRVING.

THE CONQUEST OF FLORIDA BY DE SOTO. By Prof. THEODORE IRVING. Author's Revised Edition. (Uniform with the Collective Edition of Washington Irving's Works.) 12mo., cloth, with a Map, $1 25.

"This is an important chapter in the early history of this country. The subject, too, is one of considerable interest to the general reader. Besides the historical value which the work possesses, it contains portions of as exciting interest as any romantic fiction."—*Cambridge Chron.*

*** This volume is eminently worthy of a place in every good library by the side of Prescott's Mexico and Peru. The adventures of De Soto and his followers in the regions now known as Florida, Alabama, Louisiana, &c.—the discovery of the Mississippi, under whose waters the chivalric leader found his grave—and the various romantic incidents connected with the expedition, render it a highly entertaining chapter of early American history, which no other work supplies.

HON. J. P. KENNEDY'S WRITINGS, Viz.:

SWALLOW BARN, (illustrated.) HORSE-SHOE ROBINSON, (with Vignettes.) ROB OF THE BOWL, (with portrait on steel.) Complete in 3 vols. 12mo., cloth, $4; half calf extra, $7 50.

*** These works have taken the same relative place in American literature as that occupied by the historical fictions of Scott in the literature of England, and they worthily fill a place by the side of Irving and Cooper.

Separate Works.

SWALLOW BARN: A SOJOURN IN THE OLD DOMINION. With Illustrations by STROTHER. Large 12mo., cloth, $1 50.

"We have always regarded Swallow Barn as one of the very highest efforts of American mind. It is exquisitely written, and the scenes are vividly described. Its features of Virginia life and manners are the best ever drawn. This is eminently a splendid edition."—*Louisv. Jour.*

HORSE-SHOE ROBINSON: A TALE OF THE TORY ASCENDENCY. Author's Revised Edition. Complete in 1 vol. large 12mo., $1 50.

*** This work is founded on actual facts connected with the annals of Virginia and South Carolina. The events have been thus chronicled, "because they intrinsically possess interest" for the lovers of adventure, and because "they serve to illustrate the temper and character of the war of our Revolution," and to bring out more vividly than political history can do, its varied, romantic, and picturesque features. The volume comprises adventures of great interest, yet in strict accordance with historic truth.

ROB OF THE BOWL. 12mo., with fine portraits, $1 25.

*** A romance illustrative of the early colonial history of Maryland under the Calverts.

BAYARD TAYLOR.

TRAVELS IN VARIOUS PARTS OF THE WORLD. By BAYARD TAYLOR. With plates, 5 vols. 12mo., cloth, $6 50; half calf, $12 50; calf extra, $15.

THE TRAVELS AND POEMS. New edition, complete in 6 vols. 12mo., uniformly bound in cloth, $8; half calf, $15; calf extra, $18.

Separate Volumes.

VIEWS AFOOT; OR, EUROPE SEEN WITH KNAPSACK AND STAFF. By BAYARD TAYLOR. Twentieth edition, revised and newly stereotyped throughout. 12mo., cloth, $1 25.

"There is a freshness and force in the book altogether unusual in a book of travels. * * * As a text book for travellers, the work is essentially valuable; it tells how much can be accomplished with very limited means, when energy, curiosity, and a love of adventure are the prompters; sympathy in his success, likewise, is another source of interest to the book."—*Union Magazine.*

"This is a capital book in whichever way it is considered, brimful of instruction. Among the hundred volumes already issued on the subject, Mr. Bayard Taylor's seems to us altogether the best and liveliest. Not only does he possess an open mind, he has also a discerning eye, and a neat hand at description. There is nothing more graphic in Defoe. It is an excellent and a lively book."—*Athenæum.*

ELDORADO; OR, ADVENTURES IN CALIFORNIA AND MEXICO. New edition, complete in 1 volume 12mo., with Illustrations, price $1 25.

"These volumes relate most striking and novel adventures, and cannot fail to be eminently popular"—*Commercial Advertiser.*

"They contain the most authentic, sparkling and best printed information and adventure yet published."—*Literary World.*

THE LANDS OF THE SARACEN; OR, PICTURES OF PALESTINE, ASIA MINOR, SICILY, AND SPAIN. With a Map and Vignettes. 12mo., $1 25.

"It is not often our privilege to read so delightful a book as this. * * What a treat for the holidays! * * What a freshness pervades every page—how full of life and beauty is every picture!"—*N. Y. Daily News.*

"There is something delightful and fascinating in Bayard Taylor's books—having its origin chiefly in their fresh unhackneyed style. * * * His descriptive powers are remarkable."—*N. Y. Dispatch.*

"The narratives of no traveller of modern times have proved more interesting and instructive than those of Bayard Taylor."—*Newark Whig.*

"Exquisite pictures of oriental life everywhere embellish the narrative, which carries the reader along without the slightest sense of fatigue or ennui."—*Charleston (S. C.) Post.*

"Better pictures of oriental life and scenery than he gives are not to be found in the English language. Certainly if any are to be found which enable us to behold "with a clearer inward eye the hills of Palestine, the Sun-gilded Minarets of Damascus, or the lovely pine forests of Phrygia," they have not been placed within our reach."—*Michigan Christian Herald.*

BAYARD TAYLOR'S WORKS—*Continued.*

A JOURNEY TO CENTRAL AFRICA; OR, LIFE AND LANDSCAPES FROM EGYPT TO THE NEGRO KINGDOMS OF THE WHITE NILE. With a Map and Illustrations by the Author. 12mo., $1 50.

"He writes eloquently, easily, and with a vivid feeling for the picturesque; he has a lively sense of humor and does not indulge it too much; and best of all, he can feel sincere enthusiasm for the beautiful in nature and art, and is not ashamed to own it." * * *—*London Leader.*

"It is very rarely our good fortune to meet with such a delightful book of travel; it comes with all the freshness of reality, and makes us long to pack a portmanteau, put Mr. Taylor's book in our pockets and set off by express train for the land of the pyramids. * * * With this beautiful passage we must leave a book which has compensated many, many weary hours in reviewing the commonplace productions of the day."—*London Atlas*.

"If it were possible to add any thing to the fascination which attracts so many travellers to the banks of the Nile, this volume would do it."—*London Daily News.*

"As a vivid delineator, it would be difficult to overmatch Mr. Taylor."—*Liv. Standard.*

"He proceeds by the Nubian Desert and the White Nile to Khartoun, penetrates to the populous Negro Kingdom of the "Shillocks," having reached a point of Central Africa beyond which modern explorers have hitherto failed to penetrate."—*London Review.*

"Treading for the most part on unhackneyed ground, he has produced a volume as fresh and original as it is brilliant, and even when gleaning from old fields, surprises us by the novelty of his observations and discoveries."—*Yankee Blade.*

"As a writer of travels, especially, he has never found his equal."—*Buffalo Democracy.*

"No other American traveller has passed over the field before him, and his narrative is a positive addition to the stock of human knowledge.

"A journey which led him into fresh untrodden fields."—*Cleveland Plaindealer.*

"There is no romance to us quite equal to one of Bayard Taylor's books of travel. Fact under his wonderful pen is more charming than Fiction."—*Hartford Republican.*

A VISIT TO INDIA, CHINA, AND JAPAN. By BAYARD TAYLOR. With Frontispiece and Vignette engraved on steel. Large 12mo, pp. 504. $1 50.

"Bayard Taylor is certainly a remarkable man. The more we see of him in his writings and the more we hear of him, the more we admire him. He is decidedly *the* American traveller and travel-writer."—*New Haven Courier.*

"We find it useless, however, to search for passages of greater length, that would afford any adequate conception of the instruction and delight promised by this work, full as it is of adventure, incident, and anecdote, woven together in a rich web of description."—*Charleston Cour*

"Commence where you will in this last book of his, and you will find yourself immediately interested, and will reluctantly leave the narrative."—*Boston Traveller.*

"In some respects it is the most valuable of the series, for though less furnished with the poetic and the historical, it contains more of description and information concerning scenes and people comparatively new."—*N. Y. Independent.*

"The fascination surrounding the visions of India which from youth-time one has carried in his imagination loses none of its enchantment as he follows Mr. Taylor through his volume; while mysterious China and Japan, though disrobed of the veil which has surrounded them, are as inviting to curiosity as ever."—*St. Louis Evening News.*

"Not a page of this book but is replete with interest, not a page but reveals some curious fact, not a page but glows with some vivid description or humorous episode."—*N. Y. Saturday Courier.*

EXTRAORDINARY NARRATIVE.

A PERSONAL NARRATIVE OF A VISIT TO EL MEDINAH AND MECCAH. By Lt. Richard Burton, Bombay Army. With an Introduction, by Bayard Taylor. With a Map and two Illustrations. Large 12mo. $1 50.

The history of this curious book is as follows:

Burton, an officer in the East India Company, having, by a long residence in Upper India, acquired a perfect knowledge of the Oriental languages and customs, projected a visit under the auspices of the Royal Geographical Society, to the Holy City of Mecca and the Tomb of the Prophet at Medina, places rarely, if ever before visited by any Englishman. This he successfully accomplished in 1853–4, disguised as a Mohammedan Dervish. The history of the pilgrimage is not surpassed in interest and originality by any book of travel ever published—embracing his residence at Cairo as Mohammedan student; the journey across the desert with the great annual caravan of Pilgrims; the visit to the tomb of Mohammed; the discovery that the sacred black stone of Mecca is an aërolite; the annual sermon preached at Mecca to an estimated audience of 150,000 Pilgrims, gathered from all parts of the Moslem world; his narrow escapes from detection; and the only accurate account of the ceremonies of the Mussulman faith.

To the religious community this work furnishes information never before made public, respecting the ceremonial laws of a large proportion of the population of the Eastern world; while for general interest Burton's narrative will compare favorably with either *Eothen*, or *Crescent and the Cross.*

MR. STEWART'S NEW WORK ON BRAZIL.

BRAZIL AND LA PLATA. Personal Narrative of a Visit there, 1850–3. By Rev. C. S. Stewart, Chaplain U. S. Navy. Author of a "Visit to the South Seas," &c. With two Illustrations. 12mo, $1 25.

*** This very interesting volume gives a variety of curious and entertaining information, which is to a great extent novel as well as authentic and reliable. It is a work eminently suited for popular reading and for school libraries, &c.

HON. MISS MURRAY'S LETTERS.

LETTERS FROM THE UNITED STATES, CANADA AND CUBA. By Hon. Amelia M. Murray. 10th thousand. 1 vol. 12mo, $1 00.

DR. KANE'S ARCTIC EXPLORATIONS.

ARCTIC EXPLORATIONS; The Second Grinnell Expedition, 1853–5. By E. K. Kane, M. D., U. S. N. With 300 Illustrations on wood and steel, beautifully executed. 2 vols. 8vo. $5.

www.ingramcontent.com/pod-product-compliance
Lightning Source LLC
LaVergne TN
LVHW020935110826
845150LV00004B/876

* 9 7 8 1 4 2 5 5 5 1 7 9 7 *